Post-Theories in Literary and Cultural Studies

Post-Theories in Literary and Cultural Studies

Edited by Zekiye Antakyalıoğlu

LEXINGTON BOOKS
Lanham • Boulder • New York • London

Published by Lexington Books
An imprint of The Rowman & Littlefield Publishing Group, Inc.
4501 Forbes Boulevard, Suite 200, Lanham, Maryland 20706
www.rowman.com

86-90 Paul Street, London EC2A 4NE

Copyright © 2022 by The Rowman & Littlefield Publishing Group, Inc.

All rights reserved. No part of this book may be reproduced in any form or by any electronic or mechanical means, including information storage and retrieval systems, without written permission from the publisher, except by a reviewer who may quote passages in a review.

British Library Cataloguing in Publication Information Available

Library of Congress Cataloging-in-Publication Data

Names: Antakyalıoğlu, Zekiye, editor.
Title: Post-theories in literary and cultural studies / edited by Zekiye Antakyalıoğlu.
Description: Lanham : Lexington Books, 2022. | Includes bibliographical references and index. | Summary: "Post-Theories in Literary and Cultural Studies brings to attention the post-theoretical discussions on the changing perceptions in literary and cultural studies. In four sections the volume presents essays that trace the engagement of post-theory with post-postmodernism, posthumanism, ethics, and politics"— Provided by publisher.
Identifiers: LCCN 2022004053 (print) | LCCN 2022004054 (ebook) | ISBN 9781666913873 (cloth) | ISBN 9781666913897 (paper) | ISBN 9781666913880 (ebook)
Subjects: LCSH: Criticism. | Theory (Philosophy) | Literature—History and criticism—Theory, etc. | LCGFT: Essays.
Classification: LCC PN81 .P626 2022 (print) | LCC PN81 (ebook) | DDC 801/.95—dc23/eng/20220304
LC record available at https://lccn.loc.gov/2022004053
LC ebook record available at https://lccn.loc.gov/2022004054

Contents

Acknowledgments	ix
Editor's Introduction *Zekiye Antakyalıoğlu*	1

Part I: Changing Climates in Theory and Criticism

1	A Liberal Humanism for the Twenty-First Century? *Cian Duffy*	9
2	The Ethical Turn: Return of Empathy *Aytül Özüm*	21
3	The Microfascistic Turn and the Question of Sympathy in the Twenty-First Century *Rahime Çokay Nebioğlu*	33
4	Enjoy Your Theory! Post-Lacanian Psychoanalytical Approaches to Literature and Culture *Aylin Alkaç*	43
5	Does Post-Colonial Still Have Relevance? *Mehmet Ali Çelikel*	53

Part II: Post-(Humanist)-Theories

6	A Reconsideration of Subjectivity? Lacan's Response to Posthumanism *Nurten Birlik*	65

7   From Theory to Literature: Posthumanism as a Post-Theoretical
    Endeavor   75
    Başak Ağın

8   The *Rhizome d'être* of Posthumanism and the Question of Ethics:
    Revisiting Braidotti with Agamben   85
    Zekiye Antakyalıoğlu

9   The Posthuman Turn: Twenty-First Century Variations of Feminism   99
    Ela İpek Gündüz

10 Reinterpreting the Anthropocene: Toward an Ecocentric Worldview   113
    Cenk Tan

11 Literary Data, Fossil, and Speculation   125
    Emrah Peksoy

Part III: Literary Landscapes

12 Reading Character in Reading or, Character Again, Post-Theoretically   139
    Ivan Callus

13 The Affective Politics of the Twenty-First Century Novel   153
    Selen Aktari-Sevgi

14 Post-Postmodernism   165
    Bran Nicol

15 Metamodernism: Is it a New Hype for "the Post-Postmodern
    Syndrome"?   177
    Enes Kavak

16 The Lines of Influence: The (In)Visibility of Poetry after Theory   187
    Seda Şen

17 The Posthuman Turn in Postdramatic Theater   199
    Mesut Günenç

Part IV: Post-Philologies

18 Post-Theory and Post-Translation Studies   213
    Evrim Doğan Adanur

19 New Directions in Corpus Linguistics   223
    Meltem Muşlu

20 Translingualism in the Context of Language Teaching in the
    Twenty-First Century: New Approaches and New Practices   235
    Gamze Almacıoğlu

| 21 | Language Education within and after the Post-Method Era
Vildan İnci Kavak | 249 |

Appendix: Tables of Differences	261
Table I: Theory/Post-Theory	262
Table II: Modernism/Postmodernism/Post-Postmodernism	263
Table III: Humanism/Posthumanism	264
Index	267
About the Contributors	271

Acknowledgments

The idea of this project on "post-theories" came from a group of fellow academics who work and teach in the department of English at Gaziantep University, Turkey. They inquired if I were interested in being the editor of a volume that would bring together various researches on post-theoretical studies. I owe special thanks to them, for it was their enthusiasm that created the motivation behind the book's inception and coming into existence. The majority of the chapters were written by scholars and academics from all around Turkey holding various degrees and affiliations in the field of English language and literature. Many thanks to them for their invaluable contribution and support that made this project a possibility. Besides them, I'd like to extend my immense gratitude to Bran Nicol (University of Surrey, UK), Ivan Callus (University of Malta, Malta), and Cian Duffy (Lund University, Sweden) for kindly accepting my invitation and being on board. Their generous contributions have reinforced the substance of the book.

Special thanks to the Lexington Books family for their assistance in materializing this volume, and to Elis Durmaz for her keen eyes in the preliminary proofreading process.

Post-Theories in Literary and Cultural Studies is not only the culmination of pure academic interest or scholarly effort; it is also the fruit of commitment and solidarity. That's why editing it has been an honor and joy.

Zekiye Antakyalıoğlu

Editor's Introduction

Editing a volume on post-theories has been challenging as post-theory is an organic field of study that engages with the current research and critique offered by academics from different backgrounds and various interdisciplinary focuses. A volume of essays on post-theoretical studies has to be aware of the risks of undertaking such a task when discussions, trends and sensibilities are changing beyond notice.

The term "post-theory" implies both a detachment from and an attachment to "Theory" which, with "T," signifies the academic, scholarly, and philosophical endeavors of the second half of the twentieth century. "Theory" generally refers to the French Theory that had a colossal effect on literary and cultural studies with the works of scholars/philosophers such as Jacques Lacan, Roland Barthes, Michel Foucault, Jacques Derrida, Paul de Man, Gilles Deleuze, Felix Guattari, Jean Baudrillard, Paul Ricoeur, Emanuel Levinas, and Jean François Lyotard who have been considered as the "stars" that formed Theory's great constellation. Theory also refers to the works of the American, British, or European scholars such as Fredric Jameson, Hayden White, Richard Rorty, Stephen Greenblatt, Harold Bloom, Judith Butler, Slavoj Žižek, Hans Georg Gadamer, Terry Eagleton, and many others that this brief introduction fails to count. Postmodernist, poststructuralist, new historicist, post-Marxist, psychoanalytical, postcolonialist, and postfeminist schools of thought have been fundamental sources of literary and cultural production, shaped our ways of thinking, and created the deconstructive tradition in philosophy by radically changing our way of perceiving the concepts such as text, language, sign, gender, race, ethnicity, society, and existence. Theory, guided by a "hermeneutics of suspicion" as pioneered by Marx, Nietzsche, and Freud, promoted symptomatic reading as the best way of interpretation and functioned as the main source of interpretation in humanities and literary studies between the 1960s and 2000s. For many years, the academy experimented on the various forms of symptomatic reading to find the latent or hidden meaning as far as interdisciplinary studies could get. With the turn of the new millennium, prompted by the changes and problems on the global scale, there has been a resurgence of scholarly interest in theories that are more embedded in the social realities and human condition. The new century with its new problems—such as terrorism, war, economic crisis, COVID-19 pandemic, climate changes, oil and water crises, Anthropocene, the impact of social media, consumerism, migration, Brexit, the question of democracy, etc.—requires a serious turn to a more ethically driven and realistic engagement with the human condition. Therefore, in the last two decades, "more genuine criticism" (i.e., evaluation, value-judgment) and "less disinterested interpretation" became the new mantra. Academia, especially (post)humanities, has recently become more auto-critical and aware of the necessity of assuming a more responsible and relevant role in the face of the grave changes in the material world. *Post-Theories in Literary and Cultural Studies* brings to the attention of an Anglophone readership selected discussions in the "post-theory" era that indicate the changing perceptions in theoretical, literary, and cultural studies.

Post-theory holds two simultaneous attitudes toward Theory: acknowledgment and critique. On the one hand, it is indebted to the legacy of Theory and forms its discursive practices in relation to it; on the other hand, it is sceptical of it. It is a critique of Theory for its lack of *ethos*, and at the same time, a return to it with contemporary anxieties and motives. Post-theory is more socially, politically, morally, empirically, and environmentally oriented in engaging with life and literature than "Theory," and is shaping itself in direct response to the social demands. It examines Theory's viability and relevance regarding the urgent matters of concern that gained significant momentum in the contemporary scene. Jean-Michel Rabaté, in *The Future of Theory*, succinctly describes the contemporary sentiment as follows,

> The problem with Theory seems to be that it is always accused of having missed something. Theory is missing out on "life," real life that is, as in the expression "Get a life!" about "real" sexuality, "real" politics, and so on. (3)

The present volume, *Post-Theories in Literary and Cultural Studies*, is, therefore, a timely and relevant source of reference for those who wish to develop an understanding of this change of attitude in literary and cultural studies toward "getting a life." Therefore, the essays are more directly and sincerely responsive to the problems in "real life," their effects on language and literature, their roots in socio-political domains, and reflections on theory.

The volume agrees with Ernesto Laclau who, in the preface to *Post-Theory: New Directions in Criticism* (1999), stated that "although we have entered a post-theoretical universe, we are definitely not in an a theoretical one." (1) It also endorses Rosi Braidotti's slogan "Theory is back!" (*The Posthuman Glossary*, xiii) and aims at demonstrating, through various essays, what this return entails.

One of the aims of this volume is to show that theory can reinvent theory and redefine criticism according to the day's demands. In this context, the volume is planned to consist of chapters that examine the relation of post-theory with the concepts such as "ethics," "aesthetics," "truth," "value," "human," "authenticity," and "reality" to understand the mindset of the new century. Critical volumes of essays such as *Post-Theory: New Directions in Criticism* (Eds. Martin McQuillan, et al, 1999), *Theory After 'Theory'* (Eds. Jane Elliott and Derek Attridge, 2011), and *Post-Theory, Culture, Criticism* (Eds. Stefan Herbrechter and Ivan Callus, 2004) or manuscripts such as Jean-Michel Rabaté's *The Future of Theory* (2008) and Terry Eagleton's *After Theory* (2004) engaged with diverse concerns that indicate either the surpassing of Theory as dated and overcome, or the legacy of Theory as still necessary but demanding upgrade. *Post-Theories in Literary and Cultural Studies*, takes shape in response to the studies as such, and offers a re-evaluation of previous research from the standpoint of current tendencies, especially when new speculations circulate the upsurge of "posthumanism" as the next big theory.

Post-Theories in Literary and Cultural Studies is compiled of twenty-one essays which are grouped in four sections:

Part I, "Changing Climates in Theory and Criticism," involves five chapters examining the post-theoretical inclinations and matters of concern in literature and social life. In chapter one, Cian Duffy offers a critique of the exponential use of Theory in the literature departments since the 1960s, illustrates its suspicious practical outcomes, and calls for a return to practical criticism and a romantic humanism in literary studies as an alternative that might bridge the gap between theory and life. Aytül Özüm, in chapter two, returns to the question of ethics from the standpoint of narratology underlining literary empathy as the nexus of the present concerns. Rahime Çokay Nebioğlu, in chapter three, draws attention to the world's mutation into a new form where swarms of hatred, racist and sexist killings, economic turmoils, and terrorism are becoming part of everyday life. She contends that contemporary capitalism's politics of negative affects marks "the microfascistic turn" in our era. Aylin Alkaç, in chapter four, discusses the importance and relevance of post-Lacanian reading in the contemporary scene by underlining the internal tensions and new directions in psychoanalytic literary theory. Mehmet Ali Çelikel, in chapter five, questions whether the term "post-colonial" is still relevant in literary studies, and rethinks the colonial and postcolonial theories to interpret the conditions of postcolonial migrants as represented in the contemporary fiction.

Part II, "Post-(Humanist)-Theories," is formed of six chapters that elaborate on the various aspects of posthumanism as the dominant "–ism" of the post-theoretical era. It traces the engagement of post-theory with posthumanism across a range of different contexts such as feminism, psychoanalysis, Anthropocene, social life, new materialism, and ethics. Nurten Birlik, in chapter six, rethinks Lacanian subjectivity from a posthumanist perspective and reconsiders the concepts of human and non-human from the psychoanalytical view. In chapter seven, Başak Ağın describes posthumanism as a post-theoretical endeavor by offering a genealogy of the concept and discussing its relevance in humanities. Zekiye Antakyalıoğlu, in chapter eight, revisits Giorgio Agamben with Rosi Braidotti to open a discussion on the irreconcilable aspects of the ethically oriented theories of the two prominent contemporary thinkers. In chapter nine, Ela İpek Gündüz, presents a survey of the twenty-first century variations of feminism mainly from the posthumanist standpoint. Cenk Tan, in chapter ten, by centering upon the pivotal term Anthropocene, lays out various interpretations of the concept from an ecocentric worldview. Emrah Peksoy, in chapter eleven, offers an object oriented, materialist, and speculative realist method in analyzing literary texts regarding their ontological qualities.

Part III, "Literary Landscapes," examines, in six chapters, the effects of posthumanism, post-theory, and post-postmodernism in literary studies from the standpoint of genres (fiction, poetry, drama), and illustrates the current tendencies and changes of perspective in literary studies. In chapter twelve, Ivan Callus analyzes the resurgence of the idea of "character" in post-theoretical era by offering a critique of the poststructuralist theories which reduced "character" into a textual element or mode of language. Selen Aktari-Sevgi, in chapter thirteen, examines the affective politics of the twenty-first century novel by focusing on the changes in narrative tone and form since postmodernism, and presents how the contemporary novel offers a communal, ethical, and political response to challenge the hegemony of neoliberalism. Bran Nicol, in chapter fourteen, discusses the reasons behind the end of postmodernism and describes whether or not the literary and artistic movement of the new millennium might be termed as "post-postmodernism." In chapter fifteen, Enes Kavak scrutinizes the relevance and viability of "metamodernism" as the successor of postmodernism and inquires whether metamodernist thinking can be an alternative to post-postmodernism. Seda Şen, in chapter sixteen, elaborates on the fate of poetry in the post-theoretical period and explores how poetry has undergone changes in form, content, and medium in the digitalized world. Mesut Günenç, in chapter seventeen, interrogates shifting critical theory by focusing on the postdramatic theater and posthumanist drama from the standpoint of posthumanist ontology and illustrates the changing perceptions in performativity.

Part IV, "Post-Philologies," involves four chapters that focus on the changing focal points and areas of research in the studies of English as a language. Generally, volumes engaging with literary and cultural theory tend to exclude sections on language studies. Even during the "linguistic turn" of Theory in the twentieth century, although interdisciplinarity was the *forte* of theoretical and cultural studies, Theory research was somehow negligent of language studies, translation studies, and linguistics as related fields. This part, therefore, aims to change this attitude by its supplementary focus on the studies of English language. The chapters will offer a survey on the changing climates in the field of post-translation studies as the catalyst that made the emergence of "world literature" possible (Evrim Doğan Adanur, chapter eighteen); the digitalization of the text/language from the perspective of corpus linguistics and data processing (Meltem Muşlu, chapter nineteen); the change of horizons regarding the global use of English and translingualism (Gamze Almacıoğlu, chapter twenty); and finally, language education, especially after the pandemic or the online-education turn (Vildan İnci Kavak, chapter twenty-one).

The volume finishes with an appendix which contains three tables of differences that may function as a practical guide for those who find it hard to draw the lines of demarcation between the concepts and terms that the book interrogates. These three tables of differences are intended, especially to serve early-career researchers and graduate and undergraduate students' interests in gaining a clear and comparative perspective while distinguishing "theory" from "post-theory" (Table I); visualizing the differences between "modernism," "postmodernism," and "post-postmodernism" (Table II); and the differences between "humanism" and "posthumanism" (Table III).

Zekiye Antakyalıoğlu, 2021

REFERENCE LIST

Braidotti, Rosi. "Preface." *The Posthuman Glossary*. Edited by Rosi Braidotti and Maria Hlavajova. Bloomsbury Academic, 2018. p. xiii.

Laclau, Ernesto. "Preface." *Post-Theory: New Directions in Criticism*. Edited by Martin McQuillan, Graeme Macdonald, Robin Purves and Stephen Thomson. Edinburgh U.P., 1999. p.1.

Rabaté, Jean-Michel. *The Future of Theory*. Blackwell Wiley, 2008, p. 3.

I
CHANGING CLIMATES IN THEORY AND CRITICISM

1
A Liberal Humanism for the Twenty-First Century?

Cian Duffy

A few years ago, I asked the students on an MA survey course in literary theory to discuss this statement in their final paper: "the history of literary theory in the twentieth century can best be understood as a debate about the validity of liberal humanist ideas." My intention, as it had been throughout the course, was to get my students thinking about the historicity of "Theory," about the fact that theoretical texts are just as much the product of specific personal and historical circumstances, and carry just as much ideological freight, as the literary texts to which they can be applied. Put differently, my intention was to challenge the scienticity of Theory, to get my students thinking about how theoretical texts and literary texts are not really so very different as proponents of theoretical reading often assume. In this respect, the topic for the final paper was the natural conclusion to a course which had understood New Historicism as the *ne plus ultra* of Theory, of a course which had turned New Historicism back upon Theory itself.

It goes without saying that claims to have identified an "end of Theory" are just as likely to prove premature as Fukuyama's announcement of "the end of history" following what seemed like the denouement of the Cold War. But in asking my students to think about the historicity of Theory, about the *end* of Theory, I was also asking them to think about its *beginning*. What did it mean to suggest that Theory *began* with liberal humanism? To posit *origins* is no less hazardous an exercise than to posit *endings*. Theory, broadly defined, is as old as literature itself. Aristotle's *Poetics* is Theory. But (as I had argued on the MA course) it is possible to talk about Arnold's "The Function of Criticism at the Present Time" as marking, in various and very real senses, the beginnings of the modern discipline of academic literary criticism. I am thinking, in particular, of Arnold's insistence that

> a critic may with advantage seize an occasion for trying his own conscience, and for asking himself of what real service, at any given moment, the practice of criticism either

is, or may be made, to his own mind and spirit and to the minds and spirits of others. (*Essays in Criticism* 4)

In an obvious sense, this statement represents the *beginning* of what became Theory because Arnold's subsequent assessment of "the function of criticism" defined the parameters of future debates. Key early twentieth-century critics of English literature—Eliot, Leavis, and Richards—all demonstrably owe to Arnold, either directly or through opposition, much of their own thought: about the *purpose* of criticism; about the relationship between literary texts and their historical and biographical contexts; about whether or not it is possible or desirable to make evaluative judgments of literary texts; and about the inseparability of meaning and form. Arnold's assessment of the "real service" of criticism also played, through its influence on the *Newbolt Report* (to which I return below), an instrumental role in the establishment of English literature as a subject of academic study in schools and universities in Britain.[1] In this sense, too, his essay stands as a *beginning* for our subject, in terms of pedagogy as well as research praxis: for how and why we *teach* our students to study literature as well as for how we approach it ourselves, as professional scholars. But in another, perhaps less obvious but certainly more fundamental sense, Arnold's essay represents a beginning for literary Theory because the casuistry which he proposes—the critic pausing to consider what "real service" the activity about to be undertaken can provide—constitutes, or at least *ought* to constitute, the beginning of *every* instance of critical reading: what is the *purpose* of this reading; what is to be achieved by it; and why does that matter?

In what follows, I return to Arnold's foundational question and consider how we might resolve it today: what should be "the function of criticism" in our "present moment"? Specifically, I consider how Arnold's assessment of that "function," and its legacy in liberal humanist critical praxis, could help us address the impasses which Theory has reached, perhaps even *produced* from within itself, for literary critics today. I am aware, of course, that humanism in general, and liberal humanism in particular, is viewed with increasing disapprobation by certain sections of the academy. Humanism is often now critiqued as an ideological instrument of Western thought, historically (and still) deployed to repress all forms of diversity through the policing of a normative, essentially Cartesian valorisation of subjectivity defined as rational, heterosexual, white, male, and biologically *human*. But there may be a danger that such posthumanist critiques, however well-intentioned and well-founded, involve significant collateral damage. I don't think anybody could seriously doubt that humanism, historically, has produced enormous benefits. And though we might recognize that humanism, as an ideology and attendant set of cultural practices, has also had very damaging societal and environmental consequences, we should recognize, too, that these were not *intended* consequences and are certainly not *inevitable* consequences. We might argue, in other words, that rather than *rejecting* humanism, the time has come simply to renegotiate, armed with a few centuries of additional knowledge, how humanism is *defined*. Whatever else it is, after all, *humanism* is first and foremost a conception of what it means to be human and it makes no sense at all to think that this conception should remain fixed in stone—or to view the celebration of our humanity and of human cultural productivity as inherently, or necessarily, a suspicious activity. In very simple terms, one could argue that a twenty-first-century humanism, true to the spirit, if not to the letter, of Enlightenment humanism, would insist that affording the recognition and protections of personhood not only to *all* humans, but also to the natural world around us—as indeed *some* Enlightenment thinkers did insist—is a basic prerequisite of how *humanity* (in the sense of being *humane*) should be defined. One could argue, in other words, that a renegotiated humanism, sufficiently self-aware, still has enormous, progressive potential.

This kind of thinking informs my return to liberal humanist literary criticism here. For one thing, the reputational cloud under which that criticism labors is partly due to what Siskin (216), following Kaufer and Carley, describes as "reverse vicariousness:" a process by which texts become tokens, in critical and/or popular discourse, for ideas and positions which those texts do not, in fact, represent. Much of the assumption that liberal humanist reading practices are *intrinsically* elitist or insensitive to difference is simply not correct. Hence, even if we grant that liberal humanist reading practices *did*, historically, generate positions which we might now regard as problematic, that is not the same as saying that those practices can *only* generate such positions. Again, my intention here is to examine the extent to which we might, armed with the insights of a century of Theory, renegotiate liberal humanist ideas about the "function of criticism" and make those ideas of "service" today.

In the cultural aftermath of the First World War, the British government tasked a committee, led by the writer and historian Henry Newbolt, to investigate "The Teaching of English in England." Published in 1921, the *Newbolt Report* expressed concern that "modern literature" is no longer "generally recognised as having any direct bearing" upon "the life of the people" (256). Conversely, the report pointed to an alarming "tendency to assume that literature is the preserve of the 'cultured'" (259). But "literature and life," the report insists, "are in fact inseparable [. . .] literature is not just a subject for academic study, but one of the chief temples of the human spirit, in which all should worship" (259). *Newbolt* accordingly stressed the importance, the "obligation," of "the teaching of English" as a means of counteracting that tendency and re-establishing the relevance and centrality of literature, "not merely" to the lives of "students" but also to "the teeming population outside the University walls" (259).

A century after the publication of *Newbolt*, a case could be argued that the exponential rise of Theory as the dominant pedagogic and research paradigm in university literature departments has opened up a similarly damaging gulf between the academic study of literature and what *Newbolt* calls "the life of the people." Anxieties around authorial intention, reading against the grain, deconstructive reading, symptomatic reading, mapping historical works of literature against postfactum theoretical frameworks—these are among the practices which most sharply demarcate between academic and general reading; between what we do with literature in universities and what we do with it elsewhere; and between *how* we read as critics and *why* we read as people.

The perception of such a gulf is typified in Baskin's description of studying literature at university, which traces to the "postmodern notion of 'critique,'" what Baskin calls a "hatred of literature" among professional scholars, a "hatred" which

> manifested itself in their embrace of theories and methods that downgraded and instrumentalized literary experience, in their moralistic condemnation of the literary works they judged ideologically unsound, and in their attempt to pass on to their students their suspicion of literature's most powerful imaginative effects. ("On the Hatred of Literature")

One suspects, reading this, that Baskin may not have had especially good teachers, if they did indeed altogether reject the idea of literature as "a conduit" of "timeless truths" and "trustworthy passions" and emphasized, rather, that "the more powerful of an imaginative experience a work delivered, the more important it was to learn to view it with skepticism and detachment." Be that as it may, the opposition in Baskin's account between "theories and methods" and what we can quickly recognize as an intuitive appreciation for literature and literary value, broadly aligned with liberal humanist attitudes, is both instructive and alarming.

Among professional scholars, too, we can detect anxieties about the effects of the institutionalisation of Theory as a paradigm for research and teaching praxis. Sedgwick, for example, suggests that "the very productive critical habits embodied in what Paul Ricoeur memorably called the 'hermeneutics of suspicion'—widespread critical habits indeed, perhaps by now nearly synonymous with criticism itself—may have had an unintentionally stultifying side-effect." (4) "Subversive and demystifying parody, suspicious archaeologies of the present, the detection of hidden patterns of violence and their exposure," Sedgwick explains:

> these infinitely doable and teachable protocols of unveiling have become the common currency of cultural and historical studies [and] the broad consensual sweep of such methodological assumptions, the current near-profession-wide agreement about what constitutes narrative or explanation or adequate historicization, may, if it persists unquestioned, unintentionally impoverish the gene pool of literary-critical perspectives and skills. (21)

More recently, Bate (70) has pointed to the rise of what he calls the "New Didacticism": "a kind of millennial puritanism" which "reversed an older moralism" and according to which "what were once known as 'works of literature' became 'texts' which had to be 'interrogated'" as part of a wider "critique of humanism." Leavis (169) may well have been prescient, then, when he worried about the dangers of "critical expression" falling "under the control of something in the nature of a coterie."

Let this not be misunderstood. As Sedgwick and Bate make clear, the intention was good, of course: to establish the importance of literary studies as a discipline through an appeal to its ability to uncover the ideological freight of literary works and their role in the perpetuation, albeit often unintentionally, of damaging misrepresentations. And nobody would question the real importance of the insights generated by Theory into the historical oppressions and repressions with which literary and other cultural texts have often, wittingly or unwittingly, been complicit. But too often, the practical outcome has been a suspicion, or even the "hatred" Baskin perceives, toward literature understood as a medium for discriminatory attitudes and ideologies—and faulty, anachronistic readings of literary works. The paradox we are faced with is that Theory, which was supposed to bridge the gap between literary studies and "the life of the people," has played an unintentional part in making the study of literature seem elitist and, by extension, in confirming the damaging tendency, first noted by *Newbolt* (269), to assume that literature itself "is the preserve of the 'cultured.'" And the consequences of this for university literature departments are felt daily in the slashing of government funding for subjects no longer thought to be useful or relevant, and in the broader idea of "culture wars" to which the political right increasingly makes divisive appeal.

The faltering, in other words, of what Arnold called "the function of criticism", and the faltering institutional confidence in that function, is not just a problem for the academy: it is also, and moreover, as Arnold and his successors recognized, a problem for our societies. *Newbolt*, for example, argues that a failure to engage properly with literature led not only to a stifling of critical thinking but also to the fact that "the bulk of our people, of whatever class, are unconsciously living starved existences, that one of the richest fields of our spiritual being is left uncultivated" (259). Richards, discussing the tendency of his students to make what he considered thoughtless, "stock responses" (31) to literary texts, insists on the need to combat such "mental inertia" if we "wish for a high and diffused civilization, with its attendant risks" as opposed to "a population easy to control by suggestion" (314)—an insistence we would do well to remember in these days of twenty-four-hour news and social media. Leavis similarly emphasizes the connection between the "critical function" and an "educated public": the "disastrousness of letting the critical function be forgotten," Leavis insists, would be the surrender of an "educated public" to the "conditions" which would "deprive it of organs of expression, cohesion, and effect" (170, 172).

Faced with increasing awareness of these difficulties, in the early decades of the twenty-first century, literary critics have begun to suggest alternative solutions than symptomatic reading to Arnold's question about the "real service" which can be derived from "the practice of criticism." The emergence, for instance, of the various reading and analytical practices which might be grouped together under the rubric of "ecological criticism," and to which I will return later, makes one cogent answer to that question. Other solutions have come from those critics who have advocated renewed attention to the *formal* characteristics of literary texts, a renewal very much consistent with the tenets of liberal humanist criticism. Levinson (558–9), for example, reviews the emergence of a "New Formalism" that developed as a reaction to the institutional dominance of New Historicism. All the studies Levinson surveys "aim to recover for teaching and scholarship some version of their traditional address to form," though there is no reason to assume that New Historicism *intrinsically* neglects form, and, as Levinson rightly points out, it is "regrettable" that it often "serves as a catch-all term" for a broad spectrum of symptomatic practices (599). Specifically, Levinson suggests, New Formalist approaches "seek to reinstate close reading both at the curricular centre of our discipline and as the opening move, preliminary to any kind of critical consideration" (560). One could wonder how close reading—the cornerstone of liberal humanist criticism—ever lost that central position: after all, "close reading," as Levinson insists, *ought* to produce "the basic materials that form the subject matter of even the most historical of investigations" (560). More recently, Best and Marcus describe the development of new forms of what they call "surface reading" in reaction to the prevalence and perceived interpretative shortcomings of "symptomatic reading" and its assumption that "meaning" is latent rather than apparent in texts (1, 4). Such strategies include exploring the material history of texts (9); "accepting texts, deferring to them instead of mastering them or using them as objects"; (10) and attending, in terms of "form, structure, and meaning", to what "the text says about itself" (11)—many of which strategies clearly echo liberal humanist reading practices.

Taking my cue from these echoes of liberal humanism in emergent, post-Theory methodologies in literary studies, in what remains of this essay I consider how Arnold and his successors understood "the function of criticism" and the "real service" which that "function" could provide in order to assess how relevant their ideas might still be today. I do so not only because Arnold and his successors had a similar sense to ours of the faltering of the "critical function" but also because the specific intellectual and social difficulties which they hoped that "function" could address have only grown more pressing a century later. That faltering has been made clearly visible, by researchers within the academy, through hoaxes like the Mickelson and Sokal papers, as well as through the so-called "Postmodernism Generator," a website which produces algorithmically essays in postmodernist and poststructuralist literary criticism (https://www.elsewhere.org/pomo/). And this, again, is to say nothing at all of faulty readings of literary texts based on preconceived theoretical paradigms: so-called criticism-by-numbers. But the problem, which is ultimately one of confidence in the epistemological value (in the "real service") of the kind of knowledge generated about literary texts by Theory, extends well beyond what *Newbolt* called "the university walls." Anxieties about fake news, alternative facts, conspiracy theories, and the clear and present difficulty of identifying valid and valuable information against the background noise of disparate opinion—such things seem very much of the now and very much the consequence of our information-technology and social-media driven societies. But here is Richards almost a century ago:

> It is arguable that mechanical inventions, with their social effects, and a too sudden diffusion of indigestible ideas, are disturbing throughout the world the whole order of

human mentality, that our minds are, as it were, becoming of an inferior shape—thin, brittle and patchy, rather than controllable and coherent. It is possible that the burden of consciousness that a growing mind has now to carry may be too much for its natural strength [. . .] Therefore if there be any means by which we may artificially strengthen our minds' capacity to order themselves, we must avail ourselves of them. (320)

For Richards, who draws sustained analogies between physical and mental conditioning, the reading of literature—*if done properly*—is "the most serviceable" of such "means" (320). This is so, Richards insists, not only because "there is no such gulf between poetry and life as overly-literary persons sometimes suppose" (319), and so when we read literature we read about ourselves, but also because the processes by which we make judgments about literary texts ought to be cognate with the processes by which we make judgments in a whole range of other political, social, and even existential circumstances. In other words, what Arnold calls the "function of criticism" is not merely a matter of literary criticism. "If we are neither to swim blindly in schools under the suggestion of fashion," Richards argues, "nor to shudder into paradox before the inconceivable complexity of existence, we must find a means of exercising *our power of choice* [. . .] The lesson of all criticism is that we have nothing to rely upon in making our choices but ourselves" (310–20; emphasis added). Hence, just as there should be no "gulf" between "literature" and "the life of the people," so, according to Richards, should "the function of criticism" be understood as crucial to the promotion and protection of a "high and diffused civilisation."

So far so good. But one could easily worry that much of what today passes for critical thinking, be it in literary studies or journalism or social media, represents less independence of thought than what Richards calls "blindly" following "the suggestions of fashion." Eliot (23) may have been overstating his opinion for rhetorical effect when he concluded that "criticism, far from being a simple and orderly field of beneficent activity, from which impostors can readily be ejected, is no better than a Sunday park of contending and contentious orators, who have not even arrived at the articulation of their differences." But neither does his quip fall entirely short of the mark today, either, when it comes to critical, or for that matter, to public debate. To Richards' anxieties about "fashion," we might add Arnold's concerns about the potentially blinding effects on the critic of what he calls (*Essays in Criticism* [second series] 6) the "personal estimate" and the "historic estimate" of literary texts, the former leading us to look less critically upon a text or position because we can relate to it and the latter because that text or position has been presented to us as of significance. Today we might use the term "echo chamber" to characterize these "estimates"—and we would do well to remember that literary critics are no less immune to such "chambers" than anybody else, nor left-wing thinkers any less vulnerable to them than those on the right.

So much for problems. What about solutions? The emphasis, in liberal humanist literary criticism, on attention to the formal features of texts rather than their contexts, for all its obvious risks, needs to be understood as an attempt to guarantee *independent* thinking on the part of the critic and, by extension, on the part of the citizen. Such independence is what I had hoped to enable through the exam question with which I began this essay: to ask my students to step outside the parameters of any given theoretical paradigm or assumption and to think, instead, about "Theory" *per se*. Liberal humanism is itself, of course, a Theory and no less informed (and potentially blinded) by ideological and cultural perspectives than any other Theory. But liberal humanist reading praxis differs from much theoretical reading on two key points—and the continued "service" which might be made of these is worth re-evaluating today.

The first is Arnold's insistence on the need for constant *self-reflection* on "the function of criticism:" that literary critics should constantly reassess not only *what* they are doing but also *why* they are doing it, rather than starting from some preconceived Theory or standpoint. In other words, liberal humanist criticism insists that a meta-perspective on "the function of criticism" should be the beginning of every specific instance of critical reading—and that is surely an irrefutable argument, though of course critics can and will come up with very different estimates from Arnold and his successors about the "service" which "criticism" can provide. As critics, and as citizens, we must not, to quote Richards again, blindly follow "the suggestions of fashion:" rather, we must continually reassess, for "ourselves," on the basis of our own experience, *what* we are reading, and *how* and *why* we are reading it. Every exercise of the "function of criticism" should begin with such reassessment.

The second signal feature of liberal humanist reading praxis is its willingness to *listen* to what literary texts have to say rather than to treat those texts as objects of suspicion, as is the case with much Theoretical or symptomatic reading. We should, in other words, remain open to what literary texts can tell us, on their own terms, about ourselves and about our world. In one respect, this is only common sense: surely if literary texts were really to be understood as dangerous vehicles of ideological manipulation, the simplest solution would be not to read them at all? And of course, through practices like cancel-culture, no-platforming, and excision, we see, today, moves toward exactly such a censoring attitude. But I really doubt if anyone picks up a book with the intention of being manipulated or misled. And I wonder what author would willingly put pen to paper in the first place if they genuinely felt their work could be an agent of such misleading. Authors write to tell stories, to record facets of human experience, and readers read to learn what others have thought about such things. Hence, an adequate understanding of "the function of criticism" should surely take its point of departure, as liberal humanism does, in a recognition of these facts about *why* we write and read.

Here, though, we encounter potential complications. *Trusting* the text, understanding "the function of criticism" to involve at least as much *exposition* as *critique*, requires what Arnold calls a "high order of excellence" (*Essays in Criticism* [second series] 3) in the literature we read and that we avoid what *Newbolt* calls the "weeds of literature"—which, it suggests, "have never been so prolific as in our day." (257) But how do we identify what "really excellent" literature *is*, and, even more problematically, *who* gets to decide? Here liberal humanism is certainly vulnerable to critique and it offers no better answer to the first question than that we can learn to recognize "excellence" when see it by familiarizing ourselves with works already agreed to be excellent and using them as a "touchstone," as Arnold (*Essays in Criticism* [second series] 17) famously puts it—an answer which is in one way common sense and in another way little better than a chicken-and-egg paradox. To the second question, however, about *who* gets to decide, liberal humanist criticism offers the more progressive than is now generally recognized affirmation that *anyone* can *learn* how to recognize and appreciate "excellence"—but also that everyone needs to be *taught* how: nobody is born with the skill. Richards designed "practical criticism" precisely to provide this kind of training, again using analogies between mental and physical conditioning,

> If it is easy to push up the general level of performance in such "natural" activities as running or jumping (not to insist upon the more parallel examples of mountaineering, fly-fishing and golf) merely by making a little careful enquiry into the best methods, surely there is reason to expect that investigation into the technique of reading may have even happier results. (309–10)

It is crucial to remember, then, that while liberal humanist ideas about *quality* in literature have sometimes been made the basis for accusations of elitism, and while individual critical judgments do often reflect the prejudices of their time, liberal humanist critical praxis is not *per se* elitist. Conversely, from Arnold to Leavis, liberal humanist critics insist that everyone *can* and *should* be *taught* to recognize quality and to read only the best, not just for their own sake but also, and moreover, in order to promote "high and diffused civilisation." Far from being intrinsically elitist, liberal humanist critical praxis would make "excellent" literature accessible to all; it would make literary critics (and good citizens) of us all by enabling us to think for *ourselves* through introducing us to the best of what others have thought. It is, or at least can be, a *method* rather than an ideological program. What liberal humanist criticism makes apparent, in other words—and again, paradoxically, in view of the reputational clouds under which it has labored—is that *education* and access to the fine arts, as the key to independent critical thinking, is fundamental to stable and progressive societies and that such education cannot simply be the preserve of the few. If academic praxis has suggested otherwise, then that must surely have been a grievous, even if unintentional, misstep.

It would require substantially more scope than I have at my disposal here to enquire into what role "the function of criticism," as understood by liberal humanist thought, might play in (re)forming educational- and educational-access policy today, and not least because these are wider issues of social and economic justice. Nor is that really the purpose of this essay or of the volume of which it is part. But we should remember that liberal humanism's insistence on the need to evaluate the quality of *literary* works is paralleled by an insistence on the need to evaluate works of criticism too. Even if we reject as too vulnerable to prejudice the liberal humanist idea of ranking literature according to quality, we can surely accept the need to evaluate the quality of criticism just as we would evaluate the quality of research in STEM-subjects? It cannot be that "anything goes" when it comes to literary criticism. I have already noted how Sedgwick and others sought to re-establish the importance of close reading. But we might also point to a wider, systematic problem with symptomatic or deconstructive methodologies. Such methodologies are undoubtedly useful in exposing, critiquing, and breaking down structures of authority. But they are of rather less use in creating or constructing meaning, precisely because they are suspicious of such creative activity. For this kind of Theory, in other words, literature and criticism are opposed activities. But that is not a distinction which liberal humanist criticism would recognize. "The critical activity," Eliot writes, "finds its highest, its true fulfilment in a kind of union with creation in the labour of the artist" (30). Criticism is *itself* a creative act and therein lies its individually and socially transformative potential. And in such ideas, we arguably find the germs of much later, neo-modernist refutations of postmodernism and poststructuralism.

In closing, I will look briefly at how liberal humanist reading practices could help us evade some of these impasses into which Theory-driven, or symptomatic reading, have led us. When Bate diagnosed what he dubbed the "New Didacticism" in literary studies, he noted that it had been until then largely blind to what works of literature can tell us about environmental damage: "it was too busy worriedly manipulating the words 'nature' and 'man' to pay attention to man's manipulation of nature through technology" (248). That situation has since been remedied and "a flourishing literary ecocriticism" (71) has emerged. But the extent to which ecological criticism has begun to read symptomatically is undeniably a problem. What might we gain by recalibrating ecological criticism away from the "hermeneutics of suspicion" and toward the reading practices outlined by liberal humanist thinkers, by listening to what literary texts say to us about everything from species loss to how we experience being in nature? Symptomatic readings of literary texts frequently present *nature* as a sign for something else, something repressed, something human. And this kind of anthropomorphic reading typifies exactly the commoditization of nature for human purposes which deep ecologists diagnose not only as detrimental to the biosphere but as predicated upon a fundamental misunderstanding of the relationship between humans and the rest of the natural world. *Humanism* may be a problem here, or a particular flavor of humanism at least, but liberal humanist reading praxis could give us a way of resetting our approach to literary representations of the natural world and our place in it—not through critique, but to listening to what those texts tell us. This could be as simple as remembering that the *literal* meaning of a text is important, that the range of possible figurative meanings in a text is delimited by the literal meaning, that "surface reading" or practical criticism ought to be the beginning, at least, of all exposition and interpretation. Let's take an example. If we insist on reading a poem like William Wordsworth's "Nutting" symptomatically, we may well decide that it narrates the fall from grace, the emergence of the ego into Freudian self-consciousness and/or sexual self-awareness, or the formation of a

Cartesian subjectivity in which human and nature are opposed. But we risk missing the child's "sense of pain" (50) at having destroyed, in his remorseless quest for hazelnuts, "a dear nook/ Unvisited [. . .] beneath the trees [. . .] among the flowers," (14–15, 25–6) and the "sweet mood" (37) that place occasioned. The symptomatic interpretations are possible, of course, but are they worth the price of the poem's own assessment of the situation: "move along these shades/ In gentleness of heart; with gentle hand/ Touch,—for there is a Spirit in the woods" (51–3)? Should the academy tell the general or student reader that such a reading is naive, that *this* is not what the poem is *really* about? In our days of industrial agriculture, industrial fishing, fracking, strip mining, could Theory really make any point of more "service" to us than the poem makes itself? What we need to learn is how to listen to what texts tell us about ourselves and our place in the world—and then decide, for ourselves, whether we agree.

NOTE

1. For recent scholarly appraisals of the *Newbolt Report* and its influence on English Studies, see Lawrie (2014) and Aldridge and Green (2019).

REFERENCE LIST

Aldridge, David, and Andrew Green. "Newbolt and the Construction of Subject English," *English in Education*, vol. 15, number 3, 2019, pp. 195–198.
Arnold, Matthew. *Essays in Criticism*. Macmillan, 1895.
———. *Essays in Criticism*, second series, Macmillan, 1896.
Barry, Peter. *Beginning Theory*. Manchester University Press, 2002.
Baskin, Jon. "On the Hatred of Literature," *The Point*, 21, 26 January 2020, https://www.thepointmag.com/letter/on-the-hatred-of-literature/ (accessed June 2021).
Bate, Jonathan. *The Song of the Earth*. Picador, 2000.
Best, Stephen, and Sharon Marcus. "Surface Reading. An Introduction," *Representations*, vol. 108, no. 1, 2009, pp. 1–21.
Eliot, T.S. *Selected Essays*. Faber & Faber, 1932.
Fukuyama, Francis. *The End of History and the Last Man*. Free Press, 1992.
Lawrie, Alexandra. "Coda: the Newbolt Report and University English Studies in the Twentieth Century," in Alexandra Lawrie ed. *The Beginnings of University English*, Palgrave, 2014, pp. 149–57.
Leavis, F. R. *New Bearings in English Poetry* (1932). Faber and Faber, 2008.
Levinson, Marjorie. "What is New Formalism?" *PMLA*, vol. 122, no. 2, March 2007, pp. 558–69.
Newbolt, Henry. *The Newbolt Report* (1921). British Board of Education, Stationary Company, 1926; quoted from: http://www.educationengland.org.uk/documents/newbolt/newbolt1921.html.
Richards, I. A. *Practical Criticism*. Kegan Paul, 1929.

Sedgwick, Eve Kosofsky, editor. *Novel Gazing: Queer Readings in Fiction.* Duke University Press, 1997.
Siskin, Clifford. *The Work of Writing.* Johns Hopkins, 1998.
Wordsworth, William. *The Major Works.* Edited by Stephen Gill, Oxford World's Classics, 2008.

2

The Ethical Turn

Return of Empathy

Aytül Özüm

Contemporary discussions on ethical literary criticism and the role of empathy no longer have an imperative tone in terms of how, when, or why to empathize with characters in fictional narratives. Instead, they mostly describe the ontology of art and the artist. Today's descriptions about different facets of ethical reading and empathy take their roots from Emmanuel Levinas's controversial essay, "Reality and Its Shadows," first published in 1948 in *Les Temps Modernes*. While comparing artistic representation with the realistic, Levinas especially stresses the ambivalent nature of art as follows:

> To go beyond is to communicate with ideas, to understand. Does not the function of art lie in not understanding?. . . Art does not know a particular type of reality; it contrasts with knowledge. It is the very event of obscuring, a descent of the night, an invasion of shadow. To put it in theological terms, which will enable us to delimit however roughly our ideas by comparison with contemporary notions: art does not belong to the order of revelation. Nor does it belong to that of creation, which moves in just the opposite direction. (132)

Accordingly, fictional art creates an illusion, and therefore, the contents of a fictional narrative might not be accompanying its readers to achieve a meaningful target that would unite both sides. Being one with the fictional *other* in fictional texts is another illusion for Levinas. In the excerpt below Levinas refers to the communication between the reader and fictional art, another topic of many contemporary discussions. Under the circumstances which he describes in "The Other in Proust," the kind of reading which targets the fusion of the self and the other can hardly be ethical: "This is the last vestige of a conception that identifies being with knowledge, that is, with the event through which the multiplicity of reality ends up referring to a single being and where, through the miracle of clarity, everything that encounters me exists as coming from me. It is the last vestige of idealism" (164). This "ideal" unity does not acknowledge difference and, hence, empathetic interpretation, in this case, cannot be ethical as it disregards the solitary existence of the other. So, regarding the theoretical arguments of the critics, some of whom believe in the morally edifying value of both literature and empathetic reading of it, and some of whom stress literature as morally anarchic and hence empathy as oppressive, this chapter aims to discuss the ambivalent relationship between ethics and empathy on the ground where the borders of the subjectivities of the writer and the reader/critic are always already blurred, and narrative dynamics are complicated.

Among the theories and critical approaches to literary texts that appeared at the turn of the century, cross-disciplinarity and interdisciplinarity have been valued as essential tools uniting the previously active stance of the reader/critic and the passive but authorial status of the writer with narrative and its components instead of prioritising one over the other. However, parallel to what has been discussed for the last two decades about Levinas's ethics, it is quite noticeable that the double-edged sword of empathy neither aims to achieve a moral target, nor it helps the reader/critic get closer to the intended message of the writer; it can create caring but ethically ambivalent individuals, devoid of authenticity. It might terminate the autonomy of the inner dialogue and the authentic relationship between the reader/critic and the writer. In the realm of ethical criticism today, it is conspicuous that empathy does not necessarily promote ethical behavior; in fact, it may paralyze ethical judgment and action.

From within ethical criticism, new readings of literary texts and redefinitions of terms such as morality, self, other, autonomy, authority, authenticity, and truth have been reformulated at the dawn of the twenty-first century. Marshall Gregory discusses how and why readers/critics and texts are inseparable by stating the necessity and inevitability of ethical criticism because humans are social beings. Thus, they identify mostly with the characters in various moral circumstances in fiction. He also emphasizes the necessity to formulate a "theoretical basis" ("Ethical" 194) that would ideally connect ethical echoes in literature with dynamics in the narrative. In their attempts to construct certain precise values, some of the readings of ethical literary criticism naturally aim to narrow down the gap between the text at hand and the reader/critic on the other side. However, Gregory seems to limit the communication between the reader and the text by defining a latent moral capacity for all the fictional texts by stating that "[t]he portraits we draw of other people in our minds' eye—the picture that tells us whether and how much we can afford to trust and love them—are portraits drawn almost entirely in ethical and moral colours" ("Ethical" 198). In contrast to this, it might be argued that poststructuralism, in its praise of rhetoric, methodologically disconnects morality and the content of the texts. For this reason, for Gregory, poststructuralists cannot explain why literary representations of race, gender, class and politics are crucial for human improvement ("Ethical" 202). The real world tends to intrude. In one of his earlier articles, Gregory states that the terrorist attacks on America of 9/11 were also an attack on postmodern grandiosity.

It is hard to disagree with him because witnessing that violence resulted in an urgency to revitalize the priority given to ethical concerns. Still, it must be remembered that there are many fictional works categorized as posthuman that aim to highlight such an urgency by employing postmodern literary techniques in their own way. Concerning ethical criticism's second turn in literary critical studies, Gregory mindfully asks, "how is it going to avoid making the same mistakes that plagued it in the past: fatuity, doctrinaire shrillness, empty moralising for the sake of moralising, and fruitless debates with critical 'enemies' over the imputed ethical purity or ethical rot of one preferred or reviled work over another?" ("Redefining" 282). This concern, too, is about the methodology of ethical criticism, which includes the long-debated role and function of empathy.

Most of the theoretical manoeuvres recently shared by academics in the West to save not only the text's value but also the reader/critic's autonomy are derivatives of hermeneutical and phenomenological questions around ethical criticism such as: "What does the literary text mean?" "Why is it written?" "What is the affect of the text?" "What does the fictional world in the text represent?" "Does the materiality of the text matter?" and most significantly "What does the text do to its reader?" While the common emphasis of these questions has been on the urgency to impact the reader and crystallise the tripartite relationship among the writer, the text, and the reader/critic, the status of the writer as the supplier of literary representation has not been highlighted much. In contrast, by sceptically shattering the claims of truth, postmodernist literary theory asserted that all sorts of representations are distortions. However, recent studies on the echoes of poststructuralism in the ethical turn have revealed that faith in the viability of representation does not diminish. Literary studies about narrative empathy in the ethical turn address many issues about the form of the text and the meaning it discovers, the role of the critic in retelling the story of the text, representations of characters from different races, genders, and ethnicity, and also about the essential agency of the participatory reading activity that connects two subjectivities.

Studying literary empathy just at the nexus of these concerns lays bare various roles previously attributed both to the text and the reader/critic. It investigates various possibilities embracing the writer's position and possible claims upon their text. The role of language and the operative status of the writer's intended meaning still play a significant role in empathy studies. There is much research on the moral value that a literary text adds to the receiver due to the empathetic relationship between the reader/critic and the text and how to narrow down the gap between the intentionality of the writer and the expectations of the reader/critic.

For Lawrence Buell, one of the pioneers of ecocriticism, ethical criticism derives from the collapse of Deconstruction in the 1980s. In his essay entitled "In Pursuit of Ethics" (1999), he refers to the fall that gained pace with the republication of Paul de Man's *Wartime Journalism* that includes passages echoing pro-Nazism. Accordingly, the event marks the beginning of the debates about the contents and discontents of the ethical turn and ethical literary criticism (Buell, 8–9). On the one hand, mostly with the constructive and progressive theoretical research in sociological, psychological, and narratological interpretations of a great variety of literary texts, popular and canonical, many critics became sceptical toward the value of exclusive engagement with the text itself to annihilate its core meaning. On the other, as Buell explains, regarding the dialogue between Jacques Derrida and Emmanuel Levinas, two specific approaches, or rather attitudes in deconstructive ethical criticism concerning the status of the text, invigorated reconsiderations of the self and the other. One of them is the belief that distrust toward the reliability of the text is an ethical approach, and the other is the idea that prioritizing the content of the co-text is an "ethical obligation" (9). Levinas is one of the central figures in the post-poststructuralist era, and he gives non-ontological authority to the *other* over the *I*, which means the text. For Levinas, the other has a claim. Although he does not name ethical literary criticism in his theory, the other can possibly be interpreted as the reader or the writer of the text. Amiel-Houser and Mendelson-Maoz's evaluation of ethical criticism in the twenty-first century refers to Levinas's criticism of Western philosophy's "imperialistic project" (205), characterized by a ferocious search for something that can be identified with the self. Accordingly, empathetic reading is not ideal for ethical criticism. It is a risk to indulge oneself in such a reading for substituting one's feelings and thoughts for those in a literary text. In that search, one might ignore the differences between oneself and the other and therefore might not fully understand the plight of the other that does not correspond to his own.

As human beings, we have been recounting, writing, criticizing, re-evaluating, and trying to find meaning in various narratives; while living with the narratives, we try to detect why and in what forms we respond to them. We know that for Levinas, an ethical relationship with another person/character is not about understanding or knowing them, but it is about embracing the foreign other with all its incomprehensibility. The concrete face of the other for Levinas "resists my powers" (*Totality* 197), so it would be wrong to claim that the other asks for "my" empathy. On the contrary, the face makes one feel uncomfortable, and as a result, one feels compelled to be responsible for that face. For Amiel-Houser and Mendelson-Maoz, the ethical difficulty is to visualize the other person/character as a "radical alterity, totally exterior and inaccessible" (206) and simultaneously be on their side to help them. However, while interpreting Levinas, they touch upon the fact that the reader/critic might disrespectfully cross the boundaries between himself and what he reads (207).

To understand the desired, though not defined as the ideal, state of mind that the new ethical criticism aims to discuss, Gregory's explanations and remarks about the transforming nature of the reading process are worth referring to. He, in a way, redefines the empathetic identification as a feeling or rather as a reverberating "influence" of the text upon the reader/critic; from the perspective of new ethical criticism, the literary text invites the reader to reformulate what they imitate in the interactive process of reading: "An 'ethical' influence looked at from this perspective, then, we may define *as any influence that exerts shaping pressure on one's ethos, on who we become as a result of bending with or internalising that influence*" ("Redefining" 296). For

Gregory, only through such a process can the reader/critic preserve their "autonomy" or solitariness. Autonomy is enhanced through observing the change the reader/critic experiences in their perception of the authentic self. For better or worse, the change is therefore appreciated after being engaged in the literary text at hand.

Today, among other issues, the core of ethical criticism values the connection between the artistic, in other words, the narrative performance of the author in the text, and how life and culture, with many of their facets, invigorate that performance. So, in general terms, both the analysis of human behavior and the form of the literary text interactively participate in the formation of the concerns of ethical criticism. The author's intention, design in the narrative, and readers' expectations play a significant role in understanding the shift to the human matter from the textual matter in ethical criticism. Schwarz agrees that one of the most dominant beliefs is that literary texts, by nature, are connected to their readers because they transfer "sayings" (5) that make them potentially loaded with ethical concerns. Most literary critics believe that the readers are more sensitive toward what they read than what they live. In line with this thought, Wayne Booth strongly believes that the transformative ethical power of art, in general, cannot be denied, and he continues, "Even the most ardent opponents of censorship or ethical criticism do not deny that many stories can actually harm at least some of those who 'take them in.' And even the most ardent attackers on immoral artworks imply by their every gesture that certain other works, in contrast, are not just morally defensible, not just beneficial, but essential to any human life . . . the power of narrative to change our lives, for good or ill, becomes undeniable" (17–18).

Booth, whose concerns are rather deterministic about the existence of the implied author's intentions, in a way, regards the literary text as a merger between the author (whose responsibility is important for the ethical evaluation for Booth) and the reader/critic no matter which movement or ideology influences the reading motifs or circumstances. Accordingly, even those who deny the assumed "unity" of the selves in a text seek "a reduction of multiple or divided selves" (20). This definition of the self should also include the self of the reader/critic. While comparing the postmodern and modern approaches to ethics, Zygmunt Bauman in *Postmodern Ethics* draws attention to the modern tendency in law and philosophy toward the driving force of unity disguised as a bundle of constructed moral codes to help gather the "loosely related aims and functions" (6) of human lives. As for the postmodern condition, Bauman highlights the role of "care," which is a significant concern for ethical criticism in general, and also for empathetic identification in particular:

> . . . the impulse to care for the Other, when taken to its extreme, leads to the annihilation of the autonomy of the Other, to domination and oppression . . . The moral self moves, feels, and acts in the context of ambivalence and is shot through with uncertainty. Hence the ambiguity-free moral situation has solely a utopian existence of the perhaps indispensable horizon and stimulus for a moral self, but not a realistic target of ethical practice. (11–12)

Empathetic unity between the reader's self and the writer's selves in the literary text, which Booth describes as such, must end with "the reader's judgment" (26). It is not compatible with the postmodern perspective that "shows the relativity of ethical codes and of moral practices they recommend . . ." (Bauman 14).

For Schwarz, however, Booth does not disregard the essential place of "rhetoric," in other words, the art of meaning-making in ethics. He quotes from Booth: "If 'virtue' covers every kind of genuine strength or power, and if a person's ethos is the total range of his or her virtues, then ethical criticism will be any effort to show how the virtues of narratives relate to the virtues of selves and societies, or how the ethos of any story affects or is affected by the ethos-the collection of virtues-of any given reader" (8–9). The form and style of narratives play a significant role in the mutual transmission of ethos between the narratives and the readers. This connection has a reciprocal and interactive effect upon/between the psyches, both of the reader/critic and those portrayed in fictional narratives. As Booth also highlights, the stories we read invite us to evaluate some ethical concerns in content and encourage us to decipher and agree/disagree with the conflictual matters through the arrangement of action and plot (26–27). Empathetic identification with the characters or events in the fictional text depends on the narrative's aesthetic success. What Booth calls "aesthetic achievement" (27) is possible only if the narrative has enough capacity for juxtaposed interpretations of the readers. If empathy is taken as an experience that would respectfully separate the two sides, it also leads to awareness. Schwarz's point adds a moral side to that: "Literature provides surrogate experiences for the reader, experiences that, because they are embodied within artistically shaped ontologies, heighten our awareness of moral discriminations. Yet, I suggest, what distinguishes moral philosophy from literature is its specificity, its nominalism, and its dramatised particularity" (5).

Charles Altieri carefully approaches the role of morality in ethical criticism, its impositions by the narrative, and the function of aestheticism. He tends to favor deconstructive and Levinasian ethical criticism, although he gives voice to its aporias. He differentiates between the moral and the ethical. Accordingly, the value of deconstructive ethical criticism is in its ability to see the strength of inner textual forces above the moral values that the reader might want to impose upon what they read. Under the circumstances he articulates, empathy does *not* have to be one-sided, selfish, or floating freely to the narrative from the reader/critic. For him, once the reader/critic can separate the subjectivities within the text from their own, this attitude would project itself in social relationships (35). The approach to the text defined above brings about respect for the boundaries mentioned earlier.

Although there are agreements upon the boundaries of ethical criticism, there is still no consensus about the value of ethical considerations and approaches. In addition to explaining the return to the value of the "authorial agency" ("Introduction" 12), Buell also highlights the significance of the reading process in the new perception of ethical criticism as being more than "a free reading," for him it derives from "conscienceful listening," which differs from the approach of reader-response critics.

In fact, what is signalled by Buell is a thoughtful, sensible, and empathetic concern toward the literary texts' content and origin. Derek Attridge proposes the model of "the work as stranger." As he puts it, "[R]ather than the familiar model of the literary work as friend and companion, sharing with the reader its secrets, I propose the work as stranger, even and perhaps especially when the reader knows it intimately" (26). Accordingly, although the reader knows the work closely, the work that stands before the reader as an *other*, as discussed earlier, needs to be read meticulously since the act of reading itself requires responsibility. Therefore, morality and empathetic identification, defined variously in the terrain of ethical criticism, has different resonances. How is responsibility shared? How is the hypothetical boundary between the narrative and the reader/critic defined? What is the writer's role/function in the moral repercussions of empathetic identification? These questions preoccupied many writers and academics who are interested in ethical criticism today. The proposed methodology brings together the postmodern analysis and the edifying role of ethical criticism without devaluing the potential impact of the fictional narratives by respectfully acknowledging the distance between the self and the other.

Amiel-Houser and Mendelson-Maoz argue that "postmodern thinking motivates us to challenge the idea of empathy as a basis for ethical reading, a notion that has overshadowed both the theory and the practice of modern ethical criticism" (200). It still plays an important role in the renewed interest in ethical criticism, even though this approach has challenged the established doctrines of modern ethical thinking. Specifically, the writers in their article give voice to the stress upon the place and value of empathy in ethical criticism and state that ethics of narrative empathy, to some extent, would limit the sphere of ethical criticism. However, for Martha Nussbaum, empathetic reading is ethically significant, "Life is never simply presented by a text; it is always represented as something . . . The responsibility of the literary artist . . . is to discover the forms and terms that fittingly and honourably express, adequately state, the ideas that it is his or her design to put forward; and to bring it about that the reader . . . is active in a way suited to the understanding of whatever is there for understanding . . ."(*Love's* 5–6). Also, Martha Nussbaum sees novel reading as one means that would connect people unknown to one another. She believes that the works evoke certain political and moral sensibilities and states in the readers' minds, "The habits of wonder promoted by storytelling thus define the other person as spacious and deep, with qualitative differences from oneself and hidden places worthy of respect" (*Cultivating* 90). She also strongly highlights that reading should have a purpose to narrow the gap between the reader and the fictional characters. She does not undermine the aesthetic significance of the narratives for ethical criticism. On the contrary, she highlights its core function: "I argue that literary works can help us cross these barriers, if they display the person on the other side of the barrier in a certain way; as a human being worthy of sympathy. But to do this they will need to address, and undermine, the very specific stereotypes that block us from seeing the humanity of specific groups with which we interact" ("Exactly" 69). What is explained here also points at the significance of raising awareness through narrative means without emotionally abusing the readers and therefore not aiming to address a specific group of readers who would feel fulfilled enough after feeling for the misery of the other.

Levinas deals with a critical problem on subjective experience that can be related to the similar relationship between the narrative accounts and those who interpret them, "Expression does not consist in giving us the Other's interiority. The Other who expresses himself precisely does not give himself, and accordingly retains the freedom to lie" (*Totality* 202). It is another questioning perspective about the effective and realistic nature of that relationship, decreasing the credibility of the fictional narratives one reads while at the same time cognitively aims to empathize with the characters in them. Probability is in the nature of almost all fictional accounts; evaluating them as forms of expression, in the way defined by Levinas, might seem to lessen or even annihilate the accuracy of narrative empathy. Empathic inaccuracy for Keen is "the discordance arising from the gaps between an author's intention and a reader's experience of narrative empathy" ("A Theory" 215). It is a serious obstacle hypothetically placed before the practice of ethical criticism; However, Levinas' thoughts on the relationship between the self and the other do not mean that communication between both sides is impossible or infertile. On the contrary, this communication is based upon a respectful distance, and it is ethical, so empathetic identification, which is generally termed as such, is not about the merger of both parties. It would be relevant to state that when the respectful distance between the one engaged in empathetic identification and the fictional character empathized with is well-defined, the boundaries between their territories will be intact. In line with this relationship, Levinas's definition makes more sense: "The resistance of the other does not do violence to me, does not act negatively; it has a positive structure: ethical" (*Totality* 197). Therefore, when considered from that perspective, empathetic engagement with any fictional narrative denies "radical separation between the self and the other" (*Totality* 36). Still, the improvement of empathy is possible and more fruitful when accompanied by "(dis)approbation" and "impartiality" (Prinz 228).

Amiel-Houser and Mendelson-Maoz analyze with examples the disadvantages of narrative empathy for ethics and put forward that ". . . even when acknowledging the suffering of the other, an empathetic reading risks ignoring the concrete circumstances and the radical uniqueness of the sufferer" (204). They read Levinas's ideas in terms of "comprehending" the other, and accordingly, while trying to do that, one compares themselves with the other, which is not an ethical deed. The other for Levinas is always "inaccessible," and we are infinitely responsible for it (*Totality* 197). For this reason, empathy is read as a problematic relationship between the two sides. They also elaborate on the question they ask about the mechanics of feeling into/for the fictional other: "how can the subject attend to the other and act—to use the Levinasian terminology—'for-another' without professing to be the other?" (208). The problem they raise is about the preservation of the boundaries of both sides while at the same time working hard to feel the other's emotions. The most important point they discuss is that empathy, when imagined as a term closer to the relationship defined by Levinas, turns into an "ethical challenge" since the empathizer internalizes the obligation to feel into the other who is an inaccessible being (206). The situation itself is therefore not only complicated but also paradoxical in its nature.

Suzanne Keen's *Empathy and the Novel* is an extensive study of this complicated relationship between the novel as a fictional genre and empathy both as a contemporary issue reconsidered and revisited by various fields of study and as a term taking its origins from the definitions related to intersubjective studies in psychology. She puts forward that empathetic reading does not always entail a moralistic behavior that would activate a pro-social deed and that positive influence depends upon the context (*Empathy* 65). For Keen, when the readers are engaged in empathetic reading, they are also involved in an aesthetic process because they imitate the narrators' emotional experiences and characters portrayed within formal narrative devices (93). She also illustrates the negative points of empathy, which is parallel to the generic structure of all fictional accounts. One does not always expect to read about happiness, fairies, or all the beautiful and positive sides of life. Fiction has no limits in that sense. As she puts it, "[t]he extreme risk entailed in empathising or identifying with others underscores the problems of empathic inaccuracy and the amorality of empathetic responsiveness to suffering. The victim with whom the empath resonates emotionally may be an assassin, an assailant, a person with blood on his hands" (158–159). In form and content, Anna Lindhé's detailed reading of *Silas Marner* illustrates how problematic and intricate the ethical dilemma is in the novel. She points out that when literature is conceptualized to trigger only "empathy and compassion," (38) that perspective would paradoxically limit the reader's role in the potentially fertile relationship. Literature enables the reader to see what they really are and comprehend more about the human and humanity. The comment she makes at the end shows that literature exposes the reader to complicated situations, hence to the paradox of "the responsibility towards the Other *as well as* the denial of the Other" (38).

Richard Posner is frequently quoted due to his challenging thoughts against ethical criticism. He is against the idea that good literature is also a proper tool to convey the conventional tie between "great literature" (7) and its readers' moral improvement. Moralistic content does not mean, for Posner, that the work is good. He strongly believes that good work should "cause the reader to suspend moral judgements" (6–7). He prioritizes the aesthetic features of a work over its content by stating that "[the moral content] of a work of literature is merely the writer's raw material. It is something he works up into a form to which morality is no more relevant than the value of the sculptor's clay as a building material is relevant to the artistic value of the completed sculpture" (7). He exemplifies why readers are motivated to continue reading a literary work despite the evil or the unpleasantness depicted in content by implying that it is not about what the work morally transfers to its readers, but about which means the writer employs while doing that. While questioning ethical criticism, one of his targets is Nussbaum's argument that "literature can enlarge our empathetic awareness of injustice and of moral issues generally" and continues, "I do

not think that a better understanding of people makes a person better or more just
... Nussbaum is echoing Socrates' unsubstantiated claim that people do wrong only
out of ignorance of what is right" (10).Posner does not believe that we read literary
works to have better ideas about religion, morality or politics, but to "make sense
of our lives" and to "fashion an identity for ourselves" (20). Literature encourages
empathy and reading it makes one "realise that it *is* what you think, and so may serve
to clarify yourself to yourself" (20). Another issue he discusses is about the readers'
feelings. When he defines empathy as "amoral" (19) he means that what the reader
empathises within the process of reading is only an imitation of genuine sadness,
happiness, grief, or ecstasy. Therefore, literature does not create a moral person; for
Posner, it only plays a role "to fashion an identity for ourselves" (20). When it is pondered from this perspective, it is evident that empathic accuracy or the inaccuracy
explained earlier with another reference to Keen is an irrelevant concern for Posner.
So, the reader should concentrate on the formal characteristics of a literary work, not
on what the author morally aims to project in his work.

Gregory, on the other hand, underscores the positive link between ethics, art,
and human potential by stating that, "[w]hat's at stake in ethical criticism is the
centrality of both ethics and literary art to human beings' lives as morally deliberative, socially embedded, imaginatively fertile, and persistently emotional creatures
who are capable . . . of submitting their moral deliberations . . . to ethical evaluation" ("Redefining" 283). He explains the current situation as follows, "there is both
space and need for fruitful and enlightening arguments about the dynamics between
ethics and literary art . . . postmodern theorists . . . never manage to live their way
around ethics, and most of the time . . . they do not even attempt to do so. . . . Ethics counts because it is an evolved adaptation that served the survival interests of the
individuals . . ." (283–284). While referring to Posner's views among other ethical
critics, he states that there is an emphasis upon literature's "capacity for corrupting
readers' moral character" (287). Posner is not against literature, but he highlights that
capacity against those who strongly believe in literature's moral content. Breithaupt
is another critic who stresses the negative sides of empathy and disconnects it from
morality to align it more closely with aesthetic perception. For him, empathy is not
always morally positive because it might be manipulative, self-centered, imaginative or misleading in various cases. Empathy is interpreted as "co-experiencing," it
emphasizes that readers are not simply passive observers but active creators and co-creators of the real or imagined situations of others (171). While co-experiencing,
the sides do not learn lessons or agree/disagree with the feelings in a literary text; they
gradually become aware of the differences.

While ethical criticism is becoming a more "descriptive" rather than "prescriptive"
form of analyzing texts (Davis x), it is important to see the complex unity among the
writer/narrator, the reader/critic, and the narrative. After empathising with various
selves in the texts, the readers discover what they really are, despite the risk of empathic inaccuracy, an edifying function of ethical criticism. Empathetic situatedness
is more closely linked with the means that lead to the construction of the third party,

fed and structured by the self and the other. Donna Orange's remarks about the ethical turn in psychoanalysis are also worth mentioning. As she points out, "[e]mpathy has nothing to do with merger: it requires separated otherness … [and] …mak[es] a space for the patient in my homeless heart, so that the devastated other may have a developmental second chance" (37). Narrative empathy is not enhanced or inspired by the fantasies and the imaginative powers of the reader, which are thought to be stimulated by the moral content. Rather, it is about the productive intersubjective space between the text and the reader/critic that makes both sides ask questions for mutual understanding and respect.

REFERENCE LIST

Altieri, Charles. "Lyrical Ethics and Literary Experience." Davis, *Mapping*, pp. 30–58.
Amiel-Houser, Tammy and Mendelson-Maoz, Adia. "Against Empathy: Levinas and Ethical Criticism in the Twenty-First Century" *Journal of Literary Theory*, vol. 8, no. 1, 2014, pp. 199–218. https://doi.org/10.1515/jlt-201–0009.
Attridge, Derek, "Innovation, Literature, Ethics: Relating to the Other." *PMLA*, vol. 114, no. 1, *Special Topic: Ethics and Literary Study* (Jan. 1999), pp. 20–31. JSTOR, www.jstor.org/stable/463424.
Bauman, Zygmunt. *Postmodern Ethics*. Blackwell, 1995.
Booth, Wayne C. "Why Ethical Criticism Can Never Be Simple." Davis, *Mapping*, pp. 16–29.
Breithaupt, Fritz, "The Bad Things We Do Because of Empathy," *Interdisciplinary Science Reviews*, vol. 43, no. 2, 2018, pp. 16–174.
Buell, Lawrence, "Introduction: In Pursuit of Ethics." *PMLA*, vol. 114, no. 1, *Special Topic: Ethics and Literary Study* (Jan. 1999), pp. 7–19. JSTOR, https://www.jstor.org/stable/463423.
Davis, Todd F. and Kenneth Womack, editors. *Mapping the Ethical Turn: A Reader in Ethics, Culture, and Literary Theory*. University Press of Virginia, 2001.
———. Preface. Davis. *Mapping*, pp. ix-xiv.
Gregory, Marshall W., "Ethical Criticism: What It Is and Why It Matters." *Style*, Summer 1998, vol. 32, no. 2, *Literature and Ethical Criticism* (Summer1998), pp. 194–220. JSTOR, www.jstor.org/stable/40859548.
———. "Redefining Ethical Criticism: The Old vs. the New" *Journal of Literary Theory*, vol. 4, no. 2, 2010, pp. 273–301. JSTOR, https://doi.org/10.1515.
Hand, Sean, editor. *The Levinas Reader: Emmanuel Levinas*. Basil Blackwell, 1989.
Keen, Suzanne. "A Theory of Narrative Empathy" *Narrative*, vol. 14, no. 3 (Oct. 2006), pp. 207–236. JSTOR, https://www.jstor.org/stable/20107388.
———. *Empathy and the Novel*. Oxford University Press, 2007.
Levinas, Emmanuel. "Reality and Its Shadows." Hand, *The Levinas*, pp. 129–143
———. "The Other in Proust." Hand, *The Levinas*, pp. 160–165.
———. *Totality and Infinity: An Essay on Exteriority*, translated by Alphonso Lingis. Martinus Nijhoff Publishers, 1979.
Lindhé, Anna, "Paradox of Narrative Empathy and the Form of the Novel, or What George Eliot Knew," *Studies in the Novel*, vol.48, no. 1 (Spring), 2016, pp. 19–42.

Nussbaum, Martha C., "Exactly and Responsively: A Defense of Ethical Criticism." Davis, *Mapping*, pp. 59–82.
———. *Love's Knowledge: Essays on Philosophy and Literature*. Oxford University Press, 1990.
———. *Cultivating Humanity: A Classical Defense of Reform in Libera lEducation.* Harvard University Press, 1997.
Orange, Donna.*Nourishing the Inner Life of Clinicians and Humanitarians:The Ethical Turn in Psychoanalysis*. Routledge, 2016.
Posner, Richard A. "Against Ethical Criticism." *Philosophy and Literature,* vol. 21, no. 1, 1997, 1–27.https://chicagounbound.uchicago.edu/journal_articles/39/
Prinz, Jesse J., "Is Empathy Necessary for Morality?" *Empathy: Philosophical and Psychological Perspectives.* Edited by Amy Coplan and Peter Goldie. Oxford University Press, 2011, pp. 211–229.
Schwarz, Daniel R. "A Humanistic Ethics of Reading." Davis, *Mapping*, pp. 3–15.

3

The Microfascistic Turn and the Question of Sympathy in the Twenty-First Century

Rahime Çokay Nebioğlu

Brecht once asked: "How can anyone tell the truth about Fascism, unless he is willing to speak out against capitalism, which brings it forth?" (137–138). The history of fascism has never been truly separated from the history of capitalism. Fascism has always been on capitalism's agenda as a toolbox to reach out whenever it confronts challenges in maintaining its extension and meeting its ends. Even Nazism itself was not a single-handedly political problem but a response to an economic crisis. It was, as Samin Amir indicates, "[t]he fascism of the major 'developed' capitalist powers that aspired to become dominant hegemonic powers in the world, or at least in the regional, capitalist system" just as Mussolini's fascism was a response to the economic crisis in Italy in the 1920s. Thinking of fascism only as a political ideology of totalitarian systems or periodizing it as a thing of the past would be misleading in understanding arising tendencies in the contemporary world. "[T]he analysis of fascism", as Guattari underlines, "is not simply a historian's speciality," and "what fascism set in motion yesterday continues to proliferate in other forms, within the complex of contemporary social space" ("Everybody" 163). Fascism, Deleuze and Guattari emphasize, is not an ideology or a political phenomenon but rather a form of "desire" (*TP* 165). Desire is multiple and productive, and it can enter into numerous different assemblages and relationalities. Fascism alike can be characterised by multiplicity and capacity to adapt to new conditions and take different forms accordingly.

The mutability of fascism as a desire runs parallel to the mutability of capitalism. The reciprocal relation between fascism and capitalism is often overlooked because fascism is reduced to historical phenomena. Historical phenomena like totalitarianism or Nazism are indeed the articulations of fascism at the macro level. Considering fascism only at the macro level through its most immediate and visible forms would suggest that fascism can disappear or survive only in totalitarian regimes. Fascism, however, never disappears. It has always survived and keeps surviving even in (seemingly) democratic societies as it does today. The true nature of fascism can be grasped if we can examine it at the micro level. There have been some moments in history in which fascism seemed to be waning around the world. The waning of macro fascisms has become possible only because capitalism could no longer expand its growth under purely fascistic regimes and had to be transformed. Capitalism needed flexibility and mobility to infinitely broaden its market economy and market forces. It needed democracy so that it could liberate itself from any restrictions. It is no coincidence that we witnessed the rise of democracy (and/or the waning of macro fascism) in simultaneity with the rise of late capitalism. Yet this is not to say that the shift to late capitalism marked the end of fascism. Fascism as a desire has continued to exist under late capitalism and recently turned back in the form of microfascism as late capitalism began to face new challenges and went in dire need of another transformation. The microfascistic turn in the contemporary era is not a turn back to Fordism or fascism at the macro level. It is an outcome of capitalism's impossibility to retrieve macro fascisms and its growing need to repurpose its neoliberal agenda.

We are facing the microfascistic turn in our current political and economic affairs with the shift from late capitalism to crisis capitalism, which I define as a new Cerberus-like capitalism that contains not only already-existing conventions of late capitalism (e.g., axiomatic) but also reappropriates the conventions of primitive and despotic socius (e.g., declension and new alliance principle) as a reaction to its ongoing crisis since the early 1990s. My understanding of crisis capitalism as the latest stage of capitalism draws partly upon Naomi Klein's conception of disaster capitalism, but it departs from Klein's conception at certain points. Klein defines disaster capitalism as a type of capitalism that treats disasters and catastrophes as "exciting market opportunities" (6) on the grounds that "only a large-scale disaster—a great unmaking—can prepare the ground for [capitalist] 'reforms,'" and "by inflicting an array of shocks to the human brain, [one] could unmake and erase faulty minds, then rebuild new personalities on that ever-elusive clean slate" (29). Despite agreeing with Klein on capitalism's opportunist treatment of disasters, I prefer calling the latest form of capitalism "crisis capitalism" in lieu of disaster capitalism for two reasons. First, capitalism not only benefits from and feeds on real disasters, as Klein suggests, but it also perpetually creates the permanent atmosphere of crisis and the permanent state of exception without the existence of real *large-scale* disasters themselves. Second, crisis hereby also marks the crisis of capitalism's own making, the crisis that pushes it to be always more creative in inventing new ways of exploitation. The shift to crisis capitalism is likewise late capitalism's response to its own crises with a turn of "microfascism."

Microfascism, coined and elaborated by Guattari and Deleuze, is a useful term to comprehend the nuances of emergent cultural production in the contemporary world. Microfascism marks a sense of heaviness and fatigue that makes people not only "desire [their] own repression" (Deleuze and Guattari *TP* 215) but also become a source of repression for others by imposing their own desire. It is a desire to sub-mit to power, adhere to extreme views and convictions, and become intolerant of difference as one is too exhausted to imagine another way. As the most insidious form of fascism, microfascism has always been in the states' political agenda. In the older political and economic programs like the authoritarian regimes of the Nazi's, Mussolini, or Stalin, numerous forms of microfascisms scattered into the spheres of everyday life. Microfascisms were then the outcome of the disciplinary project that moved from the top (a despotic leader/state) to the bottom (the masses/nation). They were only complimentary to fascisms at the macro level. They were enacted through what Althusser called "ideological state apparatuses" and "repressive state apparatuses" (127–186). With the transition from disciplinary societies to societies of control, microfascisms have begun to be intensively enacted not through disciplinary and enforced mechanisms but an affective politics without necessarily resorting to a fascist molar aggregate at the macro level. The affective politics of crisis capitalism has invented more insidious and effective ways of perverting the desire of the masses and addressing "fascism in us all, in our heads and in our everyday behaviour" (Foucault xiii) to the point that every individual has either willingly taken over "the mission of self-appointed judge, dispenser of justice, policeman, neighbourhood SS man" (Deleuze and Guattari *AO* 228), or has become indifferent and apathetic to the sufferings of the others as well as to their own misery. Unlike the fascist mobilization of the masses in the previous eras, the microfascistic turn of crisis capitalism has locked the masses into a paralyzing oscillation between repurposed anger/hate and comforting substitutes of sympathy, which eventually renders revolutionary action ineffective.

Over the last two decades, there have been numerous attempts to understand and interpret the constellations of the new emotional and cultural dynamic we witness daily in all platforms of life. Some have recognized it as a turn to affect (Tomkins 49; Sedgwick and Frank 496–497; Massumi "Autonomy of Affect" 88; Clough 1; Leys 434; Gregg and Seigworth 3–4; Probyn 74). Others have interpreted it as the emergence of New Sincerity and drawn novel attention to sincerity (van den Akker and Vermeulen 5; Kelly 145). In the growing literature on the emergent cultural production, the emphasis largely falls on how and why feelings have been intensified in the recent decades (Ahmed "The Politics of Fear"; Sedgwick and Frank *Shame and Her Sisters;* Massumi "Everywhere You Want to Be"*;* Stewart *Ordinary Affects*; Cvetkovich *Depression: A Public Feeling;* Klein *The Shock Doctrine;* Probyn "Writing Shame"). The crystallisation of microfascism can certainly be traced through the intensified affects such as fear, anxiety, shame, hate, and rage. But we can get the larger picture of the microfascistic turn and its dangers by tracing affects that, despite their seeming abundance, have been flattened in the last few decades. The affective politics of crisis capitalism not only aims to intensify, produce, and reproduce negative affects as part of its microfascistic agenda but it also aims to flatten some particular affects such as sympathy and compassion to the extent that they are replaced by flat affects of indifference and apathy. The flattening project of crisis capitalism is complimentary to its politics of negative affects, and flattened affects are symptomatic of crisis capitalism's triumph in capturing, nullifying, and automating what these affects are capable of, that is, the possibility of taking action against the forms of violence, injustice, and power.

The intensifying and flattening projects of crisis capitalism inherently intersect and serve to the same end. "Capitalism starts intensifying or diversifying affect, but only in order to extract surplus-value," says Brian Massumi, and he continues: "It hijacks affect in order to intensify profit potential. It literally valorises affect. The capitalist logic of surplus-value production starts to take over the relational field that is also the domain of political ecology, the ethical field of resistance to identity and predictable paths" (*Politics of Affect* 20–21). Contemporary capitalism seeks to *intensify* negative affects, particularly fear, hate, and anger, through its affective politics that uses technology, mass media, and the internet as channels to organize affective encounters. By setting up a perpetual atmosphere of crisis and working through the bombardment of negative images, capitalism seeks to drain these affects of their potentiality and make microfascism the permanent state of being. In this regard, the intensification of negative affects is another constellation of capitalism's flattening project. The affects of anger and hate can open up a site for resistance, be translated into an intellectual agency and creative action, and be destructive for the system itself. These affects can be driving forces to speak out against diverse forms of power and to construct counterpower. One fine example can be found in the relation between feminism and anger as Sara Ahmed tackles in her famous article on "Feminist Attachments," where she defines anger as "a form of 'against-ness'" (174) and as "what gives us 'the energy' to react against the deep social and psychic investments in racism as well as sexism" (175). For Ahmed, feminism is "a response to pain and as a form of anger directed against that pain" (ibid.). Knowing the creative and transformative potential of negative affects, crisis capitalism intensifies and directs them against an unknown, invisible enemy that is always out there as the cause of any existing or prospective pain. The logic behind the intensification of affects is to discharge these affects of their revolutionary energy and control the subject of their *against-ness* before the masses recognize the actual cause of their pain or the pain of the others and direct their anger and hate against the system. This is indeed another way of flattening, paralyzing, and automating these affects to the point of unresponsiveness to one's own pain—let aside the pain of the others. Resistance requires a response to the intolerable and recognising what is wrong and what needs to be changed. Crisis capitalism de-territorializes the possibilities of resistance by guiding the masses to the wrong enemy and making them blind to their real condition. Their feelings are carefully curated through the organization of their daily encounters with the images of violence, the narratives of anger, hate and shame, and the flow of lies, made-up stories and crises. The circulation and sociality of these emotions eventually make them establish a toxic relationship with themselves and others.

The same holds true for the feelings of sympathy today. The flattening of sympathy indeed hides a much grimmer picture of the microfascistic turn. Many scholars from various disciplines ranging from aesthetics to neurobiology have attempted to define sympathy so far. Despite the differences in their focus, perspective, and methodology, these scholars have more or less arrived at a consensus on sympathy's being a tendency to feel what another is feeling or might feel, and feel a need to take an altruistic action as suggested in its most commonly used synonyms "emotional contagion" (Hatfield et al. 2), "fellow-feeling," "analogous emotion" (Smith 10), "imitation of emotions" (Spinoza 183), and "motor mimicry" (Bavelas et al. 317). Without delving into subtle differences and conflicts within/between these definitions, I treat sympathy as an intersubjective emotional experience in which one is affected by and mutually shares the emotional states of others. In so doing, I lay stress not on what sympathy is but on what sympathy can do to demonstrate why and how sympathy today has been strategically encaptured, automated, and flattened by crisis capitalism. Perhaps the best answer to this question lies in Spinoza's following notes:

> That, which painfully affects the object of our pity, affects us also with similar pain (by the foregoing proposition); therefore, we shall endeavour to recall everything which removes its existence, or which destroys it (cf. III. xiii.); in other words (III. ix. note), we shall desire to destroy it, or we shall be determined for its destruction; thus, we shall endeavour to free from misery a thing which we pity. (184)

As suggested here, sympathy arises out of our affective encounter with another's pain. As we begin to suffer as much as the object of our pity does, our conatus requires us to end this mutual pain by finding out its source and seeking to eliminate it. This implies two important points about what sympathy can do. First, sympathy is an affective experience through which one *sees the intolerable*. Second, it is a driving force through which one *acts against* what is wrong and unjust. These two aspects, as Nussbaum marks, make sympathy "a social emotion" that could provide "an essential bridge to justice" by bringing the individual and the community together (37). The capacity of sympathy to unite the people and motivate them to react against the intolerable immediately makes it a threat that needs to be flattened.

The flattening project of crisis capitalism is more complex and insidious than its politics of intensification. To begin with, it ironically operates through its discourse of compassion. Crisis capitalism deploys the rhetoric of compassion first used during the presidency of Bush, who, in his address on April 30, 2002, called for being "compassionate to actively help [their] fellow citizens in need" and later proved how compassionate he was not only for his own fellow citizens but also for the others with his "war on terror," and then employed by Obama, who, in his commencement speech, underlined the necessity of attaining "the ability to put ourselves in someone else's shoes; to see the world through those who are different from us—the child who's hungry, the laid-off steelworker, the immigrant woman cleaning your dorm room." Naming this call for compassion as "empathic imperative," Alissa G. Karl rightly argues that the capitalist discourse of compassion is indeed "a specific requirement within today's labor markets" and aims at "the commodification of such capacities in service work and consumer markets" (272). Following a similar line of thought with Karl on seeing the call for compassion as an effort to "trai[n] labor and cas[t] worker subjectivity in accordance with requirements for affective and immaterial labor in the contemporary workplace" (274), I add up to it by saying that it is simultaneously an effort to incorporate sympathy into the capitalist axiomatic in order to purge it of its revolutionary potential. The more crisis capitalism calls for compassion, the more it demands people to be uncompassionate. This demand for flattening sympathy to the point of rendering it ineffective is met through the same affective channels capitalism uses to drain the revolutionary potential of anger and hate.

The microfascistic turn challenges the possibilities of sympathy or sympathetic action in the contemporary world. Microfascism and sympathy are primitive tendencies inherent to human nature waiting to be activated or automatically respond to the relevant stimuli (Deleuze and Guattari *TP* 9–10; Preston and de Waal 12). When activated, however, microfascism and sympathy cannot coexist. The former always seeks to address its own needs and desires, although it ironically fails and ends up making one desire their repression. The latter, in contrast, seeks to care for the well-being of the other. Microfascism incapacitates sympathy because they are two opposite drives that clash with each other. One cannot be engaged in any true altruistic behavior when they are too much indulged in their egotistical interests. I propose that sympathy can coexist with microfascism only when it is flattened, and there are two flattened forms of sympathy today that can exist in perfect harmony with microfascism: sympathy as a microfascistic fellow-feeling and sympathy as (veiled) indifference. My take on this partly relies on Martin L. Hoffman's insights into the limits and problems of empathy. In his book *Empathy and Moral Development: Implications for Caring and Justice*, Hoffmann points out two major limitations of empathy. One is empathy's "vulnerability to familiarity bias and here-and-now bias," and the other is "empathic over-arousal" (Hoffmann 13). The first refers to the fact that although anyone in pain can arouse sympathy, it is more probable for one to feel more for their own kin/d, that is, for those "who are similar to themselves," and those "who are present in the immediate situation" (Hoffmann 13–14). The second refers to the fact that when one is exposed too intensely to the pain of the other, it can transform into their own pain and become too much to handle, which may eventually move them out of their fellow-feeling mode entirely (198). I contend that the affective politics of crisis capitalism carefully works on these two limitations to flatten the true potential of sympathy, and sympathy evolves into its current crippled forms.

To begin with the first crippled form of sympathy in the twenty-first century, microfascistic fellow-feeling is sympathy converted into ideological extremism (in the form of nationalism, patriotism, or right-wing fanaticism) and/or antipathy for the other. This form of sympathy no longer bears any ties with true altruism. It no longer seeks justice or equality, which are the goals typically intended in any sympathetic act. It is rather terribly toxic in the sense that it either aims to normalize pain under the name of sacrifice or simply aims to maintain the privileges and superiority of one group over the other. The atmosphere of chaos and insecurity is the primary tool that crisis capitalism has used since the 9/11 attacks to convert sympathy into microfascistic fellow-feeling. With the flow of media images of violence, people are drawn into an omnipresent state of insecurity. They are made to believe that what has happened to their fellows could happen anywhere and anytime (to themselves as well) and that they would be safe only if they make sacrifices for their state and their people as a patriotic act. The call for sympathetic sacrifice closely resonates with the motives behind the microfascistic turn: firstly, to make the masses not only willingly accept their pain but also willingly accept any prospective pain that would follow—if necessary—and secondly, to allow the governments to exempt themselves from the responsibility of taking care of their people in times of need. One fine example of this can be found in President Bush's call to his people to contribute to the economy and the state's war on terror by making individual *sacrifices*. This form of sympathy can be called upon, not always necessarily by those in power. As the microfascistic turn has made everyone a self-assigned judge, one can be drawn into the pool of ugly comparisons of who suffers more and who deserves more sympathy and can be blamed for showing sympathy for the less-deserved, that is, those who happen to be not of one's kin/d. As this suggests, microfascistic fellow-feeling always holds potential for transforming into antipathy for *the other*. This flattened and toxicized type of sympathy can be observed in Trump's politics, which has released strongly anti-immigrant sentiments during election campaigns, scapegoating the immigrant population for the economy going bad and unfair job competition. His politics immediately translates the sympathy of his base voters (for their fellows) into violent antipathy for the immigrants.

As for sympathy as (veiled) indifference, it is a form of sympathy that is performed and yet not felt. It is surrogate sympathy. Sympathy, in essence, derives "the tendency to automatically mimic *and synchronise* facial expressions, vocalisations, postures, and movements with those of another person and consequently, to converge emotionally" (Hatfield et al. 81). This means that when one is exposed to a particular image of pain in the other, he inherently tends to sympathize and feel that pain. Crisis capitalism puts effort to break this immediate self-induced response to the pain of the other with its affective politics. Through mass media, technology, and social networking platforms, crisis capitalism subjects the masses to a continuous bombardment of images of violence and pain. The overexposure to this affective image loop serves two ends: It either makes the images of violence and pain fall into the automatic perception of the receiver, which in turn desensitizes the receiver and makes them indifferent to the pain of the other, or it makes the receiver feel exhausted with/by the pain, which in turn makes them consult to temporary solutions, that is, substitutes of sympathetic behavior, to relieve it. In the first case, sympathy turns into sheer indifference because the receiver is no longer triggered by the external stimuli, so they neither mimic the pain of the others nor feel an urge to respond to it. Even if the receiver responds to the stimuli, the sympathy performed is not true sympathy, but surrogate sympathy that targets not at the relief of the pain in the other but the self-esteem and/or the guilty pleasure of the receiver (for being privileged and superior enough to help). In the second case, sympathy turns into veiled indifference because overexposure to emotional stimuli exhausts the receiver's power to act and pushes them to look for easy, quick, and temporary ways to cope with the pain of themselves rather than with the pain of others. The receiver's pain is often accompanied by a slight sense of guilt of not being able to help. To minimize this pain imbued with guilt, the receiver, who now confronts a "compassion fatigue" in Hoffmann's words (199), performs unemotional and ineffective sympathetic behavior, which can be considered equivalent to veiled indifference. Typically, true sympathy would lead to performative action to change and transform the conditions of the intolerable. In this flattened form of sympathy, however, sympathetic behavior is automated. It is performed only to overcome the sense of guilt and the pain of the receiver without necessarily seeking to change the conditions that cause the pain of the other in the first place. The closest example to this can be found in social media heroism today. Although the circulation of posts asking for or performing sympathy on social media still holds the potential to raise awareness and even trigger larger social movements, the driving force behind most, if not all, constellations of sympathy is veiled indifference, born out of compassion fatigue. These substitutes of sympathy set the stage for ineffectiveness by pushing sympathetic action into habituation. Automated performances of sympathy like clicking, forwarding, and reposting replace authentic, sympathetic action and suffice to expel the sense of guilt like a defence mechanism that copes with the pain even before it surfaces. This is particularly alarming considering that in the face of political irresponsibility, individual sympathy and ethical responsibility are the only kind of responsibility left for the possibility of any change.

In his *Ethics*, Spinoza points out that "[s]ympathy (misericordia) is love, in so far as it induces a man to feel pleasure at another's good fortune, and pain at another's evil fortune" (236). He adds: "He who is moved to help others neither by reason nor by compassion, is rightly styled inhuman, for (III. xxvii.) he seems unlike a man" (311). True sympathy requires one to go beyond their microfascistic desires to unite with the people and feel and take action for them; to be a human requires one to feel sympathy for the other. We are, however, witnessing the most challenging phase of humanity and the cruellest stage of capitalism in which we are losing control over our emotions, emotions conditioned upon us begin to control us. The flattening of sympathy is symptomatic of capitalism's advanced dehumanizing project. It is not only the processes of production and reproduction but also emotions conducive to revolutionary action that are automated in today's capitalist system. The more capitalism seeks to develop machines capable of feeling and acting with reasoning, emotion, and moral agency, the more it seeks to strip humans of their capacity to feel, reason, and act. The more microfascisms are enacted, the more dehumanized the world becomes. What is to be focused on is not machines replacing humans but the automation of altruistic emotions, behaviors, and cognition, which risk replacing the possibilities of resistance and new political imagination. What is to be done is not to lament the impossibility of abolishing capitalism which keeps transforming and multiplying into innumerous permutations, but to contemplate the possibility of inventing new means of resistance. The problem we face now is severe; the virus we are coping with is cancerous; the forms of resistance we know of are locked up.

Under the conditions of the microfascistic turn, the lines between sympathy and indifference and resistance and apathy blur.

By attempting to define and describe the microfascistic turn in the contemporary world, my aim is not to instil pessimism about how dystopian the twenty-first century has turned out to be. It is rather to draw attention to the state of heaviness that we are currently drawn into. What is at stake here is our capacity to be a human; in Spinozan terms, our capacity to love and to sympathize. By being perpetually made exhausted of feeling, we are gradually turning inhuman and indifferent to the intolerable. We are gradually losing our power to feel and act. This, in turn, signals the slow disappearance of transformative political action. I propose that imagining new creative ways of resistance today can be possible only through recognizing the change in our current sociopolitical and economic affairs. If there is a way out, it is only from within. Even if we cannot abolish capitalism, we can still reverse the way it operates; even if we cannot stop its transformation, we can still deal with its permutations. But we must know our enemy better before being completely emptied and turned numb. True resistance begins where life is most exhausted and most cramped. As Deleuze declares in his Postscript, "There is no need to fear or hope, but only to look for new weapons" (4).

REFERENCE LIST

Ahmed, Sara. "The Politics of Fear in the Making of Worlds." *International Journal of Qualitative Studies in Education*, vol.16, no.3, 2003, pp. 377–398.

———. "Feminist Attachments." *The Cultural Politics of Emotion*. 2004. 2nd ed., Edinburgh UP., 2014, pp.168–191.

Althusser, Louis. "Ideology and Ideological State Apparatuses." *Lenin and Philosophy and Other Essays.* Translated by Ben Brewster, Monthly Review Press, 2001.

Amir, Samin. "The Return of Fascism in Contemporary Capitalism." *Monthly Review*, vol. 66, no. 4, 1994, https://monthlyreview.org/2014/09/01/the-return-of-fascism-in-contemporary-capitalism/. Accessed 10 January 2021.

Bavelas, Janet B., et al. "Motor Mimicry as Primitive Empathy." *Empathy and Its Development*, edited by Nancy Eisenberg and Janet Strayer, Cambridge UP., 1987, pp. 317–339.

Brecht, Bertolt. *Galileo*. Grove Widenfeld, 1966.

Clough, Patricia T. "Introduction." *The Affective Turn: Theorizing the Social*, edited by Patricia Ticineto Clough and Jean Halley and with a foreword by Michael Hardt, Duke UP., 2007, pp. 1–34.

Cvetkovich, Ann. *Depression: A Public Feeling*. Duke UP., 2012.

Deleuze, Gilles. "Postscript on the Societies of Control." *October*, vol. 59, 1992, pp. 3–7.

———. Cinema II: The Time Image. 1985. Translated by Hugh Tomlinson and Robert Galeta, U. of Minnesota P., 2001.

———. *Desert Islands and Other Texts 1953–1974*, edited by David Laoujade and translated by Mike Taormina, Semiotext(e) Foreign Agents Series, 2004.

Deleuze, Gilles and Félix Guattari. *Anti-Oedipus: Capitalism and Schizophrenia*. 1972. Translated byRobert Hurley, Mark Seem, and Helen R. Lane, U. of Minnesota P., 1983.

———. *A Thousand Plateaus: Capitalism and Schizophrenia.* 1980. Translated by Brian Massumi, U of Minnesota P., 1987.
Foucault, Michel. "Preface." *Anti-Oedipus: Capitalism and Schizophrenia.* 1972. Translated by Robert Hurley, Mark Seem, and Helen R. Lane, U. of Minnesota P., 1983, pp.xi–xv.
Gregg, Melissa and Gregory J. Seigworth. *The Affect Theory Reader.* Duke UP., 2010.
Guattari, Felix."Everybody Wants to be a Fascist." *Caosophy: Texts and Interviews 197–1977,* edited by Sylvere Lotringer, translated by David L. Sweet, Jarred Becker, and Taylor Adkins and with an introduction by François Dosse, Semiotext(e) Foreign Agents Series, 2009, pp.154–176.
Hatfield, Elaine, et al. *Emotional Contagion.* Cambridge UP.,1994.
Hoffman, Martin L. *Empathy and Moral Development: Implications for Caring and Justice.* Cambridge UP., 2000.
Karl, Alissa G. "Empathize! Feeling and Labor in the Economic Present." *Criticism,* vol. 62, no. 2, 2020, pp. 271-295.
Kelly, Adam. "David Foster Wallace and the New Sincerity in American Fiction." *Consider David Foster Wallace,* edited by David Hering, Side Show Media, 2010, pp. 131-46.
Klein, Naomi. The Shock Doctrine: The Rise of Disaster Capitalism. Metropolitan Books, 2008.
Leys, Ruth. "The Turn to Affect: A Critique." *Critical Inquiry,* vol. 37, no. 3, 2011, pp. 434-472.
Massumi, Brian. "Everywhere You Want to Be: Introduction to Fear." *Politics of Everyday Fear,* edited by Brian Massumi, U. of Minnesota P., 1993, pp. 3–39.
———. "The Autonomy of Affect." *Cultural Critique,* no.31, 1995, pp.83–109.
———. *Politics of Affect.* Polity, 2015.
Nussbaum, Martha C. "Compassion: The Basic Social Emotion." *Social Philosophy and Policy,* vol. 13, no.1, 1996, pp. 27–58.
Preston, Stephanie D., and de Waal, F. B. M. "Empathy: Its Ultimate and Proximate Bases." *Behavioral and Brain Sciences,* vol. 25, no.1., 2001, pp. 1–20.
Probyn, Elspeth. "Writing Shame." *The Affect Theory Reader,* edited by Melissa Gregg and Gregory J. Seigworth, Duke UP., 2010, pp. 71–93.
Sedgwick E. Kosofsky and Adam Frank. "Shame in the Cybernetic Fold: Reading Silvan Tomkins." *Critical Inquiry,* vol. 21, no. 2, 1995, pp. 496–522.
Silvan Tomkins, *Shame and Her Sisters: A Silvan Tomkins Reader,* edited by Eve Kosofsky Sedgwick and Adam Frank, Duke UP., 1997.
Smith, Adam. *The Theory of Moral Sentiments.* 1759. Edited by D. D. Raphael and A. L. Macfie, Liberty Fund, 1984.
Spinoza, Benedictus de. *Ethics.* 1677. Translated by R. H. M. Elwes, The Floating Press, 2009.
Stewart, Kathleen. *Ordinary Affects.* Duke UP, 2007.
Tomkins, Silvan S. *Exploring Affect: The Selected Writings of Silvan S. Tomkins,* edited by E. Virginia Demos, Cambridge UP., 1995.
van den Akker, Robinand Timotheus Vermeulen. "Periodising the 2000s, or, the Emergence of Metamodernism." *Metamodernism: Historicity, Affect, and Depth after Postmodernism,* edited by Robin van den Akker, Alison Gibbons, and Timotheus Vermeulen, Rowman & Littlefield, 2017, pp.1–19.

4

Enjoy Your Theory!

Post-Lacanian Psychoanalytical Approaches to Literature and Culture

Aylin Alkaç

Since their inception around the turn of the twentieth century, Freud's theories have been engaged with various reactions, ranging from being seen as products of an epoch-making genius to those of a conservative propounder of white bourgeois morality. As one of the fathers of the hermeneutics of suspicion, in Ricoeur's terms, alongside Nietzsche and Marx, Freud himself has been the most suspected of all. Neither his nor his followers' analyses of literature and culture fared differently. Even Lacan's return to Freud within the post/structuralist linguistic turn could not retrieve psychoanalysis from the depths of suspicion it has been thrown into. A strong wave of critique came from feminist psychoanalysts who mainly took issue with Freud's and Lacan's phallogocentrism, without really considering if they were descriptive or prescriptive in their arguments. In her "Laugh of the Medusa," for example, Helene Cixous condemns psychoanalysis as a "phallocratic ideology," arguing vehemently against the metaphor of the "dark continent" Freud used to refer to women to attest to his inability to understand the female psyche fully, and accuses Lacan of "standing erect in his old Freudian realm" and "preserving the sanctuary of the phallos" (884). Lacan's philosopher contemporaries also attacked his style and teaching and psychoanalysis in general. In their *Anti-Oedipus*, arguing against the centrality of the Oedipus complex in psychoanalytical analysis, Deleuze and Guattari declare that "a schizophrenic out for a walk is a better model than a neurotic lying on the analyst's couch" (2). The list is long. So eminent were the rivals, and their discourses resonated so well with the deconstructive momentum in theoretical circles of the time that psychoanalysis was discredited as a universalising metanarrative about human subjectivity. Consequently, its use for theoretical analyses of literature and culture became obsolete in academia for a few decades. However, the true Lacanian irony is that it is partly the (mis)readings of his adversaries that lead to the revival of psychoanalysis as a pertinent approach to analyses of literature and culture in the new millennium.

It would also be a psychoanalytically interesting observation to note that it has been possible with the passage of time and elimination of the controversies surrounding Lacan's personality and clinical practice to revisit Lacan's texts and appropriate his approach in different fields of study.

There are two main reasons for the incessant return to psychoanalysis in theory, apart from its being a discourse that lends itself easily to controversy. One is the commonality of questions raised by psychoanalysis with literature, philosophy, and theory in general: questions regarding the constitution of subjectivity, the positioning of the subject concerning the other—in the singular or plural—the extent and limits of human thought. . . . Not only did Freud and then Lacan turn to literature and philosophy in their search for answers to these questions, but writers, philosophers, and critics turned to psychoanalysis for the same purpose. In the former case, illustrations of a theoretical position by referring to texts from many fields have been unapologetic, although severely criticized. Just as Freud was an avid reader of literary and philosophical texts, Lacan, in his writings and seminars, refers to a large number of philosophers ancient and contemporary, from Plato to Hegel, St. Thomas Aquinas to Heidegger, as well as writers, from Sophocles to James Joyce, Shakespeare to Marguerite Duras. In the latter case, however, the dialogue between texts from these different fields are either openly acknowledged, and psychoanalytical terms are used to open up fields of inquiry to new dimensions even when the writer is not necessarily a proponent of psychoanalysis, as in the case of Fredric Jameson, or denied although the continuity in their theoretical arguments is evident to the unbiased careful reader, as in the case of Derrida. In the *Political Unconscious*, Jameson conceives the literary or aesthetic act as having an active relationship with the Real, a Lacanian concept distinct from reality. He suggests that the text carries the Real as its "own intrinsic or immanent subtext" (67). In the same book, he also uses the same distinction to talk about the "reality of history" as different from the Real of History—written in capital letters in the Lacanian fashion—to refer to that real which lies inaccessible beyond the textualized history that we can know. Derrida, on the other hand, was much dedicated to a rigorous critique of Freudian psychoanalysis, and his reading of Lacan was often marred with misreadings. There is, however, a curious homology between his concept of différance and Lacan's discussion of the functioning of the signifier in "The Agency of the Letter in the Unconscious." The resonance between the following descriptions is conspicuous:

> [T]he signified concept is never present in and of itself, in a sufficient presence that would refer only to itself. Essentially and lawfully, every concept is inscribed in a chain or in a system within which it refers to the other, to other concepts, by means of the systematic play of differences. Such a play, différance, is thus no longer simply a concept, but rather the possibility of conceptuality, of a conceptual process and system in general. (Derrida, "Différance," 11)
>
> [I]t is in the chain of the signifier that the meaning "insists" but that none of its elements "consists" in the signification of which it is at the moment capable.

> We are forced, then, to accept the notion of an incessant sliding of the signified under the signifier. (Lacan, 170)

Rather than mutual indebtedness, this example illustrates how, even without much difference in their terminology, the two fields speak to the same problematique in language in similar ways. However, their writers would reject any such affinity. Such commonality in arguments can be identified between contemporary texts as well as texts across time, anachronically, and even among disparate writers. In an edited volume, *Lacan: Silent Partners*, Žižek brings together articles, not only by Lacan scholars but also by those who are critical of Lacan's thought, such as Alain Badiou, that explore this convergence of interests in questions raised and answers discussed in the writings of philosophers as diverse as Schelling, Hegel, Nietzsche, and Badiou, and writers such as Kafka, Turgenev, and Henry James, to name a few. Fascinated by how Lacan's writing can be put in dialogue with a variety of texts, visual and verbal, Žižek's writing testifies to what he calls a "Lacanian paranoia" of discerning Lacanian themes everywhere. In *Looking Awry*, he writes, mockingly, that "*Richard II* proves beyond any doubt that Shakespeare had read Lacan" (9). Rather than paranoia, one can argue, it is this concurrence of questions asked that renders psychoanalysis, particularly its Lacanian renewal with specific emphasis on the role of language, a viable theoretical approach for the analyses of literature and culture today.

The other reason for the revival of psychoanalysis in theoretical analyses, especially after the 1990s, is the realization of the unique reading practice it offers—a practice that implicates both the reader and the read. The contemporary proponents of Lacanian psychoanalysis challenge the traditional view of psychoanalysis as a model of interpretation, offering only symbolic analyses of the texts with reference to theory, reducing them to symptoms of their authors' mental ailments or theoretical allegories. The traditional view was based on early Freudian discussions of literary texts. The characters in narratives were treated as real persons and were analyzed for their symptoms, or the author's life was put under scrutiny to find connections between their traumas, complexes, and obsessions with their writing. Apart from Freud's discussions of literature, well-known examples include Marie Bonaparte's analysis of the life and works of Edgar Allan Poe, Ernst Jones's discussions of Hamlet and Oedipus following on Freud. These literary studies were criticized for their failure to address the richness and specificity of a literary work, turning them simply into manifestations of psychic mechanisms and, together with Freud's other analyses of culture and religion, for instrumentalizing texts to elucidate or verify psychoanalytical theories.

Lacan himself never offered a systematic formulation of theory. Still, post-Lacanian critics define a practice of reading characteristic of psychoanalysis distinct from other theoretical approaches, based on Lacan's writings and reassessment of what psychoanalytical experience in actuality entails. This distinct interpretive approach relies on the fact that psychoanalysis is first and foremost a clinical practice based on the interaction of the analysand with the analyst as well as the unique experience of discovery, from which theoretical considerations arise. Defining the clinical experience of psychoanalysis as a singular event rather than pure cognition, Shoshana Felman explains how "the singular event of a discovery, the unique advent of a moment of illumination that, because it cannot by its very nature become a heritage, an acquisition, has to be repeated, reenacted, practised each time for the first time" (12). Contrary to what the opponents of psychoanalysis think, psychoanalysis does not posit a unitary truth to be derived from the interpretive process that takes place in a session but rather a "revolutionised interpretive stance" and "a revolutionary theory of reading," in Felman's words (9). Particularly Lacanian psychoanalysis never offers theoretical truths to be applied in clinical practice to the analysand's discourse or in reading to the texts. "The practice of psychoanalysis (as well as the experience of a practical reading) is a process, not a set of doctrines. In the process, one can implicate the doctrines, one can perhaps imply them, not apply them" (11). It is rather "an attempt to illuminate a way of reading whose unending struggle to become aware was able, in the process, to become attentive to messages or items of signification that were formerly unusable and, as such, unreadable, inaudible, invisible" (15). Similarly, in *Jacques Lacan: Psychoanalysis and the Subject of Literature*, Jean-Michel Rabaté explains how Lacan was not simply a "user" of literary examples but a reader of texts, of a special type, reading to understand something of human nature while founding his approach in the experience of psychoanalysis. For Lacan, the psychoanalytical experience is "an experience of language as living speech" as well as "an experience of 'writing' and of 'reading'" (3).Thus, rather than psychoanalyzing the work or the writer, what Lacan "does with texts, then, is similar to what he does with patients: he treats 'the symptom as a palimpsest' and tries to understand the 'hole' created by the signifier, into which significations pour and vanish. However, in both cases 'interpretation does not have to be true or false. It has to be just'" (4). This insistence that post-Lacanian psychoanalytic reading does not ascribe to a doctrine, does not seek ultimate truths, and does not claim absolute knowledge takes its basis from Lacan's writings, which are wildly misread and misinterpreted. Truth, for Lacan, is a paradoxical phenomenon, intimately associated with its opposite, lying; it can never be captured in its wholeness, forever missing but has to be pursued nevertheless.[1] Only its multiple representations can be found signified in the symbolic, and the truth of the unconscious is available solely as and through interpretation. In his discussion of knowledge and its limits, he distinguishes between *connaissance* and *savoir* as two different kinds of knowing, neither of which corresponds to truth or incontestable reality. For a theorist who conceives the subject to be constituted through a process of *méconnaissance*, generally translated as "misunderstanding" or "misrecognition," it is only paradoxical to suggest that Lacan would claim knowledge to be possible in its totality. Hence, a true Lacanian reading of literary or cultural texts and psychoanalytical texts would inevitably entail an awareness of the gaps and holes in the text read and the process of reading itself.

Today, a completely new psychoanalytical approach is at stake. Not only did Lacan revolutionize psychoanalysis with his return to and revision of Freud, but also, since his time, psychoanalysis has been radically transformed as its texts have been revisited by feminists, neo-Marxists, postcolonial critics, thinkers of the Frankfurt school and deconstruction, and members of various schools of psychoanalysis in Europe and America as elsewhere. Post-Lacanian encounters of psychoanalysis with literature and culture in the last few decades have led to the emergence of a new range of fields of critical inquiry such as trauma studies, performance studies, affect theory, as well as new readings and new applications of psychoanalytical concepts in film studies, gender studies, race and ethnicity studies, Holocaust studies, and contemporary art theory. There is also another trend, which is applying the distinct interpretive approach of psychoanalysis, as described above, to the major psychoanalytic writings of its fathers, Freud and Lacan. Some of these studies originate from psychoanalytical theories and build on them with a more interdisciplinary approach. At the same time, some incorporate psychoanalytical concepts, especially as inflected by Lacan, in their analyses. More familiar with the breadth of Lacanian corpus, some critics write with the psychoanalytical insight attentive to his conceptualisation of truth and knowledge. In contrast, others continue to challenge or apply insufficiently Freudian and Lacanian concepts in their studies. There have been estimable attempts at exploring and rethinking the relevance of psychoanalysis for a wide range of fields of critical inquiry in the last few years. Jean Michel Rabaté's *Knots: Post-Lacanian Psychoanalysis, Literature and Film* brings together critics from diverse fields of study from different parts of the world who "have absorbed the teachings of Lacan, but never repeat his ideas as if they constituted a dogma" and mostly "have taken to heart objections raised by deconstruction, feminism, Judith Butler, Gilles Deleuze, or Alain Badiou, without feeling obliged to pay allegiance to any school in particular" (4). Ankhi Mukherjee's *After Lacan: Literature, Theory, and Psychoanalysis in the Twenty-First Century* demonstrates the convergence of post-Lacanian psychoanalytic reading with film studies, disability studies, new media studies, and queer studies, with race and politics. Elissa Marder invited contributors to "think about how the relationship between literature and psychoanalysis once again needs to be reinvented" (257) for her *Literature and Psychoanalysis: Open Questions*. This is an edited issue for *Paragraph*, a journal of modern theory, on the occasion of the fortieth anniversary of Shoshana Felman's famous 55/56 issue of Yale French Studies, which had the title *Literature and Psychoanalysis: The Question of Reading: Otherwise*, aiming to (re)introduce Lacan and the new possibilities of reading psychoanalysis brought to the academia in the U.S. in 1997. It would be impossible to offer a comprehensive overview of the whole critical field fuelled by post-Lacanian psychoanalysis, which comprises a wealth of theoretical perspectives and approaches within this chapter; therefore, in what follows, the discussion will focus on the internal tensions and new directions that are sought in one of these fields, trauma studies, in an attempt to illustrate the complicated relationship between a new field and psychoanalysis, which informs it.

Trauma studies emerged in the early 1990s, especially with the writings of Cathy Caruth, Soshana Felman, Geoffrey Hartman, and Dori Laub. Drawing mainly on Freud's description of trauma as a missed encounter, images and narratives of trauma, fiction or nonfiction, were examined to reveal how the traumatic experience opens a gap in the knowledge and memory of the victim who is unable to assimilate the event by consciousness at the time of its happening and is then haunted by it. In *Unclaimed Experience*, Caruth argues that when the traumatic event is finally narrativised as memory belatedly, it loses its precision and force, and thus cannot fully attest to the specificity of the traumatic reality. This crisis in witnessing a traumatic event is also elaborated by Felman and Laub. Examining various testimonial texts, they suggest that art and literature offer access to traumatic reality that cannot otherwise be known. Their discussion in *Testimony: Crises of Witnessing in Literature, Psychoanalysis and History* also emphasizes the listener, who is implicated in the testimonial process. Invoking the Freudian notion of transference, Felman and Laub indicate how the listener can undergo secondary traumatisation by witnessing the testimony but not the event, even outside the clinical setting as in the cases of their students, readers, and viewers of traumatic narratives. Their observation opened a whole new line of discussion in trauma studies by introducing the notion of vicarious witnessing. These early writers in trauma studies were either specialised in psychoanalysis or were psychoanalysts themselves. This extremely brief introduction of the basic tenets of their work only aims to point out how their writing was based on and testified to the insight of reading that nods toward an openness to non-knowledge entailed in psychoanalysis. The field of trauma studies has since been revised and expanded with an interdisciplinary approach by later theorists.

Interestingly, criticism voiced against the founding texts of trauma studies raised parallel criticisms against psychoanalysis over the last century. Dominick LaCapra, a historian working on the relationship between trauma and historiography, criticizes Felman for sacralizing the victim and Caruth for sacralizing trauma in his *History in Transit*. Referring to Felman's discussion of vicarious witnessing, LaCapra argues that Felman conflates empathy with identification in the testimonial process, leading to the victim's idealization and turning the listener into a surrogate victim. He goes on to explain his notion of empathy as different from identification saying, "the historian puts him- or herself in the other's position without taking the other's place or becoming a substitute or surrogate for the other who is authorised to speak in the other's voice" (65). Ironically, LaCapra himself conflates the listener's position, who might as well be a student in class or any reader or viewer of a traumatic narrative, with that of the historian. While an emphatic distance may be more viable for a historical understanding of an event, Felman never idealizes secondary traumatization as desirable and even discusses how this would compromise the possibility of attaining the truth of the event, if it were possible. Similarly, in Caruth's writing, LaCapra identifies "a rather prevalent valorisation, even a negative sacralisation or rendering sublime, of trauma" (122) because she defines trauma as an irreducible singularity that cannot be integrated into consciousness as it is experienced and is resistant to articulation. Consequently, he finds Caruth too much concentrated on the acting-out of trauma than working through, both Freudian terms relevant to clinical situations. While acknowledging that there are instances in Caruth's writing which indicate the desirability of working-through, he, nevertheless, insists that delineations of acting-out in her text, and in trauma studies in general, need to be "counteracted by processes of working through" (55). According to LaCapra, "working through trauma involves gaining critical distance on those experiences and recontextualising them in ways that permit a reengagement with ongoing concerns and future possibilities" (45). Accurate though it is in terms of the ultimate functionality of working through, LaCapra's definition misses an essential understanding of working through, that it is a psychoanalytic technique which takes effect in the engagement of the analyst with the analysand, through complete freedom of acting out the analysand's repetition compulsions accompanied by an interpretation process by both parties.[2] As such, were Felman and Caruth willing to include instances of working through in their writing, this would not achieve the goal LaCapra desires, that of relief from the incapacitating effects of trauma on the victim and other witnesses. Furthermore, rather than a therapeutic effect, what is at stake in both Felman's and Caruth's writings is a reading of the traumatic experience and the implications of bearing witness to it as a victim or listener/viewer. Hence, LaCapra's critique is emblematic of the free deployment of psychoanalytical terms to analyses.

In *Trauma*, Lucy Bond and Stef Craps present an overview of the limitations they find in trauma studies, particularly in the earlier writings of the field, in their discussions of the past, present, and future of trauma theory. Their criticism has three main arguments: that analyzes of European and Western experiences are too generalized to imply a uniform global experience of trauma; that they focus on experimental representations of trauma in arts as the most suited mode of expression; that they concentrate solely on the experience of the victim, disregarding other parties implicated in the traumatic event. While acknowledging that trauma studies began with studies of the Holocaust, Bond and Craps criticize Caruth, Hartman, Felman, and also LaCapra for not including other sites of trauma and the traumatic experiences of oppressed groups in their writings, which, they argue, is called for "if the field is to have any hope of redeeming its promise of promoting cross-cultural solidarity" (110). On the one hand, they contest the event-based model of trauma studies for being too much focused on the individual's experience; on the other hand, they insist on the specificity of the suffering of the variously marginalized groups. In their attempt at justifying their position, they invoke Franz Fanon, a psychiatrist whose writing is infused with the language of psychoanalysis, as the pioneer of postcolonial trauma theory. However, by observing that his psychiatric case studies enable Fanon to describe the mental distress caused by colonial violence, they unwittingly affirm the event-based individual basis of understanding and writing about trauma, different though the setting may be. The other criticism Bond and Craps raise against the general trend in trauma studies is the narrow cannon consisting of avant-garde texts on which the readings in the field concentrate. Instead, they argue for including other nonverbal, nonfiction, popular, and vernacular forms of expression as alternative representations of traumatic experiences. As soon as they point out the need for an expansion of the cannon, however, they admit that Caruth and Felman wrote about films, documentaries, and testimonies in their founding works. Similarly, as they argue for a need to direct attention to other parties involved in traumatic events, mainly the perpetrator, in trauma studies, they acknowledge that some of Caruth's key examples of trauma have been instances of perpetrator trauma. However, they are quick to add that they find her analysis rather limited.

What stands out in the critique of trauma studies by Bond and Craps is it being wrought with inconsistencies. Missing that the point is the unique experience of reading psychoanalysis offers, reading for the gaps and holes in attempts at representing trauma through visual and verbal media, they criticize the early writers in their field for being too much universalising, too specific, too general, and too narrow, at the same time. Furthermore, their critique is at odds with the unease they express about trauma theory becoming a field. They express their determination to prevent "a set of valuable and complex ideas and insights" that constitute trauma studies from "congealing into a rigid method or creed" so that it will not lose its "capacity for self-reflection and the original investigative or ethical impulse" (107). In contrast, they expect anyone writing on trauma to embrace the totality of a field. They use the terms "trauma studies" and "trauma theory" alternatingly throughout the book. They insist on resistance to becoming a field, but it is not evident from their discourse how they distinguish study from the theory from the field. Hence, there is a circularity in their argumentation, also marked with the residual anxiety of the critic who is not specifically well-versed in psychoanalysis writing in a field informed by psychoanalysis. Failing to recognize the complex relationship between the specific and the general in psychoanalytical practice and reading, they condemn analyses that arise from specific analyses as generalizing while also trying to expand the limits of their field to include what has been left out in former writings, without becoming a field.

The critique articulated within trauma studies is symptomatic of the contemporary critic's reluctance to ascribe to or perform theory. Theory has today become a dirty word which almost no one can claim without an attending self-consciousness. In *The Future of Theory*, Rabaté distinguishes Theory, written with a capital letter reminiscent of Lacan to refer to theory in general, from particular theories. He notes the irony in the proliferation of anthologies, critical readers, conferences, books by reputable academic presses, all dedicated to ever subcategorizing or multiplying studies, fields, and theories. However, the death of Theory has long been announced repeatedly since the rise of deconstructionism. Elizabeth S. Anker and Rita Felski use the term critique rather than theory in *Critique and Postcritique* to describe the contemporary scene as the period after deconstruction, which is more marked with scepticism than confident theorizing. They offer a brilliant discussion of what they call "the series of frequently exuberant movements and 'turns'" in different types of critique to draw attention to the recurrent returns to past concepts and discussions. What seems, then, to characterize the field of theory/critique in the new millennium is a crisis of being in the "post" of all post-theories: Postmodernism, postcolonialism, postfeminism—to which this book also testifies. After all theories have been traversed and all arguments exhausted, the critic asks the question of what follows.

In *Postcolonial Poetics*, for example, Elleke Boehmer, who has been writing in postcolonial studies for more than two decades now, proposes a refreshed approach in her field, a call for attention to the aesthetics of postcolonial writing. Arguing that questions of aesthetics have been considered secondary to more political, historical, and cultural concerns, postcolonial studies has marginalized itself, offering mostly a content-based reading practice relying on a limited set of vocabulary. While highlighting the importance of a discussion for peculiarly postcolonial aesthetics, Boehmer also feels the need to defend her position since the history of aesthetics in philosophy is intertwined with discussions of universality, especially after Kant. Hence, new discussions in a specific field in theory engage in a dialogue with its recent past and the larger Theory. They try to open up to new dimensions by returning to what has been repressed in the past. It may then be deduced that, in psychoanalytical terms, this repetition compulsion pervasive in the critical scene of humanities is its symptom, a metaphorical manifestation of the unconscious and impossible desire to reach a Theory, a complete Truth that is not missing. The common response is, of course, to deny it: continuing to theorize, pretending not to theorize. However, a critic familiar with the Lacanian conceptualization of the symptom will know that resistance is futile, that repressed will return in the symptom with a different manifestation—it is incurable. Hence, the alternative, and a perhaps less painstaking response, would be to—as Žižek expresses in the title of one of his books—enjoy it! The post-Lacanian reading practice appropriated in different fields of inquiry today is theoretical enjoyments of texts—pure *jouissance*.

No writing attempting to offer a post-Lacanian reading can conclude without directing its attention to its own interpretive process if it fulfils its promise of being Lacanian. The discussion so far has been inevitably selective in its references and examples, possibly entails misreadings of the arguments put forth by the theorists mentioned, is influenced by the personal experiences of its writer who has been engaged in reading, writing, and teaching psychoanalytical criticism for some time, and will most likely be subject to criticism. Yet, it has been written with the full commitment to enjoy one's theorizing.

NOTES

1. In no single writing can one find Lacan's neat definitions or theories about how he conceptualizes truth or knowledge. Nevertheless, for a discussion of truth and its paradoxical relation to lying, see *The Four Fundamental Concepts of Psychoanalysis*, and see his Seminar XX known as *Encore* for a discussion of the intricate relations among feminine sexuality, love, and knowledge.

2. Freud develops his understanding of what is aimed at and possible in psychoanalysis over the years. An earlier but general understanding of his term working-through can be found in his "Remembering, Repeating, and Working-Through."

REFERENCE LIST

Anker, Elizabeth S. and Rita Felski. *Critique and Postcritique*. Duke University Press, 2017.
Boehmer, Elleke. *Postcolonial Poetics: 21st-Century Critical Readings*. Palgrave Macmillan, 2018.
Bond, Lucy and Stef Craps. *Trauma*. Routledge, 2020.
Caruth, Cathy. *The Unclaimed Experience: Trauma, Narrative, and History*. The Johns Hopkins University Press, 1996.
Cixous, Helene. "The Laugh of the Medusa." Translated by Keith Cohen and Paula Cohen. *Signs*, Vol. 1, No. 4 (Summer, 1976), pp. 875–893.
Deleuze, Gilles and Félix Guattari. *Anti-Oedipus: Capitalism and Schizophrenia*. The Athlone Press, 1984.
Derrida, Jacques. "Différance," *Margins of Philosophy*. Translated by Alan Bass. The Harvester Press, 1982.
Felman, Shoshana. *Jacques Lacan and the Adventure of Insight: Psychoanalysis in Contemporary Culture*. Harvard University Press, 1987.
Felman, Shoshana and Dori Laub. *Testimony: Crises of Witnessing in Literature, Psychoanalysis and History*. Routledge, 1992.
Freud. "Remembering, Repeating and Working-Through." Vol. 12 of *The Standard Edition of the Complete Psychological Works of Sigmund Freud*, 24 vols. Vintage, 2001.
Jameson, Fredric. *The Political Unconscious: Narrative as a Symbolic Act*. Routledge, 2002.
Lacan, Jacques. "The Agency of the Letter in the Unconscious or Reason Since Freud," *Écrits: A Selection*. Translated by Alan Sheridan. Routledge Classics, 2001, pp.161–197.
———. *The Seminar of Jacques Lacan, Book XX: On Feminine Sexuality, the Limits of Love and Knowledge*. Edited by Jacques-Alain Miller. Translated by Bruce Fink. W. W. Norton & Company Ltd., 1998.
———. *The Seminar of Jacques Lacan: The Four Fundamental Concepts of Psychoanalysis*. Edited by Jacques-Alain Miller. Translated by Alan Sheridan. W. W. Norton & Company Ltd., 1998.
LaCapra, Dominick. *History in Transit: Experience, Identity, Critical Theory*. Cornell University Press, 2004.
Marder, Elissa, editor. "Literature and Psychoanalysis: Open Questions." *Paragraph* Volume 40, No. 3. Edinburgh University Press, 2017.
Mukherjee, Ankhi, editor. *After Lacan: Literature, Theory, and Psychoanalysis in the Twenty-First Century*. Cambridge University Press, 2018.
Rabaté, Jean-Michel. *The Future of Theory*. Blackwell Publishers Ltd., 2002.
———. *Jacques Lacan: Psychoanalysis and the Subject of Literature*. Palgrave: 2001.
———. editor. *Knots: Post-Lacanian Psychoanalysis, Literature and Film*. Routledge, 2020.
Žižek, Slavoj. *Looking Awry: An Introduction to Jacques Lacan through Popular Culture*. The MIT Press, 1992.
———. *Enjoy Your Symptom: Jacques Lacan in Hollywood and Out*. Routledge Classics, 2008.
———. editor. *Lacan: The Silent Partners*. Verso, 2006.

5

Does Post-Colonial Still Have Relevance?

Mehmet Ali Çelikel

The literary scholars have been bold on criticism for the past five decades, covering an era of post-Second World War, postcommunism, and post-9/11. The prefix "post-" in literary theories has been overwhelmingly used in this historical and cultural milieu of the past fifty years since the beginning of what we may call the fast and furious age of critical theories. The second half of the twentieth century witnessed the disintegration of the long-standing European colonial empires, giving birth to a generation of novels written in the aftermath of European colonial rules. The novels named under the general title of postcolonial fiction necessitated the upheaval of new forms of critical and analytical reading within the umbrella term "postcolonialism" since the former critical theories were not sufficient in analyzing those as they did not consider the colonial history.

By the end of the 1990s, discussions on postcolonial theory, its contents, and discontents had already been in their crest at universities in the UK. The hot contestations in the postgraduate seminars, academic panels, conferences, and talks provoked even quarrels. As a young PhD student, I insisted on using the term with a hyphen in the middle as "post-colonial" to avoid the term's political connotations that evoked an anticolonial and anti-imperialist attitude. I argued that this usage of the term with a hyphen properly defined the historical period as opposed to the pre-colonial period and, thus, more proper to reference the fiction written in the aftermath of the colonial rule. I contended that it was possible to read scholars and writers who had already been opponents of the colonial rule during the colonial practice. At the same time, it was also possible to see and read about people who praised the colonial practices in the aftermath of the colony. While "post-colonial" refers to the historical period immediately after independence, "postcolonial" defines a territory that has been previously colonized, a cultural condition created by imperialism, as Neil Lazarus points out (2).

In *Colonial and Postcolonial Literature: Migrant Metaphors* (2005), Elleke Boehmer asserts that the history and culture of the world have been shaped by colonial ventures for the past few centuries (1). But the past few centuries in question here denote the colonial era of European colonialism. It ostensibly excludes the colonial practices in the earlier centuries by non-European imperial powers such as the Arabic (in Spain between the tenth and fifteenth centuries) and Ottoman imperialism (in the Middle East, the Balkans, the Caucasians, and North Africa between the thirteenth and early twentieth centuries). Boehmer's prioritization of European colonialism as an effective means of cultural imperialism that has shaped today's world's contemporary dominant culture and lifestyles is somehow undeniable, considering the hegemonic use of English worldwide. Therefore, in the same way, as Boehmer did (1), I would also like to limit the concerns of this chapter within British Imperialism and postcolonial literature written in English.

In the discussions of post-theory, the "post-," that has been already in question as to whether it denotes the continuation of the earlier theoretical assumptions or intensifies the previous theoretical arguments, problematizes the theory even more than it used to, especially in relation to the discussions of poststructuralism or postmodernism. In a world stripped of its old-school ethical values and barriers between high and low cultures, postcolonial fiction has rather turned into a reflection and celebration of the multiplicity of identities, cultures, and values without any center than focusing merely on the cultural problems of postcolonial migrants, because the identities in a postcolonial world live under the shadow of a pseudo-egalitarian capitalist system that suggests equality based on exchange-value. The literary theory that constantly produces novel perspectives of analysis due to the steady changes in the scope of contemporary fiction is "past the last post" as in the title of Ian Adam and Helen Tiffin's renowned book (2001). Therefore, the rethinking of the postcolonial theory in this chapter is concerned with the cultural clashes of the fictional migrant characters in postcolonial novels or the representations of geopolitical conditions in those novels and the politics of migration in sociological aspects in the twenty-first century. This study questions whether or not postcolonial fiction in the sense of the late twentieth century can still be talked about. Additional questions are how this world is interpreted in the new forms of imperialism today, how the novels representing postcolonial characteristics should be analyzed, and the countries that have never been colonized.

However, we should remember that humanities seem to have lost its permanence in sticking to solid theories with their hard-and-fast rules in catching up with the speedy developments in contemporary social life and the literary world. Novelties in theoretical approaches are no matter of time. Once a literary theory is hypothesized to criticize and analyze new forms and contents in the literary world, another novelty comes into being in literature, making a new generation of theorizing publications appear. This is not to suggest that a new genre appears in the literary world every other year. No new genre has been introduced since the emergence of the western novel. Yet, new inventions, the latest technical gadgets that offer new forms of lifestyles, fast economic and political changes in the post-Soviet era in the 1990s and post-9/11 era in the 2000s inevitably gave way to novelties in form and narration in literature. While post-1950s British fiction witnessed the emergence of postcolonial novels and cold war fiction, the post-1990s witnessed a new wave of narrative styles that undervalued the older forms and movements, as of old and prioritized concerns over new social events and crises of the contemporary age that staged huge global migrations, such as the introduction of neo-liberal economic policies, Islamophobia, military interventions in Iraq, Afghanistan, and Syria, the collapse of the Soviet-powered Iron Curtain in Eastern Europe. These, of course, took place simultaneously or in the aftermath of one another, including the disintegration of the European colonial empires. Naturally, it is hard to align all these theoretical formulations and principles.

This chapter, then, revisits and rethinks the colonial and postcolonial theories within the arguments of post-theory to suggest that postcolonial criticism takes it as its concern to analyze the cultural clashes of the postcolonial migrants to analyze hybridity, ambivalence, and mimicry observed in the characters of the novels written within the postcolonial period. Postcolonial reading is nonhierarchical, multiplicitous, and acentered, and, thus, it seeks to analyze and interpret the cultural conditions of postcolonial migrants.

Therefore, I opt to use the term without a hyphen in the middle as "postcolonialism," unlike my preference in the late 1990s, because there are various examples of fictional writing that represent the very characteristics of fiction written in the aftermath of the colonial rule in the second half of the twentieth century and the twenty-first century so far, even though they were not the texts written by writers of a formerly colonized nation. The scope of the term postcolonialism covers fiction which comes from, in Neil Lazarus's terms, "a common heritage of multilingualism and multiculturalism, a common heritage of displacement and migration" (23). The terms and concepts such as hybridity, displacement, dislocation, deterritorialization, ambivalence, mimicry, and imitation that allure postcolonial critics are no more in the framework of postcolonial fiction only.

However, it would be useful to begin with the overall definitions of conventional approaches in postcolonial theory. We might still be asking Ania Loomba's question at the end of the day: "Is postcolonial studies redundant today or more important than ever?" (14). Loomba refers to the heterogeneity of the term to point out the hardships of defining the term satisfactorily since the nature of postcolonial studies "may range from literary analysis to research" and "from the critique of medical texts to economic theory" (24). Elleke Boehmer, in *Empire* (2002), argues that the chronological definitions of "the postcolonial" are conventional as they are "mainly post-independence" as well as focusing on "Eurocentric theories of anti-colonial struggles" (6).

It is mostly true that the term has confusing and conflicting connotations as it denotes both a historical era and a cultural condition. Homi Bhabha consolidates the scope of the term on a more solid ground claiming that it "bears witness to the unequal and uneven forces of cultural representation" in the competing "political and social" dominance of the west "within the modern world order" (1). So, independently from the colonial practices backed by imperialism, the postcolonial aura is home to unequal cultural representations generated by long-standing western cultural colonialism whether or not it is commanded by politically and militaristically empowered colonial dominions. To pay homage to Edward Said, we must revisit "orientalism" that creates a perception that has been dominantly infused into the western mind and established through political and cultural media. The same perception could also be seen in what Frantz Fanon calls "the wretched of the earth" to claim that non-European and non-white peoples of the world are wretched, undermined, undervalued, and culturally despised over whom the colonial ventures are justified. Said and Fanon refer to this kind of indoctrination created through colonial discourse as in the works by Rider Haggard's *King Solomon's Mines* and *She*. According to John McLeod, colonial discourse is "formed" wherever "language and power meet," and it must be remembered that language is not merely a means of communication as it shapes our world and mindset (18).

The colonial practice that started as a lucrative act in the overseas territories is justified by labelling the natives as "savage." In Said's analysis, this was how the occupation started by several people who reside on an area establishing their habitat and borders "between their land and its immediate surroundings and the territory beyond" that they prefer to name as "the land of the barbarians" (54). To put it in different terms, it is a universal practice to label "a familiar space which is 'ours' and an unfamiliar space beyond 'ours' which is 'theirs'" and this labelling makes "geographical distinctions" arbitrary (Said 54). Hence the landscape and its cultural designations become ideological as the dominant occupying settlers name them. This turns the idea of geographical divisions into cultural and political constructs. While people are deterritorialized and redefined, they also turn into beneficial subjects of the colonial power. As put by Said, this means

> to instruct (for its own benefit) the Orient in the ways of the modern west; to subordinate or underplay military power in order to aggrandise the project of glorious knowledge acquired in the process of political domination of the Orient; to formulate the Orient, to give it shape, identity, definition with full recognition of its place in memory . . . (86)

The cultural construction built during the colonial rule creates an ambivalence toward "the past and present" as argued by Paul White, who claims that the ambivalence occurs as a result of questioning whether things were "better 'then' or 'now,'" whether or not the colonized should "design a new project without further expected movement built in" (3). White also refers to an ambivalence from the side of the colonisers who hesitate whether to "respect" or "dislike" the natives (3). The aftermath of the colonial practices as such continued to have their percussions in the post-colonial period. In postcolonial literature, examples of ambivalence occur due to historical reasons. Elleke Boehmer suggests that there is a "paradoxical development" historically because the meaning of "both colonial and postcolonial literatures" is found in the "defining parameters in history" (*Colonial and Postcolonial Literature* 7). Additionally, postcolonial literatures draw their energy "from radicals critique to intervene in situations of social injustice" (7). These paradoxes indicated by Boehmer signify ambiguities in cultural meaning and ambivalence in the cultural identity of the postcolonial migrants portrayed in the novels by authors such as Salman Rushdie, Timothy Mo, Monica Ali, and many others.

What is signified by the title postcolonial literature, Boehmer argues, is a "multifarious" or maybe a puzzling parade of texts that have been written, since the early 1980s, with their "polyglot" and "possibly disruptive aspects of postcolonial writing" which elicited the interest of poststructuralists who study "the displacement and de-formation of conventional meaning" (*Colonial and Postcolonial Literature* 237). With deconstructed meanings, the baffling use of language and polyglot, postcolonial writing attracted the attention of postmodern critics, too, since, in it, one may find all the exemplary tropes of postmodern writing. For that reason, critical theory started to involve what may be called migrant writing. Yet, as in Boehmer's questioning, what are the assumptions for "post-imperial writing" in contact with the "critical theories" mainly based in "the once—or still—colonising metropolis?" (237). The following question may also be added: Would postcolonial writing be analyzed within the critical terms of academia in the West, which caused postcolonial fiction to come out as resistance against western dominance?

Boehmer answers these by asserting that postcolonial criticism that celebrates particularly the "aspects of the postcolonial narrative" which portray and recall the theory comes out of "the intersection of postmodern and postcolonial discourses" (237). Therefore, while the interests of postcolonial criticism lie "in the provisional and fragmentary aspects of signification," its concerns lie "with the constructed nature of identity" (237). As a result, argues Boehmer, the fiction of postcolonial condition presents "ways of articulating, of putting into play, this justice- and respect-driven struggle" (258). While it is true that postcolonial fiction bears the tropes and narrative techniques of postmodernist fiction, it also presents many of the anti-imperialist political concerns. At the same time, it voices the cultural clashes in the conditions of postcolonial migrants and reflects the contradictory situations and adaptation problems during the cultural adaptation processes and cultural hybridization of all the immigrants in general. Therefore, it may well be claimed that postcolonial criticism may be used as a critical tool to analyze the fiction of postcoloniality and the texts written by and about the immigrants in general or, to be more specific: the fiction of migration.

Thus, the poetics and discourse used by the writers of the postcolonial period are also observed in the fictional works written by or about immigrants and refugees. In the same way as other kinds of writing, the fiction of postcolonial condition is naturally concerned with "questions of form, structure, perception, and reception" (Boehmer, *Postcolonial Poetics* 2). Thus it can suggest "insights of its own" on how these matters work in harmony with one another (*Postcolonial Poetics* 2). To be more specific, postcolonial fiction also creates its own poetics that also dominates and represents the texts of immigrants and refugees. Although postcolonialism might "share its problems of positionality," as Boehmer argues, "with many colonial-era disciplines" emerged in the academia of the western world that refers to "othered" subjects, it has to deal with a major concern: interrogation of such complicities (*Postcolonial Poetics* 23). In a sense, postcolonial criticism is concerned with complex structures of narration concerning many other fields in humanities, as much as other critical theories do. Among these are:

> Postcolonial feminism, ecocriticism or green postcolonialism, . . . intersectionality, gender and sexuality studies, ethically informed readings: the postcolonial field has been engaged by a host of issues-based approaches, which . . . have severally and together intensified its already existing programmatic tendencies. (Boehmer 49)

There are certainly and inevitably many uses and scopes of postcolonialism. For instance, Bill Ashcroft, Gareth Griffiths, and Helen Tiffin prefer to use the term to refer to all cultures "affected by the imperial process from the moment of colonisation to the present day," pointing out that "more than three-quarters of the people living in the world today have had their lives shaped by the experience of colonialism" (1–2). Yet, it must be remembered that world history is full of colonial ventures in many various forms, and contemporary debates on globalization and third-world exploitation suggest that colonialism is not a general "post" condition but rather a more or less constant phenomenon. Therefore, if the term is meaningful in reference to the period after colonization, it is necessary to clarify whose colonization and what post(-)colonial(ism) is in question. Peter Childs and Patrick Williams point out "early nineteenth-century Latin America and the end of Spanish and Portuguese control" (1) whereas Aijaz Ahmad stretches the "post-colonial" to cover a period from as early as Arabic, Ottoman, and Chinese colonial ventures to the ongoing British rules in the Falklands and Belize until the final quarter of the twentieth century or in Hong Kong until 1997 (9). From Ahmad's point of view, colonialism "becomes a trans-historical thing, always present and always a process of dissolution in one part of the world or another" (9).

Stephen Slemon (3) and Childs and Williams (4) find the term and concept useful only when not employed in reference to the post-independence period. They all find it more helpful when post-colonial writing functions as specifically anticolonialist, as a movement with a certain specified stance against colonialism rather than an indicator of a period. Despite the definitions of the critics above, who point out the term's political potential, post-colonial writing obstinately refuses to detach itself from the brute fact of colonization as such. It cannot help but refer to historical antecedents and to the colonial condition, which is necessarily prior to "post-colonial." In short, there are two distinct, if related, uses of the term. One signifies the historical period that comes after colonialism. The other is the style and condition in which "the colonised peoples seek to take their place, forcibly or otherwise, as historical subject," as Elleke Boehmer puts it (*Colonial and Postcolonial Literature* 3). Boehmer suggests that postcolonial must be "distinguished from the more conventional hyphenated term *post-colonial*," which she takes as a period term designating the post-Second World War era (3). Postcolonialism, in its unhyphenated form, in this sense, is a cultural and political condition designating the aftermath of all experiences of colonisation. Perhaps the term, when used in this sense, should be called "anticolonialism" and such a stance could well have existed even in texts written during colonialism by the writers of a colonized culture. Indeed, as Robert J. C. Young points out, anticolonialism in both eastern and western contexts is "as old as colonialism itself" (6). In this case, anticolonialism or anti-imperialism is not necessarily a phenomenon of the post-colonial era historically.

Postcolonialism still suggests a connection with the colonial period and its aftermath because the fiction of the post-colonial era deploys cross-cultural conditions. There are certainly legitimate questions to be asked here. Do texts written in other underdeveloped countries not also display cultural clashes and hybridity? Are there not any examples of hybridisation and/or mimicry in the countries that have never been colonized? Similarly to the fiction of writers from a formerly colonized culture, linguistic polymorphism, cultural clashes, idiosyncratic usage of the hegemonic language and cultural hybridity, which were all the consequences of a colonial experience in the post-colonial era, may also be seen in the examples of contemporary novels in the twenty-first century as a consequence of economic globalization that caused the mobility of mass populations. Some contemporary Turkish novelists foreground the multicultural social structure of Turkey, bearing similarities to the postcolonial cultural condition. For instance, Orhan Pamuk's *A Strangeness in My Mind* (2015) follows the story of Mevlut, a rural Anatolian immigrant who works as a street vendor on the streets of Istanbul. Mevlut's story reflects the migration of huge masses that started in the 1950s, from rural Anatolia to Istanbul. The metropolis, which had been modernized and secularized since the early years of the Republican period of modern Turkey, creates a feeling of unhomeliness in Mevlut, who resists the habits and behaviors of Istanbul while struggling to preserve his rural identity and traditions. One of his greatest shocks is to see homes in Istanbul where people do not take their shoes off indoors, which is quite unusual for Mevlut. In one of those flats where he knocks on a door to sell "boza," a traditional Turkish drink made of polenta, sugar, and water to be consumed on winter nights, the group of people inside the flat question his religious beliefs:

> "Are you a religious man?"
> Mevlut knew by now this question carried political connotations in the wealthier households. The Islamist party, . . . supported mainly by the poor, had won the municipal elections three days ago. Mevlut, too, had voted for its candidate. (Pamuk 28)

The above quotation foregrounds Mevlut's anxiety over losing his habits and lifestyle given to him by his religious and rural upbringing while he feels humiliated politically. Here, Pamuk highlights the societal tension between the rural and religious Turkish identity as the representative of pre-republican Ottoman identity; and urbanized, secular Turkishness as the representative of republican values. While Pamuk's text uses this social polarization as the cause of Mevlut's embracement of his rurality and religious values to refuse the westernization and secularization that he perceives as humiliation, it also underlines economic migration as a class issue that globally causes contrasting cultural identities to cohabit. On the other hand, the only reason Mevlut is in Istanbul is to make a living and, with an unavailing effort, to make a glorious return home one day. The same sort of dream could also be seen in Monica Ali's *Brick Lane,* in which Nazneen, despite her confinement in the household in London where she is forced to have an arranged marriage, desires going back home to have a fresh start. However, *Brick Lane* suggests that Nazneen's traumatic life results from postcolonial and postimperial cultural conditions and the result of her gender-based problems, which are also multiplied by her cultural origins. Her life is intermingled with cultural trauma, having been forced into an arranged marriage and lost a child. Therefore, Monica Ali's text is not to be interpreted as a consequence of post-colonial trauma only but also due to the oppression of female identity in a multicultural community. Her problems of belonging and unbelonging also stand out as one of the initiators of her search for identity. In this case, Nazneen turns into a culturally oppressed Asian woman. In short, *Brick Lane* traces the story of a trauma that has migrated to Britain. Thus, it is not only the story of a traumatized immigrant but the story of a migrated trauma. In a similar vein, Pamuk's Mevlut also suffers from the traumas caused by his migration, despite not having a postcolonial identity.

In *The Satanic Verses,* Salman Rushdie recounts the story of a Bangladeshi family as one of the subtexts in the frame story that helps us understand how conventional concepts are forced to change after migration. Muhammad and Hind Sufyan start running a café and guesthouse after migrating to London. In Bangladesh, Muhammad, a man of culture, a cosmopolitan capable of quoting from the *Qur'an* as well as the military accounts of Julius Caesar, was the breadwinner of the house by virtue of his being a teacher. However, due to his inability to cook, his wife, Hind, becomes the breadwinner in London, while Muhammad waits on customers in the café. He had to leave his homeland due to his Communist ideals but has become a second-class citizen. Hind's cooking becomes the basis for their restaurant, a typical situation where many Asian immigrants find themselves. Their two daughters, Anahita and Mishal, exhibiting the situation of immigrants, are unaware of their homeland, Bangladesh, a place that their "Dad and Mum keep banging on about," which Mishal prefers to call "Bungleditch" (259).

A more contemporary example of a suppressed cultural identity of an illegal immigrant is shown by Lawrence Osborne in *Beautiful Animals,* published in 2018. Set on a Greek Island, the novel traces the story of two young holidaying women who find an illegal immigrant washed ashore. The immigrant named Faoud turns out to be a Syrian refugee who swam to the island from a boat on the Mediterranean. Faoud, who escapes from the Syrian civil war, presents a rather different portrayal of conventional refugees' identity not only from the postcolonial migrants but also from the economic refugees. Faoud turns out to be a member of the middle class with a petit-bourgeois past when he puts on the T-shirt brought to him by one of the young women:

> He put on one of the T-shirts and suddenly he looked clean-cut, austere and curiously middle class. What he really needed was a shower, but it would have to wait. (Osborne 79)

Many similar examples may be cited as representations of multicultural identity problems from Timothy Mo's *Sour Sweet,* in which the Chens run a take-away food counter where the wife overtakes the patriarchal roles to manage the business while the husband takes a less dominant role as in the case of Hind and Muhammad Sufyan in *The Satanic Verses*. The postcolonial migration causes changes not only in cultural identities but also in gender roles. The examples of migration in Ali's *Brick Lane*, Pamuk's *A Strangeness in My Mind*, Rushdie's *The Satanic Verses*, Osborne's *Beautiful Animals*, and Mo's *Sour Sweet* all meet in similar anxieties of changing identities, cultural transformations, hybridization, unhomeliness, and mimicry, although not all of them are written by postcolonial authors. They are written by authors of various cultural origins in different historical and cultural milieus but still reflect the global economic problems that cause their migration. Thus, migration turns into a class issue.

To return to the beginning of this chapter, the issue of migration has turned into a phenomenon of an age stripped of its old-school values like solidarity, cooperation, aid campaigns, peace protests, social state policies, and public services. Migration in postcolonial conditions is no more an issue of the postindependence period historically but a matter of class inequalities. Migrants of educated, talented, and productive classes are admitted. In contrast, migrants who work as unqualified workers in underpaid jobs are considered loads over society's shoulders. This turns the global movements of mass populations into an international problem. Thus, the tenets of postcolonialism do not function only to analyze the texts written by the writers of formerly colonised nations but also to analyze the texts and conditions regarding the global migrants of economic causes. Postcolonialism is still valid in the age of post-theory, while it now covers a larger spectrum than conventional postcolonial texts.

REFERENCE LIST

Adam, I. and Tiffim, H. (eds.). *Past the Last Post: Theorising Post-Colonialism and Post-Modernism*. Harvester Wheatsheaf, 1991.
Ahmad, Aijaz. "The Politics of Literary Postcoloniality," *Race and Class*. 36/3. 1995. 1–20.
Ali, Monica. *Brick Lane*. Black Swan, 2004.
Ashcroft, B., Griffiths, G., and Tiffin, H. *The Empire Writes Back: Theory and Practice in Post-Colonial Literatures*. Routledge, 1989.
Bhabha, Homi. *The Location of Culture*. Routledge, 1994.

Boehmer, Elleke, *Empire, the National and the Postcolonial 189–1920: Resistance in Interaction.* Oxford University Press, 2002.

———. *Colonial and Postcolonial Literature: Migrant Metaphors.* 2nd edition. Oxford University Press, 2005.

———. *Postcolonial Poetics: Twenty First-Century Critical Readings.* Palgrave Macmillan. 2018.

Childs, P. & Williams, R. P. J. *An Introduction to Post-Colonial Theory.* Prentice Hall/Harvester Wheatsheaf, 1997.

Lazarus, Neil. "Introduction," in Nail Lazarus (ed.). *The Cambridge Companion to Postcolonial Literary Studies.* Cambridge University Press, 2004. 1–16.

———. *The Postcolonial Unconscious.* Cambridge University Press, 2011.

Loomba, Ania. *Colonialism/Postcolonialism.* 3rd edition. Routledge, 2015.

McLeod, John. *Beginning Postcolonialism.* Manchester University Press, 2000.

Mo, Timothy. *Sour Sweet.* Abacus, 1982.

Osborne, Lawrence. *Beautiful Animals.* Vintage, 2018.

Pamuk, Orhan. *A Strangeness in My Mind.* Faber & Faber, 2015.

Rushdie, Salman. *The Satanic Verses.* Viking, 1988.

Said, Edward. *Orientalism.* London: Vintage. 1979.

Slemon, Stephen. "Modernism's Last Post," in Ian Adam, and Helen Tiffin (eds.). *Past the Last Post: Theorising Post-Colonialism and Post-Modernism.* Harvester Wheatsheaf, 1991.

White, Paul. "Geography, Literature and Migration," in King, R. & Connel, J. & White, P. (eds.) *Writing Across Worlds: Literature and Migration.* Routledge, 1995. 1–19.

Young, Robert J. C. *Postcolonialism: An Historical Introduction.* Blackwell Publishers, 2001.

II
POST-(HUMANIST)-THEORIES

6

A Reconsideration of Subjectivity?

Lacan's Response to Posthumanism

Nurten Birlik

PREAMBLE

Due to advanced technologies, digital capitalism, biotechnological breakthroughs, and robotics in the twenty-first century, different forms of ontologies, transcorporeal, relational, or interconnected, have appeared. This is the time for the breakdown of the previous barriers between human and machine, human and non/dis/human, nature/matter and culture. In such a context, the definition of human can no more contain/exhaust the implications of humanness and anthropocentrism in traditional sense. This is the age of sophisticated technological devices that can wage war on epistemic opponents, and that can imprison the individuals in their solipsism. In technologically mediated societies, the systems have reconfigured subjectivities and organized the course of things for them differently. The previous humanist ideals or Cartesian conceptions of the self are replaced by or combined with new parameters. All these led to the problematization of humanism and triggered a series of questions regarding the definition of the human of humanism. As a result, a non-normative, postanthropocentric, biocentric, and ethical attitude, also concerned with the sustainability of the Earth and its resources, and the relation of the West to the non-West, gave way to the posthumanist turn, which has become a wide umbrella term just like humanism.

This posthumanist turn is critical and rather pessimistic to the degree of dystopianism about the humanist ideology of modernity. Humanism is both Eurocentric and European in spirit, and its Eurocentric attitude metamorphosed into a totalizing ideology in the course of the centuries. It is this aspect of humanism that is challenged by posthumanism. The ills of this ideology are listed by Rosi Braidotti, this Eurocentric paradigm, she says,

> [i]mplies the dialectics of self and other, and the binary logic of identity and otherness as respectively the motor for and the cultural logic of universal Humanism. Central to this universalistic posture and its binary logic is the notion of "difference" as pejoration. Subjectivity is equated with consciousness, universal rationality, and selfregulating ethical behaviour, whereas Otherness is defined as its negative and specular counterpart. In so far as difference spells inferiority, it acquires both essentialist and lethal connotations for people who get branded as "others." These are the sexualized, racialized, and naturalized others, who are reduced to the less than human status of disposable bodies. (15)

Posthumanism is suggested as an alternative "that refuses the dualisms of mind/body, nature/culture, and subject/object, on which the Western account of human 'exceptionalism' [...] relies" (Wingrove 461). In this context, the knowledge production mechanisms about one's body and subjectivity are reconsidered and reconceptualised, and posthumanist ideas are "supported by new advances in contemporary biosciences, neural and cognitive sciences and by the informatics sector. Posthuman subjects are technologically mediated to an unprecedented degree" (Braidotti 57). Now, knowledge production mechanisms point at open systems that refuse to be totalised by previous frames of thinking. They are beyond "human" formulation due to their unruly and differential agential potential. The nonhuman agencies, like the ecological, the robot, the animal, the virtual, and the matter, characterized by their differential becoming, are also attached significance. The previous anthropocentric view of things has been subverted. As a result, the human is regarded as one among many entities that have agential potential.

This new conceptualization of the human requires that psychoanalysis should change its ways of explaining and treating it if we still call this new category a "human." Different psychoanalytical schools (following Klein, Winnicott, Erikson, Kernberg, Kohut, and Lacan) might suggest different ways of approaching the subject. Still, their starting point is almost always the same: the identificatory processes with the significant others in early infancy, which are both constitutive and constituent in the formation of subjectivity. In posthumanism, as these significant others have undergone metamorphosis, psychoanalysis should reconsider its traditional practice.

This chapter aims to address the inadequately tackled question of what psychoanalysis might say about this new epistemological category within a Lacanian perspective. The theoretical argument is geared toward Lacanian theory, among others, because of its emphasis on the constitutive power of language, the Law, and the early identificatory processes, all of which assume different overtones in posthumanism. The process of linguistic castration and the symbiosis with the mother or the nourisher as the core of ego (*moi*), both of which are of pivotal significance in Lacanian psychoanalysis, need to be reconsidered in the age of digitalized relationalities and culturenatures, which imply a different conception of the logic of the signifiers/the Law. Due to his emphasis on language, Lacan could respond to the poststructuralist turn and evolve into a poststructuralist philosopher from a threshold figure between structuralism and poststructuralism in his early career. However, to what extent his epistemology could respond to posthumanism, the recent paradigm shift, remains unexplored. In this theoretical discussion, the chapter aims to respond to this question by creating a fruitful dialogue between different forms of posthumanism (with references mainly to Braidotti, Haraway, and Barad) and Lacanian psychoanalysis.

POSTHUMANISM AND ITS DEPARTURES

In posthumanism, the intricacies among/between the human and the nonhuman are reconsidered as the previous breach between the human and the nonhuman, the biological and the technological/natural/cultural-natural disappears. Matter and nature are taken not as passive but dynamic agentic processes. The "human" material involves not only the mental or the psychic but also the bodily site or corporeal dynamics that are important in forging agency. This opens up a new track of argument that problematizes the taken-for-granted significance of the human after entry into the symbolic.

Posthumanism departs from poststructuralism due to the emphasis on language and discourses put by the latter. The posthumanist mode of thinking challenges the constitutive power of language in different forms by emphasising the agential potential of the human and the nonhuman. Its emphasis on the formation of agency which involves the corporeal and psychic dynamics, goes the other way, and underlines the significance of a different kind of relationality. In this line of thinking, the cyborg of Haraway can be taken as a metaphor for the hybrid materiality of organism and machine, or the psychical and the virtual. It might objectify "the divergent figure of 'breached borders' or 'entangled agencies'" (Wingrove 461). Likewise, culture and politics are reconsidered in posthumanism not as "inscriptions on the surfaces of bodies but rather dynamic presences in their deep layers." The corporeal body,

> [b]ecomes an historically textured force that both initiates and responds in unruly ways. Perhaps most insistently, the relationality through which the world is transformed extends beyond the human to encompass organic and inorganic matter, a networked agency—regularly portrayed as an "assemblage" (borrowing from Gilles Deleuze) or "mangle" (introduced by Andrew Pickering)—that makes (human and worldly) being always and forever a collective and highly contingent affair. (Wingrove 462)

The concept of power is also reconceptualized concerning materiality. Discursive forces in poststructuralism are taken as material discursive forces in their entanglement or intra-action. This mode of thinking does not only introduce new vocabulary, but it also leads to a new way of reimagining, redefining, and re-positioning the human and the nonhuman through this new vocabulary:

> To restrict power's productivity to the limited domain of the "social," for example, or to figure matter as merely an end product rather than an active factor in further materializations, is to cheat matter out of the fullness of its capacity. How might we understand not only how human bodily contours are constituted through psychic processes but how even the very atoms that make up the biological body come to matter and, more generally, how matter makes itself felt? It is difficult to imagine how psychic and sociohistorical forces alone could account for the production of matter. Surely it is the case—even when the focus is restricted to the materiality of "human" bodies—that there are "natural," not merely "social," forces that matter. (Barad, "Performativity" 810)

Karen Barad lists "a host of material-discursive forces—including ones that get labelled 'social,' 'cultural,' 'psychic,' 'economic,' 'natural,' 'physical,' 'biological,' 'geopolitical,' and 'geological'" ("Performativity" 810) that shape the materialization of all bodies which are characterized by their differential constitutions in a process of intra-action, which underlines "the mutual constitution of entangled species" (Barad, *Meeting* 33). This is "an accounting of 'non-human' as well as 'human' forms of agency, and an understanding of the precise causal nature of productive practices that takes account of the fullness of matter's implication in its ongoing historicity" (Barad, "Performativity" 810). In Donna Haraway's words, the "material-semiotic actor" "accounts for the object of knowledge as an active part of the apparatus of bodily production" (208). In a nutshell, posthumanist mode of thinking "allows matter its due as an active participant in the world's becoming, in its ongoing 'intra activity.' It is vitally important that we understand how matter matters" (Barad, "Performativity" 803).

In this context, entanglement, a term constantly recurring in a posthumanist mode of thinking, deserves attention as it is a reference to a peculiar kind of relationality. This relationality explains the differential constitutions of entities not through a teleological drive but through a networked environment. This also shapes how we conceive time and space. They are no more separate but are characterized by intra-action. This is a wholesale attack on Newtonian conception of time and space, in fact, modernity, which divorced time from space (Giddens 17). This departure from the teleological drive brings with itself the need to redefine other epistemological categories, too:

> Existence is not an individual affair. Individuals do not preexist their interactions; rather, individuals emerge through and as part of their entangled intra-relating. Which is not to say that emergence happens once and for all, as an event or as a process that takes place according to some external measure of space and of time, but rather that time and space, like matter and meaning, come into existence, are iteratively reconfigured through each intra-action, thereby making it impossible to differentiate in any absolute sense between creation and renewal, beginning and returning, continuity and discontinuity, here and there, past and future. (Barad, *Meeting* ix)

In such a neo-materialist attitude to the human and the nonhuman, there is no space for essentialism(s) and the Oedipal drama. Then, how does posthumanism account for the formation of subjectivity? The response to this question comes from Butler and Haraway through Barad, who underlines the significance of performativity, which "is linked not only to the formation of the subject but also to the production of the matter of bodies, as Butler's account of 'materialization' and Haraway's notion of 'materialized refiguration' suggest." She looks at "the nature of this production" (Barad, "Performativity" 808). The performativity she proposes,

> . . . incorporates important material and discursive, social and scientific, human and non-human, and natural and cultural factors. A posthumanist account calls into question the givenness of the differential categories of "human" and "non-human," examining the practices through which these differential boundaries are stabilized and destabilized. (Barad, "Performativity" 808)

SUBJECTIVITY IN LACANIAN EPISTEMOLOGY

Before moving on to possible interfaces between Lacanian epistemology and the posthumanist subject, it is important to see how subjectivity is defined within a Lacanian frame. Lacan challenges the previous myth of autonomy and totality since he bases his idea of subjectivity on the reinterpretation of Freud's *Ichspaltung* or a splitting of the subject (*Seminar II* 3–12). Lacan's subject is formed by his conscious and unconscious parts; consciousness comes into being in a language-specific context, but the unconscious is also a closed system of a network of signifying representations. Unconscious is structured like a language and has a similar mechanism of the signifier and signified, but these representations as pure signifiers operate on their own specific logic, are elusive and alien to the conscious subject as they are untranslatable into symbolic logic.

Lacan locates this split at the source of human "I"dentity formation and takes "narcissism as the central imaginary relation of interhuman relationships" (*Seminar III* 92). In his epistemology, the subjectivity comes into being through identificatory confusion with others in a linguistic space. The infant's "self" is constituted in a process of identification with objects passively first in the pre-mirror phase (the first six months) and actively in the mirror phase (from the sixth to the eighteenth months). Pre-mirror phase perceptual fusions lead to later mirror phase identifications with the human Gestalt as an image: "in an exteriority in which this form is certainly more constituent than constituted, but in which it appears to him above all in a contrasting size (*un relief de stature*) that fixes it and in a symmetry that inverts it, in contrast with the turbulent movements that the subject feels are animating him" (*Écrits* 2). The mother acts like a mirror image to reflect a totality to the infant, who can perceive itself only in fragments. This image becomes its reality. The mother is everything to it and assumes the position of the (m)Other in this close circuit. It is captivated by the imago of the mother, which is the unconscious image that determines how the subject apprehends other people in the symbolic register, becoming the subject's structuring projections (*Écrits* 2). As the experience of the "self" in fragments gives way to the mirror-phase fusion, for Lacan, this Gestalt symbolizes "the mental permanence of the *I*," but, at the same time, "it prefigures its alienating destination" (*Écrits* 2). Thus, the infant moves from its insufficiency in empirical reality to an illusory unity. Lacan foregrounds the significance of the biological mother who becomes the infant's first Imago. This symbiosis between the mother and the infant is both constitutive of his core of ego, as it is the foundation of his ideal ego identifications and alienating at the same time. It is an illusion. Therefore, Lacan says that ego is an other and ego is fiction (*Écrits* 2–3).

The subject apprehends others in its future life against the background of its imagoes and their structuring projections. In other words, one can never get rid of our imagoes. In such a context, Lacanian ego can never belong to the living present as a unified and continuous agent. Thus, the objective perception of external reality is another fiction. Rather than a finished identity, ego is a process involving unconscious relations and associations as amorphous series of identifications. Later identificatory relations are also significant. There is a strong relationship between the Lacanian subject and its social environment in whose mirror it struggles to change its own reflection because recognition is crucially significant in this Hegelian site of being.

For Lacan, when the infant is disconnected from the mother, the result is a very deep sense of Lack, which is unfillable. The energy that strives to fill in this Lack is called desire, which comes into being simultaneously as the Lack. Desire is, likewise, insatiable, and it goes on producing itself. Anything/any object or position that promises to fill in this lack or satisfy desire is of phallic significance. Desire is the psychic energy devoted to returning to the nostalgic object, the phallus, which is structurally excluded from language. Still, its status as an empty locus or absent presence problematizes its teleological significance:

> Because the phallus is not a question of a form, or of an image, or of a phantasy, but rather of a signifier, the signifier of desire . . . it is the ultimate significative object, which appears when all the veils are lifted. . . . The phallus represents . . . what cannot enter the domain of the signifier without being *barred* from it …It is at the level of the Other, in the place where castration manifests itself in the Other, it is in the mother—for both girls and boys—that what is called the castration complex is instituted. (Lacan quoted in Wilden 188)

Unlike Freud, who gives this primary position to the biological father and threat of castration represented by him, Lacan places language/the symbolic at the centerpiece of his epistemology. Therefore, in Lacan, it is language that poses this threat and disconnects the infant from the symbiosis with the mother. When the infant is linguistically castrated, that is, when the infant has acquired the logic of the signifiers, this symbiosis is intruded upon by the Law encoded in language, and the infant is traumatized and disconnected from this narcissistic identification. This is also the time when it becomes positioned in the symbolic. This symbolic positioning or entry into language is also a move from the imaginary register to the symbolic, from the ideal ego to the space of the ego ideal, the symbolic position from which s/he looks at itself.

Neither the ideal ego nor the ego ideal, which make up "us" or constitute our subjectivity, is a finalized or a stable agent. Along with these linguistic elements and psychic processes, there is another threat to a stable identity: the imaginary residues in us. Return of the repressed subverts the stability of any form of illusory self. We constantly suffer from the return of the repressed psychic material in different forms and degrees, which in some cases blur all the clear boundaries in our psyche. The imaginary is excluded by the Law but never banished altogether; thus, it never disappears from the subject's consciousness.

LACAN AND POSTHUMANISM

As discussed in the section above, Lacanian epistemology is a radical departure from Cartesian understanding of the self, and his conception of language is a far cry from the representational understanding of language. In fact, in his epistemology, rather than a stable, self-knowing, autonomous self of humanism in which the human is the measure of everything, we find a post-Cartesian subjectivity which is fluid, unstable, and subject to the intricacy of the internal and the external as it is objectified by the Mobius strip. Although Lacanian understanding of the subject goes the other way and puts the emphasis on the identificatory processes in both the Mirror phase and after the entry into the symbolic, he still speaks about the significant others who are real human beings, in a linguistic environment, despite their fluid subject positions. This anthropocentrism makes Lacanian epistemology "humanist" as the subject needs these significant others to achieve its ideal ego and, later on, the humanizing castration in a language-specific context to have a position in the symbolic. If, in Lacanian sense, getting a position in the symbolic implies internalization of the logic of the signifiers in identificatory processes requiring a special form of reciprocity, other forms of being, that is, nonhuman forms, are denied acknowledgment in this process right in the beginning.

Then what happens to the nonhuman others in his epistemology? Or, in the absence of another human subject that enables different forms of identificatory processes, is there a way out of psychosis? Due to the signification/significance of the digital technologies and the speed the nonhuman others penetrate into our psyche, Lacanian epistemology should somehow account for this new phenomenon. What if the mother/nourisher is replaced by a robot in the mirror phase, for example? If the nonhuman others cannot enjoy the position of the significant others, how can we explain their place in our lives? For the time being, these questions remain unresolvable in Lacanian epistemology.

The argument I defend here is that, like the humanist legacy of positivist psychology, the antiessentialist legacy of the antipositivist psychoanalytical psychology is doomed to remain humanist. This is a paradoxical implication in the latter's case due to its emphasis on the constituting power of language. However, it cannot account for the significance of the robots or nonhuman organisms and matter for the human subjects. Posthumanism's attempts to emancipate the nonhuman others from the previous humanist and anthropocentric hierarchy in which the human enjoys the highest rank, and to advance material justice run counter to Lacanian epistemology which is still anthropocentric.

Lacanian epistemology accounts for the constitutive power of the "human" processes and denies this power to the nonhuman entities, whether it be animate, inanimate, or the virtual. However, this denial cannot stop the nonhuman entities from appearing in the form of a regulatory phantasy or an *objet petit a* or a source of *jouissance*. As explained above, the subject is captured by the nostalgia binding itself to the lost object and makes repetitive attempts to find the lost (and impossible) object. The energy to search for this is desire, and the "'*object-petit-a*' represents the little machine that unleashes desire. It is Lacan's formula for the lost object which underpins symbolization, cause of, and 'stand in', for desire" (Sarup 69). This implies that the breach between the materiality of the nonhuman and identificatory dynamics changes shape after the entry into the symbolic as they assume multidimensional agential significance. The *objet petit a* position of the nonhuman others, be it a mobile phone or a robot or, at times, even the natural phenomena or interspecies intimacies like the human-animal bonding, manages to speak to us in an intrasubjective dialectics, that is, they speak to and unleash our unconscious mechanisms.

However, this might also be alarming as the aesthetically rich materiality of the advanced technologies might manipulate the mechanism of desire in the subject and reconfigure it after it enters into the symbolic. In this case, Lacanian ideas might function as a cautionary tale to warn the subject against its manipulation by the system. How can psychoanalysis do this? *Objet petit a* also accounts for the psychic/ systematic or topological relationality and the multidirectional flow between the subject and the capitalist systems in the symbolically positioned subject. This is the point used and abused by the capitalist systems to encourage the "human" subjects to consume more with commodity fetishism, a form of fantasy. Objects may function "as objects of desire, which fill the gaps opened in the socio-symbolic structure. The role of fantasy in this context is to provide support for desire and its coordination" (Žižek 7). Fantasy is objectified through the object that functions as a protective screen (Lacan, *Seminar XI* 263–270). In the form of commodity fetishism, it might assume a collective nature and might become a driving force to consume more. This is one of the objectifications of the Mobius strip through which the internal psychic mechanisms merge into the external social phenomena. This is illustrative of how ideology creates a fantasmatic illusion:

> In the process of filling or repressing its constitutive lack, ideology strives to create a fantasmatic illusion of social totality by concealing its inherent antagonism, a traumatic dimension beyond signification. . . . And the socio-economic system itself embeds the

subjects into its own logic through commodity fetishism, where it finds ways to justify relentless valorisation and commodification. (Rajbar 4)

Desire is characterised by the inability to find its object, by a gap, "the *petit a* never crosses this gap. . . . This *a* is presented precisely, in the field of the mirage of the narcissistic function of desire, as the object that cannot be swallowed, as it were, which remains stuck in the gullet of the signifier" (Lacan, *Seminar X I* 270). However, in capitalist systems, it is attached to an object-cause, sliding from one object to another by promising narcissistic omnipotence, in the structurally failed quest of its satisfaction. It is this sliding process that is manipulated by the capitalist systems. Desire slides from one object to another, that is, from one signifier to another, "producing an endless stream of more desires to be satisfied. Desire is therefore sustained by fantasy with the subject following a particular object of desire. . . ." (Rajbar 7). Capitalist systems manipulate the subjects and their relation to their desire through object commodity "in the shape of new products, styles, and experiences, which unwittingly sustain the status quo of the entire socio-economic system" (Rajbar 14).

CONCLUSION

Lacanian epistemology subverts and evacuates the category of the coherent self as it problematizes the Cartesian ego, which is a stable totality of wholeness. Instead of Cartesian unity and essence, he emphasizes identificatory relations and language as the constitutional elements in the formation of the ego and the fiction of the self. For him, instead of the self, there are identifications with significant others. The shifting psychic identifications with the significant others shape what one is or what one might become. The subject emerges only within the discourse and gets to know itself from the place of language. As the subject is caught in and spoken by language, Lacan shifts Freud's emphasis on the father to the Father, or the Law and language in the constitution of the subject. In Freud, it is the biological father that disrupts the symbiotic tie with the mother that gives narcissistic gratification to the infant. However, in Lacan, this symbiosis is intruded upon by language and the Law. As language and the unconscious are distinct and operate through different lines of logic, Lacan also takes the idea that the ego of the subject is identical with the presence that is speaking to one as an illusion. For him, "I" is an other, and he critiques the objective status of the speaking I and differentiates it from the subject itself, which is positioned in language. Thus, he rereads and provides a linguistic/symbolic corrective to the classical Freudian theory.

It is never without a critical distance, but there is an intrinsic connection to humanism in Lacanian epistemology. Although Lacan explains the configuration of the subject through identificatory and linguistic processes, not through an inherent, biological essence, the human of humanism is still there. Matter, the animal, and nature, or the nonhuman in general, appears in Lacanian epistemology either as the Real or the imaginary Real waiting to be incorporated into the symbolic. As posthumanism is triggered largely by antianthropocentrism, which criticizes species hierarchy and advances ecological and species justice, its questions regarding subjectivity remain unresolved and unresolvable within a Lacanian universe for the time being. However, one should also add that although in Lacanian epistemology the non-human does not have an "actant" position in the formative years, it might have a representational significance for the linguistically castrated subject in different forms, as in the example of *objet petit a*, a psychic mechanism manipulated by capitalist systems in the form of commodity fetishism. In these cases, Lacanian epistemology might act as a warning to the capitalist systems' ways of extracting the surplus gain from the subject.

REFERENCE LIST

Barad, Karen. "Posthumanist Performativity: Toward an Understanding of How Matter Comes to Matter." *Signs: Journal of Women in Culture and Society*, vol. 28, no. 3, 2003, pp. 801–803.

———. *Meeting the Universe Halfway*. Duke UP, 2007.

Braidotti, Rosi. *The Posthuman*. Polity P, 2013.

Giddens, Anthony. *The Consequences of Modernity*. Polity P, 1996.

Haraway, Donna. *Simians, Cyborgs, and Women: The Reinvention of Nature*. Routledge, 1991.

Lacan, Jacques. *Écrits, The First Complete Edition in English*. Translated by Bruce Fink. W.W. Norton, 1998.

———. *The Seminar of Jacques Lacan Book XI The Four Fundamental Concepts of Psychoanalysis*. Edited by Jacques-Alain Miller, translated by Alan Sheridan, W.W. Norton, 1998.

———. *The Seminar of Jacques Lacan Book III The Psychoses*. Edited by Jacques-Alan Miller, translated by Russell Grigg, Routledge, 1993.

———. *The Seminar of Jacques Lacan Book II The Ego in Freud's Theory and in the Technique of Psychoanalysis, 1954–1955*. Edited by Jacques-Alain Miller, translated by Sylvana Tomaselli, W W Norton, 1991.

Rajbar, Simon. "The Ontology of Crisis: The Sublimity of *objet petit a* and the Master-Signifier." *International Journal of Žižek Studies*, vol. 12, no. 2, 2018, pp. 1–24.

Sarup, Madan. *Jacques Lacan*. Harvester Wheatsheaf, 1992.

Wilden, Anthony. "Lacan and the Discourse of the Other. Notes and Commentary." *The Language of the Self The Function of Language in Psychoanalysis*, translated by Anthony Wilden, The Johns Hopkins UP, 1981, pp. 157-312.

Wingrove, Elizabeth. "Materialisms. *The Oxford Handbook of Feminist Theory*. Edited by Lisa Disch and Mary Hawkesworth, Oxford UP, 2016, pp. 261-282.

Žižek, Slavoj. *The Plague of Fantasies*. Verso, 2008.

7

From Theory to Literature

Posthumanism as a Post-Theoretical Endeavor

Başak Ağın

Presenting a genealogy of posthumanism and the concept of the posthuman is a demanding task that needs to follow nonhierarchical and nonlinear patterns because posthumanism is rhizomatic in its structure. It is informed by several fields of study that seem originally unrelated at first, ranging from feminist philosophies, science and technology studies, marine biology to quantum physics and environmental humanities. But if one must offer a chronological outline of the development of posthumanism and its relevant concepts, it is possible to trace the term posthuman as early as the seventeenth century, when it appeared in Thomas Blount's *Glossographia* (1656), spelt arguably as "posthumian" or "posthumain" and meaning "posthumous" (Schmeink 32). This use of the word indicated a sense of "end" or "death," but it might also suggest "following or to come, that shall be" (Herbrechter 33). In differentiating the human from its anticipated descendant, the posthuman, one can assume that it signals a feeling of annihilation of the human, which is then replaced by a new, hybrid form. At least, this is what arises out of many popular interpretations of the term. However, the posthuman in one of its primary academic formulations signifies a spatiotemporal change in the linear and chrononormative understanding of the human, which is famously referred to as "an invention of recent date" (Foucault 387). From this perspective, the posthuman connotes a transitoriness in the conceptualisation of the human, thus indicating the social construction of the species as a self-contained entity.

In the contemporary forms of posthumanism, the human is restored to a flattened ontology, in which it shares many common qualities with its nonhuman counterparts. This means that the human is no longer viewed as the "measure." After all, "from ecto-parasites in the hair follicles to the microbiota in the gut flora, the human body is composed of diverse nonhuman species" (Ağın and Horzum 150).

Therefore, *Homo sapiens* is just one of the many species that undergo multiple symbiotic adaptations to survive. This view of the human implies that we have always been posthuman because we cohabitate not only the planet but also our bodies with nonhuman beings and things. Conceived this way, the posthuman is a hybrid body that bends and co-emerges with the other nonhuman inhabitants of their shared planetary home out of diverse spatialities and temporalities, within which they are all socially and environmentally situated. Hard to imagine as it is, the concept of the posthuman is therefore close to the world of fiction, although it depicts a highly factual situation in the present era.

While fictional examples that one way or another depict the multifaceted aspects of the posthuman abound, such as "the hybrid monster of Mary Shelley's *Frankenstein* (1818), the gender-, time-, and space-bending protagonist of Virginia Woolf's *Orlando: A Biography* (1928), and the techno-lab progenies of Aldous Huxley's *Brave New World* (1932)" (Ağın 15), the use of the concept to denote a different species than the human first appeared in Helena P. Blavatsky's 1888 *The Secret Doctrine*. Seeing the human as the origin of all "astral races," Blavatsky viewed all mammals as products of this original figure and thus called them "post-human" (Schmeink 32). However, leaving aside those initial and somewhat misguiding stages in the posthuman's figurative evolution and speaking from a more scientific perspective, the early roots of posthumanism depend highly on the outcomes of Macy Conferences (1941–1960), where discussions on such concepts as "information and materiality," "automaton," "self-regulating mechanisms," and "feedback loops" held a significant place (Hayles 54–56). These key phrases might evoke a sense of a dystopic posthuman, as they appear in science fictional plots like *Black Mirror* (2011–) and *Westworld* (2016–). Still, they indicate and express a turn in the Western philosophies of the late twentieth century. With a focus on the discursivity of human social practices that are believed to affect the world's materiality, the Western thought followed what came to be known as the linguistic or the cultural turn, pursuing the legacy of epistemology. Even when the feminist scholars of the era emphasized the body and difference, what they produced either left the body behind and turned to its materialization via discourse or was accused of doing so. This was a gap that posthumanism would strive to bridge from the late 2000s onwards until the end of the first half of the 2010s, especially with the new materialist veins in feminist thought.

In posthumanism's earlier journeys, before the main academic discussions of posthumanism as a theory appeared in the late 1990s and early 2000s, the first philosophical text to deal with the concept was Ihab Hassan's "Prometheus as the Performer: Toward a Posthumanist Culture? A University Masque in Five Scenes" (1977). With the linguistic turn and poststructuralism on the rise in the 1970s and 1980s and following the Foucauldian antihumanism that announced the end of the human in *The Order of Things* (1973), Hassan advanced the view that this strand of antihumanism signalled the demise of a certain configuration of the human, and thus was not implying a literal death. This postmodernist sense implicated a critique of the Enlightenment "Man" as the ultimate figure that holds a central place in the "universal" meaning-making practices. Such conceptualization of the posthuman as the embodiment of techno-cultures, which have always accompanied the human in its evolutionary processes, triggered a new, dynamic sense of the human and gave way to further scholarly conversations over the concept. Subsequently, many posthumanisms emerged, some of which implied cautionary undertones against a dystopic vision of the world, while some others embraced nano-, bio-, info-, and cogno-technologies as steps to creating a super-human, which later exhibited itself in transhumanist compositions.

The rise of the academic posthumanist discussions, which deliberately sought to distinguish themselves from imaginaries of bodiless minds and cyborg humans as later seen in liberal transhumanism or extropianism, was marked by key publications from various scholars in the late 1990s and early 2000s, making posthumanism and the posthuman aligned with anxieties that featured every turn of the century. Among those publications, Katherine Hayles's "The Posthuman Body" (1997), *How We Became Posthuman* (1999), "Refiguring the Posthuman" (2004), and *My Mother Was a Computer* (2005), Judith [Jack] M. Halberstam and Ira Livingston's *Posthuman Bodies* (1995), Elaine L. Graham's *Representations of the Post/Human* (2002), Neil Badmington's "Theorizing Posthumanism" (2003) and *Alien Chic: Posthumanism and the Other Within* (2004), as well as Andy Miah's "A Critical History of Posthumanism" (2008) can be considered some of the landmark essays and books that paved the way for the critical development of posthumanism. From diverse perspectives, these scholars and thinkers brought posthumanism from science fiction to fact, which later carried on to the level of theories, positioning it as post-theory. However, the main emphasis was on the technologisation of culture, diseased bodies, or the co-opting of culture over nature, which pointed out the anxious futures of the early twenty-first century.

For instance, Halberstam and Livingston's *Posthuman Bodies* was engaged in the debates over "the causes and effects of postmodern relations of power and pleasure, virtuality and reality, sex and its consequences" (3), while Graham's conceptualization focused on otherness: For Graham, aliens and monsters were good examples to showcase what the posthuman was, and in a posthuman world, the emphasis was on the enculturation of the human processes, spurred by novel technologies, which were "assimilated into culture as a functioning component of organic bodies" (10–11). Badmington's understanding of the posthuman thus relied on similar grounds to Graham's because he also indicated a world where aliens were "welcomed, *loved*, displayed and celebrated" (3). On the other hand, Miah's formulation resonated more with Hassan's, with its emphasis on "after" humanity, as in the changing definitions and boundaries of the human. All these positionalities were best summarized in Hayles's words, when she noted that the posthuman "signal[led] [. . .] the end of a certain conception of the human, a conception that may have applied, at best, to that fraction of humanity who had wealth, power, and leisure to conceptualize themselves as autonomous beings exercising their will through individual agency and choice" (286). For Hayles, the posthuman relied on the constant and interactive "flows of information" between virtual and/or material bodies and the environment (200).

Since then, however, posthumanism has come a long way and established itself as a post-theoretical venture. Therefore, for the purposes of this chapter, it must be underlined that the posthuman and -ism implicated here are not engaged in cyborgian, dystopic, nightmarish futures, which currently find expression in transhumanist (ad)ventures that "herald" life without bodies or pursue the possibility of transferring the entire humanity (at least the advantaged ones) to another planet. Instead, here posthumanism is discussed as a theoretical and practical endeavor that rethinks the human as one of the many agentic bodies of this very planet, thereby dethroning the Enlightenment ideals of "Man," which has inevitably led to the emergence of posthumanities instead of a commonplace notion of the humanities as the literary, historical, and philosophical study of Anthropos. In this regard, one can find traces of this posthumanism in Hassan's formulation, which evolved following the postmodern idea of life as discursive practices, supported by the posthumanist addition of materiality. This embeddedness of matter and values is strongly emphasized in the current understanding of posthumanism, which coincides with how this chapter is framed: This chapter does not designate any separation between the diverse strands of many posthumanisms, except those positioned as close to transhumanism, nor does it view new materialisms as a completely different venture than posthumanism but presents an overall evaluation of contemporary posthumanist undertakings. What follows is thus a brief but complex outline of the present-day configurations of the posthuman, posthumanism, and posthumanities, which have ecologically oriented undertones. Posthumanism and its discussions here serve as templates to evaluate its positioning as a post-theoretical set of theories, as a twenty-first-century guide to the critical discussions in the humanities and its future.

To begin with, posthumanism(s) of now, as a critique of the previous era that was marked by the linguistic turn, can be associated mostly with the Deleuzoguattarian pathways of continental philosophy, such as those outlined by Rosi Braidotti and Francesca Ferrando, which bear resemblances to the new materialist engagements that emphasize the agentic capacities of matter and its inseparability from discourse. While Braidotti's posthuman(ism) is shaped primarily by her Deleuzean reading of Spinozan monism and is therefore rhizomatic in theme and structure, Ferrando's is based more on a three-fold skeleton that follows from the same philosophical roots of Western thought, hence the reason why she calls her stance as philosophical posthumanism. What the new materialisms share with these two continental approaches is their insistence on the human configuration as a nonhierarchical and decentralized figure. Braidotti's neo-materialist and neo-vitalist readings of the Spinozan *Ethics* via Deleuze resonate in this sense with Jane Bennett's political-ecological approach, which compellingly argues for the vibrancy of matter, noting how "nonhuman powers" are "circulating around and within human bodies" (ix). Likewise, although the new materialist and material feminist scholars such as Stacy Alaimo, Nancy Tuana, Vicki Kirby, and Karen Barad follow a different school of thought than Braidotti and Ferrando, they concur with their European fellow posthumanists in the sense that they formulate a dynamic model, where the human and the nonhuman actors of life are always already enmeshed.

From another point of view, this view materializes in the posthumanist articulation of the "co-evolution and multispecies origins of life" (Nayar 53), which not only acknowledges but also dehierarchises the Darwinian understanding of evolution. Redistributing in nonlinear ways the linear formulations of historicity and temporality as in the positivist paradigm, this view of posthumanism reconfigures life as a dynamic web of interactions, in which the human and the nonhuman are undertaken from a nonprogressive perspective. Indicating the origins of life from common ancestral roots, which leads to the making of the human as a biological body, this notion partakes in reinforcing the concept of the human as yet another species. Here, there is an emphasis on the refusal of the human as a "self-contained, sovereign and independent" body, so this is the articulation of a view that "reject[s] the centrality of humankind in the world" (Nayar 53). At the same time, it refers to the spatiotemporal interplays of the emergence of many species, which means that *Homo sapiens* did not appear overnight as an able-bodied, eloquent, and unique figure bestowed with rationality. The making of the human as a species was and still is a process tied with environmental and social factors that play equally important roles in making the world as we know it. Seen as such, the posthumanist discussions of Anthropos as a social construct further find roots in the "sense of the living system not as an autopoietically closed system but one whose internal complexity accounts for the radically different external environment" (Nayar 53). Such interactive environments have thus come to signal a perpetual re-assessment and re-assignment of the human agentic powers since the very beginning of life.

Accentuating the interactive dynamics in the complex web of life, within which the material and the discursive are inseparably bound, the new materialist scholars heavily contribute to the making of posthumanism as they bring forth "the materiality of the human body and the natural world" (Alaimo and Hekman 1). By challenging the "normative sense of the human and its beliefs about human agency" (Coole and Frost 4), they consider everything, from "biological organisms to igneous rocks, from volcanoes to hurricanes, from bee communities to whales, from metals to lithic compositions" (Ağın 39) as lively, vibrant, and agentic, thus reconfiguring diverse concepts as "space, time, matter, dynamics, agency, structure, subjectivity, objectivity, knowing, intentionality, discursivity, performativity, entanglement, and ethical engagement" (Barad, *Meeting* 33). What can be understood from these theories is that, despite their different backgrounds, the contemporary theorisations on posthumanism have evolved into a merger of ontology and epistemology.

From such a continental philosophical perspective as Ferrando's, posthumanism situates itself as post-theory because it follows a *troika* in its theorization: It is post-dualistic, postanthropocentric, and posthumanist all at once (Ferrando 28). This means that, like its "infamous" predecessor poststructuralism, it seeks to deconstruct the binary oppositions on which major Western tradition is based, but it does so by bringing forth a radical view on poststructuralism itself: The idea that life is predominantly composed of our discursive practices, as many poststructuralist and postmodern thinkers have contended, is a problematized area of discussion within posthumanism. "Language," writes Karen Barad, for instance, "has been granted too much power" ("Posthumanist" 801). Barad's critical approach to the linguistic or the cultural turn is supported by the material turn: "Language matters. Discourse matters. Culture matters. There is an important sense in which the only thing that does not seem to matter anymore is matter," Barad notes ("Posthumanist" 801), with an emphasis on matter and materiality. This is where the postdualistic stance of posthumanism emerges, in a way that echoes the Harawayan concept of "material-semiotic nodes" (200) and further develops with Barad's "material-discursive practices" ("Erasers and Erasures" 450). This means that posthumanism strives to overcome those dualities that are the remnants of the postmodern thought, or rather, those that the postmodern thought could not achieve to overcome: While poststructuralism and such related sets of theories as postmodern feminism and postcolonialism have fought battles over the deconstruction of dualities within gender, race, and ethnicity categories, of which posthumanism is appreciative, the primary binaries of nature/culture, mind/body, and matter/discourse remained unresolved due to the exclusive emphasis on epistemology, leaving behind ontology. By bringing ontology back into the equation, posthumanism views these three sets of dualities as always already intertwined, hence its postdualistic position.

The postanthropocentrism of posthumanism also relies on the deconstruction of those dichotomies. Deliberately capitalised as "Man," Anthropos has always been exclusively male. As the dominant subject of the Western discourse, he is "white, European, head of a heterosexual family and its children, and able-bodied" (Braidotti, "Four Theses" 23). "Speaking," thus, "a standard language," as Braidotti notes, this so-called universal representation of the human is only acceptable as "human" only when he has the position of "a full citizen of a recognized polity" ("Four Theses" 23). The roots of delegating Anthropos as the symbol of entire humanity but portraying this symbol only as a privileged figure date back to ancient Greece, where life itself was understood as a dualism: On the one hand, there was the life of the elite, male citizens of the *polis*, with their right to representation in the political domain, and on the other hand, there was what Giorgio Agamben called "bare life" in the secondary title of his famous *Homo Sacer* (1998). Known as the *bios/zoe* distinction, this duality formed the basis of anthropocentric thinking, which placed "Man" to his throne supported by the Enlightenment ideals, while disregarding all the others that do not fall into the category of the privileged, dominant subject. Those others involved sexualised, gendered, racialized others and those who do not qualify "as human" because of their age, bodily and/or mental capabilities, religious beliefs, and so on. Problematising this alleged universality of Anthropos, posthumanism thus pursues a "*zoe*-centered" worldview, to borrow the words of Braidotti in *Posthuman Knowledge* (2019). "Displacing the centrality of Anthropos within the European world view" (Braidotti, *Posthuman Knowledge* 17), posthumanism breaks down the boundaries between the cultural space attributed to the human and the natural domain that is associated with all the others, from nonhuman bodies to "other" humans, who were originally pushed out of the category of Anthropos.

As outlined by Pramod K. Nayar in *Posthumanism* (2014), what has been discussed above echoes "the necessity of alterity to subjectivity" (53). Framed earlier in various approaches, before the emergence of posthumanism as a post-theoretical endeavor, by Jacques Derrida, Jean Baudrillard, and Gayatri Spivak, the concept of alterity in posthumanism offers an alternative to the human self and its assumedly primal subjectivity. It thus holds a significant place in the posthumanist thought because it provides an outlook from the perspective of the other. Such positioning of alterity, along the lines of "species cosmopolitanism" as Nayar underlines, "manifests in [. . .] late twentieth-century literary texts," where authors present the nonhuman others as the dominant species or as "inextricably a constituent of the human" (33–34). This presentation of alterity in literature, especially science fiction and fantasy genres, is strongly relevant to the view of the human as an "emergent condition," a "congeries," and a "moment in a network" since it emphasizes how the human "has co-evolved with both technology and other organisms" (Nayar 35). Repeating, in a sense, Hassan's mention of an "emergent [. . .] posthumanist culture" (831), it thereby refers to a new understanding of subjectivity, as opposed to one that is in humanism, which posits that only the human "is a subject, free in the decisions it takes, and therefore characterized by a self-determination," with the belief that "everything else is subjected to the laws of nature" (Marchesini 229). Instead of this false notion of the human that bestows itself with the quality of world-making and attributes this 'superiority' only to itself, reducing the nonhuman others to being "closed in their *Umwelt*" (Marchesini 229), there emerges a posthuman subjectivity, which indicates a "heterogeneous multiplicity that cannot coalesce into unity on pre-given grounds" (Braidotti, *Posthuman Knowledge* 57).

In line with this novel form of subjectivity, or rather subjectivities in the plural, "the linkage of embodied life with environments" (Nayar 53) is the third branch, which expresses itself in the rise of what is now called the ontological, material, or nonhuman turn. This linkage not only finds roots in the ecofeminist theories that highlight the interconnectedness of everything with everything else, such as the work of Val Plumwood and Greta Gaard, but is also supported by the new materialist theories mentioned above. For example, as Gaard writes, the grounds on which Plumwood's "Master Model" operates bring to life the self-identity constructed by the Western image of "Man," which posthumanism seeks to deconstruct. All the aspects of this construction, "hyperseparation, backgrounding (denied dependency), radical exclusion, incorporation, instrumentalism, [and] homogenization," both "illuminate and revise the heteronormative and humanist arguments" (Gaard 19). What follows from a combination of this view and the new materialist discussions is the emergence of material ecocriticism that combines elements from the posthumanities and environmental humanities, especially contributing to the literary criticism in the twenty-first century. Advancing the new materialist idea that matter is lively, vibrant, and agentic, material ecocriticism argues that materiality and narrativity are always already enmeshed within one another, thus forecasting the future developments in the humanities within post-theoretical spheres.

This view then leads to the position of posthumanism as posthumanism. Because humanism, especially the Eurocentric, liberal humanism, formulated itself through the bases of anthropocentric thinking explained above, posthumanism views it as problematic and as a discourse that needs to be diffracted, dissected, and reconfigured more inclusively. Embedded in such problematic visions of humanism is a "species-specific" discourse, highlighting the differences between the human and the nonhuman. From a posthumanist aspect, this discourse has become a tool to "oppress both human and nonhuman others" (Wolfe 42). If, "by tradition," *bios* "had the implication of *logos*," then it was only expected to see its underlying implications of "the discursive capacity of a certain privileged group" (Ağın 5). By contrast, *zoe* "referred to a simple form of life, mainly suggesting a lack of rationality, which was attributed to all those who were deprived of power" (Ağın 5). Therefore, posthumanism's critique of Enlightenment humanism is closely related to its critique of Anthropos due to his erasure, negligence, and overlooking of differences along with his claims of universality. To put it somewhat differently, presenting a "critique of the humanist ideal of 'Man' as the universal representative of the human," condemning "species hierarchy," and elaborating on "ecological justice" (Braidotti, "Posthuman Critical" 9), posthumanism is primarily a merger of antihumanism and anti-anthropocentrism. Calling into question the so-called superiority of the human (as a species, as the ultimate sovereign of the planetary systems, and as a white, male, Western, heteronormative subject), the complex set of posthumanist theories seek to redefine agency differently than human intentionality and to redistribute the self-bestowed agentic powers of the human among other species and beings. Conceived this way, posthumanism in its current formulations is a challenge to the discursive formations on which the "theory" of the previous century established itself.

Returning to the discussions of "the anti-humanist death of Wo/Man, which marks the decline of some of the fundamental premises of the Enlightenment and modernity" (Braidotti, "Yes" 9), then, the theory of the twentieth century has extended its dualist schemes and continued to produce critiques out of a humanly sphere only. The humanist scholars maintained their status as the followers of the Enlightenment no matter how hard they insisted on the resolution of binary oppositions because the discourses that they employed resisted against potential changes and continued, reiterating Braidotti's apt observations, to "position Man/reason/culture on the one side and Woman/matter/nature on the other" ("Yes" 9). They did so with an emphasis on "the progress of mankind through a self-regulatory and teleological ordained use of reason; secular scientific rationality allegedly aimed at the perfectibility of 'Man'; and a unitary subject position" ("Yes" 9), thereby always displacing the other. Therefore, if a literary critique of the humanities were to be presented, it would follow the idea that we are no longer in a central position, nor can we hold onto our primary *logos*, which came to be formulated as our "species throne."

If the humanities must survive, in the words of Braidotti, then it has to acknowledge that we "live in permanent states of transition, hybridisation and nomadic mobility, in emancipated (postfeminist), multiethnic societies with high degrees of technological mediation" ("Yes" 10). Only then can we reach a full state of post-theory.

REFERENCE LIST

Agamben, Giorgio. *Homo Sacer: Sovereign Power and Bare Life*. Stanford UP, 1998.
Ağın, Başak. [*published as* Başak Ağın Dönmez]. *Posthuman Ecologies in Twenty-First Century Short Animations*. 2015. Hacettepe U, PhD Dissertation.
———, and Şafak Horzum. "Diseased Bodies Entangled: Literary and Cultural Crossroads of Posthuman Narrative Agents." *SFRA Review*, vol. 51, no. 2, 2021, pp. 150–57.
Alaimo, Stacy, and Susan J. Hekman. "Introduction: Emerging Models of Materiality in Feminist Theory." *Material Feminisms*, edited by Stacy Alaimo and Susan J. Hekman, Indiana UP, 2008, pp. 1–19.
Badmington, Neil. *Alien Chic: Posthumanism and the Other Within*. Routledge, 2004.
Barad, Karen. "Erasers and Erasures: Pinch's Unfortunate 'Uncertainty Principle'." *Social Studies of Science*, vol. 41, no. 3, 2011, pp. 443–54. https://doi.org/10.1177/0306312711406317.
———. *Meeting the Universe Halfway: Quantum Physics and the Entanglement of Matter and Meaning*. Duke UP, 2007.
———. "Posthumanist Performativity: Toward an Understanding of How Matter Comes to Matter." *Gender and Science (New Issues)*, vol. 28, no. 3, spring 2003, pp. 801–31. https://doi.org/10.1086/345321.
Bennett, Jane. *Vibrant Matter: A Political Ecology of Things*. Duke UP, 2010.
Braidotti, Rosi. "Four Theses on Posthuman Feminism." *Anthropocene Feminism*, edited by Richard Grusin, U of Minnesota P, 2016, pp. 2–48.
———. "Posthuman Critical Theory." *Journal of Posthuman Studies*, vol. 1, no. 1, 2017, 9–25. https://doi.org/10.5325/jpoststud.1.1.0009.
———. *Posthuman Knowledge*. Wiley, 2019. EPUB.
———. "Yes, There Is No Crisis. Working Towards the Posthumanities." *DiGeSt: Journal of Diversity and Gender Studies*, vol. 2, no. 1–2, 2015, pp. –20. https://doi.org/10.11116/jdivegendstud.2. 1–2.0009.
Coole, Diana, and Samantha Frost. "Introducing the New Materialisms." *New Materialisms: Ontology, Agency, and Politics*, edited by Diana Coole and Samantha Frost, Duke UP, 2010, pp. 1–43.
Ferrando, Francesca. *Philosophical Posthumanism*. Bloomsbury, 2019.
Foucault, Michel. *The Order of Things*. Vintage, 1973.
Gaard, Greta. *Critical Ecofeminism*. Lexington, 2017.
Graham, Elaine L. *Representations of the Post/Human: Monsters, Aliens and Others in Popular Culture*. Manchester UP, 2002.
Halberstam, Jack, and Ira Livingston, editors [*published as* Judith M. Halberstam and Ira Livingston]. *Posthuman Bodies*. Indiana UP, 1995.
Haraway, Donna. *Simians, Cyborgs, and Women: The Reinvention of Nature*. Routledge, 1991.
Hassan, Ihab. "Prometheus as the Performer: Toward a Posthumanist Culture? A University Masque in Five Scenes." *The Georgia Review*, vol. 31, no.4, 1977, pp. 830–50. https://www.jstor.org/stable/41397536.

Hayles, N. Katherine. *How We Became Posthuman: Virtual Bodies in Cybernetics, Literature, and Informatics*. U of Chicago P, 1999.
Herbrechter, Stefan. *Posthumanism: A Critical Analysis*. Bloomsbury, 2013.
Marchesini, Roberto. "Posthuman Antispeciesism." *Angelaki: Journal of the Theoretical Humanities*, vol. 21, no. 1, 2016, pp. 21–33. https://doi.org/10.1080/0969725X.2016.1163853.
Nayar, Pramod K. *Posthumanism*. Polity Press, 2014.
Schmeink, Lars. *Biopunk Dystopias: Genetic Engineering, Society, and Science Fiction*. Liverpool UP, 2016.
Wolfe, Cary. *Critical Environments: Postmodern Theory and the Pragmatics of the "Outside."* Minnesota UP, 1998.

8

The *Rhizome d'être* of Posthumanism and the Question of Ethics

Revisiting Braidotti with Agamben

Zekiye Antakyalıoğlu

Giorgio Agamben (1942–) and Rosi Braidotti (1954–) are two contemporary scholars whose texts can be read as the epilogues to the ongoing world order and prologues to alternative futures. Although Agamben never uses the term "posthumanism" in his opus, nor aligns himself with posthumanism, he might be viewed as an unacknowledged posthumanist who seeks a new definition of "the human" and an alternative ontology that is proper to this definition. Agamben's concepts of bare life, bios/zoe, form-of-life, humanity/animality, and the state of exception (*Homo Sacer: Sovereign Power and Bare Life*, 1995; *The State of Exception: Homo Sacer II*, 2005; *Remnants of Auschwitz: The Witness and the Archive: Homo Sacer III*, 1999), his critique of the current biopolitics as well as his philosophy of potentiality and thresholds are fundamental sources in post-theory era for those who study in the fields of sociology, political sciences, literature, law, philosophy, and ethics. Rosi Braidotti, by contrast, is an acknowledged posthumanist and a publicly celebrated figure of posthumanism. Her project of nomadic/posthumanist ethics (*Transpositions: On Nomadic Ethics*, 2006; *Nomadic Theory*, 2011), understanding of "the posthuman" (*The Posthuman*, 2013), interpretation of bios/zoe, and critique of the present day have been equally influential sources in humanities for the last twenty years. Despite their new materialistic impulses, Agamben and Braidotti represent two diverse lines in contemporary thought. The main rift in the thought of the two stems from their conceptualisation of bios/zoe and their understanding of potentiality/potentia. The following discussion, with an awareness of the scholarly dangers of missing or failing to cover all significant material, will attempt to outline the merits and limitations of both scholars regarding their ethical projects.

Posthumanism chooses to treat classical humanism and humanist *ethos* pejoratively, but also remains sceptical of the antihumanist core of poststructuralism for its indifference to *ethos* and *polity*. It aims to replace "human" with an upgraded, de-centered version of "posthuman" as the better alternative for the formation of an "eco-philosophy of multiple belongings" (Braidotti, *The Posthuman* 49). *Ethos* and *polity* are common denominators in Agamben and Braidotti's work due to being integral to the contemporary biopolitics which they aim to transform. Thus, their endeavor to redefine "human" entails alternative ethics and politics, which they conceptualize differently.

Both Agamben and Braidotti are equally appalled by the pervasive character of exploitation, perversions of commodification, and the destructive aspects of advanced capitalism. They are similarly critical of the current biopolitical global order, and stand against neo-liberal, anthropocentric politics. In forming their thoughts, they are both indebted to Deleuze, and underline the philosophy of immanence in illustrating their views of potentiality/thresholds (Agamben) and *potential* transpositions (Braidotti), to achieve a Spinozist ethics of happiness, and open the possibility of a new politics that is beyond the constituted traditions. Both elaborate on the possibility of an ethics without reference to traditional understandings of the law. They attempt to reconceptualize "the human" to figure out where, how and when things went wrong in history, culminating in the ethically and ontologically wrong definition of the human.

Giorgio Agamben is a philosopher, historian, and sociologist who is genealogical and archival in method, mythical, and mystical in tone, and metaphysical in attitude. His hermeneutics involves an etymologically informed interpretation of history, centering on Walter Benjamin's messianic philosophy, Heidegger's ontology, Hannah Arendt's political theory, Carl Schmitt's concept of sovereignty, and Simone Weil's ethical philosophy. Agamben is also in dialogue with and indebted to Derrida, Deleuze, and Foucault in developing his philosophy. The supreme importance that he grants to language and its ontological significance puts him on a different plane from those who stress a turn from linguistics to ethics in contemporary philosophy and the post-theoretical era. Rosi Braidotti, on the other hand, is not a philosopher but an academic and theorist. For, if we apply the Deleuzoguattarian criteria of genuine philosophy "as the creation of concepts that are always new" (Deleuze and Guattari 5), it can be noticed that she extensively repeats and employs the concepts of Deleuze as a committed disciple of him, rather than creating new ones. In her quest for a theory of everything, she visits various other theoreticians such as Homi Bhabha, Antonio Negri, Michael Hardt, Edward Said, Gayatri Spivak, Karen Barad, Bruno Latour, Luce Irigaray, Donna Haraway, Giorgio Agamben, and Zygmunt Bauman to develop a multiversal, globally relevant, nomadic ethical vision, but finds less in them than Deleuze, and refuses any diversions from her mentor's philosophy. Her method is a posthumanist, transformational, environmentally and technologically informed form of pragmatism which directly relates to social and ecological problems. In "Posthuman Affirmative Politics" (2016), she describes her ethical project as a "neo-Spinozist expressionism which approaches events, phenomena and subject-formations as actualisations of different modes of becoming within a monistic universe" (36). Whereas Agamben's philosophy is based on nonrelationality (of law and life), Braidotti stresses the importance of relationality (of the human and nonhuman) which is shaped by an "ethical imperative to engage with the present and be worthy of it" (*Nomadic Theory* 16). Contrary to Heideggerians such as Agamben, Braidotti's emphasis of Deleuze is on generation, vital forces, and natality. Contrary to Kantians, the ethical instance is not located within the confines of the self-regulating subject of moral agency, but rather in a set of interrelations with human and inhuman forces (302).

Posthumanism, as an eco-conscious philosophy of multiple belongings, aims to replace anthropocentrism, universalist ideals of humanism, and neo-liberal capitalist biopolitics with a radically different interpretation of ontology that is revisited from an ethico-political and pragmatist standpoint. Visiting posthumanist ethics through Rosi Braidotti's gateway, and limiting the discussion to the theories of Braidotti and Agamben might provide a convenient corner of focus on the *raison d'être* of posthumanist ethics (i.e., to initiate and ensconce a different vision of the human, and reorient life with a bios-zoe-egalitarian nomadic ethico-politics), and lay out Braidotti's way of constructing the nomadic ethics of actuality in contrast to Agamben's ethics of potentiality.

Agamben's philosophy and its emphasis on potentiality are outlined by Colebrook and Maxwell as follows:

> Agamben is as critical of the present and its failure or abandonment of anything that lies outside law and language as he is of pre-modern conceptions of absolute power and the sacred that grant law a constitutive function. Rather than accept that law brings order into being and allows life to be lived in a human and political manner, Agamben theorises a new form of politics that would not begin with the polity (as a structure) nor with some constituted form of the individual or person, but with a life that can constantly be experienced as the potentiality for form, as allowing form to come into being. (6)

This "form to come into being" assumes a different outlook in the thought of Braidotti. In, *Transpositions: On Nomadic Ethics* (2006), Braidotti calls for an experimental project that involves "an enlarged sense of interconnection between self and others, including the non-human, 'earth' others by removing the Eurocentric masculinism and classical humanism to replace it with a zoe-centered egalitarianism that functions as the core of a post-anthropocentric turn" (35). She offers a new master narrative that aims to restore traditional visions of the self by simply transposing the ethical principles of nomadic subjectivity. This master narrative is inspired by "transpositions," a musical term which, in her context, "indicates an intertextual, cross-boundary or transversal transfer, in the sense of a leap from one code, field or axis into another in a qualitative sense of complex multiplicities. It involves the possibility of difference, variation, shift of scale in a discontinuous but harmonious pattern, zigzagging interconnections" (6).

Spinozist ethics of joy, for Braidotti, is central to posthumanism as an affirmative alternative to the bios-centered, humanist designs of the past that are shaped by *potestas* (restrictive force of power). It also rejects Agamben's version as an ethics of melancholy that accentuates impotentiality. The joyful ethics underlines the importance of *potentia* as a positive and motivating power that will enable the posthuman subjects to take action for ecological, environmental problems and social justice to sustain a better futurity ("The Ethics of Joy" 221). As she states in *Nomadic Theory* (2011), "the sustainability of the future rests on our ability to mobilise, actualise, and deploy cognitive, affective and ethical forces that had not been activated thus far. . . The ethical gesture is the actualisation of our increased ability to act and interact in the world" (286–287).

To do so, she envisions a non-unitary subjectivity that is nomadic in the sense of becoming-ethical and discards the old phallogocentric modes of thinking about life. She proposes the concept of "posthuman" as an empirically grounded (embodied and embedded) entity, "a navigational tool," "a vector" ("A Theoretical Framework for Critical Posthumanities" 22) that aims at achieving an adequate understanding of the process of undoing the human" (4). The posthuman subject has to be stripped of its old genderized, racialized, and normalized straightjacket, and relocated into different becomings such as becoming-woman, becoming-minoritarian, becoming-insect, becoming-cyborg, becoming-nomadic, and so on (*Nomadic Theory* 22). Therefore, in *Nomadic Theory*, she defines ethics as "a thin barrier against the possibility of extinction, as a mode of actualising sustainable forms of transformation that is based on the shared capacity of humans [collaborative morality] to feel empathy for, develop affinity with and hence enter into relation with other forces, entities, beings" (317). Accordingly, she attributes paramount attention to the reconceptualization of bios (political, social, legal, relational life, *potestas*), and zoe (nonrelational life, rhizome, becoming, *potentia*) as the precondition of founding a new understanding of "human" and "ethics" in the contemporary world.

Rosi Braidotti's critique of Agamben's concept of "bare life" rests on its emphasis on "the constitutive vulnerability of the human subject which sovereign power can kill" ("Posthuman Affirmative Politics" 38), and thereby, refuses it for identifying bare life with zoe. She regards Agamben's elaboration as a dystopic diagnosis of the present situation, criticizes him for perpetuating a historically and philosophically misguided emphasis on mortality or finitude which overrates death, and for being myopic in its vision of life ("Posthuman Affirmative Politics" 39). From Braidotti's affirmative, redemptive, and joyful standpoint, Agamben's philosophy may be perceived as mournfully melancholic, doomed, and inoperative. This view is, however, marred with the prejudiced and somewhat widely shared approaches to Agamben that tend to align his thought with the tragic vision of life. But a very solid contrary argument is possible if one recognizes Agamben's "comic paradigm" (Prozorov 31) and the emphasis of "happy life" in most of his writings. Braidotti's reading of Agamben does not fully consider the context in which Agamben introduced the concept of "bare life" to the current biopolitics, and ironically becomes a "myopic" diagnosis itself for resisting to see that for Agamben, "bare life does not precede politics, but is rather its product, a result of the inclusion of zoe into bios that cannot be identical to zoe itself . . . bare life is what happens to zoe when it is included in the bios" (Prozorov 95).

Agamben employs the term "bare life" in his critique of the state of exception/sovereign power, which reduces human to a disposable entity as an abandoned life exposed to death. *Homo sacer* (the sacred human) is what the sovereign power produces by suspending the law. "It operates in an inclusive exclusion as the referent of the sovereign decision" (*Homo Sacer* 85). In *Homo Sacer: Sovereign Power and Bare Life* (1995), Agamben describes this excepted figure's life as "a threshold of indistinction and of passage between animal and man" (105). *Homo sacer* is a subject who is caught up in the ban. Its life is "not simple natural life, but Life exposed to death (bare Life or sacred Life)" (88). This indistinction, in turn, deprives the naked figure of the subject's ability to speak. Human as a speaking being distinguishes him-/herself from animals, and Agamben tries to present a different way of approaching zoe by focusing on human's moments of silence. He, therefore, studies cases, individual situations, or experiences (such as traumatized victims of the concentration camps, patients in vegetative state, inmates of prisons, etc.) when human is reduced to inhuman, or when law and language are suspended, in order to analyze the nonspeaking impotentiality of the human. "The main claim of his major work, *Homo Sacer*, is that the untheorised conception of the sacred still inflects politics and must be dealt with in order to reconfigure politics" (Colebrook and Maxwell 7), and therefore his "turn back to life differs from contemporary vitalisms and materialisms in that it still grants language supreme importance for its capacity to articulate and render us as human subjects; he thinks that humanity can only be understood by thinking through its animality" (35).

Braidotti persistently misreads Agamben's crucial distinction between zoe (natural life, animality) and bare life (utterly naked and vulnerable, abandoned life) to present her affirmative alternative of zoe, and is unfair in her allegation against Agamben who, she believes, makes "a negative rendition" of zoe (*Transpositions* 270). She allocates her critique on his placement of zoe outside of the polity which renders it a pejorative alterity, as the inhuman other of the living human. For her, Agamben, "following Heideggerian ontology, rests on the fact that zoe has historically been feminised, classified like women alongside natives, animals and others as referents of a generative force that was reduced to a more biological function and deprived of political and ethical relevance" (270). However, Agamben never promotes bios over zoe or humanity over animality; rather, for him, "bios (political life) is both what zoe is not, and what zoe becomes" (Norris 41). The very separation of the human and inhuman forms the critique of his "ethics that would emerge from abandoning the abandonment of zoe, of what lies outside the law and the human which would require attributing more significance to the becoming of human of man" (Colebrook and Maxwell 114).

Braidotti's pragmatism, utopian impulse, and redemptive urge are the widely endorsed qualities of her project of nomadic ethics. Her pragmatist reading of Deleuze and vigorous invitation to action though, at times, resemble Lenin's reading of Marx in a way that is fundamentally different from Agamben's meditative reading of Deleuze. Compared to Agamben's solemnity and prudence, Braidotti sounds more like a politician who scatters promises about how to change the world and its established order by offering a program of alternative perspectives and practices. Yet, despite the propaganda aspect of her theory, which calls for "subjectivity," "sustainability," and "accountability" as the imperatives of nomadic ethics, she abstains from clarifying how she is planning to practice what she preaches. This reluctance might stem from the consciousness that praxis belongs to the sphere of bios (politics), and entails laws and regulations that would, in turn, necessitate moral grounding and apparatuses. Generally, morality as a field of inquiry does not score high in her ethical project which aligns itself with the legacy of Deleuze and Guattari that degrades morality as an effect of reactive consciousness. As Todd May points out, "for Deleuze, morality is to be criticised on a Nietzschean basis," and since morality assumes a transcendent figure or refers existence to a transcendent values, "Deleuze embraces a Spinozist ethics, seeking not to conform to pre-given transcendent values but to experiment with the modes of existence immanent to the world we inhabit" (103). However, nomadic ethics' emphasis on an active consciousness that evades any reactively formed moralism becomes questionable when one observes the reactive positioning of posthumanism against humanism.

If we put this aside, there is yet another incongruent aspect of nomadic ethics: it underlines *potentia* and demands for will (to act) and necessity (to change the world). Agamben's following statement from *Potentialities* (1999) points to a fundamental difference in the understanding of the two:

> Our ethical tradition has often sought to avoid the problem of potentiality by reducing it to the terms of will and necessity. Not what you can do, but what you want to do or must do is its dominant theme. But potentiality is not will, and impotentiality is not necessity. . . . To believe that will has power over potentiality that the passage to actuality is the result of a decision that puts an end to the ambiguity of potentiality (which is always potentiality to do and not do)- this is the perpetual illusion of morality. (254)

Agamben categorizes this kind of a performative ethics that is shaped by will and necessity as moralistic, because they entail "operativity and command" and, instead, he offers "an ethics that is entirely liberated from the concepts of duty and will" (*Opus Dei* 129), or imagines an ontology, a theology of being where life does not have a proper end, that is, beyond operativity and command. In this context, potentiality offers a ground, a threshold for a new flight which has no elsewhere, a flight which eschews the notion that we need to progress and actualize a better world (Frost 3). Braidotti perceives the threshold as a zone or site of plenitude expressed in the exclamation "I can't take it anymore!" (*Nomadic Theory* 317; *The Posthuman* 132; *Transpositions* 216, 217, 267) that initiates action, a flight to elsewhere, and regards *potentia* as the root of the will to act.

Agamben's difference from Braidotti's redemptive urge becomes manifest if we follow Colebrook and Maxwell:

Agamben does not seek to include bare and abandoned life within the domain of the human and political; he does not seek to grant recognition and personhood to all life. His work therefore takes a different path from forms of posthumanism or animal rights that aim to treat animals with dignity of humans, or that see no difference between animality and humanity. Rather than deem all life to be dignified and worthy of recognition, Agamben's counter manouver is to regard mere life—a life that is perfect potentiality because it need not act in order to be what it is—as the zone of a new ethics beyond humanism and recognition. He aims to release life from the bureaucracy of redemption. (103)

Agamben's ethics of threshold is beyond the distinction between human/animal, bios/zoe, dwells more in between speaking and not-speaking, on pure potentiality. In that, it attunes more with the Deleuzian understanding of rhizome or becoming which is immune to human reasoning. As Frost renders, "an experience of potentiality as a threshold cannot be reduced to waiting for a revolutionary event in order to become 'totalised' and give meaning to its existence" (3). Colebrook and Maxwell parallelly observe that, "Agamben is not a thinker with a philosophical system or theory of being that might then be applied or related to other domains" (32). But despite being contested by many "for seeking to theorise life as enigmatically silent and possessing a capacity for inactivation or impotentiality" (Colebrook and Maxwell 26), Agamben's reading of Deleuze sounds more consistent. Paulo Palladino is one of those who notices that "Braidotti's alternative to Agamben, which affirms Life, seems to be blind to Deleuze's note of caution about new diagrams and any expectations that they might overcome the difficulties of the present predicament, such that Deleuze only hoped that they would 'not prove worse than . . . previous forms'" (209).

For Agamben "bare life" comes into being when zoe and bios, animal and human are treated as opposites. He focuses on how—by way of language—humans render themselves exceptional, whereby the human is a speaking animal, but one whose animality is such that man sets himself outside the animal life that is his very being. In this context, the problem of life is that life can only become "sacred" (as in *homo sacer*, and hence, in a negative sense) when life-as-zoe has been distinguished from life-as-bios. Accordingly, Agamben conceives the ideal Life as free from the processes of sacralisation that entails this split and inflects the polity. What separates zoe and bios is polity; therefore, any ethico-political experiment, even if it aims to re-unite bios and zoe as in the case of Braidotti, or any attempt of transposing/transferring the sacredness of bios onto zoe, is likely to end up as a "bureaucracy of redemption" from which Agamben aims to release Life.

Agamben states that

> Western politics is founded upon that which it excludes from politics (i.e. zoe). The natural life (zoe) is politicised in biopolitics through abandonment to an unconditional power of death (i.e. sovereignty). It is in this abandonment of natural life to sovereign violence that bare life makes its appearance. Bare life, therefore, is not natural life or zoe, but rather, it is the politicized form of natural life. It is neither bios nor zoe, but life exposed to death by the sovereign. (*Homo Sacer* 88)

Perturbed by Agamben's "fatalistic" view, Braidotti begs "to differ from the habit that favours the deployment of the problem of bios/zoe on the horizon of death" (*Transpositions* 40). Instead, she prefers to regard zoe as a generative power, as if Agamben is only praising the superiority of mortality over vitality, humanity over animality, or relationality of bios over the non-relationality of zoe. However, she fails to notice that her attempt to design a zoe-centered egalitarian politics attributes relationality to zoe, which is incongruous with the nature of zoe *per se*.

Another essential distinction between Agamben and Braidotti becomes visible in their perception of *potentia* or *potentiality*. For Braidotti, *potentia* is an affirmative and constitutive power that will enable the posthuman to create alternative politics. In contrast, for Agamben constitutive power is a praxis which destroys law only to recreate it in a new form. "By reconsidering the distinction between being and praxis: rather than a practice or power that constitutes or *brings into being*, Agamben argues for a practice that is *destituent*, and that breaks with a long tradition of privileging creativity, act, and will" (Colebrook and Maxwell, 164; emphasis original). In other words, by proposing "destituent power" he aims to depose the law once and for all and envisions a really new historical epoch (Agamben "From the State of Control to a Praxis of Destituent Power" 28). This understanding refers to a non-relational potentiality as inoperative activity. In *The Coming Community*, Agamben defines "potentiality" as "becoming what one ought to be," "a pure taking place." For him, "the being-worm of the worm and the being-stone of the stone is divine" (15). Their taking place (being) is proper to them. Braidotti's understanding of *potentia* dwells more on a relational, constituent, operative, and active force that charges the accountable nomadic subjects with responsibility to actualise alternative states of affairs concerning the present ("Posthuman Affirmative Politics" 31). Contrary to Braidotti, Agamben's understanding of ethics does not subject life's potentiality to some external value of the proper person and is suspicious of the activist urges of utopianist projects as such.

This view distinguishes Agamben from posthumanist ideologists, and for Prozorov, it regards the limitation of potentiality by will (*potentia ordinata*) as the source of a politics that affirms certain possibilities over others exhausting potentiality in the new vision of actuality, "a better world" or a "bright future." In contrast, "if potentiality is dissociated from will, it will be possible to conceive of a politics that renders the existing order of things inoperative not in order to replace it with an actual alternative from the past or the future" (Prozorov 52).

Braidotti highlights, in her discussions of *potentia*, the importance of subjectivity in ethical conducts and believes that "for an ethics worthy of the complexities of our times, we need to redefine our understanding of the 'subject'" (*Transpositions* 18). The change that she wishes to establish is from the consumerist pseudo-individual who says "I shop therefore I am," to a liberated, non-unitary subject who, by "putting the active back to activism," and "the motion back into emotion," will create a positive difference (*Transpositions* 56, 214; *Nomadic Theory* 288, 348; *The Posthuman* 11).

Non-unitary subjectivity, sustainability and accountability, as the three constitutive elements of nomadic ethics (*Nomadic Theory* 287), presuppose a subject who has to be embedded and embodied, filled with *potentia* (potential/*conatus*) to deploy cognitive, affective and ethical forces that had not been activated thus far. "Ethics," therefore, "means faithfulness to this *potentia* or the desire to become" (*Transpositions* 163). The sustainability of the future rests on our ability to mobilize these forces. At this point, Braidotti's concept of accountability (politics, law, and police that assign humans to particular positions and set everything in its place) requires more elaboration, because Braidotti somehow avoids explaining the legal or institutional forces, such as the ideological and repressive state apparatuses, that are supposed to operate in the posthuman community to come. The concept of apparatus appears in the oeuvre of Agamben as *dispositif* and designates "a set of practices, bodies of knowledge, measures and institutions that aim to manage, govern, control and orient—in a way that purports to be useful—the behaviours, gestures and thoughts of human beings" (*What is an Apparatus?* 13). In other words, apparatuses function as the captivating forces of law that create guilt-ridden, manipulated, oppressed subjects from which Agamben aims to liberate humanity.

Braidotti's preference of a "joyfully discontinuous pragmatism" instead of a "mournfully consistent" melancholy (*Nomadic Theory* 235) entails "applicability and practicality," along with "a responsible subjectivity that can construct sustainable futures . . . and honour our obligations to the generations to come" (237). However, Judith Butler warns Braidotti for not being clear about what she means by sustainability and becoming. Focusing on our time's destructive and toxic productions, Butler questions whether we should approach "toxicity" as part of this "becoming" (23). For her, Braidotti's ethical dimension seems to imply that some forms of becoming (if they help for sustainable future) are good and some are not. However, even if toxicity seems to be the part of a process that is indisputably antilife, it is still the part of becoming which is a circulation of life and death, destruction and rebirth. The same thing goes for the concepts of love, union and agreement in terms of the concept of relationality, and Butler reminds Braidotti that people with different ideologies and political views, or belief systems may not always relate to one another peacefully (26). She cautions Braidotti not to neglect that antagonism and contestation are also part of relationality. Butler's doubt is relevant and timely in highlighting Braidotti's obscurity in illustrating how her "alchemical power of transposition" will function, "how vulnerability might be transposed into relational vitality," (28) and how one different mode of thought will be involved in the ethics of assemblage. Eventually, Braidotti's call for "putting the motion back to emotion" turns to be another problematic issue, as her understanding of "emotion," despite its transformational urge, somehow evades the negative emotions (such as envy, jealousy, selfishness, resentment, pride and prejudice) and undermines the prehumanist, primordially "evil" aspects of human.

Ethics of sustainability rests on the basic principles of intergenerational and intragenerational equity so that present and future generations can inherit a liveable planet; and conserve bio-diversity, so that all species can prosper and endure (*Transpositions* 206). Deleuzean ethics, which is informed by Nietzsche's concept of *amor fati,* becomes a crucial constituent of sustainability as it involves the transformation of negative passions (resentment) in to positive passions (affirmation). Paulo Palladino, by reference to Didier Franck, presents two meanings of *amor fati*: 1. to live in such a way that you would desire to live anew [which presupposes *Aion*/ circular time], 2. to live that there is no longer any meaning in living: that now becomes the "meaning" of life [which presupposes *Kairos*/moments of being] (209). Braidotti adheres to the former definition whereas Agamben stands for the latter. She describes her understanding of *amor fati* in *Nomadic Theory* as an "ethics of overturning the negative" (292) which implies "not passive fatalism, but pragmatic and labile engagement with the present in order to collectively construct conditions that transform and empower our capacity to act ethically and produce social horizons of hope or sustainable futures" (191). However, her constant emphasis on futurity entails operativity in *Chronos* in a way that is contrary to her supposed adherence to *Aion*.

The ambiguity in Braidotti's understanding of time becomes more visible with a closer look at her concept of accountability. Accountability requires institutions, laws and regulations which operate in *Chronos*. Braidotti, by confining her concept of time to *Aion,* claims that "only *Aion* can enable us to be creative in repetitions, retelling, re-configuring and revisiting history, tradition, philosophy, politics and culture from different angles so as to infuse them with a nomadic spin that establishes multiple connections and lines of interaction (i.e. transpositions)" (*Nomadic Theory* 229–230). While underlining the importance of "putting the active back into activism" (*The Posthuman* 16), she chooses to ignore that acting is not becoming, or that the time of acting is not *Aion*; rather, acting requires a spatio-temporally oriented subject that operates in *Chronos*. In "Posthuman Affirmative Politics" (2016), she tries to overcome this ambiguity by distinguishing "politics" from "political." The politics, for her, is postulated on *Chronos*—the linear time of institutional deployment of norms and protocols, and the political is postulated on the axis of *Aion*—the non-linear time of becoming and of affirmative critical practice. However, this distinction is far from compelling in its suggestion of implementing accountability in a circular time of political praxis. By necessity, the practice of accountability assumes a political subject to be held accountable. Therefore, any suggestion of legal force will fall into the pits of an anthropocentric, somewhat totalizing worldview or imply a posthumanist sovereignty (constitutive power) that operates within *Chronos*. Zoe or rhizome is alien to human consciousness, and cannot be subjected to law since it does not know obligations. Its *raison d'être,* if there is any, is inaccessible to us. It cannot be put to human discourse; it is the silent, unspeakable condition of Life. Therefore, Agamben's philosophy of silence is more cautious and realistic, despite its emphasis on impotentiality, than Braidotti's hyperactive, ambitious, and clamorous ethics.

As Colebrook and Maxwell render,

> Agamben asks whether we might not form an ethics based on a life of fragile potentiality-impotentiality that not only does not necessarily attain the dignity of speech and reason, but also always harbours silent and unformed life as the ongoing internal otherness against which it defines itself as regulated. He articulates a counter-ontology that begins with LIFE—which is not a being but a threshold of indistinction, a potentiality for taking on form a becoming. A life that is not based on sovereignty. (78)

Agamben's ethics seeks the radical potential neither in processual, nor in circular time, but in the moment, or *Kairos* as the threshold time to overcome the aporia of *Chronos* and *Aion*. *Kairos*, in Agamben's thought, stands for the moment of rupture within history that carries an emancipatory possibility. Agamben's ethics understandably necessitates that one acknowledges that the human might not actualise its potential. Since human progress is far from guaranteed, it remains ethically imperative to bring about this progress continually in every moment (Maxwell 64).

In *Means Without End: Notes on Politics* (2000), Agamben diagnoses what captures man in biopolitics, and reduces him to bare life as the disjuncture of man as living animal who has logos (language). For him, the aporia of bios and zoe, reason and rhizome is a threshold. Only if this aporia is overcome, a new politics without sovereignty, without reference to nation, law and democracy can lead us to a happy life, in which bare life is never separable as a political subject, and in which what is at stake is the experience and communicability itself (114–117). He calls this life "a sufficient life"—a [mere or saved] life over which sovereignty and right no longer have any hold (114). Contrary to its impractical, transcendental, inoperative, and esoteric aspects, Agamben's standpoint could still be pardoned, at least for not warranting actuality. As Sergei Prozorov points out, Agamben's understanding of inoperativity "does not affirm inertia, inactivity or apraxia, let alone dysfunctionality or destruction, but rather a form of praxis that is devoid of any telos or task, does not realise any essence and does not correspond to any nature" (33). Rather, for Agamben, it manifests the originary feature of the human condition: "Because human beings neither are nor have to be any essence, any nature, or any specific destiny, their condition is the most empty and the most insubstantial of all" (*Means Without End*, 95).

What Agamben calls for, as Povinelli maintains, is "the development of a coherent ontology of potentiality (*dynamis*) that would upend the primacy of actuality (*energeia*). For him, potentiality has a dual nature: while the actual can only be, potentiality can be or not be. And it is exactly in this ontological duality of the potential that new possibilities of life are sheltered" (106). The concept of threshold, for Agamben, is a site of indistinction in an ethics that is without a proper, predetermined, law-imposed end. In other words, the potentiality as impotentiality is the very threshold he explores. Braidotti, by contrast, perceives the threshold as a limit to be passed, and invites humanity to take a leap from the old codes to new ones, but she does not offer a logical illustration of the aftermath of this leap. In Braidotti's theory, the subject's plenitude initiates action, and the threshold is experienced when the "subject feels full in a limit and utters 'This is too much!'" (*Nomadic Theory* 311). At this point, Herman Melville's Bartleby, the scrivener comes to the scene as the emblem of Agamben's ethics. For Agamben,

> [Potentiality] does not remain actualized of a lack of will. One could say of Bartleby that he succeeds in being able (and not being able) absolutely without wanting it. Hence the irreducibility of his 'I would prefer not to'. It is not that he does not want to copy or that he does not want to leave the office; he simply would prefer not to. The formula that he so obstinately repeats destroys all possibility of constructing a relation between being able and willing, between *potentia absoluta* and *potentia ordinata*. This is the formula of potentiality. (*Potentialities* 255, emphasis original)

Similarly Deleuze reads Bartleby as:

> A Formula which is neither an affirmation nor a negation. Bartleby does not refuse, but neither does he accept, he advances and then withdraws into this advance, barely exposing himself in a nimble retreat from speech . . . and hollows out a zone of indetermination that renders words indistinguishable, that creates a vacuum within language [langage]. ("Bartleby; or, the Formula" 70, 73)

Agamben sees in Bartleby a challenge to the supremacy of the will over potentiality through manifesting his power by not entering into relation, and by remaining inoperative. "Bartleby does not refuse something in favour of something else but rather affirms a simple absence of preference as such" (Prozorov 49–50). Braidotti's ethics is ready to enter into relation, it refuses humanist laws/ontology in favor of posthumanist operativity/command and reads "threshold" as a space of transposition, a moment of plenitude, an edge from which the posthuman is supposed to leap saying: "I can't take it anymore!"

To conclude, if we imagine Agamben and Braidotti standing together on a threshold, we can read Braidotti's ethics as an invitation to this leap, an invitation which Agamben, with a gesture to Bartleby, politely declines by saying "I would prefer not to."

REFERENCE LIST

Agamben, Giorgio. *The Coming Community*. Translated by Michael Hardt. University of Minnesota Press, 1993.

———. *Homo Sacer: The Sovereign Power and Bare Life*. Translated by Daniel Heller-Roazen. Stanford U.P., 1998.

———. *Potentialities*. Translated by Daniel Heller-Roazen. Stanford U.P., 1999.

———. *Means Without End: Notes on Politics*. Translated by Vincenzo Binetti and Cesare Cesarino. University of Minnesota Press, 2000.

———. *What Is an Apparatus? And Other Essays*. Stanford University Press, 2009.

———. *Opus Dei.* Translated by Adam Kotsko. Stanford University Press, 2013.

———. "From the State of Control to a Praxis of Destituent Power." *Resisting Biopolitics: Philosophical, Political and Performative Strategies.* Edited by S.E. Wilmer and Audrone Zukauskaite. Routledge, 2016.

Braidotti, Rosi. *Transpositions: On Nomadic Ethics.* Polity, 2006.

———. *Nomadic Theory: Portable Rosi Braidotti.* Columbia U.P., 2011.

———. *The Posthuman.* Polity, 2013.

———. "Posthuman Affirmative Politics." *Resisting Biopolitics: Philosophical, Political and Performative Strategies.* Edited by S.E. Wilmer and Audrone Zukauskaite. Routledge, 2016.

———. "A Theoretical Framework for Critical Posthumanities." *The Culture and Society.* Special Issue, 2018, pp:1–31.DOI: 10.1177/0263276418771486

———. "The Ethics of Joy." *The Posthuman Glossary.* Edited by Rosi Braidotti and Maria Hlavajova. Bloomsbury, 2018.

Butler, Judith. "Reflections on Ethics, Destructiveness and Life: Rosi Braidotti and the Posthuman." *The Subject of Rosi Braidotti: Politics and Concepts.* Edited by Bolette Blaagaard and Iris van der Tuin. Bloomsbury, 2014.

Colebrook, Claire and James Maxwell. *Agamben.* Polity Press, 2016.

Deleuze, Gilles and Felix Guattari. *What Is Philosophy?* Translated by by Hugh Tomlinson and Graham Burchell. Columbia U.P., 1994.

Deleuze, Gilles. "Bartleby; or, the Formula." *Essays Critical and Clinical.* Translated by Daniel W. Smith and Michael A. Greco. Verso, 1998.

Frost, Tom. "The Limit of Thought." *Giorgio Agamben: Legal, Political and Philosophical Perspectives.* Edited by Tom Frost. Routledge, 2013.

Maxwell, James. "Ethics." *The Agamben Dictionary.* Edited by Alex Murray and Jessica Whyte. Edinburg U.P., 2011.

May, Todd. *The Political Thought of Jacques Ranciere: Creating Equality.* Edinburgh U.P., 2008.

Norris, Andrew. "Giorgio Agamben and the Politics of the Living Dead." *Diacritics* 30(4):38–58, 2000. https://www.jstor.org/stable/1566307 Accessed on 13.07.2021.

Palladino, Paulo. "The Blessed Life . . ." *Giorgio Agamben: Legal, Political and Philosophical Perspectives.* Edited by Tom Frost. Routledge, 2013.

Povinelli, Elizabeth A. "The Persistence of Hope: Critical Theory and Enduring in Late Liberalism." *Theory After 'Theory'.* Edited by Jane Elliott and Derek Attridge. Routledge, 2011.

Prozorov, Sergei. *Agamben and Politics: A Critical Introduction.* Edinburgh University Press, 2014.

9

The Posthuman Turn

Twenty-First Century Variations of Feminism

Ela İpek Gündüz

Feminist thinking is affected by the posthuman turn in reconsidering the concept of human to challenge the pre-eminence of humankind considered specifically as Western male. Posthumanists aim at getting rid of the binary oppositions that essentially create hierarchies with the exclusion of women, nonwhites, things, animals, technology, etc. Affected further from the linguistic turn that situates information as a distinct entity disjointed from the material forms, the introduction of the technological agent "cyborg," and the human transforming him/herself to "the posthuman" (Hayles 2), theory embraces new modes of thinking. As posthuman theoreticians also did, posthuman feminists benefit from different disciplines like science, philosophy, social studies, etc. This variedness leads them to re-think the subject's position, relations, environment, matter, and bodies. The consequence of the globalised concerns of capitalism and the technological and scientific developments made all the entities in the world—human and nonhuman beings—become potential sources for consumption (Braidotti, *The Posthuman* 7). In as much as the harmful effects of human power are felt through global warming, ecological changes, and technological innovations, the entanglements of human and non-human become essential. As Rosi Braidotti explains in her seminal book *The Posthuman* (2013):

> the binary opposition between the given [nature] and the constructed [culture], is currently being replaced by a non-dualistic understanding of nature-culture interaction . . . the latter is associated to and supported by a monistic philosophy, which rejects dualism, especially the opposition nature–culture and stresses instead the self-organizing (or autopoietic) force of living matter. (3)

This explanation of Braidotti may be considered the core of the varied but connected ideas of posthuman feminists. "[E]mbodied environments and environed embodiments" (Asberg and Braidotti 1) direct the contemporary theoreticians to evaluate human and nonhuman affecting each other. In this part, I will aim to explore the different but at the same time analogous theories of contemporary feminist theoreticians who were mainly inspired by the works of Michel Foucault, Giles Deleuze, Spinoza, Jacques Derrida, Luce Irigaray, and Donna Haraway (to name a few). Noticing how nature is excluded from culture, these feminists concentrate on the relational, enacting, material, multidimensional, agential, and onto-epistemological aspects of the posthuman theory throughout the intellectual historical phases. This mentality gives birth to disastrous ends regarding the life of a contemporary human. Nature is directly affected by human interventions, and the centralized privileged condition of humans may bring the end of the world.

Regarding these changes, the division between nature and culture turns out to be a blurred issue. Nevertheless, concerning the inter-relational new horizons provided by the nature-culture continuum, human-nonhuman entanglement, and focusing on ontological materialities, in the twenty-first century, feminist theoreticians mostly embrace an optimistic and "genealogical" attitude. This positive evaluation includes a "non-unitary subjectivity [that] . . . means a nomadic, dispersed, fragmented vision, which is nonetheless functional, coherent and accountable, mostly because it is embedded and embodied" (Braidotti, *Transpositions* 4). As feminist theoreticians are experienced to how the mainstream ideology imposes the pre-established ideas to minor groups like women in the posthuman era, their preparedness is effectual.

Concerning the perseverance of gender differences, as Luce Irigaray offers, human, in one way or another is allocated as man or woman regardless of the racial, sexual, national, religious, class-based, or ethnic differences. Despite the existence of miscellaneous different sexual identities like transgender, queer, gay, pansexual, bisexual, etc.: ". . . across the whole world, . . . there are only, men and women. . . . Between man and woman, there really is otherness: biological, morphological, relational" (Irigaray, "The Time of Difference" 96; *Conversations* 5). The issue of sexual difference directly affects all subjects. In other words, the difference between the two genders in terms of their sexualities continues to be a provocative topic. If posthumanism is about different and varied entities that decentralize humans, the question is: why/how gender division may be meaningful in this zeitgeist. For Braidotti: "The human norm stands for normality, normalcy, and normativity. It functions by transposing a specific mode of being human into a generalized standard, which acquires transcendent values as the human: from male to masculine and onto human as the universalized format of humanity" (*The Posthuman* 26). Apparently, the woman is out of this criterion of being "normal"; adversely, she is accepted as a freak. By considering this, posthuman feminist thinkers work on alternative ways to change the perception of existing essentialism. Posthuman feminists reconsider the acceptance of the term "difference" and surpass ". . . the difficulty of theorizing the social in relation to the natural" (Fuss 1) by "reconceiving [human] as more animal and embodied, [and] more 'natural'" (Plumwood 123).

The so-called dualistic thinking of Western mentality, which privileges males all the time, is the main factor that sets the stage for developing feminist theories.

Thus, feminist theoreticians warmly welcome alternative theories, like postmodernism, poststructuralism, postcolonialism, or posthumanism, proposing to change this hierarchical structure mentality that excludes women. In feminist theory, "sex" is accepted as biological, and "gender" is related to culture. Within social relations, the woman who is regarded as "raw material" becomes a "product" in culture (Alaimo, *Undomesticated* 5). The social structure that human has devised exploits both nature and women. "Humanism historically developed into a civilizational model, which shaped a certain idea of Europe as coinciding with the powers of self-reflexive reason" (Braidotti, *The Posthuman* 13). With this understanding, the Western man evaluates himself as the autonomous subject and the others as the "negative" and the "different" inferiors, namely "the sexualized, racialized, and naturalized others, who are reduced to the less than the human status of disposable bodies" (Braidotti, *The Posthuman* 16). As the feminist movement is about differences, "[t]he antihumanist feminist generation embraced the concept of difference with the explicit aim of making it function differently" (Braidotti, "Four Theses" 24). The difference is granted a divergent approach, and instead of embracing the notion of "sameness," women began to accept "difference." About the equality demand of feminists, Luce Irigaray asks the question: "Equal to whom?" that is to say, for her, women should avoid "homologation or reduction to a masculine standard of Sameness" (Braidotti, "Four Theses" 24).

Postmodern feminists advocate the idea that it is impossible to find a unified identity for non-Western others. They try to find solutions by claiming the significance of "differences" and "diversity." In addition,

> [p]ostmodernism as an era, paradigm, or disciplinary formation has allowed feminists to theorize the subjectivity of women and to deconstruct it at the same time… because of the deconstruction being epistemologically non-existent, feminist empiricism and the feminist standpoint have fallen into the trap of universalism. (van der Tuin 24)

There exists a paradoxical issue about the position of women in postmodern times. Braidotti asks: "how can we undo a subjectivity we have not even historically been entitled to yet?" (Braidotti, *Metamorphoses* 15). Hence, the problematic point about postmodern feminism is women's unreached subjectivity, which cannot be deconstructed. Despite the inspiration from the deconstructive approaches of antihumanists who primarily focus on the linguistic representations, posthuman theoreticians mainly emphasize the materialistic side of the argument by reminding the insufficiency of the linguistic analysis. Braidotti states in her understanding:

> … monistic philosophy of becomings rests on the idea that matter, including the specific slice of matter that is human embodiment, is intelligent and self-organizing. This means that matter is not dialectically opposed to culture, nor to technological media-

tion, but continuous with them. This produces a different scheme of emancipation and a non-dialectical politics of human liberation. (*The Posthuman* 35)

Human subjectivity is questioned in the contemporary era that heightens the effects of bio-technologic and bio-genetic advances. Instead of positioning European man as the ultimate subject by ignoring the others universally, posthumanist thinkers reach a positive transformation by "becoming minoritarian" and "nomadic" (Braidotti, *The Posthuman* 53). She further states in *Transformations* that,

> Migrants, exiles, refugees, diasporic subjects . . . have first-hand experience of the extent to which the process of disidentification . . . Multilocality is the affirmative translation of this negative sense of loss . . . becoming-nomadic marks the process of positive transformation of the pain of loss into the active production of multiple forms of belonging and complex allegiances. What is lost, in the sense of fixed origins, is gained in an increased desire to belong, in a multiple rhizomic manner. (84)

As Braidotti explains: "matter is self-organised (autopoietic)" and to "monistic philosophy . . . it is also structurally relational" (Braidotti, *The Posthuman* 59). This "vitality"[1] inherently exists in the human body and all the other living matters. The term "zoe" used in Braidotti's argument that stresses "the non-human, vital force of life" (Braidotti, *The Posthuman* 60) signifies a relational approach to reach non-human entities.

In posthumanism, the excluded "others" due to the notions about sexuality, race, ethnicity, wealth, and technological output from an "embodied, embedded" kind of "symbiosis" (Braidotti, *The Posthuman* 67) are re-examined. This notion is also linked to the term "monism" (the unity of mind-soul and man-nature) that is used by Deleuze and Guattari, who rejected dualism and created alternatives—"disidentification," and "deterritorialization" (Deleuze), and "de-familiarisation" (Gilroy) (Braidotti, *The Posthuman* 88–9). Thus, the contemporary comprehension of the masculine/feminine dichotomy is enriched with multiple options for the subject. The insights provided by monism lead the subject to reach an "open-ended, inter-relational, multi-sexed and trans-species" interconnection (Braidotti, *The Posthuman* 89). Braidotti explains Deleuze's perception of the subject who loses his/her centralized position and "the distinction between internal and external space, or inside and outside reason" as the "horror of the void" (Braidotti, *Patterns* 72). In this perception of the subject, "matter" that focuses on life rather than the dual pairings enables the human to re-evaluate the "differences" affirmatively.

> [T]he blurring of the boundaries between humans and machines is socially enacted at all levels: from medicine, to telecommunication, finance and modern warfare, cyber-relations define our social framework . . . the cyborg as an embodied and socially embedded human subject that is structurally inter-connected to technological elements or apparati, is not a unitary subject position. The cyborg is rather a multi-layered, complex and internally differentiated subject. (Braidotti, *Metamorphoses* 17)

Disregarding the gender divisions, when the notion of "difference" is thought to be a starting point for affirmative evaluations of sexuality, the transformation for the subject may begin by re-analyzing the body as an "incorporeal complex assemblage of virtualities" (Braidotti, *The Posthuman* 99).

> The body remains a bundle of contradictions: it is a zoological entity, a genetic databank, while it also remains a bio-social entity, that is to say a slab of codified, personalized memories. As such it is part animal, part machine but the dualistic opposition of the two, which our culture has adopted since the eighteenth century as the dominant model, is inadequate today. . . . The embodied subject is thus a process of intersecting forces (affects) and Spatio-temporal variables (connections). (Braidotti, *Metamorphoses* 21)

Sexuality without genders by having the "generative" and "reproductive" options of the female body comes forefront in feminist posthumanist theory (Braidotti, *The Posthuman* 98). Thus, sexuality becomes a crucial site for posthumanists to scrutinise. Theoretical past of feminist theory, especially Second Wave feminist theories, were "humanist" in their concerns about women's desires to reach equality, justice, and identity in the patriarchal society. There were criticisms directed toward these critics' Western-based evaluations of the notion of humanism. Especially with the developments in postmodernism and poststructuralism that evaluate this centralized "Western human," the Eurocentric insight began to be questioned via antihumanist concerns. The humanist heritage and antihumanist response affected the genealogy of posthuman feminism and the intersection of "anti-humanism" and "anti-anthropocentrism" (Braidotti, "Posthuman"673). Especially Donna Haraway's theories, which embrace the technological developments in the twentieth century, re-evaluated the position of humans with nonhuman entities. She favours the "nature-culture continuum" concept by changing the route with the figure of "cyborg." She interrelates technological and scientific developments with the new subject formation through which she eludes from binary thinking.

In addition to Haraway's contributions to posthuman thinking, Gilles Deleuze and Felix Guattari's "neo-Spinozist philosophy" inspires posthuman feminists to rethink the human body by situating a materialist ontology of the subject in place of "the dialectical idea of negative difference" (Braidotti, "Posthuman" 681). Instead of regarding nonhuman entities as things, new materialist thinkers find vitality in the material sphere. While accepting the significance of discursive issues, material feminists aim to re-examine the body as a matter that substantially affects human life by considering the excluded groups like women, black people, third world people, and so on. This "embedded and embodied, affective and relational structure of subjectivity . . . helps redefine old binary oppositions, such as nature/culture and human/non-human, paving the way for a nonhierarchical and hence more egalitarian relationship to the species" (Braidotti, "Posthuman" 681).With this insight provided by Deleuzian thinking, there emerged interconnected branches of posthuman feminist theory: neo-materialist feminism of Rosi Braidotti, Vicki Kirby, Iris van der Tuin, Stacey Alaimo, and Susan Hekman, including "transversal nomadism" of Braidotti;

"discourses about the non-human" of Elisabeth Grosz and "technological others" of Donna Haraway; Karen Barad's "agential realism" emphasizing new subjectivities, including nonhuman entities with the effect of "onto-epistemological turn," and Richard Grusin's "Anthropocene feminism" (Braidotti, "Posthuman" 682–683).

The era of Anthropocene compels humans to reconsider their deeds. As Claire Colebrook explains: "the achievement of the Anthropocene as our recognition that one day we, too, will be a sedimentary layer in the lithosphere, [like] fossils [that] show us our inseparability from the earth" ("We Have Always" xv). Within the existing line of thought, "human time of generations (politics)" and "times of geological change" is latent, but for Colebrook, in the Anthropocene, "these two timelines, in their dissonance and difference, intersect: geological change is occurring within human and humanly experienced time" (Colebrook, "We Have Always" 6). Accordingly, objects, vitalities, materialisms, human and nonhuman, prominence in the Anthropocene era. Thus, the concern of sexual differences is ceased to be thought of as something crucial. "Anthropocene feminism" focuses on the genealogy of Anthropocene that maintains the claim that the feminine world (natural sources) is constantly demolished by deeds of masculine power (Grusin viii). Re-examining the dominancy of this hu(Man) who destroys the universe, Anthropocene feminism specifically questions how feminists may contribute to these new evaluations of the new era.

In the Anthropocene era, hu(Man) inevitably encounters the outcomes of the development of technology and decadence of nature. Two different inclinations of posthuman perspective to lead the subject interrelated are technology and nature. When we focalize the technological developments in the contemporary era, including biological, technological, biotechnological, and digital developments, the position of women in the posthuman evaluation may be elucidated. As Kim Tofoletti states: "While technology may enframe objects by bringing them into being for human resource, people too, can be enframed by technology as objects to be used and manipulated" (11). Thus, the autonomy of human beings is intimidated both because of technological developments and the limitlessness of nature. Yet, it is understood that disentangling these technological developments is impossible, which is why the posthuman theoreticians essay the positive and negative outcomes of these alterations.

As N. Katherine Hayles expounds in detail, due to the human's unavoidable confrontation with the cybernetic, digital and robotic transformations in daily life, the boundaries between the body and the external entities become blurred. Posthumanists think there is a danger in separating "information and materiality," and there may be some positive consequences for female bodies that did not participate in Enlightenment times.

> . . . technical articles in cybernetics, information theory, autopoiesis, computer simulation, and cognitive science. Slowly this unruly mass of material began taking shape as three interrelated stories. The first centres on how information lost its body, that is, how

it came to be conceptualized as an entity separate from the material forms in which it is thought to be embedded. The second story concerns how the cyborg was created as a technological artifact and cultural icon in the years following World War II. The third, deeply implicated with the first two, is the unfolding story of how a historically specific construction called the human is giving way to a different construction called the posthuman. (Hayles 2)

Despite the questions about the positive and negative outcomes of the techno-human interactions, regarding whether they will enhance the existing position of women or worsen it, this is "a cybernetic organism, a hybrid of machine and organism, a creature of social reality as well as a creature of fiction" (Haraway 65) which will lead the subject to limitless options.

Feminist posthumanist thinkers claim that it is necessary to change existing centralized epistemologies from an onto-epistemological stance. Hayles questions: "What happens if we begin from the premise not that we know reality because we are separate from it (traditional objectivity), but that we can know the world because we are connected with it?" (48). In other words, giving too much importance to linguistic constructions of reality insistently prevents the human from realizing that s/he is consisting a part of the world, and the reality is this. Concepts like "technoscience, global media, biotics, ecologies, animals, finance, land, and other lively matters" (Asberg and Braidotti 13) generate some conceptual approaches: "the inhuman humanities" of Elizabeth Grosz, "the posthuman humanities," and "feminist posthumanities" of Rosi Braidotti and Cecilia Asberg, including "material feminisms" of Stacy Alaimo and Susan Hekman, "neo-materialism" of Rosi Braidotti, "zoontology" of Cary Wolfe, and "new materialism" of Diana Coole and Samantha Frost; and "cartography and new materialism" of Rick Dolphjin and Iris van der Tuin, "material ecocriticism" of Serenella Iovino and Serpil Opperman, "eco-feminism" of Val Plumwood, "queer ecologies" of Catriona Mortimer-Sandilands and Bruce Erickson, "vitalism" of Rosi Braidotti, and "vibrant matter" of Jane Bennett(Asberg and Braidotti 13). Hence, there is no end in the branch of feminist posthumanism that handles the inevitability of confronting nature and accepting other nonhuman beings as subjects. Instead, there is an affirmative and relational outlook including "nature-cultural" and "techno-scientific" issues.

Contemporary posthuman feminism has also expanded genealogical thinking through its renewed concern for nature. It has shifted the methods and evaluations based on human constructions like language to nature and material and has refocused on epistemology and ontology. As Elizabeth Grosz clarifies: "Matter and life become, and become undone. They transform and are transformed" (5). These new ways of "becoming" lead up feminist theory to broaden its methodology. Mainly studying the function of "inhuman," including animals, plants, and machines, contemporary posthuman feminism considers "before, beyond, and after the human" to remind "the limits of the human" (11–12). Nature exists outside representations, but it is also impossible to perceive it without "discursive construction"(Alaimo, *Undomesticated* 12). By referring to Deleuze and Guattari's *A Thousand Plateaus*, Stacey

Alaimo explains rhizomes, assemblages, and strata that blur the boundaries between human and nonhuman entities. She comments that with their different method of "cartography,"[2] they reconceptualise nature so that together with Haraway's "cyborg," feminists establish new ways for alignment (12).

One of the significant deviations of posthuman feminism is to emphasize the significance of ontology for re-evaluation of identity and condition of human and nonhuman. Grosz asks questions about the historical concerns of feminism: would it be more beneficial for feminist theory to reach freedom from dominant spheres of patriarchy, imperialism, colonialism, racism, and heterosexuality or to dig up the possibilities that women may reach by their effort? (61). This does not mean that this political domination is out of concern; instead, she proposes that if the subject can explore him/herself, only then s/he may reach autonomy by "becoming" positively. She further postulates that in the contemporary era, the problematic aspect of feminism is not related to the patriarchal hegemony from which women are demanding rights and freedom. On the contrary, for Grosz,

> If women are not, in some sense, free, feminism could not be possible. The problem, rather, is how to expand the variety of activities, including the activities of knowledge production. . . . The problem is not how to give women more adequate recognition (who is it that women require recognition from?), more rights, or more of a voice, but how to enable more action, more making and doing, more difference . . . to enable women to partake in the creation of a future unlike the present. (Grosz 73)

When the natural declinations are concerned, one of the related deviations of posthuman feminist theory is "material feminism," which is mainly based on "the materiality of the human body and the natural world," as Susan Hekman and Stacy Alaimo elucidate (1). For Hekman and Alaimo, the focus of the postmodern feminists on language entails the emphasised separation of the material reality and textuality. For flourishing the contributions of feminist theory, it is crucial to discuss the discursive reflections of the women, but real bodily experiences of women are equally important. Spontaneously, there emerged an inclination to include these real experiences related to corporeality and nature. "Nature can no longer be imagined as a pliable resource for industrial production or social construction. Nature is agentic—it acts, and those actions have consequences for both the human and non-human world. We need ways of understanding the agency, significance, and ongoing transformative power of the world" (3–4). Theoreticians like Karen Barad and Donna Haraway redirect their root from epistemology to ontology of materialities to find the relations between "material, discursive, human, more-than-human, corporeal, and technological" (5). Regarding the interest of the contemporary feminists to re-examine the relation between discourse and matter by not deporting materiality, material feminism evokes the evaluation of nature as an active agent and human bodies that are the combined corporeality of the discursive material interactions (6–7). Accordingly, the relatedness between nature, culture, environment, discourse, body, and machine is examined via human and nonhuman agents.

Object-Oriented Feminism (OOF) centralizes matter, things, and objects "while twisting it toward more agential, political embodied terrain. Object-oriented feminism turns the position of philosophy inside out to study objects while being an object oneself" (Behar 3). Mainly, OOF analyzes politics, objects, and ethics. New materialist feminism and OOF have some common concerns since both foci on the matter to prevent Anthropocene, the privileged position of humans. The significance of these two feminist theories is the return to the realities rather than linguistic constructions. Moreover, Object-oriented ontology's (OOO) view of "humans as objects" is also adopted by OOF. Still, the latter underlines the problem that women are regarded as objects by dominant subjects, men. By observing the inside and outside simultaneously, OOF contributed to the future concerns of feminism. Ian Boggost acknowledges OOF's contribution of "the value of looking for the outdoors inside," and he states, "Indeed, one of the goals and victories of feminism involves making insides and outsides accessible" (qtd. in Behar 8). The theoreticians mentioned above do not solely concentrate on women's subjectivity accepted as a political and social obligation for feminists. When they change their route from subjectivity to objectivity, these theoreticians begin to have the chance to make connections with other objects. What OOF aims to achieve is to move away from the "politics of recognition of standing *out*" to "a politics of immersion, of *being with*" (Behar 9).

By annihilating the focus on discourse and language (epistemology) to the material (ontology), to maintain an identity in the world, "bodies matter" (68) since all the acts, connections, and relations are related to the reality of the body. The materiality of body inserted into feminist studies highlights the significance of "intra-actions between materiality and the social and discursive. New materialists emphasize how bodies, substances, technologies, and environments not only are acted upon but also act" (Alaimo, *Gender* xv). Accordingly, this emphasis on materialism has common points with posthumanism (Alaimo, *Gender* xv) in centralizing the interrelatedness of the body of the unaccepted others.

The linguistic turn has been immensely fruitful for feminism in terms of learning how the terms "woman" and "reality" are constructed via language (Hekman 88). Then, the notion of "constructedness" of everything comes to the forefront, which is why questions about the "objectivity" of scientific studies as an exceptional field are reconsidered. Barad explains, "Language has been granted too much power. The linguistic turn, the semiotic turn, the interpretive turn, the cultural turn: it seems that at every turn lately every 'thing'—even materiality—is turned into a matter of language" ("Posthumanist" 801). For Barad, the inevitable tendency of the thinkers of twentieth century to view the considerable power of language to represent reality is criticized by contemporary feminists. She proposes a "performative" evaluation of discursive issues, which means a contention to language that ascertains the things, bodies, and reality. Barad proposes the term "onto-epistemology." This term leads her to "agential realism," which combines matter and discourse by "intra-action." Alaimo explains interaction as "separate entities exist before and outside their relationship" and intra-action as "entities come into being through their relationship" (Alaimo, *Gender* 408). In this way, human and nonhuman become equivalent. Barad proposes "agential intra-action" between the body and the phenomena:

> Phenomena are constitutive of reality. Reality is composed not of things-in-themselves or things-behind-phenomena but of things-in-phenomena. The world is a dynamic process of intra-activity and materialization in the enactment of determinate causal structures with determinate boundaries, properties, meanings, and patterns of marks on bodies. (Barad, *Meeting* 140)

In agential realism, "'Humans' are neither pure cause nor pure effect but part of the world in its open-ended becoming" (Barad, "Posthumanist" 821). Similarly, from this agential realist perspective, the matter is not a "thing" but a "becoming" through the intra-active agency (Barad, "Posthumanist" 822). Correspondingly, bodies through intra-activity function as "material-discursive phenomena" without margins and stable entities that culminate in relating their being with non-human bodies (Barad, "Posthumanist" 823). Thus, for Barad, to contribute to the expansion of perceiving the limitless possibilities of life and world, the matter should be re-analyzed rather than being stuck on language, epistemology, and representation. These new evaluations broaden the methods of feminist theoreticians from a posthuman scale. Inspired from Barad's theory of "agential realism," Alaimo coins the term "trans-corporeality," through which the human body is accepted as a place of "intra-action between various flows of material forces" (Alaimo, *Gender* 408).

If the subject has no longer been vital, how may a woman preserve her identity? And will "becoming-woman" be useful for theory since man is regarded as being and woman is becoming, which may propose something new? (Colebrook, *Deleuze* 10–11). Due to the vagueness of this point of "becoming-woman" in Deleuze's work, there is not a clear answer, but J. Aline Flieger asserts that "feminist identity politics" and Deleuze's "becoming-woman" are not identical since the latter "precedes all 'molar' identifications" (Colebrook, *Deleuze* 13). Inspired by Deleuze and Kristeva, Colebrook further asserts that the woman should not be regarded solely as the other of man. Still, feminism means "a new way of thinking movements or becoming: no longer a movement 'owned' by identities, but a movement of desires, bodies, flows, and style" (Colebrook, *Deleuze* 14). This becoming is beyond woman; it is a kind of infinite option.

Iris van der Tuin notes that feminism maintains diverse views and methods, and in the twenty-first century, the new generation also has varied views. The concept called "generational feminism" indicates both the generational groups of feminism like "the old, the youngish, the young; first-, second-, third-wave feminism) as well as the very active notion of 'to generate'" (van der Tuin xvii). To reach different options, as mentioned, theoreticians favor dismantling dualisms that maintain the suppression of women, races, classes, and sexualities. "Feminism is the struggle against sexism, homophobia, transphobia, and other intersecting forms of structural power imbalances based on naturalizations of inequality. It aims to dissolve difference, not feminism" (xiii). Yet, the problem is feminist theoreticians also used dualisms to support their arguments. Rather than this restricted perception of opposites, van der Tuin proposes the "generational perspective" that includes "processual becoming" and "sedimentation" (van der Tuin xviii). From this mind-set, it is understood that young and old generations of feminists are like "mothers and daughters," and "the generative force" is experienced by all feminists. In this way, feminism is all the time changing and becoming (van der Tuin xx).

Ultimately, there must be a reconstruction of philosophical thought by "nomadic thinking." The latter may switch the places of "margin" and "center" by requalifying the meaning of power so that "rhizomatic" openings will also change identity constructions. "The point is not just mere deconstruction, but the relocation of identities on new grounds" (Braidotti, *Transpositions* 69). Feminist theory is conventional and complex, but innovative methods are needed. As seen, "becoming" becomes an essential notion in posthuman thought that includes changes, transformations, and processes of human and nonhuman entities. As the essentialist notions of Western man are criticized, feminist theory, after experiencing "deconstruction," needs to reach "reconstruction" of "nomadic women-in-being" by the transformation of the ascendant Woman" (Braidotti, *Transpositions* 71).

Despite the problem that we got used to thinking from the dualist way that centralizes Western Man and disdains the others, there is a necessity to adapt ourselves to these nomadic, minoritarian, transformed selves through "becoming," which give required value to bodies, things, nonhuman entities, and machines in a rhizomatic manner. As Braidotti also clarifies, feminist theory is significant in this changing thinking process due to its ongoing questioning of the dominant systems and theories. The linguistic and material restrictions and dominations should be surpassed to reach an affirmative perspective and a process of fluidity (Braidotti, *Transpositions* 85-6). Posthuman feminism was inspired by posthumanism, primarily studied by feminist philosophers who coined the term posthuman feminism, subsidiary branches—material feminism, object-oriented feminism, Anthropocene feminism, Deleuzian feminism, generational feminism—nourish and broaden the vision of the posthuman feminist theory; thus, they enable it to redevise the future in a new fashion.

NOTES

1. "This vitalist approach to living matter displaces the boundary between the portion of life—both organic and discursive—that has traditionally been reserved for Anthropos, that is to say bios, and the wider scope of animal and non-human life, also known as zoe. Zoe as the dynamic, self-organizing structure of life itself stands for generative vitality. It is the transversal force that cuts across and reconnects previously segregated species, categories and domains" (Braidotti, *The Posthuman* 60).

2. "The methodology of 'cartography' is transversal in nature for it extends across the well-known classifications of feminism: liberal, Marxist/socialist, radical, black, and lesbian feminisms; postcolonial, queer, and transfeminisms; thinking equality, difference, and deconstruction; and feminist empiricism, the feminist standpoint, and feminist postmodernism" (van der Tuin 5).

REFERENCE LIST

Agamben, Giorgio. *Potentialities: Collected Essays in Philosophy.* Ed. and trans. Daniel Heller-Roazen. Stanford University Press, 1999.
Alaimo, Stacey and Susan Hekman. *Material Feminisms.* Indiana University Press, 2008.
Alaimo, Stacey,editor. *Undomesticated Ground: Recasting Nature as Feminist Space.* Cornell University Press, 2000.
———, editor. *Gender: Matter.* Macmillan Reference USA, 2017.
Asberg,Cecilia and Rosi Braidotti, editors. *A Feminist Companionto the Posthuman Studies.* Springer, 2018.
Barad, Karen. *Meeting the Universe Halfway. Quantum Physics and the Entanglement of Matter and Meaning.* Duke University Press, 2007.
———. "Posthumanist Performativity: Toward an Understanding of How Matter Comes to Matter." *Signs: Journal of Women in Culture and Society,* vol. 28, no. 3, 2003, pp. 801–830.
Behar, Katherine. *Object-Oriented Feminism.* University of Minnesota Press, 2016.
Braidotti, Rosi. *The Posthuman.* Polity Press, 2013.
———. "Posthuman Feminist Theory." *The Oxford Handbook of Feminist Theory.* Eds. Lisa Disch and Mary Hawkesworth. Oxford University Press, 2016.
———. *Patterns of Dissonance: A Study of Women in Contemporary Philosophy.* Trans. Elizabeth Guild. Polity Press, 1991.
———. *Transpositions: On Nomadic Ethics.* Polity Press, 2006.
———. *Metamorphoses: Towards A Materialist Theory of Becoming.* Polity Press, 2002.
Buchanan, Ian and Claire Colebrook, editors. *Deleuze and Feminist Theory.* Edinburgh University Press, 2000.
Colebrook, Claire. "We Have Always Been Post-Anthropocene: The Anthropocene Counterfactual." *Anthropocene Feminism,* edited by Richard Grusin, University of Minnesota Press, 2016.
Fuss, Diana. *Essentially Speaking: Feminism, Nature, and Difference.* Routledge, 1989, 1. 34.
Gilroy, Paul. *Postcolonial Melancholia.* New York: Columbia University Press, 2005.
Grosz, Elizabeth. *Becoming Undone: Darwinian Reflections on Life, Politics, and Art.* Duke University, 2011.
Grusin, Richard, editor. *Anthropocene Feminism.* University of Minnesota Press, 2016.
Harraway, Donna. "A Manifesto for Cyborgs: Science, Technology, and Socialist-Feminism in the 1980s." *Australian Feminist Studies,* vol. 2, no. 4, 1987, pp. 1–42.
Hayles, N. Katherine. *How We Became Posthuman: Virtual Bodies in Cybernetics, Literature, and Informatics.* University of Chicago Press, 1999.
———. "Searching for Common Ground." *Reinventing Nature? Responses to Postmodern Deconstruction",* edited by Soulé Michel and Gary Lease, Island Press, 1995.
———. 1997. "*The Posthuman Body: Inscription and Incorporation in Galatea* 2.2 and Snow Crash." *Johns Hopkins University Press,* vol. 5, no. 2, Spring 1997, pp. 241–266.

Irigaray, Luce. *Conversations*. London: Continuum, 2008.
——. "The Time of Difference." *Why Different? A Culture of Two Subjects*, translated by Camille Collins, 2000, pp. 95–102.
Plumwood, Val. *Feminism and the Mastery of Nature*. Routledge, 1993.
Toffoletti, Kim.*Cyborgs and Barbie Dolls: Feminism, Popular Culture, and the Posthuman Body.* I.B.Tauris& Co Ltd., 2007.
van der Tuin, Iris.*Generational Feminism: New Materialist Introduction to a Generative Approach*. Lexington Books, 2015.

10

Reinterpreting the Anthropocene

Toward an Ecocentric Worldview

Cenk Tan

INTRODUCTION

The Anthropocene is one of the most influential concepts put forward by the environmental sciences and humanities in the late twentieth and early twenty-first centuries. Though coined by an atmospheric chemist, the Anthropocene has profoundly impacted all areas of the humanities. Since the early 2000s, the Anthropocene has been discussed, questioned, and elaborated on from various perspectives. Today, it remains a widely discussed and interpreted concept by scholars throughout the globe. From a theoretical perspective, the Anthropocene is one of the most prominent notions in the social sciences and humanities of the last twenty years. Because of its interdisciplinary context, the concept has come into the forefront in many areas including ecocriticism and environmental studies. Therefore, post-theory would be unthinkable and unaccomplished without the Anthropocene. What makes the Anthropocene relevant and worthwhile for scholarly research is that it is an up-to-date and ever-changing theory that will continue to be a prevalent concept in the upcoming years. As a factual notion that shaped post-theory in literary and cultural terms, the Anthropocene is indispensable in all areas of study.

    This chapter aims to explore the Anthropocene from its establishment until today including its most remarkable variations and reinterpretations. To this end, the research will analyze the pivotal concept of the Anthropocene, followed by the more recent and effective formulations of the Capitalocene, Plantationocene, and Chthulucene. Despite bearing a criticism against the Anthropocene, each new formulation builds on the concept's foundation and delivers noteworthy contributions to the original notion and the broad field of environmental humanities. The chapter concludes with the extrapolation that, as a result of the grave indications of climate change, the future will be an epoch characterized by significant efforts of restoration and endeavor to establish an ecocentric worldview that will ensure the preservation and sustainability of the natural environment.

REINTERPRETING THE ANTHROPOCENE

The Anthropocene is largely popularized by the Nobel-prize winning chemist Paul J. Crutzen in 2000 (Ellis 26). However, some twenty years before Crutzen, the term had already been used by ecologist Eugene F. Stoermer (27). In 2000, the Anthropocene made its first official appearance in a scientific newsletter that associated the term with carbon dioxide emission from fossil fuels and traced the beginning of this era back to the Industrial Revolution, toward the end of the eighteenth century (Ellis 27). The Anthropocene proposed: "(i) That the Earth is now moving out of its current geological epoch, called the Holocene and (ii) that human activity is largely responsible for this exit from the Holocene, that is, that humankind has become a global geological force in its own right" (Steffen et al., "Conceptual Perspectives" 843).

Crutzen and Stoermer's endeavors have maintained the widespread acceptance of humanity's impact as an altering force on Earth's historical timeline. Thus, the emergence of the Anthropocene enabled the recognition of anthropogenic climate change. Though the human impact was visible during the Holocene, scientists affirm that before the Industrial Revolution: "Human activity did not create new, global environmental conditions that could translate into a fundamentally different stratigraphic signal" (Angus 50). However, since the Industrial Revolution, the consumption of coal, gas, and oil have resulted in substantial changes that left their mark in strata around the globe (50). Through the formulation of the Anthropocene, Crutzen laid the foundations of a discussion rather than concluding and this discussion was to remain disputed in the years to follow (52).

In a proceeding published in the *Journal de Physique IV* in 2002, Crutzen contended that over half a century, the human species consumed all fossil fuels brought about for over hundred million years, which led to a dramatic increase of air pollutants (Crutzen 2). The release of these harmful gases in a relatively short span of time resulted in major distortions within the ecosystem and caused the death of living species such as fish and other wild animals (2). In the tropical rainforest areas, extinction of species has risen by thousand to ten thousand due to human activities (3). Therefore, Crutzen declares: "There is new and stronger evidence that most of the warming observed over the last 50 years is attributable to human activities" (3). Consequently, the scientist argues that the future of the Anthropocene, specifically, global climate change, will be determined by the release of harmful chemical gases (4). Crutzen concludes his article by reminding the public that humanity will continue to be a hegemonic geological power. Due to this factor, he issues a call to establish global and sustainable environmental governance (4).

In addition, it has been manifested that the Anthropocene consists of three main stages. The first stage was traced back to the early phases of the Industrial Revolution until the end of the Second World War in 1945 (Steffen et al., "Are Humans Now Overwhelming the Great Forces of Nature" 616). On the other hand, in stark contrast to this, William Ruddiman put forward concrete evidence "for atmospheric greenhouse gas increases in response to the early impacts of Old-World farming from Neolithic times onwards" (Ruddiman 4.2). Despite this, Ruddiman openly acknowledges the boost of environmental pollution after industrialization (Oldfield et al. 6). The second stage of the Anthropocene is stated to have taken place between 1945 and 2015, which is often entitled "The Great Acceleration" (Steffen et al. 617). Finally, the third stage spans the period from 2015 until today (Oldfield et al. 6). Scientists warn that new stages of the Anthropocene are bound to occur in the future (6). As a result, the role of industrialization in the aggravation of the Anthropocene is undeniable. The use of coal and the invention of the steam engine in the 1780s are two major factors which accelerated the process of the Anthropocene with a population increase of six-fold, energy consumption about forty fold, and the world economy about fifty-fold between 1800 and 2000 (Steffen et al. 616). The third stage of the Anthropocene came to exist with the act of decision-making on various levels (618-619). Steffen, Crutzen and McNeill state that:

> The growing awareness of human influence on the Earth System has been aided by i) rapid advances in research and understanding, the most innovative of which is interdisciplinary work on human-environment systems, ii) the enormous power of the internet as a global, self-organizing information system, iii) the spread of more free and open societies, supporting independent media, and iv) the growth of democratic political systems, narrowing the scope for the exercise of arbitrary state power and strengthening the role of civil society. (Steffen et al. 619)

Thus, humanity is taking action to slow down and reverse the effects of the Anthropocene. Humans are more than ever conscious of environmental issues, global warming in particular. On the other hand, the evolution of the Anthropocene continues. Earth has reached a critical phase during the great acceleration as a result of which humanity will face crucial challenges in the decades to come (Steffen et al. 620). About 60 percent of the ecosystem's constituents are degenerated and will continue to degenerate unless vital measures are taken, and concrete administrative and societal change is brought about (620). In short, the Anthropocene is widely acknowledged throughout the globe and provided scientists with the fundamental basis of a discussion that would last for decades.

Many scholars took up the Anthropocene as a departure point and put forward an ongoing debate concerning the relationship between humanity and Earth. One such scholar, Jason W. Moore, posits that history is shaped by: "Humanity (society) and Nature or even Capitalism plus Nature" (Altvater et al. 2). Moore goes on to purport that the Anthropocene exposes the Nature/Society dualism at its utmost degree but points out that, despite making a huge impact, the Anthropocene as a concept is insufficient mainly because the "how" and "why" are left unanswered (3). Therefore, Moore proposes the term Capitalocene, which "Signifies capitalism as a way of organizing nature—as a multispecies, situated, capitalist world-ecology" (Altvater et al. 6). From this specific perspective, capitalism and the "Age of Capital" play a major role in shaping Earth's natural areas. According to the environmental historian, the Capitalocene mentions three aspects that the Anthropocene does not: firstly, it insists that capitalism is interconnected with capital, power, and nature holistically. Secondly, capitalism cannot be simplified to the emission of fossil fuels in England or other locations. It is a complex history of power relations and production which brought forward: "Successive waves of global conquest and the worldwide appropriations of Cheap Nature." Thirdly, the Capitalocene challenges the Eurocentric view that capitalism emerged in England during the eighteenth century (Altvater et al. 81). In other words, Moore breaks down the concept of the Anthropocene by arguing against the commonly accepted assumption that the Anthropocene began in England and that its major causes were coal and steam with the entire humanity as the belligerent (81). Moore criticizes the Anthropocene because it represents an oversimplification that ignores a group of complex factors such as: "Inequality, commodification, imperialism, patriarchy and the problem of humanity-in-nature" (Altvater et al. 82). On the other hand, these factors are visible in the Anthropocene argument rather than in the complementary context (82).

In addition, Moore avers that the Capitalocene responds to the questions left unanswered by the proposition of the Anthropocene which falls short of resolving how this epoch came into being (83). The definition of capitalism needs to be reinterpreted as it is not and should not be reduced to economics but stands for: "A new way of organizing nature, and therefore a new way of organizing the relations between work, reproduction, and the conditions of life" (Altvater et al. 85). Thus, the capitalist system generated a law of "Cheap Nature," which was cheap in a particular meaning, arranging the potential of empire, science, and capital to seize the unpaid energy and work of nature within the impact of the capitalist stronghold (89). Therefore, it is emphasized that: "The appropriation of women, nature, and colonies is the fundamental condition of the exploitation of labor-power in the commodity system" (Mies 77).

Furthermore, Moore adds that cheap nature possesses a central place within capitalism. The scholar relates several concrete examples concerning cheap natures such as cheap land and labor, cheap fossil fuels, oil, steel, and coal (Altvater et al. 92). These enabled the capitalist system to found its premises on the basis of cheap nature's constituents. Moore defines the concept of cheap nature as "Work/energy and biophysical utility produced with minimal labour power, and directly implicated in commodity production and exchange" (99). In addition, the proletariat is an essential requirement that supplies "Cheap Labour" to capitalism as a system of cheap nature (Moore, "The Capitalocene Part I" 19). In turn, this led to the necessity of cheap energy, cheap food, and raw materials (22). The subjugation of the new world was a major event in the acquisition and domination of cheap nature and provided the workforce to convert it into capital (22). Hence, cheap nature forms a major aspect in capitalism and its perpetual objective of accumulating wealth. All in all, Moore insists that the Anthropocene should be referred to as the Capitalocene or "the Age of Capital" (*Capitalism in the Web of Life* 86). The author argues that capitalism is neither an economic, nor a social system, but rather: "A way of organizing nature" (*Capitalism in the Web of Life* 16). The Anthropocene, on the other hand, is an environmental notion that rejects the hostility of the multispecies and capitalist inequality by claiming that all humans are accountable for the destruction generated by capitalism (Moore, "The Capitalocene Part I" 3).

Thus, the Capitalocene "[i]s a key conceptual and methodological move in rethinking capitalism as 'a historically situated complex of metabolisms and assemblages'" (Moore, "The Capitalocene Part II" 240–241). In this respect, the Capitalocene proved to be a major breakthrough as it indicates a detailed counter-account of the Anthropocene and meticulously fills in the blanks left behind by Crutzen and Stoermer in the early 2000s. From this perspective, the formulation of the Capitalocene not only stipulated a profound argument with accurate references to the social sciences/humanities but also supplied a ground for further discussion and development of the issue. Jason W. Moore concludes by drawing attention to the finite essence of nature against the infinite character of capitalism and declares that "[t]here are limits to how much new work capitalism can squeeze out of new working classes, forests, aquifers, oilfields, coal seams and everything else" ("Nature in the limits to Capital" 19). Therefore, to perceive and reflect upon nature with a capitalist mentality will have destructive outcomes.

New variations soon emerged from the foundation set forth by the Anthropocene and further elaborated by the Capitalocene. One of the most prominent variations is the Plantationocene. Coined by pioneer feminist Donna Haraway, the Plantationocene is referred to as the immense metamorphosis of various human-controlled grazed lands, farms, and forests into surrounded plantations that depend on slave labor and other forms of oppressed, discriminated, and generally transported labor ("Making Kin" 162). Scientists have acknowledged that the plantation system was an exemplary driving force for the mechanically constructed factory system, which is considered the basic ground of the Anthropocene (162). The scholar declares that: "The Plantationocene continues with ever-greater ferocity in globalized factory meat production, monocrop agribusiness, and immense substitutions of crops like oil palm for multispecies forests and their products that sustain human and non-human critters alike" (162). Thus, the Plantationocene, which was initiated with slave labor, witnessed a transformation through agribusiness and other capitalist practices that continue to exert a dominant influence on natural areas.

Moreover, the Plantationocene draws public attention to the socioecological outcome of plantation farming and the modification of the plantation throughout history (Davis et al. 2–3). The term emphasizes the: "Historical relocations of the substances of living and dying around the Earth as a necessary prerequisite to their extraction" (Haraway et al., "Anthropologists Are Talking" 557). To that end, Haraway's Plantationocene focuses on: "Networked relations forged across species lines," disintegrating the description of human manifestation and nature/society segregation (Davis et al. 4). Hence, Haraway's major objective is "to make kin," which signifies much more than living beings connected to one other through bloodline and pedigree (5). Haraway further disputes that the plantation system forms a role model for mechanized factories, which are often held responsible for the instigation of the Anthropocene (Haraway, "Making Kin" 162). The scholar specifically concentrates on the concept of "slave gardens," which she ascribes peculiar meaning to as: "Refuges for biodiverse plants, animals, fungi, and soils" (162). She asserts that the swift dislocation of: "Germ plasm, genomes, cuttings, and all other names and forms of part organisms and of deracinated plants, animals, and people" is one determining activity of the Plantationocene, Capitalocene, and Anthropocene altogether (162). On the other hand, Haraway's Plantationocene also received criticism due to the fact that it lacked an analysis concerning human involvement and preferred to prioritize the acknowledgment of biodiversity despite the severe experiences of slave narratives (Davis et al. 5). Therefore, the lack of consideration of socioecological factors concerning the Plantationocene is an apparent shortcoming (Davis et al. 5). As pointed out by Davis et al., many scholars are not content with the formulation of the Plantationocene, which: "Minimize the ways in which racial politics structure plantation life (both human and non-human)" (10). Thus, the understanding imposes limitations on the comprehensive acknowledgment of the plantation's socioecological and multiracial impact (10).

Nonetheless, another perspective discusses that the Plantationocene renders the existence of plantation economies in the sixteenth century as a turning point in human history mainly because plantations constitute a basic model for the "Carbon-consuming and emitting industrial food production system and anticipate the agribusiness monocultures, factory meat production, and simplified ecologies implicated in biodiversity loss and species extinctions" (Carney 2). Due to this reason, plantations exemplify a symbol of change in the history of nature and humanity (3). Additionally, they were described as: "The engine of wealth generation that propelled European capitalist and imperialist expansion" (Tsing 148). Thus, plantations provided European colonizers with the necessary means to establish hegemony over the world.

Anna Tsing professes those plantations were based on compulsion and lacked a crucial factor in their relationships: "Love" (148). Therefore, instead of emotional attachment, Europeans utilized compulsion and enforcement to cultivate (148). As a consequence, many people were displaced together with their crops and products, sugar canes and the people growing them were sent from West Africa to the Americas, and the unskilled Indian/Asian workforce was relocated to the Pacific (Tsing 149). Thus, the white European colonizers possessed and worked the land while at the same time oppressing and imposing forced labor on people of colour (149). All in all, the Plantationocene tackles issues related to historical and socioecological matters of the capitalist plantation system, which rise to the surface in various notions concerning exploitation of land and labor, racism, and extinction of species (Carney 20). Thus, the Plantationocene exposes subordinate economies and ecologies that originated within the sphere of plantations and also revealed: "Bio-cultural refugia that precariously exist within and against the plantation world of the present" (21). For these reasons, the Plantationocene provided invaluable contributions to the framework set forth by the Anthropocene and further carried on by the Capitalocene.

After the coining of the Plantationocene, Haraway put forward the notion of the Chthulucene in 2015 derived from the Greek words "Khthon," meaning all beings of the Earth and "Kainos," a new beginning, a time of freshness (*Staying with the Trouble* 2). The scholar indicates that all living beings, including the tiniest bacteria and all fauna and flora, ought to be considered "kin" to one another. Haraway defines the Chthulucene as: "The dynamic ongoing symchthonic forces and powers of which people are a part, within which ongoingness is at stake" (*Staying with the Trouble* 101). Through the coining of the Chthulucene, the pioneer feminist signals the foundation of a truly holistic notion with its own philosophy and unique emphasis on the non-human or other than the human sphere. The critic highlights that she is a: "Compost-ist, not a posthuman-ist: we are all compost, not posthuman" (*Staying with the Trouble* 101–102). With a holistic understanding, Haraway envisages that all living beings are part of the same ecosystem and that all living entities eventually end up in a state of compost. Thus, she questions why the Anthropocene is the name suggested for this epoch and why the naming of the age is prioritized by the same being, humanity itself (Grear 77). From this context, Haraway concentrates on her statement: "We are all lichens, we have never been individuals" (*Staying with the Trouble* 30). Through the construction of this argument, Haraway prioritizes the biological realities that interconnect all living beings and leaves out all social, evolutionary, economic, philosophical, and so on perspectives she deems to be anthropocentric (Grear 90). According to Anna Grear, Haraway defends a symbiotic perspective of life which maintains that humans have never been individuals (90). In this context, it is asserted that: "Animals are symbiotic complexes of many species living together" (Gilbert et al. 326–327).

Rather than the name of an epoch, the Chthulucene is the reinterpretation of biological reality. According to the symbiotic point of view, "the 'all' of the 'we' is profoundly interspecies—(or intra-species if we count 'earthlings' in an all-embracing way)—a lively entanglement of beings and systems that are never individual in the traditional Western sense" (Grear 91). In this respect, the interrelated symbiotic view is directly related to New Materialism as a comprehensive and contemporary school of thought (92). New Materialists possess and defend similar views brought forward through the notion of the Chthulucene. Anna Grear stresses that human acknowledgment of material issues will eventually lead to a better comprehension of the natural environment (92). As a result, the Chthulucene is a notion that tackles anthropocentric thought in general and the Anthropocene and Capitalocene altogether. The Chthulucene breaks down the assumption that humans claim right and superiority over nature (Grear 93). Grear concludes her argument by expressing that: "The newly de-centred environmental subject would no longer stand at the 'centre' of a world rendered oppressively fungible and commodified. Then, perhaps, environmental law might, by responding to the energies of the Chthulucene, become an important mode of coordinating 'something—just maybe—more liveable'" (95). In a review of Haraway's article, it is maintained that: "The strength of this book is Haraway's ability to shift our thinking and catalyze a resurgence of living well. Her use of neologisms, symbols, stories, and art illustrate the imagination that is required for ongoingness" (Wolfstone 391). Thus, Haraway's Chthulucene exposits an all-encompassing understanding that aims to consolidate the mutual relationships between humans and all other nonhuman life forms.

CONCLUSION

The Anthropocene has come a long way since the early 2000s. Crutzen and Stoermer's original concept was received with enthusiasm and proved a watershed in the humanities. On the other hand, many scholars challenged this concept to reformulate new notions so as to fill in the gaps that the Anthropocene left behind. To this end, the most influential reformulation was delivered by Jason W. Moore, who brought forward the notion of the Capitalocene. Through this conception, Moore disputed arguments of the Anthropocene and purported that the negative human impact on Earth was the obvious result of capitalist human activities, hence renaming it as the Capitalocene. In addition to Moore's effective term, Donna Haraway proposed two particular notions that exercised serious influence on the framework laid by Crutzen and Stoermer. The Plantationocene and Chthulucene were innovative from particular aspects. The Plantationocene affirmed its connection with the historical past of western civilization whereas the Chthulucene emphasized the interconnected relationship between humans and non-humans. There is no doubt that more innovative formulations will follow these preliminary notions in the future.

Though its cause remains unknown, the COVID-19 pandemic is a catastrophic event that resulted in dramatic changes. With over four million deceased worldwide, the coronavirus and its variants have proven to be a major menace for all of humanity. The pandemic's relation to climate change is an intriguing topic as there are speculations that the virus might have come into existence due to disastrous climate change. While this has not been scientifically proven yet, there seems to be a positive aspect of the pandemic as well. In 2020, during the early stages of the pandemic, many countries had applied mandatory quarantines during which millions of people had to stay home and isolate themselves from society. Research has demonstrated that this had a positive impact on the environment. From February to March 2020, there was a steep decline in carbon emission worldwide and a major decrease (about

50 percent) was observed in the emission of harmful gases (CO) in various locations such as New York and Northern Italy (Melidis 252). Other effects were the serious reduction of fuel and coal consumption throughout the world, which occurred as a result of the halt in industrial and commercial activities (252). China's coal consumption dropped by 36 percent, and the EU's power demand declined by 9 percent in 2020 (253). As a natural result of these dropping numbers, a notable increase in air quality has been observed in many cities throughout the world (Melidis 253). Along with the halt of the aviation industry, air traffic dropped by 90 percent in the UK compared to 2019 (Melidis 253). Similarly, water pollution also dropped significantly in many areas due to the cessation of tourism and water transport in various canals (254). Moreover, the Ganges River showed signs of amelioration since the lockdown in India as industrial waste dumped into the river decreased significantly. Finally, the forced lockdowns also led to the return of wildlife to inhabited urban areas such as parks, towns, and other locations (Melidis 254–255). All in all, despite having fatal effects on humans, the COVID-19 pandemic has proved nature's possibility to restore itself through minimal human intervention and within a short period of time (255). To that end, theories concerning the Anthropocene and Capitalocene have proven to be accurate and viable once again.

Besides of the pandemic, world countries have developed awareness against the global climate change problem. Facing the risk of droughts in many parts of the world, governments are taking drastic measures to halt and reverse global climate change. Germany had earlier announced the end of nuclear energy, and many European countries followed in its footsteps. Additionally, in 2019 Germany has banned diesel cars with a high degree of emission (Töller 3). Various European countries are taking steps to deliver the transition from petrol vehicles to electric vehicles and it is highly probable that the manufacture of petrol vehicles will soon leave their places to electric run vehicles. Moreover, on 19 February, 2021, the United States officially rejoined the Paris Agreement, announcing that it is ready to address the climate change threat and take joint action against it ("The US. Officially Rejoins the Paris Agreement").

All these endeavors signal the coming of a new epoch that will and has to be characterized by various effective efforts of restoration. These efforts are expected to create a significant difference in the struggle against global climate change. They will, hopefully, slow down anthropogenic climate change which, unless taken action, is likely to cause a great deal of problems to our planet. This restoration period will not only become an environmentally conscious era, but will also be an epoch of active policy-making and legislation of environmentally conscious policies by governments worldwide. The COVID-19 pandemic has demonstrated the exigency of restoring nature and provided a preview of its effectuality on the environment. Therefore, restoration will become the face of a new epoch of hope and compensation. Let us all take action and work together to restore the natural environment to a stable condition for Earth, all nonhuman beings and generations to come.

REFERENCE LIST

Altvater, Elmar, et al. *Anthropocene or Capitalocene?: Nature, History, and the Crisis of Capitalism*. Edited by Jason W. Moore, PM P, 2016.

Angus, Ian. *Facing the Anthropocene: Fossil Capitalism and the Crisis of the Earth System*. NYU P, 2016.

Carney, Judith A. "Subsistence in the Plantationocene: Dooryard Gardens, Agrobiodiversity, and the Subaltern Economies of Slavery." *The Journal of Peasant Studies*, 10 Apr. 2020, pp. 1–25.

Crutzen, Paul Jozef. "The Anthropocene."*Journal de Physique IV (Proceedings)*, vol. 12, no. 10, 2002, pp. 1–5.

Davis, Janae, et al. "Anthropocene, Capitalocene, . . . Plantationocene?: A Manifesto for Ecological Justice in an Age of Global Crises." *Geography Compass*, vol. 13, no. 5, Apr. 2019, pp. 1–15.

Ellis, Erle Christopher. *Anthropocene: A Very Short Introduction*. Oxford UP, 2018.

Gilbert, Scott F., et al. "A Symbiotic View of Life: We Have Never Been Individuals." *The Quarterly Review of Biology*, vol. 87, no. 4, 2012, pp. 325–341.

Grear, Anna. "'Anthropocene, Capitalocene, Chthulucene': Re-Encountering Environmental Law and Its 'Subject' with Haraway and New Materialism." *Re-Imagining Environmental Law and Governance for the Anthropocene*, edited by Louis Kotzé, Hart Publishing, 2017.

Haraway, Donna."Anthropologists Are Talking—About the Anthropocene." *Ethnos*, vol. 81, no. 3, 2015, pp. 535–564, doi:10.1080/00141844.2015.1105838.

———. "Anthropocene, Capitalocene, Plantationocene, Chthulucene: Making Kin." *Environmental Humanities*, vol. 6, no. 1, 2015, pp. 159–165.

———. *Staying with the Trouble: Making Kin in the Chthulucene*. Duke University Press, 2016.

Melidis, Michail. "What Are the Effects of COVID-19 on the Environment?" *HAPSc Policy Briefs Series*, vol. 1, no. 1, 2020, pp. 251–257.

Mies, Maria. *Patriarchy and Accumulation on a World Scale: Women in the International Division of Labour*. Zed Books, 1986.

Moore, Jason W. *Capitalism in the Web of Life: Ecology and the Accumulation of Capital*. Verso, 2015.

———. "Nature in the Limits to Capital (And Vice Versa)." *Radical Philosophy*, Sept. 2015, pp. 9–19, www.radicalphilosophyarchive.com/article/nature-in-the-limits-to-capital-and-vice-versa/. Accessed 28 June 2021.

———. "The Capitalocene, Part I: On the Nature and Origins of Our Ecological Crisis." *The Journal of Peasant Studies*, vol. 44, no. 3, 2017, pp. 1–37.

———. "The Capitalocene Part II: Accumulation by Appropriation and the Centrality of Unpaid Work/Energy." *The Journal of Peasant Studies*, vol. 45, no. 2, 2017, pp. 237–279.

Oldfield, Frank, et al. "The Anthropocene Review: Its Significance, Implications and the Rationale for a New Transdisciplinary Journal."*The Anthropocene Review*, vol. 1, no. 1, 2013, pp. 3–7.

Ruddiman, William. F. "The Anthropocene."*Annual Review of Earth and Planetary Sciences*, vol. 41, no. 4, 2013, pp. 1–24.

Steffen, Will, et al. "The Anthropocene: Are Humans Now Overwhelming the Great Forces of Nature." *AMBIO: A Journal of the Human Environment*, vol. 36, no. 8, 2007, pp. 614–621.

———. "The Anthropocene: Conceptual and Historical Perspectives." *Philosophical Transactions*, vol. 369, 2011, pp. 842–867, doi:10.1098/rsta.2010.0327.

"The United States Officially Rejoins the Paris Agreement." *United States Department of State*, State.gov, 26 Feb. 2021, www.state.gov/the-united-states-officially-rejoins-the-paris-agreement/. Accessed 29 June 2021.

Tsing, Anna. "Unruly Edges: Mushrooms as Companion Species." *Environmental Humanities*, vol. 1, no. 1, 2012, pp. 141–154.

Töller, Annette E. "Driving Bans for Diesel Cars in German Cities: The Role of ENGOs and Courts in Producing an Unlikely Outcome." *European Policy Analysis*, vol. 2021, no. 00, 2021, pp. 1–21.

Wolfstone, Irene Friesen. "Review of Donna Haraway, Staying with the Trouble: Making Kin in the Chthulucene (2016)." *Imaginations*, vol. 10, no. 1, 2019, pp. 389–391. doi:10.17742/IMAGE.CR.10.1.15.

11

Literary Data, Fossil, and Speculation

Emrah Peksoy

INTRODUCTION: CORRELATIONISM AND WITHDRAWN TEXT

Mapping out Speculative Realist orientations for literary studies holds immense fecundity as literary work utilizes mind-related abstract units as its object. Viewing literary units produced not by, for, on or against the human agency is a realist position that surpasses the traditional hermeneutical meaning-making process as the latter devalues the literal for the sake of metaphorical. For the aim, Meillassoux's position is conflated with Harman's Object-Oriented-Ontology (OOO) and the rationale for a textual object withdrawn from all human access is presented. The text's customary function to inform discursive mechanisms, social practices, political activism, sexual orientations, psychological, or economic power relations is problematized by juxtaposing literary knowledge with its pure mathematizable qualities. Getting in touch with the aesthetic properties of the text is excavating for its *ancestral qualities (archefossils)* withdrawn from human experience but only vaguely felt through its *mathematised object properties* within the realm of *contingent* causalities. The theoretical foundation is reified with examples from conceptual literary experiments. Then, the insights imbibed are fitted into computational literary analysis techniques and how a speculative look at the text amplifies a subjectless *reading experience*. For, reducing the text to its sheer numerical expressions creates an indirect causal link between form and content which, in turn, reverses anthropocentric interpretation.

Speculative realism is too broad to be mapped out with specific details as it is practised by many under various distinctive streaks. Indeed, one might find it quite difficult to place numerous positions as diverse as Bennett's vital materialism, Bogost's unit operations, Bryant's flat ontology, Brassier's transcendental nihilism, Latour's actor-network theory, Harman's object-oriented ontology, Meillassoux's contingency and many others under the same footing. They are not even willing to be considered so since they all, this way or another, are critical of this umbrella term and pursuing their own unique agenda in their allocated space of politics, theology, or science completely separated from the home base. Interestingly, though, the literary-cultural artefact is the elephant in the room for speculative realism since it has so far done so little to clarify its position before it. The reason lies in "an indefensible thesis," as Meillassoux identified, that "thought cannot get outside itself" (Meillassoux *After Finitude* 11). The dogma, which dictates that being and thinking are inseparable, limits us to produce knowledge that is not self-referential and self-refuting in the first place. Thus, it is no wonder that, except few core thinkers, the positions mentioned above diverted from the main agenda, either to pure materialisms or relational ontologies. The plan here is to explore the space, which is not relative to us, which a speculative realist would call "great outdoors," of the literary text in this context.

For speculative realism, the current correlationist position of philosophy, the idea that the mind-world exist only with each other, and this relation is the only meaningful relation, is the common enemy. While Meillassoux's antagonism for correlationism welcomes all other relations alongside human-world relation and argues for the possibility of absolute knowledge, Harman's path, that of Object-Oriented Ontology (OOO), does not privilege human-world relation and places it on the same ontological footing just like any other relation—say, between trees and raindrops. Thus, for the latter, absolute knowledge of reality is impossible. Aiming for absolute knowledge through literary text seems naïve. Considering the effervescent, immaterial, and illusory nature of the object of literary production, thinking on any entity outside mind and language is tautology and profanity. Yet, equating being to language and extracting social, political, and psychological musings from literary works has dire consequences of viewing reality as the correlate of mind and pure solipsism. Assiduous efforts to exalt material qualities of entities have been captivated by the centrifugal force created by "human" *textualism*. Such that, textual elements, for instance, are either treated as thematic entities constrained within provisional historical processes or elusive viewpoints that need to be deconstructed incessantly. Linguistic propositions, sensual relations, and contextual engagement are human-mind related categories of textualism and necessarily lead one again to a correlationist vicious circle. But what if the text is not what its author intended, and its readers expected? What is *Great Expectations*' significance when there is no reader present? Moretti deftly highlighted this issue when he introduced the concept of the great unread, the immense corpus of unfavoured, forgotten or lost books doomed to oblivion. The dim but should-not-be-overlooked effect of any individual text on the general textual landscape of world literature provides us with some visceral reality hidden from human access. We excavate a part of this reality through relentless decoding of the text in hand but the remaining, what is left from the tip of the iceberg, must be hidden inside the fossilized sediments of dead media, represented by forgotten, unread, never-published, then-unpopular-texts waiting to be explored. In this scenario, Dickens' text includes his own reality and contains the qualities of all other textualities that have somehow managed to creep into it. The "textualities" here refer to any "distinct set of properties [. . .] that become manifest when I interact with it, [as well as] a dog, match, ray of light, and neutrino" (Cogburn and Ohm 191). Although the text here persists, the meaning intended for us could be transformed into a completely different nature than we are accustomed to. This position is not a "only text" or "nothing but text" viewpoint in the fashion of New Criticism and Deconstruction that aim to close the text, ironically, for the sake of a homogenous metaphorical meaning. This position opens text for multifarious possible meanings, albeit unintelligible to human agents, an anticorrelationist argument that stresses the non-human nature of textuality. The rift between Meillassoux and Harman on the possibility of attaining absolute knowledge (of the text), then, becomes triviality so long as one accepts the existence of a veiled reality.

TEXT WITH FOSSILIZED MEANING

Text as an archaeological excavation site is a powerful analogy for other worldly realities that text might be harboring. This is in line with Meillassoux's *ancestrality*[1] argument which deals with pre/posthuman fossilized objects that become manifest without human intervention but have the potential to make themselves somewhat perceived. For Meillassoux, since thought cannot function without converting an object into a thought, correlationist mindset fails to grasp any reference anterior to human existence. Ancestral objects are the objects that precede the meaning-making activity of human subjectivity and arche-fossil "is a material indicating traces of 'ancestral' phenomena anterior even to the emergence of life" (Brassier 15). For example, the statement that "earth was formed nearly five billion years ago" should be unthinkable for a correlationist mindset that only imagines a one-way relation (from humans to world). We try to perceive it as if we could imagine what it was like back then and how thought would be like if we had ever lived then. Hence, the co-existence of humans and the world is a myth, a dogma that underlies human finitude. Accordingly, it is our duty "to understand how thought is able to access the uncorrelated, which is to say, a world capable of subsisting without being given" (Meillassoux *After Finitude* 28). Scientific methods, through carbon-dating or starlight measurement, inform us about these *uncorrelated* realities, the arche-fossils, which refer, unlike fossils that prove the existence of prehistoric life, to ancestral realities preceding life itself.

The issue here is the vexed issue of materials produced by humans, such as the text. Reading geological and archaeological data as archaic texts accentuates the need for mining for meaning. Jussi Parrika's concept of media archaeology reifies this view when he sees geology and astronomy as pure media elements that need hermeneutical decoding. For, geology is not about physical entities but also about meaning. We need to excavate meaning from the sediments of the deep time of the planet because "[t]he readability of the earth is still a continuing trope. The earth is constantly read as if it were a script needing to be interpreted, a trace of hermeneutics" (Parikka *Geology* 138). As such, the fossils left for us and the new ones we are producing for the future accentuate the material-realist nature of textual media. Since "[m]edia archaeology sees media cultures as sedimented and layered," then textual media produced by humans never grow old or become obsolete but is "continuously remediated, resurfacing, finding new uses, contexts, adaptations" (Parikka *Media* 3). Considering the infinite number of textual materials, their persistence in deep time as they are preserved on rare earth minerals such as silicon, selenium, coltan, cobalt, and so on in the age of advanced technology, meaning preserved inside the fossilized media acts as an expansion to reconsider usual concepts of time. In a way, it becomes a zombie-media waiting to be revived in future under different circumstances and in different contexts prone to different interpretations. The issue underlined here is not the act of interpretation but the reality that an abstract entity, textual meaning, might be harboring more/less (or nothing) than it was intended in the first place. For a reader of text, literary fossils refer to a limited set of loose interpretations perceived by humans. Yet, arche-fossil is the recognition that the text that has managed to make itself visible through an infinite set of possibilities (say, its writer or historical conditions and social structure in which it is created). This way, the necessity of the beholder, the human subject, is questioned in the presence of a text stripped from its qualities. Text with compound meanings is exemplified with Brendan Howell's live text installation, *exquisite_code* project, a human-computer co-authored performance novel, which features a director software de/selecting and editing prompts and text segments provided by several human collaborators. As the textual selection process is arbitrary and authorial intention is annulled, reading becomes "trying to detect the signatures of the particular collaborators in the mash" (Marino 284). Though narrative expectations might not be answered while reading the book, the Python code used for the process provided in the appendix preserves the text's aesthetic core. Readers could recreate the whole process but with different textual output on each execution. Subsequently, the text becomes a surplus material radiating from the fossilised language of the code. In a way, "the text fossilizes the product of the execution" (Marino 285), and readers are transformed into miners who read the code, not the textual façade, that inhabits archaic aesthetic possibilities.

CONTINGENT MEANING

This situation accentuates the *contingent* nature of entities as stressed by Meillassoux. Cutting the causal link between entities, the principle of contingency in his version of speculative philosophy renders a world separated from natural laws. For him, "[c]ontingency expresses the fact that physical laws remain indifferent as to whether an event occurs or not—they allow an entity to emerge, to subsist, or to perish" (Meillassoux *After Finitude* 66). In this world of chaos, there is no reason for anything to happen or not happen. Everything exists independently of each other, and physical laws are not absolute principles but contingent happenstances. Coupled with correlationist thinking, this principle annuls the givenness of any entity and creates a world in a vacuum where the fire's capacity, for example, to burn paper is completely accidental, provisional, and inconsistent. We tend to favor one theory of nature over another as it seems like the only logical solution for now. On the side of textual knowledge, the principle of contingency is not an utterly viable option for literary texts since the text is treated as an extension of the human mind. Yet, the contingency closes the text for humanistic interpretation and allows us to see it as is, in isolation from the correlationist contamination. The text is an ever-changing entity with no assertion on the truth. The literary reader is a nostalgic decoder that is bound to view the text through their subjective viewpoints, taking its meaning too literally or too figuratively. Consider, for example, the oscillation of voice between the author and the narrator in a literary text. The reader's endless quest to decide who is who in which context impugns the credibility of interpretation let alone the purely subjective readerly experience. In the latter case, this experience is elusive to the extent that one could never finalize or objectify it. As known, putative secrets of text are incessantly deconstructed or mined until they are no longer secrets. Still, this objective proves to be futile as the interpreter is stuck in a vicious cycle under each veil she uncovers. Here, she is overburdened with trivialities to the degree that "her immense baggage of learning, blinds her to the knotty specificities of the text in question" (Eyers 29). These "specificities," then, lead us to develop analyses too formulaic in nature and to lose our critical stance to develop ramifications such as "negativity, pessimism, vigilance, diagnostic gaze, suspicion"(Marling and Marling 99) rather than an objective stance. In the end, the text is overly fetishised as new forms of reading are incessantly produced.[2]

The current literary trope is currently producing abundant literary objects which explicate this speculative treatment. Consider, for instance, experimental poet Christian Bök's ongoing The Xenotext Experiment[3] in which he attempts to write an eternal poem encoded into the genome of an extremophile bacterium. Though storing information on DNA is already conducted, the novelty of Bök's project lies in his herculean effort to make a bacterium—*Deinococcusradiodurans*—write poetry as well as store one. By utilising RNA transcription, Bök assigned the letters of the alphabet to twenty-six nucleotide pairs and fed the genetic translation/transformation of his poem *Orpheus* to the bacteria's DNA, which, in turn, replies with another poem *Eurydice* in the form of protein ciphers to be decoded with the software he constructed. The bacterium is the most durable organism identified and is believed to outlive any life, the earth and the sun, "facilitating the postapocalyptic survival of the poem" (Waidner 31). In Bök's own words, through the poem we might conceivably "transmit messages across stellar distances or even epochal intervals [. . .] like a secret message in a bottle flung at random into a giant ocean" ("The Xenotext Experiment" 231). This initiates nonhumanistic speculation which urges us to experience the past in future. Through defeating human temporality, the attempt is a challenge to produce an already-layered-fossil-matter that surpasses the givenness itself as it could "ensur[e] that future humans could access lost data from the past" (Bök "From the Xenotext" 399). The whole process is linguistically highly constrained, for the poem the microbe will produce has limited vocabulary, with only 120 words. The creativeness lies with the experimenter who must create distinctive conditions for the microbe to produce it. The strain here is the linguistic genius of human poets juxtaposed with the inventiveness of the experimentation. The microbe does not produce language except proteins translated into human language. Unlike textual artefacts produced on paper, this protein language has no cultural signification, reference, intertextual operant, or signifying units except its capacity for interpretation without meaning. The biological constraints of the microbe, Bök states, "tell[s him] what to do" and hence, it "address[es] [. . .] life itself in its own language" ("Silliman's Blog"). Consider that the protein poem resists reading and interpretation as it is generated via a decoding software that has created a lexicon of only 120 words in syntactically correct arrangements out of eight trillion possibilities. Bök does not address the remaining options that are nonsensical for us. This way, he underlines the inherent limitation of linguistic constructs and leads us to consider "what lies beyond subjective interpretation in spatial, temporal and semiotic terms" (Skibsrud). By juxtaposing the poet as the subject with subject-with-no-agency, Bök aims for a pristine nonhuman aesthetics in which the text exists outside the confines of language. This way, the whole process creates an autopoietic textual systems world in which all textual units—agency, reading, interpretation—account for one another in single biological unit, leading to a preemptive, contingent speculative reasoning.

MEANING IN NUMBERS

The speculative formula offered for a text that is contingent (and withdrawn as arche-fossils) is reminiscent of Toril Moi's timely question: "What good does it do to know that something we love is contingent, or socially constructed?" (32). Or how do we get access to that great outdoors with our humanoid perception? Though Harman's vicarious causation and Meillassoux's *mathematizable object properties* offer seemingly distant answers to this question, the argument is that they share a similar core that allows us to gain access to the real. Viewing objects as residing in encrusted shells "withdraw[n] into obscure cavernous underworlds, deprived of causal links"(Harman "On Vicarious Causation" 179), Harman imagines a world in which objects encounter/experience each other in a buffer zone where they interact "through sensual profiles found only on the interior of some other entity"("On Vicarious Causation" 184). Since this encounter is never direct but through some vicars unbeknownst to both parties, it creates a distinct third object of encounter. To explicate, whenever I read *Great Expectations*, I the reader and the book as an object are conflated into a distinct reader-text object without disturbing the inner realities of each other. The resulting truth statements are true only for me under specific physical or abstract conditions. There are billions of reader-text encounters but neither the reader nor the text in question is transformed. Each encounter is a brand-new experience not completely different from a dog sniffing the book. Consider the alternative ending to Pip's story provided by Dickens. Though we see a change in the narrative progression, the textual object remains unaffected by the inner and outer consumption. On Meillassoux's side, the problem is easier to solve. He argues for an accessible ontology that can "discourse about the great outdoors; to discourse about a past where both humanity and life are absent" (Meillassoux *After Finitude* 47). This capacity can only be attributed to science, or the mathematization of nature, as he prefers to call it. Since mathematics can only grasp an autonomous world independent of its sensible qualities, its peculiar language acts as our only proximity to reality. As "every mathematical statement describes an entity which is essentially contingent" (Meillassoux *After Finitude* 206), it provides an entry into the realm of absolute ancestral statements. Yet, it is necessary to note that mathematical statements are not sole absolutes, but an arbitrary (or not) solution to spatio-temporal positioning of humanity in nature. Hence, the mathematizable object properties "are effectively in the object in the way in which [we] conceive them, whether [we are] in relation with this object or not" (Meillassoux *After Finitude* 10). The assumption is that the intermediary agent that we get in touch with entities is their mathematizable qualities. Though Harman assigns mathematics only to material entities, the speculative position differentiates pure mathematics from mathematical statements as a formal linguistic construct.[4] The former is the objective while the latter is what we contingently have. The proof is in *The Number and the Siren* where Meillassoux offers an ingenious reading of Mallarmé's poem *Un Coup De Des*. The poem, in content and form, perfectly reflects the speculative agenda described here. With his reading of the content, he first rejects poets' genius to create the most beautiful lines and attributes literary success only to pure chance. Then turning to the form, he decrypts a unique number, a cipher, a secret code—which is 707—to interpret this enigmatic poem with a new perspective, by studying the numbers of word senses, meters, syllables, line and word counts, pagination, editorial revisions, and so on. This way, the content is reinforced with "the precise determination of the 'unique Number' enigmatically evoked in the poem" (Meillassoux *The Number* 3). This brilliant exploration, that the poem holds a three-digit encryption, which accentuates a kabbalistic reduction of ideas into numerals, enables speculative viewpoint to verify its position—that the meaning is there (as an ancestral statement illegible for us) in numbers (as it permits mathematical thought) but in completely coincidental terms (contingency).

As seen, generic principles of textual form are provided only as a possibility, as contingent against customary implementations. For instance, an individual text's deviation from certain generic norms does not put it in the periphery. It is strictly preserved in the center through its aesthetic core which remains unaffected. One might question whether a text is historical fiction or not, but its—hypothetical— avant-garde position is incontestable, though speculative. So, the question of how we might get access to this speculative, aesthetic core of the text is still valid. We could mobilize Harman's question when he questions Meillassoux's speculative mathematical decoding of Mallarme in the fashion of gematria. "Where to next," he asks, "is there any way to extend this method to other literary works?" such as Dante, Shakespeare, or Stevens. Yet, he answers his own question: "it seems unlikely" (Harman "Speculation" 5). That is why his and few other disciples' treatments of literary texts fail to propose a full-fledged implementation of speculative agenda.[5] To explicate, his mobilization and reading of Lovecraft and Poe remain only at the topical level, and it is so as long as these topics coincide with his OOO agenda. Lovecraft's universe is highly favored by anticorrelationist thinkers since it "hint[s] at some ineffable reality over and above all the object's manifest features" (Harman "Poe's Black Cat" 219). Similarly, Joy expresses her longing for a new mode of reading which "might discover a non-projective, non-hermeneutic wedge" ("Weird Reading" 34) inside interpretation, rather than a methodology.

However, the argument is that the speculative potential of textual objects is also manifested through the computerized treatment of literary text in its reception and interpretation. In fact, the methods kill two birds with one stone: they suture OOO's indirect access to objects with their mathematical enactment. Unlike Meillassoux who accidentally discovered a numeric code deliberately planted, computer-based textual analysis (CTA) requires a deliberate attempt for a contingent code. CTA is considered an umbrella term for various practices such as topic modeling, sentiment analysis, network modeling, character mapping, stylometry, metadata analysis, visualizations, geocoding, frequency distribution, and their statistical significance. These act as intermediary agents that transform what we read as humans into mathematical abstractions in principle. Individual words and their relations are quantified to explore the withdrawn realities behind them. This is what the hermeneutical process aims to achieve, but "words are [. . .] the means by which reader comprehension happens but not that which is comprehended" (Algee-Hewitt et al. 190). An individual word does not exist in a vacuum but relative to the sentence, paragraph, book, writer, epoch, century, or all other textualities within which it was imagined. These methods take that individual word out of its humanistic context and represent it in nontemporal and nonspatial Cartesian space. Do it for all other words or units for inspection in a book or literary period and then, we get a grand narrative to inspect. This kind of quantified representation informs us of the self-reflexive potential of textuality. Quantity becomes narration itself which gives us the deep story of either an individual text or the whole literary history. Through computation, algorithms, machine learning, and statistics (*vicars*), we get to the meaning *proper* in mathematized language.

Coming back to our example *Great Expectations* and considering its literary units, one could ask: what is this book then? Who is Pip? What is London? Why am I moved by it? These questions were and still are being answered by students of the hermeneutical process with no emancipatory result. Yet, speculative reasoning should take place in "a carnal realm" (Joy "Weird Reading" 34), where literary objects interact with each other without our agency. For instance, plot with respect to characters or overuse of function words interacting with third-person narration articulated in mathematical terms, which in turn expresses, to borrow from Joy, "new modes of reading that would allow texts a certain anti-reductionist and autopoetic [. . .] ontology" ("Weird Reading" 32). An example is creating word embeddings models of the vector representations of words through various algorithms.[6] Each word in a literary unit is represented in the vector space of the textual units explored. Computing the mathematical representation of the word *pip* in lowercase in vector space in its relation to all other words in a corpus, we gain access to the periphery of the textual world, in which its narrative potential is consumed in an instant. "*meantersay, chap, ay, partickler, wery*" (0.8111134, 0.7880545, 0.7538747, 0.7511464) reside in closest proximity to *pip* (1.0), which reflects the character's close association with Joe Gargery, his brother-in-law.[7] These figures continually change when processed with another element added or subtracted (say, another book by Dickens or his whole corpus, the whole nineteenth century, British novel, English prose, and so on). The previous exploration is not a new discovery of the book's universe of meaning. Yet, the fecundity of possible meanings inherent is limitless. They are there, just like *Deinococcusradiodurans*' protein poem (with eight trillion possibilities), waiting for its aesthetic potential to be unearthed.

CONCLUSION

In his treatment of Western cannon, Harold Bloom shows us how porous the term cannon is, in that different genres fall out of favor or rise in favor in each century. This is a natural process as each book, writer, and era shapes its successors for better or worse. The reason is attributed to the contingent feature that "governs literature" (Bloom 11). Though, he blames the *school of resentment*, that is, the established critical methods that value social and political activism instead of aesthetic signification, for faulty treatment of literature, he looks for this aesthetic value in the personal, visceral responses of individual human beings. Yet, between the lines, he accepts its withdrawn, inaccessible, unexplorable quality: "literature is not merely language; it is also the will to figuration, [. . .] the desire to be different, the desire to be elsewhere" (Bloom 12). This aesthetic core is preserved no matter how much so-called canonical works are favoured or replaced by new works. It is deposited into sedimented layers of literary deep time and as arche fossils, will flicker data into distant futures. Maybe they will be forgotten or wiped out of the literary arena but their dim manifestations in the fossilized core of each text will be there to be appreciated as lofty but ambivalent mathematical formulations. This is valuable as it offers inexhaustible speculative potential rather than consumptive theory.

NOTES

1. Meillassoux chooses the term *ancestrality* for the phenomena anterior to life and *diachronicity* for the phenomena posterior to life. But for convenience, I will stick to the first one to refer to both.
2. New formalism (Levinson), expressive (Kuiken), surface (Best and Marcus), reparative (Sedgwick), distant, enumerative (Piper), postcritical (Felski) reading, thin description (Love), and so on.
3. See Bök, Christian. *The Xenotext: Book 1*. Coach House Books, 2015.
4. This issue needs further elaboration, but due to space limitation, I leave this to another article.
5. For further information see Joy, Eileen A. "Like Two Autistic Moonbeams Entering the Window of My Asylum: Chaucer's Griselda and Lars Von Trier's Bess Mcneill." *Postmedieval-a Journal of Medieval Cultural Studies*, vol. 2, no. 3, 2011, pp. 316-28, doi:10.1057/pmed.2011.20.; Dodson, Matthew J. "The Objects Within: An Applied OOO Literary Criticism." Masters Thesis, Oregon State University, 2014-07-02 2014. ScholarsArchive@OSU, http://localhost/files/qj72pb24x2020-07-09; Lovasz, Adam. "Object-Oriented Literary Studies and Melville's Cosmos: Writing as Dissemination In Moby-Dick." *Textual Practice*, 2020, doi:10.1080/0950236X.2020.1789205.
6. *FastText, Word2Vec, Glove*
7. The numbers were extracted with Word2Vec package in *R* programming language by feeding the book into the algorithms.

REFERENCE LIST

Algee-Hewitt, Mark et al. "The Novel as Data." *The Cambridge Companion to the Novel*, edited by Eric Bulson, Cambridge University Press, 2018, pp. 189-216. *Cambridge Companions to Literature,* Cambridge Core.

Bloom, Harold. *The Western Canon: The Books and School of the Ages*. Riverhead Books, 1994. *History of the Human Sciences.*

Bök, Christian. "From the Xenotext." *The Routledge Companion to the Environmental Humanities*, edited by Ursula K. Heise et al., Routledge, 2017, pp. 379-400. https://www.routledgehandbooks.com/doi/10.4324/9781315766355.ch37.

———. "Silliman's Blog," edited by Ron Silliman, vol. 2021, 2011. https://ronsilliman.blogspot.com/2011/05/christian-b-o-k-this-is-one-of-notes.html.

———. "The Xenotext Experiment." *SCRIPTed*, vol. 5, 2008, p. 227, doi:10.2966/scrip.050208.227.

———. *The Xenotext: Book 1*. Coach House Books, 2015.

Brassier, Ray. "The Enigma of Realism: On Quentin Meillassoux's after Finitude." *Collapse II Speculative Realism*, edited by Robin Mackay, vol. II, Sequence Press, 2007, pp. 15–54.

Cogburn, Jon and Mark Allan Ohm. "Actual Qualities of Imaginative Things: Notes Towards an Object-Oriented Literary Theory." *Aesthetics in the twenty-first Century Speculations V*, edited by Rıdvan Aşkın et al., vol. V, Punctum Books, 2014, pp. 180–224.

Dodson, Matthew J. "The Objects Within: An Applied OOO Literary Criticism." Masters Thesis, Oregon State University, 2014–07–02 2014. ScholarsArchive@OSU, http://localhost/files/qj72pb24x2020–07–09.

Eyers, Tom. *Speculative Formalism : Literature, Theory, and the Critical Present*. Northwestern University Press, 2017. *Diaeresis*.

Harman, Graham. "On Vicarious Causation." *Collapse II Speculative Realism*, edited by Robin Mackay, vol. II, Urbanomics, 2007, pp. 171–205.

———. "Poe's Black Cat." *Romanticism and Speculative Realism*, edited by Chris Washington and Anne C. McCarthy, Bloomsbury Academic, 2019, pp. 217–36.

———. "Speculation." *Oxford Research Encyclopedia of Literature*, 2020.

Joy, Eileen A. "Like Two Autistic Moonbeams Entering the Window of My Asylum: Chaucer's Griselda and Lars Von Trier's Bess Mcneill." *Postmedieval—a Journal of Medieval Cultural Studies*, vol. 2, no. 3, 2011, pp. 316–28, doi:10.1057/pmed.2011.20.

———. "Weird Reading." *Speculations: A Journal of Speculative Realism*, no. IV, 2013, pp. 28–34.

Lovasz, Adam. "Object-Oriented Literary Studies and Melville's Cosmos: Writing as Dissemination in Moby Dick." *Textual Practice*, 2020, doi:10.1080/0950236X.2020.1789205.

Marino, Mark C. "Reading Exquisite_Code: Critical Code Studies of Literature." *Comparative Textual Media: Transforming the Humanities in the Postprint Era*, edited by N. Katherine Hayles and Jessica Pressman, vol. 42, University of Minnesota Press, 2013, pp. 283–310.

Marling, Raili and William Marling. "Reparative Reading and Christian Anarchism." *Lit: Literature Interpretation Theory*, vol. 32, no. 2, 2021, pp. 99–116, doi:10.1080/10436928.2021.1901200.

Meillassoux, Quentin. *After Finitude : An Essay on the Necessity of Contingency*. translated by Ray Brassier, Continuum, 2008.

———. *The Number and the Siren : A Decipherment of Mallarmé's Coup De Dés*. translated by Robin Mackay, Urbanomic; Sequence Press, 2012.

Moi, Toril. "'Nothing Is Hidden': From Confusion to Clarity; or, Wittgenstein on Critique." *Critique and Postcritique*, edited by Elizabeth S. Anker and Rita Felski, Duke University Press, 2017, pp. 31–49.

Parikka, Jussi. *A Geology of Media*. University of Minnesota Press, 2015. *Electronic Mediations*, vol. 46.

———. *What Is Media Archaeology?* Polity Press, 2012.

Skibsrud, Johanna. *The Poetic Imperative: A Speculative Aesthetics*. McGill-Queen's University Press, 2020.

Waidner, Isabel. "Christian Bök's Xenotext Experiment, Conceptual Writing and the Subject-of-No-Subjectivity: Pink Faeries and Gaudy Baubles." *Configurations*, vol. 26, no. 1, 2018, pp. 27–46, doi:10.1353/con.2018.0001.

III
LITERARY LANDSCAPES

12

Reading Character in Reading or, Character Again, Post-Theoretically

Ivan Callus

I

Deluded about the performativity, a disclaimer for this chapter might read as follows:

> All the writers, critics and individuals discussed in this text are real. Any resemblance to imagined or assumed character(s) is either fortuitous or deceptive.

To which it might be added that the most self-aware discourse cannot self-analyze, cannot read its own character, even as it sees itself (mis)read. In the words of Geoffrey Hartman, "What is at issue is the character of self-analysis" (22).

II

It is the winter of 1987, still the heyday of theory. Picture somebody in the character of an undergraduate reading up on structuralism, in preparation for poststructuralist discourse. It might even have been *me* (pronouns and their reference, together with their unabashed use, are going to matter in this chapter about the apparent resurgence of the idea of character in post-theoretical criticism).

The student stops in their reading tracks when coming across this passage:

> Under the aegis of semiotic criticism, characters lose their privilege, their central status, and their definition. This does not mean that they are metamorphosed into inanimate things (à la Robbe-Grillet) or reduced to actants (à la Todorov) but that they are textualized. As segments of a closed text, characters at most are patterns of recurrence, motifs which are continually recontextualized in other motifs. In semiotic criticism, characters dissolve.

The undergraduate (or "I") would likely not have read the passage—by Joel Weinsheimer (195), noteworthy for his fine scholarship on Hans-Georg Gadamer and hermeneutics—at source. "I" read it in quotation: in the third chapter, called "Story: Characters," of Shlomith Rimmon-Kenan's *Narrative Fiction: Contemporary Poetics* (32). At the time, Rimmon-Kenan's book was one of not many texts available that served as accessible guides to literary theory. Others included Jonathan Culler's *Structuralist Poetics* and Catherine Belsey's *Critical Practice*. The suggestion across those books appeared to be, in line with the broader drift of theory as it was establishing itself in various literature programs in the United States, the UK, and beyond, that it was now only a quaint student who in good critical (or should one say *uncritical*) faith would write a character study, an exercise for which there would have been assiduous training in Sixth Form or high school. You know the kind of exercise in question (again, the use of the "you," in further artless pronominal deployment, is appropriate in reflection on character): the one in which you take to heart questions like why Iago seems driven by "motiveless malignity," why Pip is so intent on the qualities of a gentleman, and why Sebastian Flyte is carrying a teddy bear around called Aloysius. For criticism more broadly, and as Toril Moi discusses extensively in her essay "Rethinking Character" in the book co-written with Amanda Anderson and Rita Felski, *Character: Three Inquiries in Literary Studies*, L. C. Knights's quippingly titled 1933 article, "How Many Children Had Lady Macbeth?," had already chipped away at the innocence and viability of that rather pleasing practice. Years earlier, D. H. Lawrence's disdain for "the old stable *ego*—of the character" (87) had already done something of the same, and that's without even going into the effect of psychoanalysis, which Lawrence didn't much like but which his century rather did. More strongly still, structuralism and semiotics would leave little doubt that even the most vivid characters and their impressing of line and dimension upon the reading mind were a conjuration bodied in language and pre-established pattern. "Character is the major aspect of the novel to which structuralism has paid least attention and has been least successful in treating," Culler noted, before adding: "Although for many readers character serves as the major totalizing forced in fiction—everything in the novel exists in order to illustrate character and its development—a structuralist approach has tended to explain this as an ideological prejudice rather than to study it *as a fact of reading*" (230; emphasis added, in view of considerations below that connect with this chapter's title). And with the death of the author, too, following seminal essays by Roland Barthes and Michel Foucault, what price character? (See Burke 2010.)

Before long, like a hapless *picaro*, the undergraduate would come across poststructuralism, with its further talk on the linguistic turn, on being written into being, on (the death of) the subject. As Catherine Belsey, paraphrasing Louis Althusser and Jacques Lacan among others, explained, "Subjectivity, then, is linguistically and discursively constructed and displaced across the range of discourses in which the concrete individual participates" (61). Furthermore, "the displacement of subjectivity across a range of discourses implies a range of positions from which the subject grasps itself and its relations within the real, and these positions . . . may be incompatible or contradictory" (65). The sense was that in the move to subjectivity the idea of character was being disdained. It was becoming a fond but displaced remnant from less sophisticated repertoires of critique.

This presented a dilemma. It is apparent in a title from 1991, which is almost cleverer than Knights': *Who Comes after the Subject?* Eduardo Cadava, Peter Connor, and Jean-Luc Nancy's collection brought together essays by Sylviane Agacinski, Alain Badiou, Etienne Balibar, Maurice Blanchot, Mikkel Borch-Jakobsen, Jean-François Courtine, Gilles Deleuze, Jacques Derrida, Vincent Descombes, Didier Franck, Gérard Granel, Michel Henry, Luce Irigaray, Sarah Kofman, Philippe Lacoue-Labarthe, Emmanuel Levinas, Jean-François Lyotard, Jean-Luc Marion, and Jacques Rancière. This full listing is important. There is a curriculum of theory embedded there. To be sure, it is not quite comprehensive. Barthes and Foucault, for instance, could not be included in the collection because by 1991 they had passed on, while the characters here are decidedly (and by editorial choice) Parisian, even by the demographics of theory's genealogies. But it is, otherwise, anchoring enough. And all the contributors were responding to a question concerning "one of the great motifs of modern philosophy: the critique or deconstruction of subjectivity" (Connor and Cadava, n.p.). In Jean-Luc Nancy's words, "the question therefore bears upon the critique or deconstruction of interiority, of self-presence, of consciousness, of mastery, of the individual or collective property of an essence. Critique or deconstruction of the firmness of a seat (*hypokeimenon, substantia, subjectum*) and the certitude of an authority and a value (the individual, a people, the state, history, work)" (4).In this reading, subjectivity, never mind character, is precarious.

This year, as I write, is the thirtieth anniversary of that landmark collection. It is not by any means certain that in the present, when the term *post-theory* is apt to be taken literally, literary criticism has quite absorbed the collection's import. (The time of post-theory was announced long ago, alongside the tendency in theory to problematise the prefix "post-"; see, for instance, a number of the essays in Lyotard 1992, as well as McQuillan, Purves, and Macdonald 1999, and Callus and Herbrecher 2004; what has since changed, arguably, is the readier acceptance of the literal meaning of the term "post-theory"). The reasons can be ascribed to different considerations. Among them is the "ethnogeographical" and "ethnonational partitioning of 'philosophy'" involved (2), this latter term and category itself being one of the points at issue, as acknowledged by Nancy himself (the launch two years later of *Angelaki*, with the subtitle, "Journal of the *Theoretical Humanities*," afforded a suppler term). Significant among the other reasons, and the one focused on in this chapter, is the act of reading character in reading.

III

"Reading Character in Reading," the title-phrase to this chapter, can be understood in more than one way. Let me mention three. First, it can refer to how characters on the page strike and impress themselves upon the reading mind. It conjures the equivalent, for the reader, of Charles Dickens surrounded by his characters in Robert W. Buss's 1870 painting, *Dickens's Dream*. It brings back the immediacy, in a vividness felt almost on the skin, of characters in books we read as children, or, why not, more recently (if we are now not all entirely miserable and jaded, post-theoretically). It is the kind of relation that the critic Werner Wolf powerfully studies under the label of "the aesthetic illusion," that is, "a feeling of being recentred in a possible world as if it were (a slice of) life, a feeling that prevails in spite of the fact, and our latent awareness of it, that this impression is triggered by a 'mere' artefact" (325). Notice, accordingly, that beside the charm in Buss's painting lurks something unnerving. Perhaps it is not good, after all, for characters to take on a life of their own, alongside our recentred one. The boundaries between the diegetic and what we take as real are not innocently transgressed, as Jane Austen's Catherine Morland and Ian McEwan's Briony Tallis discovered. For there is some unsettlement when characters report, "Reader, I married him," or when they step out of and down from the screen, or when in games they appear to emancipate themselves—themselves, *them*selves, them*selves*?—from code.

Second meaning. What reading character do we have, while reading? And here again, incidentally, the artless use of the pronoun, in this case "we," is not out of place. Note how Nancy himself used it, in his introduction to *Who Comes after the Subject?*: "We are the second half of the century. A 'we' without 'we,' a 'we' without philosophical community" (2)—with that lack of community not in and of itself undoing the use of "we" (2). And so, to move non-theoretically on for a moment: as we read, are we avid and focused, or casual and distracted? Do we annotate compulsively as we read, pencils continually hovering? Do we rather rely on the resonance of the moment, for the later recall we are able to command? As if it is so simple: we read differently all the time, with shifting dispositions across newspapers and magazines, social media and web browsing, textbooks and monographs, chronicle and science, fiction and poetry. Still, it is irrepressible to wonder whether there is a correspondence between reading character and broader personality, whether one is reflected in the other. Are we at odds with ourselves when reading? With the world? Do we come away more equilibrated, enacting what I. A. Richards said in *Principles of Literary Criticism* (1924) about reading appetencies, before and amid the pitfalls of the intentional fallacy and the affective fallacy, as W. K. Wimsatt and Monroe C. Beardsley had it? What, indeed, are we to read into our reading character? But that is doubtless a different question for a different conversation.

Or perhaps not. Allow this interlude. "The house was quiet and the world was calm," Wallace Stevens's well-known poem about the experience of being lost to, *in*, reading is as good a reveal of reading disposition as any. You (allow, again, this mode of addressivity in an academic context, for this too is part of the post-theoretical language game) . . . you will want to ask yourself whether you find the poem to be luminous or suspect in its stilling of the "truth in a calm world" whereby "The reader became the book; and summer night // Was like the conscious being of the book." Stevens's poem is about a particular experience (one could say *phenomenology*) of reading. It relates to the equilibrating intensity (if that is not an oxymoron) when the act of reading can appear graced (or charged, if less mystical language is preferred) with the apperception of oneself before a book read in that sense of stilled truth-time, with character(s)—of self, book, reading, (un)world(ed)-time—revealed therein. So: there you have it, or there you have yourself (or not): in your disposition and reaction to Stevens's poem. Your character, or something of/like it: in the response to a poem on the conscious being of the book in the reading.

But, to move on to the third meaning of "reading character in reading." Some readers, we know, are not like us. Because they are so different, we suffer them to tell us what and how to read. Depending on our dispositions and inclinations, we trust them to read for us, these reading characters on whom we imprint ourselves and who, depending on our affinities, may be variously liberal humanists or formalists or structuralists or Marxists or post-Marxists or postcolonialists or poststructuralists or postmodernists or New Historicists or feminists or queer theorists or critical race theorists or posthumanists or new materialists or—since there's always one, or ones—the awkward outlier, the cussed crew of indeterminate affiliation. The phrase "reading character in reading" therefore and accordingly also suggests how a reading of a character or text—Johnson's or Coleridge's or Eliot's or Steiner's or Derrida's reading of *Hamlet*, for instance, just to go with six very real characters—can convey a sense not only of the personality and temper behind the reading, but also a sense that the interpretation or critique can itself appear to have a character that goes beyond style. It is why it was possible, for instance, to have spoken with any purpose about a Leavisite reading or a Barthesian one. It is also, incidentally, why yet another title-phrase, *Later Derrida* (see Rapaport), acquires point and purchase, signalling that a signature mode of reading, if that is what is in the frame, can change over time.

On the basis of these three understandings of the phrase *reading character in reading*, three further paths for discussion, I suggest, open up. They are paths that consider:

1. the ways in which the critical orientations of an age can be gauged from what it says, or refuses to say, about questions surrounding literary character;
2. the receding and resurgence, in literary criticism of the past decades, of interest in character; and
3. whether it is possible, or even makes sense, to discern a distinct and changed character in literary criticism in the present.

Without the time available to look at each of these comprehensively, I am reflecting instead on some of criticism's trajectories along the question of character, in the hope that they bring into relief what is at stake in the idea that character may be making a post-theoretical comeback.

IV

I pick up a document from a different age of literary criticism, Miriam Allott's *Novelists on the Novel*, from 1959. A section called "Characterization" collects novelists' reflections upon that theme. Surprisingly, Henry James's lines from his 1884 essay, "The Art of Fiction," are not included: "What is character but the determination of incident? What is incident but the illustration of character?" (James, 55). But here is Samuel Johnson, to distinguish between "characters of nature" and "characters of manners" (Allott, 202); Anthony Trollope, to say, "I have lived with my characters . . . There is a gallery of them, and of all in that gallery I may say that I know the tone of voice, and the colour of the hair, every flame of the eye, and the very clothes they wear" (285); E. M. Forster, on flat and round characters (288–9); Virginia Woolf, to assert that "I believe that all novels . . . deal with character," but, warningly, "You see one thing in character, and I another. You say it means this, and I that" (290). Here too is George Eliot, observed by Allott in her "reluctance to . . . adopt any formula which does not get itself clothed for me in some human figure and individual experience" (208). This is the idiom, the character, of debates that we can think criticism has outgrown, much as with Shakespearean criticism we shrink from the characterizations by A. C. Bradley and Lily B. Campbell of Shakespeare's tragic heroes but somehow always assume that undergraduates have internalised them, so that we can move on with them, ready-equipped, to work by Stephen Greenblatt and Jonathan Bate and Jonathan Dollimore and Margreta de Grazia. Curiously, though, the tone, texture, tenor of those debates persists in the representation of character in other media. The debates around adaptation insofar as character migration is concerned would not otherwise hold.

V

In a sense the issues under discussion all revolve around the readerly and critical instincts bearing upon one question. Does Hamlet exist? We know the answer to that one. "Of course he does not." But also, "Of course he does." Moi captures the comic paradox: "We [academic critics] are not more likely than others to mistake fictional characters for other people. Yet our discipline is replete with warnings about doing precisely this" (28). Disingenuous it may therefore be, but the question of Hamlet's existence does matter. For all that it is tendentious, Hamlet remains not just any character. If he doesn't exist, then neither does any imagined life or mind. "I have a smack of Hamlet myself, if I may say so," Coleridge famously exclaimed. In *I Am Hamlet*, the actor Steven Berkoff wrote,

> In every actor is a Hamlet struggling to get out. In fact, in most directors too.
> For whatever reason, and there are many, Hamlet is the accumulation of all our values and beliefs. In him are set out the rules for the perfect human, the perfect rationalist,

plus the adventurer, all rolled into one. No other play gives an actor such words of compassion, charm, wisdom, wit, moral force, insight and philosophy.
. . .
    Hamlet is a feast for the actor since there is something naturally of Hamlet in us all. . . . Since Hamlet touches the complete alphabet of human experience every actor feels he is born to play it. (vii)

And Bloom, in *Shakespeare and the Invention of the Human*, argued as follows:

More even than all the other Shakespearean prodigies—Rosalind, Shylock, Iago, Lear, Macbeth, Cleopatra—Falstaff and Hamlet are the invention of the human, the inauguration of personality as we have come to recognise it. The Idea of Western character, of the self as a moral agent, has many sources: Homer and Plato, Aristotle and Sophocles, the Bible and St. Augustine, Dante and Kant, and all you might care to add. Personality, in our sense, is a Shakespearean invention, and it is not only Shakespeare's greatest originality but also the authentic cause of his particular greatness. (4)

And of course, no character has been more read, critiqued, interpreted, than Hamlet. Nor more inhabited. It is materially—*politically*—important, to be Hamlet, as is attested by those who have played him against conventional perceptions of who it is that can non-incongruously say, "It is I, Hamlet the Dane!": from Charlotte Clarke in the eighteenth century to Ian McKellen at eighty. And a good deal of literary criticism and a fair space of philosophy can be mapped on to reactions to *Hamlet*. It is, in fact, possible to characterise a reading sensibility, a critical temper, through its reactions to Hamlet: Voltaire's, Hegel's, Nietzsche's, Eliot's. It is also true that every major school or method of critique has had a landmark reading of *Hamlet*: New Historicism in Stephen Greenblatt's *Hamlet in Purgatory*, for instance, deconstruction in Derrida's *Specters of Marx*.

    And if it is possible to characterize a phase in criticism through its approach to Hamlet, consider some signs of the times. In her recent book *Character,* Marjorie Garber observes how "Perhaps the most cited phrase about the actor's job in delineating character is Hamlet's 'to hold as 'twere the mirror up to nature'—but it is worth considering that a mirror produces a *reversed* image. Is character intrinsic, or reflected?" Her response—"character is in fact often produced by interactions *between* people, by perception and performance"(20)—is curiously in accord with the conclusion to Kazuo Ishiguro's *Klara and the Sun*, published more recently still. There a nonhuman character, an "AF" or "artificial friend," expresses one of literature's most disarming, or most cloying (which of two it is depends upon your reading character in reading) expressions of intersubjectivity:

Mr Capaldi believed there was nothing special inside Josie that couldn't be continued. He told the Mother he'd searched and searched and found nothing like that. But I believe now he was searching in the wrong place. There *was* something very special, but it wasn't inside Josie. It was inside those who loved her. (306)

The relationality to character is clearly something that is very much a concern of our times. Mario Aquilina speaks persuasively about this in his introduction to *The Edinburgh Companion to the Essay*. He demonstrates a resetting of focus even within study of the genre of the essay, traditionally so invested in "individual thought and personality," to take in instead how the essayist's "consciousness . . . is always more than single and always more than mine."

But back to Garber: interestingly, possibly tellingly too in this book by a significant Shakespearean, not that much more is said about Hamlet. Contrastingly, John Frow's *Character and Person*, published six years earlier and described by Moi as "the most monumental recent attempt to theorize characters" (29), is full of references to Hamlet. Then again, Anderson, Felski, and Moi's book is not, not quite. Felski's *Hooked*, about identification in literature, is not, either. O brave new world, that has no Hamlet in it.

Post-Hamletic. That's us. Maybe.

VI

I exaggerate, of course. So let me change tone.

The title of my chapter echoes the 1989 collection of essays edited by Lindsay Waters and Wlad Godzich, *Reading de Man Reading*. Paul de Man's centrality to literary theory hardly needs remarking. He is the very embodiment of rigorous reading, uncovering how critical blindness and critical insight interrelate. Yet his legacy is forever marked by the consequence of the discovery in 1987, by Ortwin de Graef, of his wartime writings with a distinct anti-Semitic turn. The historical and situational ironies have been amply commented. Here is a theorist whose criticism was successful in checking character's propensities for whatever it is that character in reading does, now being discussed for the soundness of his character. Geoffrey Hartman, in the first essay in *Reading de Man Reading*, points to the further irony that "In *Allegories of Reading*, [de Man] proposes that autobiography . . . is built on self-accusations that allow the writer to write, that is, to excuse himself . . . It is as if de Man . . . feared that writing would always be implicated in such an effort of exculpation" (22). Hartman's essay thereby itself becomes a reflection on reading character in reading. "It also seems appropriate to have those who were close to the Yale critics tell us what they know of his character," he suggests, after observing that "To fall . . . into a pattern of either/or, of denunciation or defense, is a trap that shows the poverty of our speech when it comes to moral statement" (23). It need hardly be said that reading this with the character of our own times in mind is a curious exercise. To re-engage the disposition—"De Man's critique of every tendency to totalize literature or language, to see unity where this is no unity, could be a belated, but still powerful, act of conscience"(23)—is to re-encounter the stamp and character of a different critical time.

Rereading character in rereading is inevitable.

VII

There is no escaping pronouns.

"One" is no pronoun for discussing character: it is too evasive, surely. The definitiveness of the other options seems so much more apt. Writing of *Les Liaisons Dangereuses*, Frow remarks that "we," as readers, "occupy every pronoun in the novel, and possess a knowledge that belongs to none and transcends each of them" (67). But this is only one instance of sustained interest, across his book, in how "Name and pronoun are inscriptions and identifications of personhood or quasi-personhood in language." (228). They are essential, clearly, for the relation of, to, character.

It is curious, therefore, that Nancy writes:

> [T]he *subject*—the property of the self—is the thought that reabsorbs or exhausts all possibility of *being in the world* (all possibility of existence, all existence as being delivered to the possible), *and* that this same thought, never simple, never closed upon itself without remainder, designates and delivers an entirely different thought: that of the *one* and that of the some *one*, of the singular existent that the subject announces, promises, and at the same time conceals.

Referring then to his title, he notes: "This is what I tried to indicate with the verb 'comes,' and with the pronoun 'who?': With which 'one' have we henceforth to-deal?"(5) It was left to Blanchot, in his essay to the collection which he titled, simply, "Who?", to point out the curiosity in the choice of the relative pronoun. For what if the subject should be followed by a "what," not a "who"?

Reading that passage in the context of posthumanist discourse and its predilection for nonhuman characters, the question of the "what" and the inescapability of the pronominal seems more trenchant than ever. Felski notes, rightly and reasonably: "Characters do not have to be deep, well-rounded, psychologically complex, or unified to count as characters; nor, of course, do they need to be human. They need only to be *animated*; to act and react, to will and intend" (78; emphasis in the original). Except literature will have in reserve at least one test case for the most right and reasonable assertion: in this case, possibly Tibor Fischer's *The Collector Collector*, a novel in which the narrator is inanimate, or should be, since it is a 5,000-year old Sumerian bowl. Even there, though, the pronominal is inescapable. Nonhuman characters, even if inanimate, will always be given that much anthropomorphism and anthropocentrism.

It is in the fate and character of the times—a mark of the post-theoretical and the temper and character of its self-analysis—to worry for the non-anthropocentric without being able to cast off, for all of that awareness, the character of the anthropomorphic.

VIII

Eliot, in "The Perfect Critic," deplored impressionistic reading and "the pernicious effects of emotion" (13). The theory of poetry ought to be impersonal, the character of reading depersonalised. One learns all this early, relearns it across the theoretical humanities. That is one aspect of the *bildungsroman* of the undergraduate at the start of this chapter. But reading character in reading and the beguilements of identification will not be easily checked—or unlearned. Nor will rereading oneself, rechecking oneself doing so. The receding and resurgence of the idea of character in literary criticism is part of this dynamic. "I have . . . been pained, even when I have been exhilarated, by the mounting impulse to discount the human element in literature," writes Baruch Hochman in *Character in Literature* in 1985. It is possible to sympathize with that line while taking on the (post)structuralist perspectives it also feels cogent to uphold. By the end, Hochman was arguing, "It is not only that . . . we seem 'naturally' to envision and extrapolate characters from texts, but that we *should* do so if we are to apprehend those texts in the richest way possible." Anderson's, Moi's, and Felski's "inquiries" are all, in their different ways, conceding that there is point to this even as they problematize it. They allow for all of theory's perspectives on subjectivity while understanding that, though not named as such, post-theory may also coincide with this resurgence of critical interest in the way in which attachment to reading character works, as studied further by Felski in *Hooked*. They help reframe the character of criticism by refocusing attention on the criticism of character.

In so doing, they follow in the wake of Frow, dispelling discomfiture around critical talk on character. "What kind of things are literary characters," asks Frow in *Character and Person*, referring to that questioning as "this most inadequately theorized of literary concepts" (vi). Dissatisfaction within literary criticism with that inadequacy is, perhaps, the sign that character's time has really come again. If so, it would be important to characterize the character of that coming, in simultaneous portrayal of the post-theoretical moment in this aspect. Considerations of space mean that this chapter is not the context in which to do so. It has had to suffice merely to suggest that there is renewed credibility in critical chatter around character, that there is more of that "kind of criticism requir[ing] a more forthright and noncynical acknowledgement of our profound interest in character as we read" (Anderson 166).

Nevertheless, quick observations can be attempted. Frow's question is not a new one, of course, as he is at pains to demonstrate. But it is notable that it is ideas of personhood that he more prominently positions alongside character in his study, not subjectivity. Moreover, it is reading that actuates the connection:

> [This] is, above all, a book about reading: about the kinds of knowledge and emotional investment that you need to do it well, and about the centrality of fictional character— and by extension, of social models of personhood—to reading of almost any kind. (xi)

It would be facile to suggest on the strength of all the above that the answer to the question, "Who Comes after the Subject?," is "Character, again." But it would be careless not to note that character never went away anyway, even in the heady days of theory (narratology ensured that retention, though its aliases and schemata for character may have deadened the effect), or to disregard the signs that it has been coming "back" strongly for some time (for instance, since Shauna Deidre Lynch's *The Economy of Character*, in 1998). Whether it does so with a vengeance (to "come after" has that meaning too) would be a further fine question.

IX

In conclusion, three final points.

The first is to sound a note of caution. The late Jean-Luc Nancy, in his introduction to *Who Comes after the Subject?*, warned thirty years ago against trying to read the character of the time. "It is very likely that no one 'philosophy'—if something like this still exists, and is not merely something shelved in our libraries—is able to grasp this situation, nor to think it through. It is very likely that there is no 'Weltanschauung' for it. 'Weltanschauungen' belong to the epoch when the world had not become the world, world-wide" (1). It is tempting to be discerning trends, something "in the air." But in these times of intensified complexity, of inscrutable infinities of signs, it is impossibly hard to read their character and orientations. It would be ironic indeed, therefore, to think it might be possible to read with any confidence or certainty the character of criticism around character, or to characterize the present or impending time around that theme. Some apparent currents can be sensed and can be reported on. But it is all that can be assayed.

The second point is that we would be out of character with our times if we neglected the import of a remark by Frow: "[C]haracter is specific to the genres in which it is formed" (ix). This is truer than ever in the context of new media. It is significant that Frow's book breaks with earlier (and later) studies of literary character to devote non-tokenistic attention to digital games and game studies. The specificity of games' contribution to character studies, opening onto considerations of player-characters (Vella 2016) and on the reconsideration of agency, immersivity, and the particular ontologies and aesthetics therein (Calleja 2011; Nguyen 2020), prompts the thought that a feature of post-theory must surely be the normalization of that reference.

The third point arises from the currency of the world-wide being overtaken by the futurity of the metaverse. The possibility of the metaverse (online, virtual, hyperconnecting, reality-augmenting), something like which has been amply predictable for a long time, cannot but reframe discussion of character. That will be the case even if the actuality falls short of what is potentiated there. Meanwhile, there are many things for which Facebook could be berated, but to some critical sensibilities its move on the metaverse, signalled through its rebranding to Meta, will not in and of itself be as bad as the fact of that exercise forever spoiling a perfectly good prefix. Then again: as readers, we were already in metafiction; as scholars, already all too meta. So in reality: as you were then, as we were then—virtually. This merely extends the subject matter, the matter of the subject. All that's needed is to stay, read, in character.

Or perhaps not. Not (in) character, not again, not post-theoretically.

REFERENCE LIST

Allott, Miriam. *Novelists on the Novel.* Routledge and Kegan Paul, 1959.

Anderson, Amanda. "Thinking with Character." *Character: Three Inquiries in Literary Studies*, by Amanda Anderson, Rita Felski, and Toril Moi. Chicago: University of Chicago Press, 2019. pp. 127–70.

Aquilina, Mario. "Affinities and Contestations: The Self and the Other in the Essay." *The Edinburgh Companion to the Essay*, edited by Mario Aquilina, Bob Cowser, and Nicole B. Wallack. Edinburgh University Press, forthcoming.

Belsey, Catherine. *Critical Practice.* Methuen, 1980.

Berkoff, Steven. *I Am Hamlet.* Faber and Faber, 1989.

Blanchot, Maurice. "Who?" *Who Comes after the Subject?*, edited by Eduardo Cadava, Jean-Peter Connor, and Jean-Luc Nancy. Routledge, 1991. pp. 58–60.

Bloom, Harold. *Shakespeare: The Invention of the Human.* Fourth Estate, 1999.

Burke, Sean. *The Death and Return of the Author: Criticism and Subjectivity in Barthes, Foucault and Derrida*, third edn. Edinburgh University Press, 2008.

Cadava, Eduardo, and Peter Connor. "Preface." *Who Comes after the Subject?*, edited by Eduardo Cadava, Jean-Peter Connor, Jean-Luc Nancy. Routledge, 1991. n.pag.

Calleja, Gordon. *In-Game: From Immersion to Incorporation.* MIT Press, 2011.

Callus, Ivan, and Stefan Herbrechter. *Post-Theory, Culture, Criticism.* Rodopi, 2004.

Culler, Jonathan. *Structuralist Poetics: Structuralism, Linguistics and the Study of Literature.* Routledge and Kegan Paul, 1975.

Derrida, Jacques. *Specters of Marx: The State of the Debt, the Work of Mourning and the New International*, trans. Peggy Kamuf. Routledge, 1994.

Eliot, T. S. "The Perfect Critic." *The Sacred Wood*, 7th edn. Routledge, 1960. pp. 1–16.

Felski, Rita. *Hooked: Art and Attachment.* Chicago University Press, 2020.

Felski, Rita. "Identifying with Characters." *Character: Three Inquiries in Literary Studies*, by Amanda Anderson, Rita Felski, and Toril Moi. Chicago: University of Chicago Press, 2019. pp. 77–126.

Fischer, Tibor. *The Collector Collector.* Secker & Warburg, 1977.

Frow, John. *Character and Person.* Oxford University Press, 2014.

Garber, Marjorie. *Character: The History of a Cultural Obsession.* Farrar, Straus, and Giroux, 2020.

Greenblatt, Stephen. *Hamlet in Purgatory.* Princeton University Press, 2001.

Hartman, Geoffrey. "Looking Back on Paul de Man." *Reading de Man Reading*, edited by Lindsay Waters and Wlad Godzich. University of Minnesota Press, 1989. pp. 3–24.

Hochman, Baruch. *Character in Literature.* Cornell University Press, 1985.

Ishiguro, Kazuo. *Klara and the Sun.* Faber and Faber, 2021.

James, Henry. "The Art of Fiction." *Literary Criticism, Volume One: Essays on Literature, American Writers, English Writers*. The Library of America, 1984. pp. 44—65.

Knights, L. C. *How Many Children Had Lady Macbeth? An Essay in the Theory and Practice of Shakespeare Criticism*. Haskell House, 1973.

Lawrence, D. H. Letter to Edward Garnett, 5 June 1914.*D. H. Lawrence: The Critical Heritage*, ed. Ronald P. Draper. Routledge, 1997. 86–7.

Lynch, Shauna Deidre. *The Economy of Character: Novels, Market Culture, and the Business of Inner Meaning*. University of Chicago Press, 1998.

Lyotard, Jean-François. *The Postmodern Explained to Children: Correspondence 1982–1985*, trans. Julian E. Pefanis. Turnaround, 1992.

McQuillan, Martin, Robin Purves Graeme Macdonald, and Stephen Thomson. *Post-Theory: New Directions in Criticism*. Edinburgh University Press, 1999.

Moi, Toril. "Rethinking Character." *Character: Three Inquiries in Literary Studies*, by Amanda Anderson, Rita Felski, and Toril Moi. Chicago: University of Chicago Press, 2019, pp. 27-75.

Nancy, Jean-Luc. "Introduction." *Who Comes after the Subject?*, edited by Eduardo Cadava, Jean-Peter Connor, and Jean-Luc Nancy. Routledge, 1991. pp. 1–8.

Ngueyn, C. Thi. *Games: Agency as Art*. Oxford University Press, 2020.

Rapaport, Herman. *Later Derrida: Reading the Recent Work*. Routledge, 2003.

Richards, I. A. *Principles of Literary Criticism*. Kegan Paul, Trench, Trubner, 1924.

Rimmon-Kenan, Shlomith. *Narrative Fiction: Contemporary Poetics*. Methuen, 1983.

Stevens, Wallace. "The House Was Quiet and the World Was Calm." *Wallace Stevens: Collected Poetry and Prose*. The Library of America, 1997. p. 311–2.

Vella, Daniel. "A Structural Model for Player-Characters as Semiotic Constructs." *DIGRA: Transactions of the Digital Games Research Association*, vol. 2, no. 2 (2016) http://todigra.org/index.php/todigra/article/view/37(accessed 12 November 2021).

Waters, Lindsay, and Wlad Godzich, eds. *Reading de Man Reading*. University of Minnesota Press, 1989. pp. 3—24.

Weinsheimer, Joel. "Theory of Character: *Emma.*" *Poetry Today*, vol. 1 No. 1/2, 1979, pp. 185–211.

Wimsatt Jr, W. K,, and M. C. Beardsley. "The Affective Fallacy." *The Sewanee Review*, vol. 57, no. 1, 1949, pp. 31–55.

———. "The Intentional Fallacy."*The Sewanee Review*, vol. 54, no. 3, 1946, pp. 468–88.

Wolf, Werner. "Aesthetic Illusion as an Effect of Fiction." *Style*,vol. 38, no. 3, 2004, pp. 325–350.

13

The Affective Politics of the Twenty-First Century Novel

Selen Aktari-Sevgi

In their "Introduction" to *The Routledge Companion to Twenty-First Century Fiction*, Daniel O'Gorman and Robert Eaglestone admit that an attempt to outline the fictional trends of the present time, "*as it is taking place*" (original emphasis, 1), is challenging when it is very well-known that the critical discussions presented in their project will either evolve or lose their critical importance and vanish completely in time. By referring to Giorgio Agamben's influential essay "What's the Contemporary?," they explain one's paradoxical relationship with the contemporary: "Contemporariness is . . . a singular relationship with one's own time, which adheres to it and at the same time, keeps a distance from it" (O'Gorman and Eaglestone 1; Agamben 41). Therefore, the experience of/in the contemporary, one of liminality, particularly because the contemporary, "as a periodizing category . . . can be untimely" (2).

In a similar vein, Peter Boxall also states that "contemporary is always unavailable to us" since we are inhabiting the present shaped "by a specifically twenty-first century speed" (3). With the "invention of communication at the speed of light" (4), our experience with the contemporary has become "an extended instantaneity, an infinity without duration" (5). This is why, he contends, he cannot offer a "stable new critical paradigm, a common nomenclature or critical vocabulary within which we might accommodate the new novel" (17). In this respect, Boxall aims to express rather than explain the dynamics of contemporary fiction. He announces: "It is the opening up of these fracture lines in the present that I set out here to trace in the fiction of our century, the discovery of forms of freedom, forms of transformation, that are only now coming to a fragile novelistic expression, and that cannot be easily accommodated within any critical paradigm, or any existing idea of the world" (18). What Boxall underlines here is the "newness" of this new literary period, which cannot be pinned down yet due to the closeness and, paradoxically, the distance one feels toward his own historical period. He attempts to make his readers familiar with "a certain kind of novel thinking, a kind of literary thinking, that does not belong fully to the present, does not conform to any existing school of thought, but that opens the present up along its 'lines of fragility'" (18).

Since one's relationship to the contemporary is one of being familiar with one's historical, political, social, and cultural period as well as being estranged from it, in-betweenness characterizes the contemporary experience. Arpad Szakolczai states that "free market economy, political democracy and technological change . . . do not seem to offer any kind of stability" (32). In this respect, in Szakolczai's opinion, contemporary times are one of permanent liminality. "Modernity, or the combination of market economy, liberal democratic polity and a society driven by technological progress, we are led to believe, is the end-state of history; the glorious condition of a fully enlightened society of free citizens equipped with equal rights at which all traditional societies are bound to arrive, after a period of transition which might involve some temporary difficulties or 'sacrifices'" (46). However, modernity has turned into an "infinite period of transition" (46). According to Szakolczai, the traditions, which have served the dominant ideology and, thus, have oppressed people, but which also offer "meaningful life" are liquidated, in Zygmunt Bauman's terms, and since new structures are not built, society has remained in permanent liminality. While such a structureless state is regarded as "the blissful ideal state," it is also a void, a realm of the absurd that has become one's reality (47). For Szakolczai, permanent liminality is a trap and "the really urgent task of *thinking* is the retrieval, recovery, reconstruction of traditions—in terms of ecological harmony, human crafts, and sustainable forms of human co-existence, among many other things" (original emphasis, 46-7). Contemporary fiction reflects these concerns discussed above. Permanent liminality might be an alternative state of resisting oppressive neoliberal structures or, ironically, an ideological apparatus of neoliberal capitalism that allows structures to be destroyed because it knows it cannot be replaced by any alternatives. Mark Fisher's definition of capitalist realism (neoliberalism) explains this vicious circle as follows: Capitalist realism is "the widespread sense that not only is capitalism the only viable political and economic system, but also that it is now impossible even to *imagine* a coherent alternative to it" (original emphasis, 2). Twenty-first century fiction shows an aspiration to revive and reconstruct the individual's communal bonds with its others and to evoke an ethical responsibility for the world we inhabit by dealing with political, social, cultural matters, and as well as ecological problems, for the extinction of species and climate change, for people in need, and to develop sympathy for one another, disregarding our differences in terms of class, gender, ethnic, national, and religious identities particularly by employing mimetic forms such as trauma and disability narratives, memoirs, autofiction, diary, journal, and documentary forms.

The literature of the present moment displays an attempt to divert from the established paradigms that have defined what postmodernist writing is. Recent theoretical debates on contemporary fiction define the transitional literary period we are in as the age of authenticity and draw attention to a new kind of realism emerging in the novel, which indicates a shift from sceptical cynicism to sincerity and ethics, and from a linguistic turn to an affective one. Such observations mark a new phase, starting roughly around the 1990s, which is often termed as post-postmodernism. While such a coinage emphasizes the post-ness of postmodernism and implies an attempt to move beyond it, the term also insists on an ongoing interaction with postmodernism through reassessing its methods and conceptions, and reveals a potentiality which no longer acclaims the oppositional positioning of postmodernist and realist aesthetics. By "deemphasiz[ing] the self-referentiality in their fiction . . . yet still insist[ing] on the indeterminacy of reality" (McLaughlin 289), contemporary writers adopt a reconstructive approach rather than a deconstructive one to reassert the "possibility of meaningful intersubjective communication based on a notion of referentiality" (Huber 28). Such communication is performed by the transmission of affects, asignifying intensive states of the material body that circulate across individuals and communities, and their emotional codification in the cognitive world. Affects can be briefly defined as liminal somatic experiences that resolve the boundaries of the subject and provide possibilities of connections and interactions with others. As bodies communicate with other bodies and forms, including inorganic objects, non-human organisms, and technologies, they change through affective contacts. In this respect, affect is endowed with political potential.

The critical studies on twenty-first century fiction frequently refer to David Foster Wallace's "E Unibus Pluram: Television and U.S. Fiction" (1993) to map the beginnings of a new formation of literary, cultural, and critical production at the end of the twentieth century. In his essay, Wallace declares that the rebellious, anarchic, and liberating power of postmodern irony became attenuate in the 1990s: "[Irony]'s critical and destructive, a ground-clearing. Surely this is the way our postmodern fathers saw it. But irony's singularly unuseful when it comes to constructing anything to replace the hypocrisies it debunks" (183). Wallace draws attention to the fact that "persistent irony," emptied of its radical potential, has become "tiresome" (183) and turned into a pop-cultural tool. Therefore, it cannot offer new alternatives for the institutions it criticizes anymore. In such a literary and cultural atmosphere, he foresees a new generation of writers, "the next real literary rebels" emerging out of "anti-rebels," who overcome the ironic distance with sincerity, defend "single-entendre values" and risk "[a]ccusations of sentimentality, melodrama. Credulity" (192–3). Wallace's assumptions, presented in the early 1990s, "1.) the fiction writer can become reactionary and turn to conservatism . . . 2.) the fiction writer can risk being deemed 'sentimental'" (Eve 42), are still the main concerns that are voiced in the theoretical debates on contemporary fiction.

In light of Wallace's arguments, Adam Kelly calls this new cultural movement in contemporary American writers' fiction "The New Sincerity." By drawing on Lionel Trilling's definition of sincerity, "a congruence between avowal and actual feeling" (Trilling 2; Kelly 199), Kelly explains what he means by the "old sincerity" as follows: "[t]ruth to one's own self should be conceived of not as an *end*, but as a *means* of ensuring truth to others" (original emphasis, 199). However, the development of modernism in the twentieth century turned the focus on the representation of objective reality by realistic aesthetics to the representation of subjective reality by experimental aesthetics. Thus, sincerity had been "superseded by the ideal of authenticity, which conceives truth to the self as an end and not simply as a means" (199), and finally regarded as a fallacy by the New Critics' formalistic approaches to authorial intention. In the second half of the twentieth century, postmodernism did not differentiate between sincerity and authenticity when it treated them as linguistic constructs. Both public and inner life, truth and reality, became fiction.

The New Sincerity is "new" because it points out a blending of a sense of sincerity with the self-conscious emphasis on the artistic process. Contemporary authors employ shared experiences as their subject matter, attempt to construct a "sincere communication" between the reader and the writer (Kelly 200) by avoiding the disaffected postmodern irony, and endorse "authenticity . . . with . . . constructive moral engagement and the recovery of language's referential function" (Savvas and Coffman 195). Pursuing sincerity and authenticity in terms of form and content suggests a possibility to return to the realist aesthetics as a reaction to postmodern playfulness. Thus, in brief, it can be claimed that three main strands are observed in contemporary fiction: sincerity, associated with the literary work's tone and representation of truth; authenticity, associated with the revival of the author's authority on the text, representation of authentic experiences, and authentic formal strategies; and realism, associated with the nostalgic practice of nineteenth-century social realism and the return of the humanist subject. The New Sincerity movement in contemporary fiction deploys these premodernist characteristics with a postmodern spirit by exposing the narrative construction and using self-reflexive methods to draw attention to the aesthetic peculiarities of the novel. Although the characteristics listed seem to be completely distinct from the postmodern agenda, they are still informed with deconstructive practices that remind us of the discursive construction of these concepts. As Imtraud Huber declares, "The new kind of realism does not revoke postmodernist claims about the power of discourse and the inaccessibility of the real, about the fragmentation of the subject and the impossibility of truth. Instead, it acknowledges them even while it asserts itself in spite of them" (6).

O'Gorman and Eaglestone note that various terms, "altermodernism, hypermodernism, supermodernism, hysterical realism, digimodernism, The New Sincerity and metamodernism," are used to describe this new literary period by the scholars and "[o]f these, the last two have held most sway in literary studies, though by no means uncontroversially so" (3). Metamodernism, very much like The New Sincerity, also "identifies at the heart of contemporary culture a persistent fluctuation between irony and sincerity, emphasizing a dissolution in the boundary between the two" (O'Gorman and Eaglestone 3). Being a liminal term, it "oscillates between what we may call—but what of course cannot be reduced to—postmodern and pre-modern (and often modern) predilections: between irony and enthusiasm, between sarcasm and sincerity, between eclecticism and purity, between deconstruction and construction and so forth" (van den Akker and Vermeulen 11). As is observed in these attempts to describe the features of the new literary period, twenty-first century fiction is mostly regarded as a period of reconciliation between realistic and experimental practices that induce "a sense of earnestness and hope" (van den Akker and Vermeulen 27). The changes that poststructuralism has brought into literature and culture can never be ignored. As Mary K. Holland says, "[l]iterature today remains postmodern in its assumptions about the culture and world from which it arises, and remains poststructural in its assumptions about the arbitrariness and problems of language, and yet still uses this postmodernism and poststructuralism to humanist ends of generating empathy, communal bonds, ethical and political questions, and, most basically, communicable meaning." (17). Thus, contemporary fiction is "born out of a paradox" (Greenwald Smith, "Introduction" 4). It blends the deconstructive, revolutionary, and subversive ideas, and narrative techniques that the linguistic turn has brought with the communicative, authentic, sincere attitude and storytelling that the affective turn has evoked. Thus, post-postmodern fiction is liminal in terms of form as well as content. There are two main central subjects that the discussions on the post-postmodern novel are built on: tone, which is aimed to be sincere, warm, and authentic, and form, which is aimed to be a personal—memoir, life, and trauma narratives to capture a realistic mode. However, as is discussed further below, these narratives are considered as neoliberalist literary products by certain critics due to their emphasis on the individual.

Post-postmodernist literature has evolved under the impact of the 9/11 attacks and the rise of fundamentalism in its aftermath, the War on Terror, neoliberal capitalism and consumer culture, global financial crisis and recession, technological developments, electronic communication, digitalization of experience, social media, climate change, and extinction movement. These economic, social, technological, political, and ecological developments are also the reasons why contemporary writers have searched for new ways of expression and narrative strategies imbued with a desire for realism, feeling, and "the restoration of a humanist subject to the core of the novel" (Greenwald Smith, "Postmodernism" 425) in the face of traumatic lived experience. In this respect, the theories of affect, although varying considerably in their critical approaches and theoretical arguments, respond to the need for mapping and moulding the traits of post-postmodernist fiction and are used to identify the differences between and common features of postmodernism, which, in Fredric Jameson's words, displays a "waning of affect" (10) and post-postmodernism, which is considered to be affective in form and content.

The relation between experience and representation is defined in linguistic terms in postmodernism and affective terms in post-postmodernism. Authenticity, sincerity, empathy, belief, ethics, and ethical responsibility, connecting and communicating with others, which are the common concerns of twenty-first-century fiction, call for affect and form. Since affects belong to the corporeal life and turn into recognizable and accessible commonly felt emotions after they reach the cognitive level by the accumulation of past experiences and spontaneous contacts with others in their environments, contemporary authors rely on invoking and circulating these affects in their literary works to make the reader emotionally engaged with their works.

Rachel Greenwald Smith defines this inclination to represent emotions and to demand emotional responses in the twenty-first century novel as "the affective hypothesis," which is "the belief that literature is at its most meaningful when it represents and transmits the emotional specificity of personal experience" (*Affect and American Literature* 1). Greenwald Smith is sceptical about the political potential of the affective hypothesis because she thinks it serves neoliberal capitalist culture rather than rebelling against it. By explaining social structures in terms of economic profit, monetizing every aspect of life by its ideological interpellation, reinforcing and enforcing individualization, associating freedom of the subject with freedom of personal choice in consuming process, marketing the notion of every individual responsible for itself in a competitive system based on the perception of human as capital, and privatizing the public, neoliberalist ideology is against communal and collective living. What it demands from the subject is conformity to its hegemony. Greenwald Smith claims that neoliberalism and the affective hypothesis share the same ideologies and reinforce one another because they both revolve around the individual.

> These subjective aspects of neoliberalism coincide startlingly with the assumptions underlying the affective hypothesis. While neoliberalism casts the individual as responsible for herself, the affective hypothesis casts feeling as necessarily owned and managed by individual authors, characters, and readers. Neoliberalism imagines the individual as an entrepreneur; the affective hypothesis imagines the act of reading as an opportunity for emotional investment and return. The neoliberal subject is envisioned as needing to be at all times strategically networking; feelings, according to the affective hypothesis, are indexes of emotional alliances. (*Affect and American Literature* 2)

Greenwald Smith's critical studies on the relation between the contemporary affective novel and neoliberal culture argue against the personal-affective literary production and personal-affective ways of reading, which, she thinks, aestheticize neoliberal investment in emotions and the personal, and alternatively, she promotes "disaffectedness" or a focus on "impersonal feelings" as a method of subversion. She criticizes the critical studies that embrace the affective hypothesis to advocate that "postmodern literature is characterized by an absence of tonal warmth and that the absence of tonal warmth in a given work signals an absence of affective charge inherent to the work" ("Postmodernism" 423). In addition, she disagrees with the notion that postmodern aesthetics, composed of "metafictional strategies, scepticism toward subjective consistency, and deferral of narrative closure," are perceived as "obstructing affective transmission" (424). She claims that it is in this disaffectedness the political alternatives to the oppressive dominant ideologies lie. In this line of thought, post-postmodernist literature, in response, is regarded to have this tonal warmth, sincerity, as Wallace has already announced, and he celebrates a revival of realism and "with it a renewed commitment to representing the emotional lives of real people" (424). This tonal warmth allies with the concept of psychological depth and desire mechanisms in the portrayal of characters. Therefore, as Greenwald Smith holds, this depth-model de-politicizes the individual by treating it as a psychoanalytical subject and cannot provide a critique of the existing political and social structures. "Impersonal feelings" that emerge from the mobile interaction of unnamed affects that always already exist outside the subject and persist themselves in contact with the others, human and non-human forms can move beyond subjectivity and reach a social level to offer transformation. Since "impersonal feelings" rely on the "unpredictability of affective connections" (Greenwald Smith, *Affect and American Literature* 2), they are not easily noticed as common forms of feelings, and therefore cannot be identified with. This is why they undermine the traditional liberal humanist subjectivity and demonstrate a relationship with the larger social, cultural, and political structures. According to Greenwald Smith, "impersonal feelings" are more valuable since they function at a collective level.

Pieter Vermeulen supports Greenwald Smith's critical stance to the affective novel. In *Contemporary Literature and the End of the Novel*, he also suggests that the novel form traditionally promises its readers identification through depicting the characters' inner world and portray the resonances of their experiences on the societal level. This process is based on the meaningful communication of emotions. However, "disaffected" twenty-first century novels, which do not portray the inner world of the protagonist, any character development or transformation, events and experiences that have a meaningful register on the character and the reader, have the potential for "imagining life and affect differently" (6). Such novels "sabotage the genre's cultural power, while at the same time make room for affective registers that cannot so easily be codified through desire and identification . . . [T]hey activate generic expectations only to frustrate them" (7). This is how impersonal feelings emerge in the contemporary novel. The formal characteristics of a novel, which unravel the ties between the individual and emotions, open up an affective space where impersonal feelings can circulate. By disrupting generic codes and readers' expectations, a disturbing, dissociated, and disoriented atmosphere is formed. This is where the transformative power of affects start to function.

Vermeulen draws attention to the difficulty of specifying such impersonal feelings or disaffectedness and the transformation they bring into the narratives because the affects resist recognizable emotional codifications and meaningful change. Defining them as "dysphoric, awkward, and uneasy, and at other times excessive, even farcical," Vermeulen perceives such narratives as "communicat[ing] both a sense of powerlessness and an opportunity for novel combinations, connections, and assemblages to emerge" (11). After this critical discussion, he proposes his own approach to affect's literary usage in the twenty-first century: "Affect . . . serves . . . for *formal operations that aim to undo emotional codification*" (original emphasis, 11).

In "Neoliberalism and the (Im)possibility of the Affective Novel," Jason Goldfarb argues that there are two opposite positions, capitulationist and subversionist groups of critics, who interpret the relation between affect and the contemporary novel as either reinforcing or attacking neoliberal culture. Capitulationists, like Greenwald Smith, perceive formal techniques in contemporary fiction, which aim to build emotional connections, as a strategy of neoliberal capitalism that commodifies literature and intellectual pursuits. By portraying the personal experiences by personal narrative forms such as memoir, autofiction, diary form, and trauma narratives, these "personal-affective" novels are considered to be lacking a radically subversive potential and evading attacking larger oppressive structures. On the other hand, subversionists see "personal-affective" fiction as the critique of neoliberal entrepreneurial individualism, which separates people from one another by entrapping them in the competitive capitalist system, thus preventing them from pursuing collective ideals. Greenwald Smith's contribution to the field is very crucial in this respect because, as Goldfarb stresses, she "has a foot in both camps" (6). She agrees with the capitulationists because she thinks that the "personal-affective" novel written in the forms of memoir and trauma narratives cannot rebel against the neoliberal culture. On the other hand, she stands with the subversionists because "impersonal-affective" novels, deprived of the tonal warmth and preventing identification, work toward subversion. They are cold and distant, and they produce an estrangement effect so that the novel can touch upon social matters rather than personal ones. Vermeulen's approach to the affective novel is also like Greenwald Smith's, a blend of capitulationist and subversionist views.

Goldfarb declares that "each view is ultimately one-sided: capitulationists fail to see how the social mediates the personal, thus missing the possibility of self-critical affective novels; the subversion view fails to see how the social is caught up in the personal and neoliberal, thus missing the capitulatory aspect of so-called 'impersonal' affect" (1). He concludes that "the affective novel" is "antagonistically situated" between these two opposite critical camps (1). As Goldfarb reveals, the subversionists associate the affective form with the personal and ignore how affects are interpreted, constructed, and socialized within the framework of the dominant ideology. Besides, since affects ceaselessly circulate, move across the individuals and communities, resist form and definition, and remain in the form of becoming, they lay bare how the dominant ideology works to control these affects to make them perform neoliberalist policies. However, from the point of view presented below, personal is always social and political. Therefore, affect, by moving through the individual, already revolts against the neoliberal entrepreneurial subject.

> [I]n demonstrating the irreducibly socio-political nature of affect (to the extent that even something as private as one's inner feelings may be read as collectively constituted), one subverts the atomized neoliberal subject and the ideology of so-called 'responsibilization', the transfer of responsibility from higher authorities to particular groups or individuals. The personal, with this in mind, is re-read as always-already social. Affect, properly conceived in its systemic and social dimension, works against—rather than with—neoliberal individualization. (Goldfarb 7)

Like Goldfarb sees affective novel as an in-between liminal form by positioning it antagonistically between capitulationists and subversionists camps, Ralph Clare, in "Metaffective Fiction: Structuring Feeling in Postpostmodern American Literature," also posits a middle ground for these positions. He implies he does not perceive post-postmodern return to affect as neoliberal capitulation. He suggests that post-postmodernism does not rely on affect only, but also it lays bare its limitations and its construction. Drawing on Patricia Waugh's widely known definition of metafiction, he offers a term, "metaffective fiction": "[M]etaffective fiction is that fiction that self-consciously calls attention to the way in which emotion and affect are represented in order to interrogate the relationship between them" (266). He notes that this can happen in many ways; metaffective fiction may expose the process of construction of emotion and character; it may form an interactive and affective relationship with the reader by estranging or appealing to her; it may represent emotions in excess so that emotions overshadow the characters and become the tone of the text; it may highlight the materiality of texts as "embodied" experiences through formal constructions; it may present an affect-in-excess so that it cannot be represented or signified in linguistic terms. Metaffective fiction posits an awareness of affect as well as textuality and also transmits affect's potentiality. He adds that metaffective fiction may move beyond "shallow representations of emotions" (266). In parallel with Greenwald Smith's and Vermeulen's arguments, Clare states that affect may establish sincerity and connection only to deprive the reader of these warm feelings or become cold and impersonal rather than establish a mediocre tone right from the start. It may present affective states or impersonal feelings that cannot be sold by the neoliberal market.

> [F]or metaffective fictions seek, though not always successfully, to renew the potential of affect in a neoliberal age that is increasingly commodifying affective labour, leisure, and our everyday emotional lives. Metaffective fictions comprise a literature that has arisen within and in response to neoliberalism and its affective economics. Metaffective fiction, does not involve emotion recollected in tranquillity, but affect reconstructed in adversity. (266)

Clare also refers to Vermeulen's arguments that expose no matter how hegemony tries to control affect, affect always exceeds these efforts. Metaffective fictions produce new literary forms, new potential affects, new affective relationships, and new subjectivities. It is inevitable for the affective novel to not draw attention to its affectivity in a neoliberal culture where efforts are commodified.

As the discussion above reveals, the critical approaches that define affect as personal or impersonal, individual or social, particular or universal, subjective or collective, and capitulating or subverting neoliberal policies indicate that the affective novel of post-postmodernism is politically controversial in its reception. The reason for this controversy stems from the different definitions of and approaches to the affect in philosophical, theoretical, and literary fields. Another important reason is like the concept of affect itself, the post-postmodern novel is in the form of becoming; it is open-ended. As Vermeulen holds, "the affective work of contemporary fiction does not so much point to the need for a more global *scope* in addressing current ethical and political challenges, but rather to the need to imagine a radically different *scale*" (original emphasis, 16). It attempts to conceptualize a political, ethical, and material subjectivity, different forms of narrativity and strategies of reforming genre norms that express such subjectivity. Still, its ideological commitments have not been determined yet. It offers possibilities rather than a set of conventions. The politics of the post-postmodern novel lies in the transformative potential of the affects, which cannot be identified at the cognitive level yet, and therefore cannot attain the form of recognizable emotions. When these affects find their place in the psychosocial life, new kind of emotions will be defined out of them. These new emotions, derived from object-oriented ontology, will set the post-postmodern novel's political agenda to challenge neoliberal capitalism.

REFERENCE LIST

Agamben, Giorgio. *What Is an Apparatus? and Other Essays*. Translated by David Kishik and Stefan Pedatella, Stanford UP, 2009.

Boxall, Peter. *Twenty-First-Century Fiction: A Critical Introduction*. Cambridge UP, 2013.

Clare, Ralph. "Metaffective Fiction: Structuring Feeling in Postpostmodern American Literature." *Textual Practice*, vol.33, no: 2, 2019, pp. 263–279. *Taylor & Francis Online*, https://doi.org/10.1080/0950236X.2018.1509269.

Eve, Martin Paul. "Sincerity." *The Routledge Companion to Twenty-First-Century Literary Fiction*, edited by Daniel O'Gorman and Robert Eaglestone, Routledge, 2019, pp. 36–47.

Fisher, Mark. *Capitalist Realism: Is There No Alternative?* Zero Books, 2009.

Goldfarb, Jason. "Neoliberalism and the (Im)possibility of the Affective Novel." *Textual Practice*, Ahead-of-Print, 2021, pp.1–18. *Taylor & Francis Online*, https://doi.org/10.1080/0950236X.2021.1900368.

Greenwald Smith, Rachel. "Postmodernism and the Affective Turn." *Twentieth-Century Literature* special issue of *Postmodernism, Then*, vol. 57, no.3/4, 2011, pp. 423–446. *JSTOR*, https://www.jstor.org/stable/41698760.

———. *Affect and American Literature in the Age of Neoliberalism*. Cambridge UP, 2015.

———. "Introduction." *American Literature in Transition: 2000–2010*, edited by Rachel Greenwald Smith, Cambridge UP, 2018, pp. 1–16.

Holland, Mary K. *Succeeding Postmodernism: Language and Humanism in Contemporary American Literature*. Bloomsbury, 2013.

Huber, Irmtraud. *Literature after Postmodernism: Reconstructive Fantasies*. Palgrave Macmillan, 2014.

Kelly, Adam. "The New Sincerity." *Postmodern/Postwar—and After: Rethinking American Literature*, edited by Jason Gladstone et al., University of Iowa Press, 2016, pp. 197–208.

McLaughlin, Robert L. "After the Revolution: US Postmodernism in the Twenty-First Century." *Narrative*, vol. 21, no.3, Oct. 2013, pp. 284–295. *Project MUSE*, doi:10.1353/nar.2013.0021.

O'Gorman, Daniel and Robert Eaglestone. Introduction. *The Routledge Companion to Twenty-First-Century Literary Fiction*, edited by Daniel O'Gorman and Robert Eaglestone, Routledge, 2019, pp. 1–10.

Savvas, Theophilus and Christopher K. Coffman. "American Fiction after Postmodernism," *Textual Practice*, vol.33, no:2, pp.195–212. *Taylor & Francis Online*, https://doi.org/10.1080/0950236X.2018.1505322.

Szakolczai, Arpad. "Living Permanent Liminality: the Recent Transition Experience in Ireland." *Irish Journal of Sociology*, vol.22, no:1, 2014, pp. 28–50. *SAGE Journals*, https://doi.org/10.7227/IJS.22.1.3.

Trilling, Lionel. *Sincerity and Authenticity*. Oxford UP, 1972.

van den Akker, Robin and Timotheus Vermeulen. "Periodising the 2000s, or, the Emergence of Metamodernism." *Metamodernism: Historicity, Affect and Depth after Postmodernism*, edited by Robin van den Akker et al., Rowman& Littlefield, 2017, pp.1–20.

Vermeulen, Timotheus. *Contemporary Literature and the End of the Novel: Creature, Affect, Form*. Palgrave Macmillan, 2015.

Wallace, David Foster. "E Unibus Pluram: Television and U. S. Fiction." *Review of Contemporary Fiction*, vol.13, no.2, summer 1993, pp.151–193.

14

Post-Postmodernism

Bran Nicol

THE DEMISE OF POSTMODERNISM

In the first decade of the 2000s, amid all the excitement and trepidation brought on by a new century, theorists and critics were keen to declare the end of something they considered was typical of the previous century and superseded by something new: postmodernism. Many of the major voices in the postmodern debate in the late-twentieth century declared postmodernism to be over: Linda Hutcheon in the 2002 edition of her book, *The Politics of Postmodernism*, Ihab Hassan in his essay "Beyond Postmodernism" (2003), Brian HcHale in his 2007 paper "What Was Postmodernism?," and the stellar cast of theorists, from Robert Venturi to Fredric Jameson, who contributed to the 2011 collection *Postmodernism. What Moment?* (Goulimari). Numerous recent studies of contemporary fiction began to be written from the perspective of being after the postmodern, such as *Martin Amis: Postmodernism and Beyond* (Keulks, 2006), *Jonathan Franzen at the End of Postmodernism* (Burn, 2011), and *Ethics and Desire in the Wake of Postmodernism* (Matthews, 2012). As McHale put it, in this decade there was an important "change of tense." The question, "What is postmodernism?," had become, "What was postmodernism?"

Why was this? What are the grounds for the claim that postmodernism was over? The most obvious rationale has a kind of self-fulfilling circular, albeit reasonable, logic to it. Because theorists decided that we are after postmodernism, they no longer used postmodernism as a paradigm to understand society or culture. This meant that the postmodern paradigm had indeed passed, that is, as a framework for cultural analysis. Strictly speaking, postmodernism had never been anything other than a "critical construct," a descriptive term rather than something "in the world" (McHale B., *Constructing Postmodernism*, 1992) (Nicol, 2009).

A second reason for the passing of postmodernism is a variation on this argument about the shift in critical fashion. Critics—literary critics, in particular—became suspicious of the idea of periodisation. Analyzing literature by fitting it into "named periods" (as Fredric Jameson disparagingly describes the superficial postmodern approach to history (Jameson, *The Antinomies of Realism*, 2013, 299), was regarded as imposing a single "big tent" reading on to complex social, cultural, and aesthetic elements. As Ted Underwood has argued in his provocative study, *Why Literary Periods Mattered*, literary studies had always depended on the application of named periods (the Victorian, the Modern, etc.) in order to emphasize discontinuity as a means of sustaining "cultural prestige" for the discipline (Underwood, 2013). Now there was a move away from periodized literary analysis to an approach to period which conceives of it differently—not as a linear construction but, in Susan Stanford Friedman's words, as "multiplicitous and multi-dimensional" (Friedman, 2019).

A third explanation approaches the question from precisely the opposite point of view. There began to be a recognition that postmodernism could no longer be a suitable label for social and cultural analysis because the things that it describes in the world are no longer suitable for the kind of descriptive framework it used. To put it differently, the world has changed in the twenty-first century in ways that postmodernism could not anticipate—or if it did, the changes are so significant that a new paradigm is required to explain them. Most significantly, the development of neo-liberalist capitalism has exceeded what the category of "late capitalism"—the acknowledged context for postmodernism—could encompass. The last decade or so has been marked by a regulation and transnationalisation of finance and political power, a shift from the hegemony of the state to a new or newly visible "global overclass" of transnational conglomerates and individuals. The consequences of neo-liberalism are to do with dissolving borders. The literal mobility that results from developments in travel (or at least were a feature of everyday life before the COVID-19 pandemic in 2020–2021), are paralleled by *"capital sans frontières,"* the situation where information, privacy breach, finance, are all able to have an effect freely across borders with unpredictable results. Related to this is the accelerated puncturing of faith in agreed facts and stable "truths," once established and sustained by a few national broadcasting companies which constituted an "official" shared agreement about reality, but now filtered through multiple social media sources which allow users to filter news voluntarily and to be subject to manipulation as they inhabit a personally tailored information "bubble."

One thing postmodernism did not anticipate was the transformative social and cultural effect of digital technology, especially as a result of the "second internet age," or what was once known as Web 2.0 (a title which now itself seems somehow anachronistic). This began in the early twentieth century and meant that the internet was transformed by user-generated content—a more dynamic, interactive, multi-authored, and continually updating, phenomenon, typified by "microblogging" social media sites such as Facebook and Twitter—and by the fact that the advent of the smartphone made it portable. The novelist Douglas Coupland has characterized the first decades of the twenty-first century as pitching us into "an aura-free universe in which all eras coexist at once—a state of possibly permanent atemporality given to us courtesy of the Internet" (Coupland 24). Ours is a world, he contends, with no dominant "era" because of the advent of the internet, the smartphone, Wikipedia, Google, YouTube, Twitter—all of which have collapsed both temporal and geographical distance.

All this may have been predicted by postmodernism, but the reality far exceeds what it could conceive of. Coupland shows how our attitude to temporality, our uncertainty, complements the academic lack of faith in periodizing principles of analysis. As his insights suggest, all three of these reasons I have outlined—the change in critical fashion, the lack of faith in periodization and time, the perceived change in global conditions—have led twenty-first century artists and writers themselves, a category distinguished to an unprecedented degree by the fact that they are products of the "theoretical age," and therefore aware of what postmodernism was and how their work relates to it, to become disillusioned by postmodernism. The British-Asian writer, Hari Kunzru, for example, whose first novel *The Impressionist* was published in 2002, recently stated that, as a young writer, he had been convinced that postmodernism, with its embrace of fluidity and hybridity, was the pathway to countering the idea of authentic identity ("I'm insufficiently white and insufficiently brown") and articulating a more liberatory kind of mixed identity: "to allow us to put together a new way of understanding identity that wasn't on this spectrum between those perceived as having a 'fully present' authenticity and the rest of us, who were a bit lacking or broken in some way." However, almost two decades later, he feels that "[t]he limits of that theory and those politics have emerged now" (Piccarella, 2019). Kunzru once admired Thomas Pynchon's ability to depict, in novels such as *Gravity's Rainbow* (perhaps *the* exemplary postmodern novel), the liberatory potential of "informational excess, and our inability to process everything and the kind of absence of stability in tone and reality." Now, however, he argues, these exact same things have become "in this political moment, [. . .] a very threatening force" (Piccarella, 2019).

THE RETURN OF MODERNISM

This apparent consensus that postmodernism was now a thing of the past has led some theorists to try to make sure the concept is well and truly buried by defining the new era we have supposedly entered after postmodernism, or by identifying the mode of cultural expression that has replaced it. There are too many of these to discuss in detail, other than to list some examples: digimodernism (Kirby, 2009), altermodernism (Bourriaud, 2009), metamodernism (Vermeuelen T. &., 2010) (James D. &., 2014), cosmodernism (Moraru, 2011), transmodernism (Onega, 2020). Other critics, such as Mary K. Holland, assume that postmodernism has in fact been a "success" as a ground-clearing exercise (the neatly dually signifying title of her book, *Succeeding Postmodernism*, suggesting both that postmodernism has been surpassed but has also made a lasting positive impact) (Holland M. K., 2013), establishing understandings about the fluidity of structure, language, and identity that enable a return to ethical concerns. Other critics still prefer simply to assume that postmodernism and perhaps all periodizing labels are dispensed with and there is no need to dwell upon them in discussions of contemporary literature (Boxall, 2013).

What has taken the place of postmodernism? One striking conclusion when we consider the list of alternatives I have just cited, is that there has been a broad consensus that if there is a new paradigm to replace postmodern it is governed by a return to the shaping forces and practices of modernism. Let us take one powerful example: Gilles Lipovetsky's account of postmodernity and its succession by what he calls *hypermodernity*. This approach both involves an analysis of what is new in the cultural landscape but also a revision of what we understand postmodernism to have been. Postmodernism was, in its heyday, explicitly regarded as a way of understanding the contemporary (Connor, 1989)(Altieri, 1998). But, once surpassed, this can no longer be the case. Lipovetsky conceives of the postmodern as a moment within modernity, a period of "parenthesis," a necessary step in what he considers the shift from the first stage of modernity to its second stage.

To make this case he offers a suggestive account of the temporality which distinguishes both postmodernity and hypermodernity. Lipovetsky contends that the "nightmare of the twentieth century" resulted in a loss of faith in rationality as it became clear that reason was merely a tool to ensure domination. This meant that modernity had failed to realize goals of Enlightenment and this was reflected in a crisis of temporality. It meant that, by the postmodern era, both the past and the future were "discredited" (Charles 2)—or, at least, the faith in the future as the time when suffering would be alleviated by the modernist project, had collapsed. Postmodernism was distinguished by its presentism, that is, by its faith in the present rather than the future.

In his 2005 essay, "Time Against Time, or the Hypermodern Society," Lipovetsky announces the demise of postmodernism. The most significant characteristic of the hypermodern phase which replaces it is that the temporality typical of postmodernism—its productive condition of being frozen in the present—is no longer applicable. Instead, the future has returned, only it is a future which is not narrativized, not bound up with postreligious narratives of progress or happiness. Hypermodernity is distinguished by the modernist logic of change, renewal, and supersession done to excess, to the extent that it represents the very consummation of modernity—an *absolute* modernity where the first stage was only "limited modernity" (Lipovetsky 31). Where once the modernist logic of change and supersession was driven by the aim to harness rationality to improve life and ensure the survival of the species, it is now driven by the logic of change for its own sake, what Lipovetsky calls "hyperchange." The climate of "epilogue" in postmodernism is being followed, he contends, by the awareness of a headlong rush forwards, of unbridled modernization comprised of galloping commercialization, economic deregulation, and technical and scientific developments being unleashed with effects that are heavy with threats as well as promises' (Lipovetsky 30-31).

POST-POSTMODERN LITERATURE AND ETHICS

What kind of literature has emerged in this new period, after postmodernism? Generally speaking, there has been an emphasis on two related elements: 1) mobility in our globalized world; and 2) a new ethics centered on an attitude of respect to the other. To begin with this first element, a number of theorists have pinpointed a turn to the global—or to the transnational, or even the "planetary"—as a new context for surveying the contemporary cultural field after postmodernism. Postmodernism was, as David James has said, "inherently 'transnational' from the start"(James D., 2017) in that it registered the effects of the commercial expansion across the globe, as theorized in landmark studies by David Harvey (Harvey, 1990)and Fredric Jameson (Jameson, *Postmodernism, or the Cultural Logic of Late Capitalism*, 1991). However, as a cultural paradigm which purported to describe contemporary culture, it is now widely regarded as fatally compromised by—in the words of Amy Elias and Christian Moraru—its "ties to late socio-aesthetic modernity, market globalization, and the society of spectacle, simulation, and empty pastiche" (Elias, 2015) and by its function as a totalizing, blanket paradigm. Moreover, as a number of recent studies have shown, with their treatment of a remarkably numerous and wide-ranging group of especially North American novelists, there would seem to be sufficient evidence of a significant shift not just in the newly global conditions which go to make up the contemporary novel, but in its outlook and subject matter, to validate a transnational flavor as a definitive characteristic of the contemporary novel after postmodernism (Jay, 2014) (Walkowitz, 2015) (Moraru, *Reading for the Planet: Towards a Geomethodology*, 2016).

Adam Kirsch has even defined a category he calls "the global novel," which he regards not as a genre, but as "a perspective that governs the interpretation of experience." It is a form which does not abolish place but uses "the global" "as a theme by which place is mediated" (12). Kirsch argues that the global novel is "a basic affirmation of the power of literature to represent the world" (13), and contains a built-in consciousness, which permits critique, of the fact that novel and novelist are part of "a world system." The global novel, Kirsch suggests, in different ways "addresses the question of what it means to write across borders" (24). It is important to note here the distinction between the "global" and the "planetary" which Amy Elias and Christian Moraru have insisted upon. They contend that where the global cannot shake off connotations of "economic, political, and technical administration" the planetary shifts the focus onto a (re)turn to ethical interconnectedness which they term "relationality." By this model any category of the global novel denotes fiction which is both produced as a result of globalized practices in publishing and transmission, but also contains a critique of or a focus on the effects of globalization (economic, political, etc.). Planetary fiction, by contrast, places the emphasis on "new models of transnationality, internationality, or multinationality," and on "our moment [. . .] measuring time, space, and culture [. . .] on the planet at large." As Elias and Moraru insist, focusing on the planet means an emphasis not simply on human practices and their effects the world over, but on the position of the human being on a planet which, by definition, turns and changes. Planetarity is thus a deterritorializing perspective on the global, opening up spaces and crossings between places and people at various points in the globe.

By implication this perspective aligns the global with the postmodern, whereas after postmodernism the emphasis should be placed on the position of the human being on the planet. In a similar vein, the art critic Nicolas Bourriaud's definition of "altermodernism" privileges a kind of global art. The newly globalized perception which characterizes our post-postmodern (or "altermodern") age now means, he argues, that the role of the artist is to become "homo viator, the prototype of the contemporary traveller, whose passage through signs and formats refers to a contemporary experience of mobility, travel and transpassing." For Bourriaud this signifies more than literal mobility, or global traveling, it means a world and art characterized by an expanded notion of "translation": "Artists traverse a cultural landscape saturated with signs, creating new pathways between multiple formats of expression and communication" (Bourriaud, "Altermodern Explained: Manifesto," 2009).

To turn to the second common element of post-postmodern fiction, these global, planetary, or transnational accounts of contemporary cultural production are all driven by an ethics which place at the center the respect for difference and otherness. Again, something similar can be traced through postmodernist theory, but the difference here is articulated by Bourriaud's insistence that the art of the twentieth century "spoke the abstract language of the colonial west," and postmodernism in particular, tended to "enclose[-] artistic phenomena in origins and identities." Postmodernism valued difference but its emphasis on "multiculturalism and the discourse of identity" did not fully allow for a twenty-first-century "planetary movement of creolisation; cultural relativism and deconstruction" (Bourriaud, "Altermodern Explained: Manifesto," 2009).

Beyond the emphasis on the global the ethical concern with respecting otherness has dominated analysis of what are perceived as new, post-postmodern, forms of literary production in the twenty-first century. The key figure here is the American novelist David Foster Wallace, who in his writing and in interviews and essays repeatedly urged a move beyond the postmodern. His rationale began with the acknowledgment that irony in literature once had a valuable function in postmodern American culture because it functioned as an oppositional, critical force. This was the great value of the relentlessly ironic, metafictional work of the great "high postmodernist" American writers, such as John Barth, Robert Coover, and Kurt Vonnegut. But the ironic mode was then taken up by TV, and suddenly it was everywhere. Throughout the seventies the kind of ironic, self-reflexive humor which was initially the preserve of American literature became one of the dominant modes in television, especially in sitcoms or comedy shows, and in magazines and advertising. This meant that any oppositional value became absorbed into the mainstream, into the *status quo*, and thereby lost its critical value. The antidote, Wallace contended, was the advent of a "new sincerity" in fiction.

In an influential essay, "The New Sincerity," which develops this idea ("David Foster Wallace and the New Sincerity in American Fiction," 2010), Adam Kelly makes the point that the position adopted by post-postmodernist writers like Wallace is the opposite to the one identified in Tom LeClair's book, *The Age of Excess*, which concludes that the effect of the vast novels produced by postmodernists like Pynchon, Coover, and Barth, is to "master the time, the methods of fiction, and the reader" (LeClair, *The Art of Excess: Mastery in Contemporary American Fiction*, 1989, 1). In postmodern literature, according to LeClair's thesis, it is a matter of the author being in control, treating the reader like someone enlisted as a witness or a sounding-board for the author to work through his or her problems. The recognition of didacticism in postmodern narrative was common in studies of postmodern fiction during its heyday. Linda Hutcheon, in her early study of metafiction *Narcissistic Narrative*, for example, points to a characteristic doubleness about metafiction, that it is both open and didactic at the same time (Hutcheon, *Narcissistic Narrative: The Metafictional Paradox*, 2014). The author of classic postmodern metafiction comes across as a didactic "ancient mariner," continually interrupting the "guests" in his (and it is usually 'his') text to put his side of the story. As a test case we might take John Fowles's classic postmodern work of "historiographic metafiction," *The French Lieutenant's Woman* (Hutcheon, *A Poetics of Postmodernism*, 1988). There may be two people "present" in his famous chapter thirteen of—that is, author and reader, or addresser and addressee, sender and receiver of the message—but it is not a dialogue. It may be "dialogic" in the Bakhtinian sense in that Fowles's discourse is driven by his "anticipation of a future answer-word," but the author's point of view is not challenged in the text, nor is it open to challenge.

Where postmodernism is about mastery and didacticism, the fiction of the new sincerity is founded on "the passive decision to relinquish the self to the judgment of the other, and [. . .] thus structured and informed by this dialogic appeal to the reader's attestation and judgement" (Kelly, "David Foster Wallace and the New Sincerity in American Fiction," 143). Beyond the specific concern with sincerity, the value of mutual respect between author and reader has been a key part of recent approaches to what was once undoubtedly the postmodern literary technique *par excellence*, metafiction. Some literary critics have analyzed what they consider a new kind of self-reflexive literary technique which departs from postmodernism. In a reading of Dave Eggers's "autobiography" of Valentino Achak Deng, *What Is the What?* (2006), Peter Boxall argues that the device Eggers deploys, are markable ventriloquial conceit whereby he writes "in the voice of" its central character (i.e., scripting Deng's autobiography) continually invites the reader to consider how the book was written and is being narrated. But such self-reflexivity exemplifies a new kind of metafiction governed by the desire to "think one's way into a shared space between one being and another," as Boxall puts it, rather than invest in "the wearily 'postmodern' conclusion that all life is a fiction, that we are all fictional characters in search of an author" (Boxall 116). Similarly, Eggers's writing has been described by James Clements as creating a "pact, rather than a dialogue between writer and reader, which reduces the danger of authorial insincerity to enable ethical communion between author and reader" (Clements, 2015).

THE RETURN OF POSTMODERNISM

These are ways, then, in which theorists and art and literary critics evidence their assumption that postmodernism is over, and we have moved into a new paradigm. The suspicion lingers, however, that many of the apparently new emphases, values, and practices, are in fact continuations of postmodernism rather than full departures. I referred above to David James's view that transnationalism was "inherent" in postmodernism. Sure enough, postmodern "high" theory often contains a critique of how globalisation eliminates difference and must be resisted. We might cite in support here Fredric Jameson's convictions about the flattening-out of historical difference (*Postmodernism, or the Cultural Logic of Late Capitalism*, 1991), or Lyotard's famous statement that "Eclecticism is the degree zero of contemporary general culture: you listen to reggae; you watch a western; you eat McDonald's at midday and local cuisine at night; you wear Paris perfume in Tokyo and dress retro in Hong Kong" (76).

Similarly, Nicolas Bourriaud's emphasis on aesthetic nomadism is more like an intensification or the next stage in the condition of postmodernity rather than its replacement. The postmodern debate provided approaches to art which are compatible with Bourriaud's "homo viator," such as J. G. Ballard's depiction of the postmodern novelist as a "scientist on safari." Lacking the "moral authority" of the nineteenth-century novelist, the postmodern writer has to assume he or she "knows nothing any longer" and must therefore adopt the role "of the scientist, whether on safari or in his laboratory, faced with an unknown terrain or subject [. . .] devise various hypotheses and test them against the facts" (ii-iii).

The same is true of sincerity, or the ways in which post-postmodern metafiction values shared space between writer and reader rather than author achieving a kind of didactic mastery over the receiver of the text. The irony and didacticism of postmodern writers such as Fowles or Coover or Auster, do not prevent them being sincere or genuinely touching in their dialogue with other people. One of the most compelling examples of this effect is Kurt Vonnegut's *Slaughterhouse 5* (1969). This is a novel cloaked in layers of irony, from the title page onward, including its notorious preface, which purports to be directly from Vonnegut himself. But one of the reasons this novel is so moving is that the ironic elements—the sci-fi story and the authorial intrusions—function as displacements, as defence mechanisms, to enable Vonnegut to write as directly as he is able to about the experience which haunted him personally: being present in Dresden during the horrific bombing of that city by the Allied forces in February 1945.

Josh Toth has recently expressed his uncertainty about whether postmodernism has in fact been overtaken by an alternative paradigm. "[P]ostmodernism's demise," he argues, "along with the cause and subsequent ramifications of that demise, have yet to be determined with any certainty, any real consensus" (Toth 4). Despite the misgivings of writers like Hari Kunzru, whom I quoted earlier, the primary technique associated with postmodernism, metafiction, which Toth calls "the postmodern modus operandi par excellence" (4), has never let up. After postmodernism "the production of metafiction continued, and continues, undaunted" (6). Toth argues, quite logically, that the writers we would automatically assume represent something different to postmodernism, such as Mark Z. Danielewski, Dave Eggers, Jonathan Safran Foer, and David Foster Wallace, are all nevertheless writers who deploy metafictional techniques. This is combined with the fact metafictional techniques remain prominent (as Wallace noted) in innumerable films and television shows. The obvious conclusion is that metafiction has continued, albeit in different forms, and postmodernism, which is inseparable from the technique, has simply moved into a new, perhaps "late" phase (Green, 2005).

While it is clearly no longer tenable to say that postmodernism is "the present," it is equally problematic to say that it is firmly in the past. Postmodernism haunts us. It is a cultural term and critical framework that many are relieved to see the back of, but it has not yet been definitively put to rest. We do not—yet—have the confidence of having moved into a new phase. This is something Toth argued in a previous book, using the Derridean concept of *hantologie*, or "hauntology" as a guide (Toth, *The Passing of Postmodernism: A Spectroanalysis of the Contemporary*, 2010). Where ontology is about presence and being, hauntology—as the connotation of spectrality indicates—is about an ontology which is neither present nor absent, neither dead nor alive, but present in the way a ghost would be present. Postmodernism is spectral in that it exists no longer (i.e., it is no longer the crucial construct of choice), but nevertheless remains effective as a remnant, a critical force successive phases or modes of analysis still need to reckon with. This is ironic given that postmodernism itself—as writers and critics of its era repeatedly observed—was distinguished by a sense of belatedness, of exhaustion, and so on.

What does it mean to decide that literature now is being produced self-consciously in the shadow of the postmodern, that the strategies deployed by writers now are reminiscent of postmodernism? It seems that the unlikeliness of a consensus emerging about what we call our era after postmodernism is evidence of a crisis in our experience of temporality (Jameson, "The End of Temporality," 2003). This is perhaps the best definition of our age—albeit a very loose one—which we can reach for. As Lyotard once argued about the postmodern, it is the limit which paradoxically points the way forward, and postmodernism must therefore be understood as "the paradox of the future anterior (modo)." Critics and theorists now, like Lyotard's examples of artist and writer "then," are still "working without rules in order to formulate the rules of what will have been done" (81).

REFERENCE LIST

Altieri, Charles. *Postmodernisms Now: Essays on the Contemporary: Essays on Contemporaneity in the Arts*. Pennsylvania State University Press, 1998.
Ballard, James Graham. "Introduction." In J. G. Ballard, *Crash* (pp. i–iii). Vintage,1993.
Bourriaud, Nicolas. "Altermodern Explained: Manifesto." Retrieved from Tate Gallery London: https://www.tate.org.uk/whats-on/tate-britain/exhibition/altermodern/altermodern-explain-altermodern/altermodern-explained, 2009.
Bourriaud, Nicolas. *Altermodern: Tate Triennial*. Tate Publishing, 2009.
Boxall, Peter. *Twenty-First Century Fiction: A Critical Introduction*. Cambridge University Press, 2013.
Burn, Stephen J. *Jonathan Franzen at the End of Postmodernism*. Continuum, 2011.
Charles, Sebastien. "Paradoxical Individualism: An Introduction to the Thought of Gilles Lipovetsky." In G. Lipovetsky, *Hypermodern Times* (pp. 1–28). Polity, 2005.
Clements, James. "Trust Your Makers of Things!: The Metafictional Pact in Dave Eggers's You Shall Know Our Velocity." *Critique*(56), 121–137, 2015.
Connor, Steven. *Postmodernist Culture: An Introduction to Theories of the Contemporary*. Blackwell, 1989.
Coupland, Douglas. "Convergences: Gods Without Men by Hari Kunzru." In D. Coupland, *Shopping Jail: Ideas, Essays, and Stories for the Increasingly Real Twenty-First Century* (pp. 24–28). Sternberg Press, 2013.
Derrida, Jacques. *Spectres of Marx: The State of the Debt, the Work of Mourning and the New International* . Routledge, 2006.
Elias, Amy J. &. "The Planetary Turn: Relationality and Geoaesthetics in the Twenty–First Century." In A. &. Elias, *The Planetary Turn: Relationality and Geoaesthetics in the Twenty-First Century* (pp. xi–xxxvii). Northwestern University Press, 2015.
Goulimari, Pelagia. *Postmodernism. What Moment?* Manchester University Press, 2011.
Green, Jeremy. *Late Postmodernism: American Fiction at the Millennium*. Palgrave, 2005.
Harvey, David. *The Condition of Postmodernity: An Enquiry into the Origins of Cultural Change*. Blackwell, 1990.
Hassan, Ihab. "Beyond Postmodernism." *Angelaki*, 8(1), 3–11, 2003.
Holland, Mark K. *Succeeding Postmodernism: Language and Humanism in Contemporary American Literature*. Bloomsbury, 2013.
Hutcheon, Linda. *A Poetics of Postmodernism*. Routledge, 1988.
———. *The Politics of Postmodernism*, 2nd Edition. Routledge, 2002.
———. *Narcissistic Narrative: The Metafictional Paradox*. Wilfrid Laurier University Press, 2014.
James, David. &. "Metamodernism: Narratives of Continuity and Revolution." *PMLA*, 129(1), 87–100, 2014.
James, David. "Transnational Postmodern and Contemporary Literature." In Y. Goyal, *The Cambridge Companion to Transnational American Literature* (pp. 122–140). Cambridge University Press, 2017.

Jameson, Fredric. *Postmodernism, or the Cultural Logic of Late Capitalism*. Duke University Press, 1991.
———. "The End of Temporality." *Critical Inquiry,* 29(4), 695–718, 2003.
———. *The Antinomies of Realism*. Verso, 2013.
Jay, Paul. *Global Matters: The Transnational Turn in Literary Studies*. Cornell University Press, 2014.
Kelly, Adam. "David Foster Wallace and the New Sincerity in American Fiction." In D. Hering, *Consider David Foster Wallace: Critical Essays* (pp. 131–46). Slideshow Media Group Press, 2010.
Keulks, Gavin. *Martin Amis: Postmodernism and Beyond*. Basingstoke: Palgrave, 2006.
Kirby, A. *Digimodernism: How New Technologies Dismantle the Postmodern and Reconfigure Our Culture*. Continuum, 2009.
Kirsch, Alan. *The Global Novel: Writing the World in the 21st Century.* Columbia University Press, 2017.
LeClair, Tom. *The Art of Excess: Mastery in Contemporary American Fiction*. University of Illinois Press, 1989.
Lipovetsky, Gilles. *Hypermodern Times*. Polity, 2005.
Lyotard, Jean-François. *The Postmodern Condition: A Report on Knowledge*. University of Minnesota Press, 1984.
Matthews, Graham. *Ethics and Desire in the Wake of Postmodernism*. Continuum, 2012.
McHale, Brian. *Constructing Postmodernism*. Routledge, 1992.
———. "What Was Postmodernism?" Retrieved from Electronic Book Review: http://electronicbookreview.com/essay/what-was-postmodernism/#:~:text=Brian%20McHale%20looks%20back%20on,world%20lived%20%22in%20the%20ruins, 2007, December 12.
Moraru, Christian. *Cosmodernism: American Narrative, Late Globalization, and the New Cultural Imaginary.* University of Michigan Press, 2011.
———. *Reading for the Planet: Towards a Geomethodology*. University of Michigan Press, 2016.
Nicol, Bran. *The Cambridge Introduction to Postmodern Fiction*. Cambridge University Press, 2009.
Onega, Susanna &Ganteau, Jean-Michel. *Transcending the Postmodern: The Singular Response of Literature to the Transmodern Paradigm*. Routledge, 2020.
Piccarella, Stephen. "An Interview with Hari Kunzru". *The Believer*, pp. https://believermag.com/an-interview-with-hari-kunzru/, 2019, December 2.
Timmer, Nicole. *Do You Feel it Too? The Post Syndrome in American Fiction at the Turn of the Millenium*.Rodopi, 2010.
Toth, Josh. *The Passing of Postmodernism: A Spectroanalysis of the Contemporary.* SUNY Press, 2010.
———. *Truth and Metafiction: Plasticity and Renewal in American Narrative*. Bloomsbury, 2021.
Underwood, Ted. *Why Literary Periods Mattered: Historical Contrast and the Prestige of English Studies*. Stanford University Press, 2013.
Vermeuelen, Timotheus & Robin van den Akker. "Notes on Metamodernism." *Journal of Aesthetics and Culture*, 2(1), 2010 https://www.tandfonline.com/doi/full/10.3402/jac.v2i0.5677.
Walkowitz, Rebecca. *Born Translated: The Contemporary Novel in an Age of World Literature*. Columbia University Press, 2015.

15

Metamodernism

Is it a New Hype for "the Post-Postmodern Syndrome"?

Enes Kavak

The prefix "*post-*" has been a cultural and intellectual signifier of the Western world in the second half of the twentieth century. It was not surprising to encounter terms such as "postspatial," "postenvrionmental," "postgeographic," or "postfeminism" even in the morning posts as J. Douglas Porteous humorously inquired in "The Post-It Generation" (83) since a barrage of confusing post-terms were persistently fabricated and circulated in socio-cultural realm. Being the most pervasive and documented of all, postmodernism enjoyed a sweeping hegemony over cultural and literary theory until the end of the century. In the 1990s, nonetheless, scholars and critics began to claim the demise of postmodernism. They proposed new literary and cultural concepts, among which post-postmodernism, metamodernism, transmodernism, automodernism, altermodernism, digimodernism, the new sincerity, object-oriented ontology, new romanticism, and new realism have attracted most of the critical interest. Although each is distinct in its portrayal and reading of the new epoch, they have commonly characterized contemporary culture under the constant assault of the capitalist financial system, rampant neoliberal politics, cultural frivolity, epistemological and ontological confusion, antifoundationalism, deep-rooted irony, and insincerity. For instance, in his critique of the scholarly obsession with postmodernism in the modules of English departments at British universities, Alan Kirby points out that outside the physical and intellectual confines of British universities, the cultural weight of postmodernity has vanished for long ("The Death of Postmodernism and Beyond," par. 3–4). As a possible cause, he notes "the emergence of new technologies restructured, violently and forever, the nature of the author, the reader and the text, and the relationships between them"("The Death" par. 5). Those academics appear to deny that the material world has been shaped swiftly and constantly by popular culture, neoliberal politics, the market economy, and digitalized society. He thus offers a new term for the state of cultural production and the participatory nature of new consumerism: "pseudo-modernism"("The Death", par.7). Internet blogs, interactive console/computer games, reality TV shows, digital messaging, and sharing platforms all offer users the option to record and stream videos or digital content and allow a superficial and pseudo-democratic interaction as well as repetitious, transient, and uncultured exchange, which highlights the consumerist and shallow nature of cultural mechanisms in the postmodern world.

Another response to the loss of meaning in the last half-century has emerged on the other side of the Atlantic in the form of a literary movement entitled "the New Sincerity." Jon Doyle asserts that the New Sincerity's stylistic distinction is in its "ways to transcend the ironic game-playing of [its] forebears and re-establish not only imagination and innovation but also a sense of value and moral importance within fiction"(259). According to the critic, the deconstructive nature of postmodernism and its literary works undermined the main bourgeois dynamics and its deceitful assertions and appeals. However, the late twentieth century exhibited that the revisionist and sceptical critique of belief, identity, and truth has constrained the ability to "provide resistance and enlightenment in the postmodern culture of post-Cold War capitalism" (Doyle 260). This argument can also be traced back to Francis Fukuyama's *The End of History* (1989). He also states that "just as postmodernism is intrinsically linked to and informed by modernism, post-postmodernism must assess and utilize thematic and stylistic aspects of postmodernism and employ them against the strategies and beliefs of its predecessor . . ." (260). In Doyle's account, post-postmodern authors and artists venture to offer a new cultural and philosophical approach, either interacting with postmodernism or addressing its failings by stimulating belief, meaning, and sincerity in culture and its textual/artistic representations.

Among this proliferation of theories, metamodernism stands out as a popular response to the limitations of postmodernism through the adoption of modern values without disregarding the cultural embeddedness of postmodernity in our lives. Timotheus Vermeulen and Robin van den Akker introduced metamodernism in their "Notes on Metamodernism" in 2010, which does not signify a complete detachment from postmodernism, but a more idealistic yet ironic consciousness by recognizing the impossibility of pure idealism in contemporary cultural endeavors. The authors explain their notion of the new art as a contemporary approach, which is informed by modernist experimentalism, idealism as well as postmodernist consciousness of the unattainability of the objective truth and universal standards. Hence, metamodernist art corresponds to the growing concerns for meaningful artistic interaction. It is mainly influenced by modernism, Kantian idealism and new romanticism by merging them with postmodern art techniques and cultural theory. In 2011, Luke Turner published an online manifesto outlining some of the key principles of the metamodernist worldview as follows:

- We must liberate ourselves from the inertia resulting from a century of modernist ideological naivety and the cynical insincerity of its antonymous bastard child.

- Artistic creation is contingent upon the origination or revelation of difference therein. Affect at its zenith is the unmediated experience of difference in *itself*. It must be art's role to explore the promise of its own paradoxical ambition by coaxing excess toward presence.
- The present is a symptom of the twin birth of immediacy and obsolescence. Today, we are nostalgists as much as we are futurists. The new technology enables the simultaneous experience and enactment of events from a multiplicity of positions.
- Just as science strives for poetic elegance, artists might assume a quest for truth. All information is grounds for knowledge, whether empirical or aphoristic, no matter its truth-value. We should embrace the scientific-poetic synthesis and informed naivety of a magical realism. Error breeds sense.
- We propose a pragmatic romanticism unhindered by ideological anchorage. Thus, *metamodernism* shall be defined as the mercurial condition between and beyond irony and sincerity, naivety and knowingness, relativism and truth, optimism and doubt, in pursuit of a plurality of disparate and elusive horizons. We must go forth and oscillate!

("Metamodernist Manifesto")[1]

Turner's manifesto is a liminal and paradigmatic cultural/artistic declaration for the modern world. He appears to acknowledge the shifting state of culture and art between idealism and dialectics. His artistic concept offers a new romantic perspective largely as a remedy to the artistic stagnation of the postmodern world and calls for a more open-minded acceptance of the past. He claims that metamodernism does not theorize a utopian vision and it is thus "descriptive rather than prescriptive" ("Metamodernism: A Brief Introduction"). Metamodernism can instead be defined as a "rumination" rather than a philosophy, school of thought, ideology, and art theory ("Metamodernism: A Brief Introduction"). He seems to defend the decision to distance the idea from an ideological and political stance. His designation of metamodernism is mostly an evaluation, or in the simplest sense, a contemplation of today's artistic and cultural scene. Nonetheless, as a manifesto is an act of declaration of political or individual motives and principles, this attempt seems naïve and greatly ambitious for such a young artist and intellectual. Moreover, the manifesto fails to propose a complete and conclusive theory of art and literature, drawing mostly on a projection for the postmillennial artistic endeavors and outlining a collective search for new artistic models. Therefore, metamodernism embodies artists' dissatisfaction with the current limbo in the philosophy of contemporary art and reveals a growing desire to define the dominant artistic and cultural tendency of the early twenty-first century. In this respect, this chapter attempts to examine the rudiments and claims of metamodernism by considering whether it can offer a likely alternative by achieving the cultural reach of its predecessors and stemming the emerging current of the post-postmodernism.

AN AESTHETICS OF "METAXIS": METAMODERNISM AND POST-POSTMODERNISM

In the cultural *fin-de-siècle* of the1990s, Western art and literature showed an inclination to return to the modernist and realist traditions to deflect the ironic and deceptive representations of the human subject and its relationships in postmodern works. Particularly, American authors welcomed the arrival of a new wave of *sincere* literature in the new century amid all the socio-political crises and deviations around the world. Savvas and Coffman note that:

> [C]ontemporary American fiction has, since roughly 1989, increasingly valorised such seemingly naïve literary qualities as a return to mimetic verisimilitude, a display of historical awareness, and a preoccupation with the physical nature of the textual artifact as keys to the revitalisation of a constructive textual authenticity, one that reinvigorates the exchange between reader and literary text. (196)

This new orientation toward a post-postmodern aesthetics of literature and art is characterized by the adoption of mimetic portrayals of contemporary life, more sincere and authentic human interaction. These have increasingly been traced in David Foster Wallace and Thomas Pynchon's late works. With the arrival of *Infinite Jest* in 1996, Wallace embraces a postironic and *hysterical realistic* position, defending the notions of connectedness, empathy, and sincerity. Although his use of quirky narrative structure and exhaustive erudite endnotes in his fiction, his characters' artless language following the single-entendre style, the verisimilitude of details as well as his specific touch on human feelings and mutual empathy locate Wallace in the ranks against the scepticism and ironic indifference to life in the earlier postmodernist works. One of the aspects of his late fiction is to reveal the fact that the particular interest in human feelings lost in contemporary America, in which individuals are given too many choices and pleasures but not a moral and humanistic framework to understand and command the all-too-complicated life outside. In the story, the pleasure-seeking and idle public are obsessed with a film called *Infinite Jest* or "the Entertainment," which strangely enthrals and even kills people, being too funny and addictive. As Nicole Timmer states in her elucidation of "the post-postmodern syndrome" in *Do You Feel It Too?*, the film in the novel represents "a thoroughgoing fatigue that is the result of having to choose constantly without knowing how to. It appeals, ultimately, to an overall desire not to choose . . ." (312). With lack of a moral frame and ethical borders, *Infinite Jest* depicts a future (in an imaginary country consisting of America, Canada, and Mexico), in which the pervasive capitalist system, degraded family relations, and emptied human relationship lead various characters (ranging from the members of the upper class, the Incandenza family, to the addicts in Ennet House Drug and Alcohol Recovery House) to feel disoriented and alienated by being spent in a culture of material gains, addictions, and artificial human interactions. Wallace's work shows how postmodernist literature should transform its ironic style and non-conformist form for more ethically framed objectives by representing real and urgent issues touching people's lives. *Infinite Jest*, in this sense, combines the elements of imaginative setting and realistic characters, fragmented linearity and cohesive thematic concern together with postmodern narration and documentary-like details.

This changing state of American fiction can also be compared to the European metamodernist art movement, which proposes an exchange between a modern desire for progress and empathy in conjunction with postmodern irony and detachment.Vermeulen and van den Akker assert, "new generations of artists increasingly abandon the aesthetic precepts of deconstruction, para-taxis, and pastiche in favor of *aesth-ethical* notions of reconstruction, myth, and metaxis" ("Notes on Metamodernism" 2). This designation snubs the dominance of cynicism, deconstruction, and fragmentation in premillennial art and literature. The authors elucidate the conceptual and lexical foundations of metamodernism as follows:

> When we use the term "meta," we use it in similar yet not indiscriminate fashion. For the prefix "meta-" allows us to situate metamodernism historically *beyond*; epistemologically *with*; and ontologically *between* the modern and the postmodern. It indicates a dynamic or movement between as well as a movement beyond. More generally, however, it points towards a changing cultural sensibility—or cultural metamorphosis, if you will—within western societies. ("Etymology of the term metamodernism")

Metamodernism draws on the platonic idea of "*metaxis* [, which] translates as "between" ("Notes on Metamodernism" 6). The label has often led to conflicting readings and interpretations, yet *meta*-embraces all three meanings of the prefix: "with," "between," and "beyond" ("Notes on Metamodernism" 2). Plato uses *metaxis* to elucidate human beings' relationship with the divine or, in other words, the interaction between the material and the spiritual. *Metaxis* also means "the state of belonging completely and simultaneously to two different autonomous worlds" (cited in Linds 114; Boal 43). Therefore, it stresses the unsettled foundations of the modern subject and its art. It denotes a search for meaning and desire for "repositioning" ("What Meta Means and Does Not Mean") between the often conflicting and doubtful yet independent state of an artistic mind. The authors point out that in contrast to the various uses and concepts of metamodernism, their version stresses "irreconcilability" and doubt as "oscillation" rather than a state of "harmony" or "the absorption of contrasts into the whole" ("Misunderstandings and Clarifications"). They also note to have implied a form of "elasticism," "swing," or "paradox" ("Misunderstandings and Clarifications"). In the context of art criticism, Vermeulen and van den Akker use "downcycling," a term that originates from the environmental sciences ("Art Criticism and Metamodernism"), to stress the metaxis of metamodernist "reappropriation" of the original art ("Art Criticism and Metamodernism"). They argue that European artists like David Thorpe and Rob Voerman have learned from the past and integrate these in thepresent or the potential future in a counter-strategy of "upcycling" by reacting to postmodernity ("Art Criticism and Metamodernism"). The intertextuality in these works generates a pastiche ironically responding or commenting on the work itself or the artist's temporal stance. For example, in David Thorpe's work *Covenant of the Elect* (2002), the artist reconstructs and revisions other past utopias and impossible utopic visions whose eclectic strategy of reappropriation reject the conventions of the works by generating an "impossible harmony"("Art Criticism and Metamodernism"). Thorpe's strategy seems to create an impossible and doubtful vision of the future by adopting more conventional techniques for new effects and meanings. The authors argue that the modernist artist does not "imitate" but "revisit" in "a search for substance" and foundations ("Art Criticism and Metamodernism"), which reminds us of the modernist artists of the early-twentieth century. This constant search for substance is both a metamodernist concern about the meaningful use and adaptation of previous ideas, which can be compared to the post-postmodernist sensibility of defending human values and social standards as critical means to shape human understanding of self and the material world.

Metamodernism has stimulated and increased academics and artists' critical interest and engagement in scholarly examinations of and debates about the term and its scope. Vermeulen and van den Akker state "there are well over fifteen hundred scholarly engagements with metamodernism" ("Ongoing Research"). The academic events such as the University of Chicago "After Postmodernism" Conference in 1997, the Free University of Berlin conference on cultural practices in 2007 and Metamodernism Network Conference at the Radboud University sponsored by AHRC in 2019 prove that postmillennial scholars show a growing interest in metamodernism as a potentially rich and stimulating cultural paradigm at the time of intellectual stalemate and philosophical ambiguity. Furthermore, the term has achieved a relatively respectable status thanks to published and online literature on post-postmodernism and metamodernism. The books such as *The Death of Postmodernism and Beyond* (2006) by Alan Kirby, *Post-Postmodernism: Or, the Cultural Logic of Just-in-Time Capitalism* (2012) by Jeffrey T. Nealon, *Metamodernism: History, Affect, and Depth After Postmodernism* (2017) (eds.) by Robin van den Akker, Alison Gibbons, and Timotheus Vermeulen and *Metamodernism: The Future of Theory* (2021) by Jason Ananda Josephson Storm showed that postmillennial theories opened a productive space for academics to collaborate and speculate on the future and peculiarities of art and culture in the new age.

Perhaps, one of the key mediums that metamodernism contributed to digital humanities most is the internet. Websites such as "www.metamodernism.com," "whatismetamodern.com," and "www.metamodernism.org" have promoted criticism, theoretical debates, and art news. They have seemed to provide metamodernist art and criticism with relatively good circulation for further academic and artistic appraisals of the concept in a participatory, democratic, and productive space. Metamodernism's contemporary strategy of utilizing and expanding in the milieus of digital humanities strongly emphasizes its contemporary roots and forward-looking ontology. Considering that metamodernism was based primarily on the concept of *metaxis*, the digital world offers a new medium of liminality and creativity for artists and their audiences. The digitally empowered metamodernism thus encourages contemporary artists to be original and conscious of the change in a new cultural epoch, in which art will be in a state of *metaxis*, a continual negotiation between the past and present, knowledge and unknowingness, origins and prospects. In today's technology- and the innovation-driven world, unsettling social developments such as the COVID-19 pandemic, the climate crisis, and all too recent the US pull-out of Afghanistan have shown once more the unavoidable interdependence of our lives and the increasing necessity of ethical approaches to life, politics, and arts. The new art and literature, in this sense, may "[provide] the flexibility needed to come to terms with our rapidly changing, interconnected world, as individual pieces are adjustable and expandable when new insights and developments arise" ("Art Criticism and Metamodernism"). It is possible that new theories and ideas can broaden their horizons and demonstrate fictional and material prospects in contrast to the negative ontological baggage of postmodern politics on humans.Metamodernism's best bet for success thus lies within a synthesis of the steady and stimulating creation outside academia and attracting a large base of an audienceby pursuing the principle of progressive yet purposeful art and philosophy.

CONCLUSION

Rebuffing the claim that theory is dead and we have come to the end of theory, we must enquire what literary and cultural theory or concept can replace postmodernism today. The turn of the century and the new millennium have paved the way for a new world where deep-rooted views and ideologies cannot offer reasonable answers to the growing tide of problems and deviations in a world based on dialectics. Since the 1990s, the academic efforts to produce a popular cultural and literary label for the new age have brought about the growing number of scholarly claims for the rightfulness of certain ideas and an inevitable upsurge of new concepts. This productive but disconcerting space has shown inherent contradictions and overlappings of all-too-ambitious manifestos over a potential path and direction for art, literature, and culture. The prefix of *post-* (as well as *trans-*, *neo-*, *digi-* or *meta-*), in this sense, hails the exodus of the grand philosophy of postmodernism. Post-postmodernism and metamodernism appear to be two alternative proposals, in which the former depends more on the literary representations of the human subject as dependable, social, and sincere individuals. The latter suggests the world of art as a potent medium of imagination and meaning-making for contemporary society.

In Timmer's examination of self in today's material life, "the post-postmodern syndrome" signifies the Western world and American writers' growing dilemma between empathy and denial, "it" and "we" (305), and deception and sincerity. Somewhat oblique and greatly ambitious definitions of metamodernism are mostly projections and inferences rather than the widely recognized values of deep-rooted cultural phenomena.Turner, for instance, changed his designation of a manifesto of metamodernism, most probably to distance it from other too ambitious and too academic concepts ("Metamodernism: A Brief Introduction"). The underlying impasse of such manifestos is their self-professed entitlement to truth, legitimacy, and authority for such a role. Given that even postmodernism was baptized and contextualized decades after its inception, a grave mistake here would have been plunging in the waters of solipsism by claiming metamodernism to be a completely new and unique set of values and attitudes. However, these claims have long been dropped and metamodernism's decades-long circulation has been acknowledged in detail by the authors in their laterwritings ("Misunderstandings and Clarifications").

As an alternative strategy, it would be sensible to emphasize the potential of such an effort as a serious and stimulating cultural and artistic concept, which can guide other post-theoretical experiments and parallel developments from within and outside postmodernism. A seeming problem would be to map how and to what extent metamodernism can expand its reach to other forms of cultural products such as literature, theater, film, performing arts, painting, or architecture in various medialities and modalities to situate itself as a dominant mode of thinking and represent contemporary culture in Europe and the rest of the world. This can only be possible if metamodernism may break the straps of academia and touch upon real audience and readers as the post-postmodernist literature has attempted, to a certain extent, by transforming itself from a scholarly hype to a cultural attitude and symptom.

NOTE

1. A complete version of Luke Turner's "Metamodernist Manifesto" can be reached at http://www.metamodernism.org/.

REFERENCE LIST

Boal, Augusto. *The Rainbow of Desire: The Boal Method of Theatre and Therapy*, translated by A. Jackson. London and New York: Routledge, 1995.
Doyle, Jon. "The Changing Face of Post-postmodern Fiction: Irony, Sincerity, and Populism." *Critique: Studies in Contemporary Fiction*, vol. 59, no. 3, 2018, pp. 259–270.
"Etymology of the Term Metamodernism." Metamodernism.org, 2010. http://www.metamodernism.org/.
Kirby, Alan. "The Death of Postmodernism and Beyond."*Philosophy Now*, vol. 58, 2006, pp.34–37.
Linds, Warren."Metaxis: Dancing (in) the In-between." *A Boal Companion: Dialogues on Theatre and Cultural Politics*. Edited by Cohen-Cruz J. and Mady Shutzman, Routledge, 2006.
"Ongoing Research."*Metamodernism.org*, http://www.metamodernism.org/
Porteous, J. Douglas. "The Post-it Generation."*Area*, vol. 27, no. 1, 1995, pp. 83–84.
Savvas,Theophilus, and Christopher K. Coffman. "American Fiction After Postmodernism." *Textual Practice*, vol. 33, no.2, 2019, pp. 195–212.
Timmer, Nicoline. *Do You Feel It Too?: The Post-Postmodern Syndrome in American Fiction at the Turn of the Millennium*. Rodopi, 2010.

Turner, Luke. "Metamodernism: A Brief Introduction."*Metamodernism.org*, 2015. http://www.metamodernism.org/.
———. "Metamodernist Manifesto." *Metamodernism.org*, 2011. http://www.metamodernism.org/.
Vermeulen, Timotheus, and Robin van den Akker. "Art Criticism and Metamodernism." *ArtPulse*, vol.19, 2014, pp. 22–27.
———. "Misunderstandings and Clarifications." *Metamodernism.org*, 2015. http://www.metamodernism.org/.
———. "Notes on Metamodernism."*Journal of Aesthetics and Culture,* vol. 2, no.1, 2010, pp. 1–14.
"What Meta Means and Does not Mean." *Metamodernism.org*, 2010. http://www.metamodernism.org/.

16

The Lines of Influence

The (In)Visibility of Poetry after Theory

Seda Şen

Charles Bernstein once said that poetry is "a secret society hiding in plain sight, open to ear and mind's eye" ("Manifest Aversions"). His words can be interpreted as a playful remark on one of the well-known myths about poetry: that it is not written anymore, it is a thing of the past, and good poets are nowhere to be found. Poetry is likened to "a secret society," and only select members can identify each other in the crowd thanks to a wink or a special salute that binds them to this mysterious subculture (Bernstein "Manifest Aversions"). One may return to the statements of modernist poets and find similar statements on the "invisibility" of poetry. Ezra Pound claimed that the reason for at least the lack of great poets was a combination of the absence of good taste among readers and the critics overlooking the endeavors of new poets who were seeking to innovate poetry ("How to Read" 17; "The Renaissance" 223). T. S. Eliot, likewise, pointed out that even if great poets existed, they were only read by smaller intellectual circles (840). The invisibility of an entity, by nature, implies that they exist, even though the public cannot see them. The concept of invisibility, thus, suggests that there is the potential that it may be brought to light if need be. A contemporary evaluation of poetry's development over the years shows that poetry has been adding new branches in form, content, and the medium(s) it uses. Even though poetry is regarded by some to have fallen out of favor or is "invisible," one may argue the opposite; poetry has become visible in our everyday lives, found in unexpected places and spaces.

Critical theory, over the years, addressed concerns over authorship, the shaping of society, language, and the approaches to the text, which are common with the concerns of contemporary poetry. Before modernism, as Peter Barry points out, Sidney, Johnson, Coleridge, Keats, Shelley, and Wordsworth were some of the poets who were concerned with questions concerning the poet's role, the form and content of the poem, poetic diction, and the audience of poetry. Today, these questions continue to be asked by contemporary poets, critics, and readers, building upon some of the recurring concerns of critical theory. According to Barry, critical theory has frequently touched upon notions one may take for granted today. For example, identity and gender being fluid, unstable, and anti-essentialist, all texts and their authors being under the influence of ideologies, language, and texts as constructs entities, texts and their meanings as multifaceted and ambiguous, and that there can be no totalizations (Barry 38-39). Thus, one may see the impact of theory over the years, which arguably resonate in some of the concerns of poetry. As such, the questions that follow may be regarded as an indication that theory has had a great impact on how poetry is written today.

Some of the questions asked by poets, critics, and readers over the years focus on one of the following concerns: (1) the poet: who they are (a prophet, a bard, a transparent eyeball, or just a regular citizen in the street), whether they write to inspire and influence the society, or isolate themselves from it, if their voice is to be heard in the poem or will the poet construct a mask in the poem; (2) the form and content of the poem: will they write their poems using rigid forms or question closed forms of poetry, will they subvert form or abandon it entirely and invent new forms, will they talk about their experiences and observations, will they touch upon history or literary history, will they allude to other classical, canonized texts and subvert them or will they describe the song they heard on the radio and juxtapose it with Dante's *Divine Comedy* to shake up the canon entirely; (3) poetic diction: to subvert and problematize the canon, what type of diction will the poet use? Should poetry have a special type of diction, or should it use colloquial speech patterns and rhythms? (4) the reader's role: what impact shall the poem have on society? What will its function be? Should the audience participate in the meaning-making process, or should they expect to be informed and educated by the all-knowing poet? If the poet is dead and the poem is born, in the Barthesian sense, what happens to poetry? And where is it heading? These questions have concerned mainly the poets of the previous centuries, who, according to Peter Barry, were the first ones to plant the seeds of theory (28).

Theory in the 1930s emerged as a reaction to liberal humanism steadily broadened its scope. For some, the rising of theory in the 1960s eclipsed in the new millennium, when the age of theory was declared "over." Much like the fate of poetry, theory has been declared "a thing of the past," a concern of the twentieth century. Accordingly, theory has generated discussions on language, culture, the human psyche, and society. One of the arguments put forward by Barry is that theory has not only enabled one to understand their environment, gender, and identity, the texts and their creative process and ways of interpreting them, but also shaped and transformed them. That is, after theory, phenomena such as identity, gender, and nation are no longer regarded as fixed entities, language, the meaning of a text, even those of theoretical texts, are not single or stable (Barry 242-243). In other words, theory created a world of instability that has impacted the development of contemporary poetry.

Neil Turnbull distinguishes theory into two to illustrate the transformation of theory from the macro or grand-scale interpretations to micro or individualistic struggles in the historical development of theory:

> [. . .] a useful distinction can be drawn between what might be termed *traditional theory*—the Freudian, Positivist, Marxist, Weberian, Symbolic Interactionist, Structuralist 'grand' or 'macro' forms of theory that dominated the Anglophone academy prior to the late 1970s - and what might be termed *contemporary theory* - the later poststructuralist 'discursive' and 'aestheticist' variations on these themes that were generally concerned with more micro-political struggles centred on questions of ontology, power and representation. (Turnbull 3)

This distinction by Turnbull shows the impact of poststructuralism in theory; the transition from grand forms of theory into specialized ones could be seen as a progression toward the ultra-specialization of issues raised in post-theory. In poetry, too, there was such a transformation.

Theory has transformed the opinions about the literary text from having single, definitive meanings under the control of the intentions of its writer into having unstable meanings. This influence of theory on how poetry is regarded is also manifested in their critical evaluations. The evaluation of literary movements, their position in literary history, poets belonging to these movements, and important figures contributing to their emergence or development have all been questioned. In other words, the fluidity and all-inclusiveness of theory have provided ground for the re-evaluation of canonical texts and has brought new poets into the spotlight that were previously marginalized.

Thus, the twenty-first century may be regarded as a period of re-evaluation. This includes a re-interpretation of theories and new ways to look at canonical texts that had been declared as "exhausted" by being the subject of hundreds of scholarly articles. With the emergence of each new theoretical approach, or the use of a different combination of theories, enables new readings of former texts. Thus, *The Waste Land* today may be read from an ecocritical perspective, or literary cartography may trace the multiple layers of maps depicted in the poem. Similar to the state of theory after "Theory," these different readings of poems do not cancel each other out; rather, they open up new territories for the discussion of other texts.

THE INFLUENCE OF THEORY ON POETRY

After the Second World War, poetry may be regarded as a time in which poetry schools were influenced by the recently emerging discussions of critical theory. As such, movements such as Confessional, Beat, L=A=N=G=U=A=G=E poetry and schools of poetry like the San Francisco School or Black Mountain School, and the Movement in Britain have challenged notions of poetic language: such as "high" art and the literary canon, the poet's role in society, poetry's relationship to the status quo of the world, the content and limitations of poetry and its relationship to other forms of expression, and how poetry is evaluated. These were all made possible with the emergence of theoretical developments, including poststructuralism, psychoanalytic, Marxist, new historical, and postcolonial theory. These poetic movements, as mentioned, derived their arguments from issues raised in theoretical discussions and carried them into their manifestoes, as exemplified in the essay of Lyn Hejinian, entitled "The Rejection of Closure":

> I can only begin a posteriori, by perceiving the world as vast and overwhelming; each moment stands under an enormous vertical and horizontal pressure of information, potent with ambiguity, meaning-full, unfixed, and certainly incomplete. (Hejinian)

The spatial image of "vertical and horizontal" used in the essay refers to how the structure of the poem "Resistance" may be composed. The poem's form visually imitates the topics the poet aspires to talk about through its broad horizontal lines, long enough to express the horizontal depth of the historical timeline used in the poem (Hejinian). As Hejinian remarks, the poem becomes a container in which language is filled with information. The use of language is in the fashion of the poststructuralist view, which problematises the relationship between word and meaning, L=A=N=G=U=A=G=E poets use it as a tool to break the fixed, rigid, and totalizing meanings of the word to decenter and open up the possibility for new meanings in the poem. Likewise, a similar example of theory influencing the manifestos of poetry may be found in Charles Bernstein's essay where he refers to Barthes's "death of the author": "The author dies. The author's work is born," to declare that the poet "dies" once the poem is composed, and L=A=N=G=U=A=G=E demands the reader to participate in the meaning-making process of the poem (Bernstein).

These uses of theory by language poets have been part of a critical debate that foregrounds the influence of creating such open forms to revolutionize poetry. For instance, Marjorie Perloff identifies Adorno's concept of "resistance," that is, "the resistance of the individual poem to the larger cultural field of capitalist commodification where language had become merely instrumental" as the birthplace of the idea known today as the desire to "Make It New." Writing a poem that resisted earlier models enabled poets to innovate poetry, particularly in modernist poetry (Perloff 9). According to Perloff, a new poetic turn is emerging since the 1980s; a poetic turn that breaks away from the "resistance model" into a "dialogue with earlier texts, or texts in other media, with 'writings through' or ekphrasis that permit the poet to participate in a larger more public discourse" (11). In other words, theory has opened a dialogue in which rigid, clear-cut binarisms in poetic diction have been problematized. The distinctions between such concepts are gradually shifting and becoming more inclusive and emerge as hybridized forms.

This hybridization of poetry, Reena Sastri argues, may be seen in the poems written by Louise Glück, whose poems Sastri identifies as the direction toward a twenty-first-century poetics of poetry. According to Sastri, by looking at emerging poetry anthologies and critical work, poetry evolves into a new hybrid mode that severs the distinction between lyric and experimental poetry writing modes (191). Glück's poetics exemplifies this hybridity in poetry, as it severs the binarisms of the 1970s and 1980s and instead brings the binary opposites together and blends them into new hybrid modes of expression (190-191). In literary criticism, this hybridity and breaking down of binarisms have also been recognized by critics.

For instance, Bob Dylan's Nobel Prize was given "for having created new poetic expressions within the great American song tradition," which was one of the instances in which the distinction between poetry and song was removed ("The Nobel Prize"). Ramazani, in his article on the relationship between American poetry and song, points out that the characteristics of the song are returning to poetry through the works of twenty-first-century poets (717). He points out that even though many modern and contemporary poems used the word "song" in their poems, none could fully eclipse and assume the characteristics of the song (718). This appropriation, however, enables the lines between poetry and song to become traversable, if not fully blend into one another: "[. . .] even as poetry appropriates and mimics other genres, becoming ever more porous, it also asserts its specificity, its difference from them, including song" (721). In light of Ramazani's words, one may regard Bob Dylan's Nobel Prize win as a surprise and part of a contemporary tendency of poetry toward song and performance (Desta). Taken together, both Glück's and Dylan's success show that poetry in the twenty-first century is a fluid, fragmented, unstable genre. One may argue that under the influence of ideas raised by theory, poetry also aims toward diversity manifested personal and political statements, a fluid interplay of words, music, and meaning. In response to the modernist poets' experimentations, postmodern poetry explored the extremes and in-betweens of the limitations and liminalities of poetry. Fragmentation in poetry, has resulted in versatility in form and subject matter in twenty-first-century poetry (Gioia).

The variegated forms of poetry and the wide range of topics suggest that poetry is moving toward self-expression that links the microcosm to the macrocosm by expressing social, political, and environmental concerns and more recent topics such as the effects of the new coronavirus pandemic on the individual and the society. In terms of the content of poetry, contemporary poetry may be grouped into two; poems that focus on the individual's well-being and those that concentrate on society by voicing issues of politics, ecology, and civil rights. The former, coming from the tradition of confessional poetry, makes use of personal experiences and observations in their poems as subject matter and express concerns over the body, identity, gender, mental health, and self-discovery, while the latter addresses issues including terrorist attacks, the pandemic, the environment, or racial discrimination. Considering both groups, one may argue that the poet's role in society once again becomes a leading one in contemporary poetry. The poet is expected to be an inspiring figure who will lead the people from their individual and social chaos into a place of peace.

As an example of poetry and its relationship to activism, the collection entitled "Poems of Protest, Resistance, and Empowerment" on the *Poetry Foundation* webpage underscores that one needs poetry during times of crisis. In this brief introduction, the editors of *Poetry Foundation* underscore the poet's role as the voice of the people.

> Speaking truth to power remains a crucial role of the poet in the face of political and media rhetoric designed to obscure, manipulate, or worse. The selection of poems below call out and talk back to the inhumane forces that threaten from above. They expose grim truths, raise consciousness, and build united fronts. ("Poems of Protest")

In his article on L=A=N=G=U=A=G=E poetry and activism using language, Peter Middleton claims that the movement, since it breaks away from the previous associations in language that are assumed to be fixed, rigid, and unchangeable, may be regarded as a medium of activism. "A poetry that suspects language of collusion can start where it finds itself, where you, and I, they and we find ourselves, if we start arguing and listening. To words, words and their actions," suggesting that language poetry can become a battleground in which fixed ideas may be put into question (Middleton 252).

The "Peace is Loud" poet Sonya Renee talks about the meeting of art, activism, and peace building in the interview conducted by Joanna Hoffmann:

> Art is an essential element of how we make the messages of activism accessible and how we invite new people into the dialogue and how we open up new minds to the issues. [. . .] everybody is not going to go to a protest. But you can find someone at the spoken word event, at the art gallery, picking up a poet's book, and being changed by what they hear or read. It's a more subversive way to change the minds of the masses. (Hoffman)

As Taylor's words reveal in the interview conducted by Hoffman, art and poetry can generate a hopeful spark to change the minds of individuals and may cause a ripple effect in starting that spirit of change. McDonagh, likewise, believes that in times of distress and gloom, poetry can create a piece of hope for change implicitly:

> When everything seems dark, [. . .] poetry can be a sign of the never-to-be-extinguished alternative. Poetry can be the mode in which our reason brings very disparate subjects, incommensurable subjects, into a single frame of reference. Poetry will not define the future. But by crediting a logic inherent in the heart of situations, crediting the statements implicit in poetry, we find starting points from which to develop our politics. (McDonagh 29)

In one of the darkest moments in American history, shortly after the terrorist attacks on September 11, 2001, poets from all around the country, and citizens who needed a kernel of hope, turned to poetry. In the weeks after the 9/11 attacks, the need to communicate as a community was manifested through public gatherings around Ground Zero, leaving commemorative objects and writing poetry to respond to the attacks. Matthew Zapruder states that poetry "acknowledges the impossibility as well as the need to say that which cannot be said" and even though poets may "lose words," as stated in the first lines of the collective poem project initiated by poet Bob Holman responding to 9/11 "Tower One," there is still the potential to "give birth" to new poems, as underlined by the 9/11 poem by the U. S. Poet Laureate Joy Harjo ("2000–2009: The Decade in Poetry"; Harjo "When the World"; Holman "Tower One" lines 1–2).

Another grim moment in recent human history, the global coronavirus pandemic, has also been one of the subjects for contemporary poetry. When the first lockdowns and restrictions due to the COVID-19 pandemic began and staying home meant several new things, poetry continued to be written. Several poetry collections were published, and countless poems appeared in other media. For Joy Harjo, dealing with the global pandemic for the individual was only possible through poetry, as in any significant moment, she claims, poetry helps provide a clear mental state in times of great transformation:

> We always go to poetry in times of transformation, you know—birth, death, marriage, falling in love, out of love. But here we are at a time of tremendous transformation—and where do we go? And here we are with poetry. And I get to help during this huge, transformative event that we're all part of." (Harjo "Interview")

However, this great transformative moment which Harjo is hopeful of does not register in the same way with other poets. In an interview with Cathy Park Hong, Crystal Hana Kim reveals the rising tension caused by racism. Hong's essay collection *Minor Feelings,* which is part of the subject of the interview, aims to overthrow the monolithic construction of Asian American identity, which "started out as poetry, then fiction, and then it became this collection" (Kim).

The poet Amanda Gorman has become a cultural icon, and her influence as an activist and poet is transgressing the borders of her nation. After her inauguration poem "The Hill We Climb," the former national youth poet laureate of the United States, has appeared on the covers of *Vogue* and *Porter* magazine and has been under the public eye with her involvement in discussions about female empowerment and racial liberation. She has become a figure who brings poetry to the forefront. Although some have criticized the media outlets foregrounding her personal life by focusing on her life as a young college student or her appearance through her fashionable looks, instead of her poems, another way of looking at her instant fame would be to evaluate it as an opportunity to show that poetry is alive and well, and it may once again become central in shaping the ideas of the public (Gorman "Porter Magazine"; "Vogue Magazine"). Thus, her activist background and topics she addresses in her poetry may be regarded as an opportunity to help the marginalized voices be heard. Gorman's voice represents that of the rising new generation that has concerns over the environment, civil rights, and gender liberation; it is particularly significant because it goes up against the voice of the white Anglo-Saxon male politician's voice. Thus, poets today have this difficult yet important role of registering the discussions that theory has been bringing up ever since its emergence through their poems.

THE VISIBILITY OF POETRY

McDonagh sees this new digitalization as the beginning of a new epoch for poetry, an epoch of globalization (28). Such an epoch, one may argue, needs a medium other than the printed paper to realize the necessary means of communication in a globalized society. As such, Ian Davidson and Marjorie Perloff claim that the internet and the digital universe may be the place to witness the birth of globalized poetry. Ian Davidson in *Ideas of Space in Contemporary Poetry* (2007) points out that the internet has redefined the notion of space:

> The structure of the Internet itself is "rhizomatic"; it can be broken into at any point and has no centre or periphery. The Internet and the digital technologies also produce spaces within which a variety of ideas about literature and "literary theory" can be applied or examined; a hypertext is both an application and a demonstration of intertextuality and of the importance of context to the production and reception of texts. (Davidson 163)

Davidson's emphasis on the rhizomatic space of the digital world brings into mind theoretical discussions on center and margin. It creates a space that is inclusive to established poets and those who are beginning their careers. In *Unoriginal Genius*, by using *The Waste Land* as her example of a collage and cut-ups of borrowed lines from everyday life and other texts, Perloff identifies the starting point of the twenty-first-century condition of poetry (1–3). That is, in the new information age, Perloff notes that communication has radically transformed spatially and temporally due to the introduction of digital discourse, namely "the Internet, e-mail, cell phone, and Facebook" (4).

While some poets are using the digital medium as part of their vision and stance in poetry, others have used them to adapt to the compulsory restrictions caused by the global COVID-19 pandemic. During the lockdowns, some poets also turned to digital communication tools. Regular poetry communities, such as Oxford University Poetry Society, who were meeting face to face, held events via Zoom, and slam poetry contests were organized on YouTube (Oxford University Poetry Society, "Virtual Poetry Slam 2021").

The twenty-first century is witnessing poetry appearing on digital platforms. Initially popping up in personal blogs or webpages dedicated to the genre, poetry now appears on video-sharing platforms such as YouTube and other social media platforms, including Instagram. It is common today in these platforms to encounter slam poetry contests, live poetry readings, illustrations by the poets accompanying their voice, or sharing through the descriptions their accounts about how and why this or that poem came to be. Although these poems carry no literary value for several people, having millions of followers on a social media platform suggests their influence is much larger than a local poet giving a reading in the neighborhood third-wave coffee shop or the local library. Thus, the effect of influence and the possibility of shaping others' opinions seem to show that poetry and its visibility is changing rapidly.

Perloff points out that the twenty-first century may be identified as an age of globalized communities, exemplified by the nature of the internet, where geographic locations or local circles have been transformed: "The word community thus takes on an entirely new meaning: the community now exists on particular websites or in the blogosphere—a situation whose far reaching implications we have not even begun to understand" (4). Perloff's description of the new community could be used to refer to the "follower" culture seen on social media. In fact, on Instagram, poets share their poems accompanied by a special background wallpaper or illustrations close to the post's frame (Kaur). Like the nineteenth-century poet who would participate in drawing room readings of their poems with their select society, Instagram poets organize live events online to sell tickets to the performative reading of their poems.

One such poet, Rupi Kaur, who has more than three million followers, organizes performances and readings to which one may purchase an online ticket and writes prompt cards for aspiring writers who want to get past their writer's block. Apart from these promotional uses of social media, many poets, like other artists and platform users who promote their work through social media, conduct "check-ins" to see how their followers are holding up. To elaborate, poets may ask their followers, like in a self-help retreat, if they are having a good day or whether they could finish their procrastinated work. Although this may initially seem as if poets and their digital circles are bonding through these questions, social media platforms have changed their apps in such a way that it requires artists to do these interactive "check-ins" to ensure an actively used account that makes sure they remain "visible" in the suggestions page.

In conclusion, in an age in which explorations on possible fields of post-theory continue, contemporary poetry is covering grounds in various mediums. The digital medium particularly enables what Pound emphasised in his essays on poetic diction: a three-layered melopoeia, phanopoeia, and logopoeia, as such examples have been made possible through video sharing, image, and voice performances uploaded on social media. The role of the poet, who assumed an "impersonal" voice in the poem in modernism, was "dead" for L=A=N=G=U=A=G=E poets. Yet, they managed to find their way back into the heart of the society as "influencers" with special nomadic communities that "follow" their work in the digital world.

Ron Silliman finds the emerging of poets who use communication technologies or abandon the printed page entirely and move toward new forms of technology-based visual poetries and the closing down of well-established publishing houses and journals as a symptom of poetry under construction, building itself anew through experimentation: "What's apparent is that (a) this joyride isn't over, and (b) we're all in this together. [. . .] I just hope we can find time to read & enjoy this great bounty" ("2000–2009: The Decade in Poetry"). As a final word that brings together the influence of poetry and theory in their "after-lives" one may read poetry and theory, meet, play, and leave the stage to their successors, it seems fit to use the words of Hélène Cixous: "Then, I am a poet—you know things come to me [. . .] There and then there is simply no time for Theory, only time for Thee, then, out brief candle" (212).

REFERENCE LIST

"2000–2009: The Decade in Poetry." *Poetry Foundation*. 21 Dec. 2009. https://www.poetryfoundation.org/articles/69457/2000-2009-the-decade-in-poetry.

Barry, Peter. *Beginning Theory: An Introduction to Literary and Cultural Theory*. Manchester UP, 2017.

Bernstein, Charles. "Manifest Aversions, Conceptual Conundrums, & Implausibly Deniable Links." *Poetry Foundation*.

Cixous, Helene. "Post-Word."*Post-Theory: New Directions in Criticism*. Editor Martin McQuillan.

Davidson, Ian. *Ideas of Space in Contemporary Poetry*. Palgrave, 2007.

Desta, Yohana. "Bob Dylan Lands Surprise Win for Nobel Prize in Literature." *Vanity Fair*. 13 Oct. 2016.https://www.vanityfair.com/culture/2016/10/bob-dylan-nobel-prize-literature.

Eliot, T. S. "Tendency of Some Modern Poetry."*The Complete Prose of T. S. Eliot: The Critical Edition: English Lion, 1930–1933*, editors Jason Harding and Ronald Schuchard, Baltimore, The Johns Hopkins University Press and Faber & Faber Ltd, 2015, pp. 840–845.

Gioia, Dana. "Can Poetry Matter?" *The Atlantic*. May 1991. https://www.theatlantic.com/magazine/archive/1991/05/can-poetry-matter/305062/.

Gorman, Amanda [@amandascgorman]. "Porter Magazine Cover." *Instagram*. https://www.instagram.com/p/CRzKbFxlWwN/?utm_medium=copy_link.

———. "Vogue Magazine Cover" *Instagram*. https://www.instagram.com/p/CNX1HJRFrgY/?utm_medium=copy_link.

Harjo, Joy. Interview. By Joshua Barajas, 19 Nov. 2020, PBS NewsHour, https://www.pbs.org/newshour/arts/joy-harjo-will-serve-a-rare-third-term-as-u-s-poet-laureate.

———. "When the World As We Knew It Ended—." *Poetry Foundation*. *How We Became Human: New and Selected Poems: 1975–2001*. Norton, 2002.

Hejinian, Lyn. "The Rejection of Closure." *Poetry Foundation*. *The Language of Inquiry*. U of California P, 2009.

Hoffmann, Joanna. "Poetry Is Not a Luxury: Art, Activism, and Peacebuilding." *Peace is Loud*. https://peaceisloud.org/art-activism-peacebuilding/.

Holman, Bob et al. "Tower One." *Peoples Poetry Gathering*,30 Jul. 2021. https://web.archive.org/web/20120306144919/http://www.peoplespoetry.org/pg_spotlighttwr.html.

Kaur, Rupi [@rupikaur_]. "Page 146 from Chapter 4." *Instagram*. https://www.instagram.com/p/CNdioerhenf/?utm_medium=copy_link.

Kim, Crystal Hana. Interview. "'Anti-Asian Racism Has Come Roaring Back with Covid-19': Cathy Park Hong on Being Asian American." *The Guardian*. 1 Apr. 2020. https://www.theguardian.com/books/2020/apr/01/cathy-park-hong-minor-feelings.

McDonagh, Philip. "'The Future Lies with What's Affirmed from Under': Reflections on the Ambassadorship of Poetry." *The Poetry Ireland Review*, No. 111 (December 2013), pp. 16–29.*JSTOR*. Stable URL: http://www.jstor.com/stable/43967825.

Middleton, Peter. "Language Poetry and Linguistic Activism." *Social Text*, No. 25/26 (1990), pp. 242–253.*JSTOR*. Stable URL: https://www.jstor.org/stable/466249.

"The Nobel Prize in Literature 2016." *NobelPrize.org*. Nobel Prize Outreach AB 2021. Thu. 29 Jul 2021. https://www.nobelprize.org/prizes/literature/2016/summary/.

Oxford University Poetry Society [@oupsox]. "An Evening with Taylor Biedler: Poetry and Healthcare." *Instagram*. https://www.instagram.com/p/COtLXR8BjnW/?utm_medium=copy_link.

Perloff, Marjorie. *Unoriginal Genius: Poetry by Other Means in the New Century.* U of Chicago P, 2012.
"Poems of Protest, Resistance, and Empowerment." *Poetry Foundation Collection.* https://www.poetryfoundation.org/collections/101581/poems-of-protest-resistance-and-empowerment.
Pound, Ezra. "How to Read."1929. *Literary Essays of Ezra Pound*, edited by T. S. Eliot. New Directions, 1968, pp. 15–40.
———. "The Renaissance." 1914. *Literary Essays of Ezra Pound*, edited by T. S. Eliot. New Directions, 1968, pp. 214–226.
Ramazani, Jahan. "'Sing to Me Now': Contemporary American Poetry and Song Contemporary Literature." Winter 2011, Vol. 52, No. 4, *American Poetry*, 2000–2009 (Winter 2011), pp. 716–755.*JSTOR.* Stable URL: https://www.jstor.org/stable/41472492.
Sastri, Reena. "Louise Glück's Twenty-First-Century Lyric." *PMLA*, March 2014, Vol. 129, No. 2 (March 2014), pp. 188–203.*JSTOR.* Stable URL: https://www.jstor.org/stable/24769447.
Turnbull, Neil, "Post-theory: Theory and 'the Folk.'" *New Formations* (51), 2003, pp. 99–112. ISSN 0950–2378.
"Virtual Poetry Slam 2021" Central Texas College. *YouTube.* 9 Mar. 2021. https://youtu.be/W1hndFdngVk.

17

The Posthuman Turn in Postdramatic Theater

Mesut Günenç

POSTDRAMATIC THEATER

Theater and dramaturgy have undergone radical transformations since the second half of the twentieth century. One of the key forces of change has been incorporating media and technology into theater and performing arts. Therefore, theatrical practices, theories, and debates about dramaturgical issues have changed. To reveal the new perception of theatrical practices and theories, before Lehmann's periodisation, Peter Szondi clarifies periods when examining the development of the dramatic form, which encompasses Greek drama, Renaissance drama and seventeenth-century drama (pure drama). "As a specific literary-historical event" (6), the core of the concept of drama in drama theory and philosophy has shifted from action (Aristotle) to a character (Hegel) from there further into the character's inner space, even out of the human world to the supernatural and spiritual field. According to Szondi, periodization has been the main criterion for understanding the drama, which is built on the depiction of human relationships:

> The drama of modernity came into being in the Renaissance. It was the result of a bold intellectual effort made by a newly self-conscious being who, after the collapse of the medieval worldview, sought to create an artistic reality within which he could fix and mirror himself on the basis of interpersonal relationships alone. Man entered the drama only as a fellow human being, so to speak. (7)

Szondi points out that the drama was developed in the sense of an absolute worldview: drama's self-isolation and complete human-centeredness were created/formed in the Renaissance as a reflection of the humanistic worldview/viewpoint. The character appeared whole and the subject became the hero/heroine of the drama with his internal conflicts until he fell on his dispersed subjectivity due to enlightenment and romanticism of ideas and Hegelian theory. This tradition continued until the modernist drama, which Szondi calls the crisis of drama. This crisis was shaped by the disappearance of the dramatic regime's hegemonic superiority over theater and through avant-garde movements (Expressionism, Futurism, Surrealism, and Dadaism) and later the rise of postdramatic theater. By rejecting traditional artistic practices, avant-garde movements succeeded in subverting Western philosophy, which places people at the centre of life and nature, uses the world as a testing ground and suppresses art.

Szondi puts Brecht and Epic theater as opposed to the Aristotelian norms of theater. With his postdramatic theater theory, which responds to Szondi's work (*Theory of Modern Drama*), although Lehmann acknowledges that Brecht deconstructs the dramatic roots, he points out that the Epic theatre, based on the story (fable), remained within the border of dramatic theater. However, Brecht has been very influential in paving the way for postdramatic theater with his innovations in staging the play and the art of watching.

Integrating theatrical form, Lehmann first used "Postdramatic" as a theatrical term in his book *Theater and Mythos* (*Theatre and Myth*). Eight years later, he theorized this in his work *Postdramatisches Theater* in 1999. The concept of postdramatic theater describes the aesthetics that emerged in the second half of the twentieth century (Lehmann 2006). In his book, whose roots dated back to the 1880s (Lehmann 49) and theorized the postdramatic theater practices, which can be considered as the inheritors of the Absurd Theater and Brechtian tradition, Lehmann deals with the work of experimental theater practitioners Tadeusz Kantor, Heiner Müller, and Robert Wilson, who adopted the postmodern staging methods of recent times. However, Lehmann, analyzing the theory of drama, divides dramatic forms into predramatic (ancient periods), dramatic (pure form, Racine's period in the sixteenth and seventeenth centuries), and postdramatic. In other words, Lehmann scrutinizes Western theater through the lens of chronological change: "the classical era, the dramatic theater of Europe from about the beginning of the early modern era to the downing of the twentieth century and the rise of postdramatic theatre in the wake of the aesthetic disruptions of the historical avant-garde" (Günenç 639) to prevent a radical break.

The prefix "post" does not represent a periodic category or a chronological meaning; it is only a deconstruction, a transcendence supplement without forgetting the dramatic past. It does not indicate a neglected or progressive rupture in the theatrical past, but rather separation, a state of transcendence in the entertainment relationships that continue to exist alongside the art of drama. "There is not necessarily a distinction between theatre as a drama-driven performance, creating a linear narration on stage, and performance art as a contradiction of everything that would describe the other" (Alloa and Krempl 177). In this sense, there is no such thing as a Cartesian duality as modern-postmodern in an epoch or temporal context because a total separation from the roots is impossible. However, postdramatic theater encounters early forms and traditional concepts, and scrutinizes open-ended and chaotic structures, textual forms, and narrations, representing nonhierarchical structure for readers and spectators. Instead of the interconnectivity of the earlier texts, postdramatic theater forms interconnectivity among sounds, lights, scenes, bodies and spectators, times, spaces, ideologies, and cultures and societies. At the same time, it breaks down, disassembles and disrupts within the drama itself.

Based on oral language poetry, the concept of poiesis, which is contained in Aristotle's *Poetics* and implies making, creating and producing, in conjunction with other aspects such as music, dance, rhythm, and choir, has long guided the history of the theater and structure of the play. The concept of poiesis in postdramatic theater contradicts Aristotle's idea of poiesis. Postdramatic structure dismantles identities and binary oppositions by replacing distinctions for verbal structure, the relativity of linear time, and the nonhierarchy of hierarchical structure. In the stylistic traits and aspects of postdramatic theater, it can be understood that postdramatic structure does not have a defined structure and definition. Postdramatic theater supports the parataxis/nonhierarchical, participatory, and immersive structure formed by combining signs that differ from each other and whose connection with each other is not obvious. "A non-hierarchical use of signs that aims at a synaesthetic perception and contradicts the established hierarchy" (Lehmann 87). A nonhierarchical trait disrupts dramatic conventions and forms heterogenic links in theater. Within this context, Lehmann refers to both Gilles Deleuze and Guattari's machine (schizo analytical machine) and their famous term "rhizome." On the one hand, Lehmann makes a connection with Robert Wilson's theater of metamorphosis which "leads to viewer into the dreamland of transitions, ambiguities, and correspondences" and "like Deleuzian machine, metamorphosis connects heterogeneous realities, a thousand plateaux and energy flows" (Lehmann 78). On the other hand, the rhizomatic structure reflects multiple roots "for realities in which unsurveyable branching and heterogeneous connections prevent synthesis" (Lehmann 90). Deleuze and Guattari define rhizome as a multifaceted alternative to the unity of a tree. Rhizome connects in any direction unendingly. As a dramaturgical form, rhizome links the continuing transformative progress in our performance (Hovik and Perez 106). With the help of heterogeneous elements and the density of signs, the theater forms a multitude of rhizomatic connections. The rhizomatic structure is exposed by dividing the dramatic time into minimum sequences, deconstructing the dramatic form using sound and visual effects, and rendering the space multiple, the reproduction of the signs, and simultaneous use without generating dignity.

DEFINITION OF POSTHUMANISM

Posthumanism, accepted as an umbrella term, has no single definition. Posthumanism embraces "philosophical, cultural, and critical posthumanism, transhumanism, new materialisms (a specific feminist development within the posthumanist frame), and the heterogeneous landscapes of antihumanism, posthumanities, and metahumanities" (Ferrando 26). Posthumanism refers to a divergence from both humanism and man himself. It is concerned with a technology-saturated society (technoculture) and a profound shift in civilization and human experience or rethinking man's interaction with nature and the world. Rosi Braidotti's "The Posthuman" is a sharply critical work of humanism, in which the same liberal individualistic subject is struck, whose perfection lies in his autonomy and self-determination (23). Posthumanist theory offers a deconstruction of alienating the integrity of nature to man and the other.

The understanding of posthumanism rejects the foundations of western humanism originating from the seventeenth and eighteenth centuries. In *Discourse on the Method,* Descartes claims that human reason ascertains the human existence with his famous dictum, "I think therefore I am," and describes human as independent and rational beings. Human's distinctive sense of individualism was also central to Locke's philosophy. To Locke, the human being is "a thinking, intelligent being, that has reason and reflection, and can consider itself as itself, the same thinking thing in different times and places" (335); however, other thinkers such as Darwin, Nietzsche, and Freud reject the idea of the human being as a liberal individual in the center of the world and humanist ideal. Discourse for Darwin is to deconstruct the thought that humanity was created in God's image, questioning the truth for Nietzsche and "the unconscious for Freud" (Davies 70). On the other hand, Martin Heidegger differs from the Cartesian thought by pointing that "Da-sein can explicitly discover beings which it encounters in the environment, can know about them, can avail of them, can have world" (58). In the twentieth century, interaction with the environment is the driving force behind identity formation. In the second half of the twentieth century, defending the decentralization of human perception and deconstruction of grand narratives, self, and the other, the postmodernists view heralded a new period. The plan to depose a central subject in favor of more marginalized concerns continued in poststructuralist, feminist, and postmodern thought (Causey 52). The acceptance of the human as a perfect being has vanished as a result of the change that began with Barthes, Derrida, and Foucault, Lyotard's *Postmodern Condition* (1979), Fredric Jameson's *Postmodernism or, the Cultural Logic of Late Capitalism* (1991), Baudrillard's *Simulacra and Simulation* (1981), and Deleuze and Guattari's *A Thousand Plateaus* (1987).

Like postmodernism, posthumanism hones in on several critical situations toward the traditional understanding of life and it refers to the deconstruction of patriarchal order and "our current maze of dualism" (Haraway 181). Haraway's essay "Cyborg Manifesto" (1991) identifies "a hybrid of machine and organism" (Haraway 149) that supports the transformation in society. To Jay David Bolter, posthumanism is a reaction "to what are perceived as totalizing practices and rhetorics of the modern era. In each case, the reaction was an attempt to subvert claims to unity, simplicity, or universality" (2). Posthumanist theory opposes the ideas of humanism that have been accepted and applied as the great western narrative that dominates the whole world. Posthumanists claim that the prevailing western ideas and humanism have come to an end because human thoughts, feelings, desires, and forms have changed radically in the historical process. For that reason, "[w]e need to understand that five hundred years of humanism may be coming to an end as humanism transforms itself into something that we must helplessly call posthumanism" (Hassan 843). Louise Lepage, analyzing N. Katherine Hayles's work *How We Became Posthuman* (1999), clarifies the posthuman term "as a point of view constructed within and by historically specific and emergent configurations of embodiment, technology, and culture" (139) and specifies that the posthuman view "configures human being so that it can be seamlessly articulated with intelligent machines" (Hayles 2). According to Hayles, a posthuman subject does not function like an interpersonal drama does. A character's relationship in drama is usually based on their mind, emotions, and/or physiological urges (sexuality). Within this context, the idea of united humanity and liberal subject boundaries is deconstructed.

Decentralizing human identity undermines binary oppositions such as man/animal, "male/female, physical/virtual, meat/machine, local/foreigner, normal/pathological" (Jurani 245). Decentralization creates the emergence of hybridization and hybrid identities that lose their integrity and boundaries. Artificially, hybrid identities contain mutable human minds and bodies. This change and the emergence of the media and digital culture represent the posthumanist subjects by deconstructing liberal subjects. In this sense, the metaphor of a rhizome opposes the hierarchical structure and supports a pluralistic structure is central to posthumanist theory and posthuman drama. Rather than a binary opposition, one can speak of a rhizomatic structure that evolves spontaneously in the required direction and maintains the self-nourishing ones of the related bonds. With its chaotic and anarchic structure, "the rhizome is anti-hierarchical and a-centred. No single organizing principle predetermines the consistencies and compatibilities between the network of its elements" (O'Sullivan 84). Posthumanism thus attempts to decenter the root and supports an antihierarchical structure. This section of the chapter has presented a brief history of how the key ideals of Western humanism developed, how historically ideals of humanism were decentralized, and the path posthumanism was opened. The following section of the study will analyze rhizomatic creative process in posthuman drama and postdramatic theater.

THE POSTHUMAN TURN IN POSTDRAMATIC THEATER

In his study "Postorganic Performance: The Appearance of Theatre in Virtual Spaces" Matthew Causey coalesces the term Posthuman with theater in 1999 to describe performances that drive the theatrical aesthetics of media and technology. Posthumanism focuses on technological issues and change, where no character and actor is at the center of the work, takes its place in the performing arts. Posthumanism adapts to changing cultural contexts and aesthetics. By their subject matter, some contemporary texts evoke a posthumanist way of reading or create new dramaturgical structures and characters. Posthumanist dramaturgy occurs, for example, in technological theater, which is far from text-based performing arts. In this regard, the posthuman series envisage an alternate space for a theater that responds to the changes of its time. Katherine Hayles noticeably proposes significative four stages of posthumanism. In the third stage, Hayles hones in on posthuman thoughts on the body "as the original prostheses becomes a continuation of a process that began before we were born" (3). Just as we need to return to the origins and aspirations of humanism to understand posthumanism, the development, innovations, new boundaries, and nonhierarchical structure in drama, as in Hayles' prosthetic feature, we need to turn to the interconnected dramatic origins, historical changes, and stages. "While the prefix 'post' indicates that the posthuman comes after the human, i.e. that it is subsequent to the human chronologically, it also suggests that it is in the proximity of the human, in the sense that it still depends on the human ontologically" (Giannachi 61). Karen JursMunby defines postdramatic theater as the "anamnesis of dramatic theatre" because anamnesis represents "the rediscovering of knowledge already inside us, the re-emerging of knowledge generated during past incarnations" (Cassiers et al 47). Similar to Hayles's prosthetic feature, historical stages and different periods are connected in the name of hypertextuality in postdramatic theater.

Like the concept of posthumanism, posthuman theater is an evolutionary concept. In this evolutionary concept, posthumanism hones in on aesthetics, art theory, media, and digital spectacle in performance art and theater. Matthew Causey, analyzing "the appearance of theatre in the virtual space [. . .] establishes a unique aesthetic object" (51) and technological mediatised devices in the twentieth century, identifies the place of theatre in the "posthuman phase" (52). Within this context, the virtually mediated performance creates posthuman bodies referred to Kantor's works, which shape the understanding of contemporary theater. In his manifesto "The Theatre of Death," Kantor asserts that "[t]he 'first actor' brought with him 'the revelatory MESSAGE, which was transmitted from the realm of DEATH, [and] evoked in the VIEWERS [. . .] a metaphysical shock" (114). The dissolution of the first actor and body-centered thought is one of the main elements of postdramatic theater; the body no longer represents the human subject in the central sense and essential aloneness or hybrid existence is observed. In Kantor's theater, "the performer's human body disappears under the weight of texts and objects" (84), which disrupts the definition of dramatic theater with its mysterious and animistically animated objects (81). In other words, the central human subject no longer represents "performative truth" (86).

Researchers such as Causey, Giannachi, Haraway, and Hayles contributed terms such as virtual theater, cyborg theater, multimedia theater, and cyberformance forming concepts such as posthuman body, posthuman theater, and hybrid subjects. Through integrating technology and media with performance, subjects and identities are hybridized. Spectators are impelled to see the posthuman subject on stage. The posthuman subject means that the subject is now technologically transformed into a performance-integrated entity, contrary to traditional western theatrical thinking. Thus, the new stage needs "the creation of hybrid forms of performance, forms of a monstrous theatre that bridge, extend, and explore the gaps between the live and the mediated" (Causey 182). Gaps between real and virtual sides and the posthuman subject cause argument and confusion among spectators because the posthuman subject is no longer fixed, unchangeable; however, it can be formed as hybrid subjects (Giannachi 76).

Carl Lavery and Clare Finburgh Delijani, who discuss nonanthropocentric aesthetics in theater in *Rethinking of the Theatre of the Absurd*, LePage, and Louis van den Hengel are among the scholars who form links between non-anthropocentric view and theater. Theater, by its very nature, is an anthropocentric art form. Aristotle puts forward theater as an art of mimesis and representation. This anthropocentric art form needs a human performance and privileges it. However, several avantgarde and modern genres have shattered anthropocentric ideals. Human identities and conflicts have "been the matter of theatre for thousands of years, not only for the tragic, but through comedy, irony, the absurd, allegory, the epic, naturalism, Brechtian and post-Brechtian theatre, and the many inventive, contemporary hybrids of performance praxis" (Heim 291).

There is also an indisputable link among both the theory of Lehmann and the roots of posthumanism. Like rhizomatic structure, posthuman drama and postdramatic theater do not have a certain explanation or form. Both postdramatic theater and posthumanism are "umbrella terms for various, often hybrid, theatrical forms to which all or some of the following assertions apply" (Jurani 247). Thus, "postanthropocentric theatre would be a suitable name for an important (though not the only) form that postdramatic theatre can take." (Lehmann 81). Instead of a traditional rule that automatically adopts linear thought; a polycentric structure emerges with posthumanism. As the principle of polyglossia represents "multi-lingual theatre texts" (Lehmann 147) in postdramatic aspects, the nonlinear paradoxical structure of the posthuman structure emerges with heteroglossia. A method that further changes the non-linear linearity evoke a rhizomatic way of thinking. "Because posthumanism is symptomatically rhizomatic, surveying its genealogical roots as a movement and a body of theoretical works cannot easily follow a linear, chronological path" (Ağın Dönmez 3) thus the text is necessarily deconstructed. Through the rhizomatic structure, postdramatic theater is more than texts "the viewer is no longer entirely in one location, they are also no longer viewing something that has a clear beginning, middle and end" (Gabriella 11). Rewriting texts is becoming increasingly important. Texts that emerge from fixed roots and traditions can acquire variable and unbalanced features through technological devices, the media, and the density of signs. Lehmann, sharing Gertrude Stein's thoughts: "there will be no drama, not even a story; it will not be possible to differentiate protagonists and even roles and identifiable characters will be missing. For postdramatic theatre Stein's aesthetics is of great importance" (Lehmann 63) analyzes how dramatic root and role of characters are deconstructed and how audiences behave and think freely without abiding plot of the story and thoughts of hero/heroines. In this context, posthuman and postdramatic theater is in an ongoing process.

When the relationship between postdramatic theater and posthuman drama is analyzed, we can find the purpose of deconstructing anthropocentrism and a character's thoughts in both. When focusing on the concepts of postdramatic theater and posthuman drama, besides removing the traditional form, body, and character from the central position, deconstructing text-based drama, subject, and forming a nonhierarchical structure, the position of the center itself has started to be questioned. As Elinor Fuchs discusses the logic of three giving examples from Aristotle's tragic structure: reversal, recognition, and suffering, Hegel's universal dialectical theory: thesis, antithesis, and synthesis, Szondi's and Lehmann's division of forms of drama: predramatic-dramatic and postdramatic theater, Rosi Braidotti divides the accurate study of humanity as man, human and posthuman: "if the proper study of mankind used to be man and the proper study of humanity was the human . . . the proper study of the posthuman condition is the posthuman itself" (159). Postdramatic theater, representing the proper study of drama, can form new discourse and theatrical signs about experimental performances, the role of audiences, new media tools, the use of technology on the scene, and the deconstruction of the character's existence. Matthew Causey, while explaining cyber or computer-aided theater, mentions "another possibility of computer-aided performance which is to allow audiences interactive access to the performance with hypertextual, image and sound data banks, in which audience members are able to access and to direct the process of a performance" (49).

Both posthuman drama and postdramatic theater, without completely rejecting the previous theories and philosophical views, form multiple structures by feeding on different roots, as in the rhizomatic structure. Supporting this structure and thinking, Ihab Hassan asserts that "both Foucault and Lévi-Strauss, I am convinced, mean not the literal end of man but the end of a particular image of us, shaped as much by Descartes, say, as by Thomas More or Erasmus or Montaigne" (845). Along with the ideas that have been deconstructed since the Enlightenment era, "gender, feminist and post-colonial studies are the prototypes" (Braidotti148) of new experimental work in posthumanism. In this context, avant-garde theories, Peter Szondi *Theory of the Modern Drama*, Antonin Artaud's *Theatre of Cruelty*, and Bertolt Brecht's *Epic Theatre* concept are the prototypes of experiential work in postdramatic theater. Like Ihab Hassan's thought *not the literal end of man*, postdramatic theater does not support the literal end of drama but the end of pure dramatic form because "we should reverse our point of view and see theatre as a phenomenon explainable by other concepts and theories (transgressing the field boundaries). The specific theatre mimetic behaviour (involving professional actors and audience) should be understood as an instance of mental strategies and cognitive faculties, which makes us able to live in a community" (Motal 251). Nontraditional and nonanthropocentric theatrical thoughts and developments may create chaos and crises in drama, however, support cognitive strategies, active participation, and experimental structure.

Laurens De Vos and Louise Lepage, scrutinizing Mark Ravenhill and Sarah Kane's plays, are among both posthuman drama and postdramatic theater scholars. Lepage published her articles as "Posthuman Perspectives and Postdramatic Theatre:

The Theory and Practice of Hybrid Ontology in Kate Mitchell's The Waves" and "Rethinking Sarah Kane's Characters: A Human(ist) Form and Politics." De Vos also edited the work *Sarah Kane in Context* with Graham Saunders. In his article "Faust Is Dead. Mark Ravenhill's View on a Posthuman Era," De Vos deconstructs the dramatic notion of character by the way struggle "between inhumanity and posthumanity is represented in contemporary drama" (652) and hero/heroine transforms into active participants in the performance, explaining postmodern sensibility of character death. In her articles, Louise Le Page scrutinizes that Kane encounters Cartesian dualism and "binaries such as mind/body, subject/object and here/there" (Lepage 253) starting from *Blasted* to *4.48 Psychosis*. The same purpose of decentering the human perspective is shared in postdramatic theater and posthuman drama. Humankind is still set at the center of the words in postdramatic and posthuman; however, this center has moved or been replaced (Hovik and Perez 103). Kane's distinctive play *Crave* deconstructs the traditional centralized subject. Instead of specific character identity, Kane uses the letters A, B, C, and M. In this way, different identities, genders, and thoughts can be constructed instead of names, bodies, and thoughts determined by the reader or the audience.

In both Ravenhill's and Kane's plays, the concept of the character, originally in the theater, has been deconstructed, and a more paradoxical character/performer has emerged.

With the deconstruction of the characters, postdramatic play as a model marks the rhizome progress in performance. The text, which is decentralized with its rhizomatic structure, supports the editing of different events and the audience's active participation with unlimited character creation. The postdramatic text can create the posthuman process for contemporary theatre. Wallace Heim lays bare the relationship between postdramatic theater and posthumanism: "Lehmann does remind us of the need for theater production not to represent the facts, but to present, rather than spell out, a situation or human condition. The postdramatic, for Lehmann, may make evident more of the hidden dynamics of conflicts (. . .). Lehmann finds that the postdramatic may be a reflection of, rather than a resistance to, contemporary social structures" (300). These social structures are opposed to Western thought reflecting the root, linear connections, and hierarchical structure.

CONCLUSION

Since the past, through avant-garde movements and theories, Cartesian thought, Da Vinci's universal model of Vitruvian Man and binary oppositions have been deconstructed, and the concept of posthuman has replaced anthropocentrism. The roots of Aristotelian thought, which continued its influence in the dramatic structure until the twentieth century, has been unsphered by avant-garde movements, Epic Theater, *Theory of Modern Drama* (1956) by Peter Szondi, *The Death of Character: Perspectives on Theatre After Modernism* (1996) by Elinor Fuchs, and Gertrude Stein's ideas on "Landscape Play." Furthermore, instead of linear time/space and traditional structure, new spaces/locations and original movements emerged. At this point, postdramatic theater emerges, which technically involves the audience during the performance, supports and includes the concepts of the density of signs, and the irruption of the real and landscape.

Both posthuman and postdramatic plays share a rhizomatic structure that does not follow a linear and chronological route. Such plays are inundated with identity and role changes in which characters exchange clothes and even bodies; hybridity, boundaries, and potentials of corporeal existence are explored artistically and philosophically by envisaging a posthuman future. While the dramatic hero/heroine was ruled in a god-centered position in the ancient period, he/she came to an anthropocentric position in the Elizabethan era. In postmodern and later postdramatic theater, the epistemological phenomenon has been deconstructed, and subjects of essential character, hierarchical structure, and a meaningful universe have been dismissed. Deconstruction of borders, nonhierarchy, and a chaotic environment is represented by posthuman and postdramatic drama. Wholeness is disrupted. Rootlessness is created, thus "there is no dramatic, beginning, middle and end and there is no single privileged spectacle, character or point of view" (Lepage 145). Theater will produce new performances in the following cycles in which nonhuman beings, performances in nature, the chaotic framework of the action, and new (s)cenes will be at the heart of drama. It denotes the end, not of humanity, but the central human image, not of the theater, but also the conventional and traditional theatrical image.

REFERENCE LIST

Alloa, Emmanuel and Krempl, Sophie-Therese. "Philosophy and Theatre: Incestuous Beginnings, Looking Daggers and Other Dangerous Liaisons—a Dialogue," in *The Routledge Companion to Performance Philosophy* (eds.). Laura Cull O Maoilearca and Alice Lagaay. Routledge, 2020, pp. 174–182.

Braidotti, Rosi. *The Posthuman*.Polity Press, 2013. Print.

Causey, Matthew. *Theatre and Performance in Digital Culture from Simulation to Embeddedness.* Routledge, 2006.

Cassiers, Edith, De Laet, Timmy and Dries, Luk Van Den. "Text: The Director's Notebook", (Eds. Michael Shane Boyle, Matt Cornish and Brandon Woolf), in *Postdramatic Theatre and Form,* Methuen Drama, 2019, pp. 33–47.

Davies, Tony. *Humanism.* 2nd ed. Routledge, 2008. Print.

Dönmez Ağın, Başak. *Posthuman Ecologies in Twenty-First Century Short Animations.* Ph.D Dissertation. Hacettepe University, 2015.

Ferrando, Francesca. "Posthumanism, Transhumanism, Antihumanism, Metahumanism, and New Materialisms: Differences and Relations," *Existenz*,Vol. 8 No. 2,2013, pp. 26–32.

Giannachi, Gabriella. *An Introduction.* Routledge, 2004.

Günenç, Mesut. "A Paradigm of Dramatic and Postdramatic Tragedy: Simon Stephens's Motortown," *Folklor/Edebiyat*, Vol. 25, No. 99, 2019, pp. 635–644.

Haraway, Donna. "A Cyborg Manifesto: Science, Technology, and Socialist-Feminism in the Late Twentieth Century," in *Simians, Cyborgs and Women: The Reinvention of Nature*. Routledge, 1991, pp. 149–181.

Hassan, Ihab. "Prometheus as Performer: Toward a Posthumanist Culture?" *The Georgia Review*, Vol.31, No. 4, 1977, pp. 830–50.

Heidegger, Martin. *Being and Time*, trans. Joan Stambaugh, Revised and with a Foreword by Dennis J. Schmidt, Albany: State University of New York Press, (1953), 2010.

Heim, Wallace. "Theatre, Conflict and Nature," *Green Letters, Studies in Ecocriticism*, Vol.20, no.3, 2016, pp. 290–303.

Hovik, Lise and Perez, Elena. "Baby Becomings Towards a Dramaturgy of Sympoietic Worlding", *Nordic Theatre Studies*, Vol.32, No. 1, 2020, pp. 99–120.

Jurani, Milo. "Breaking away from Egocentrism Posthumanism as a Way Contemplating Non-human Matters on Stage," *The Slovak Theatre*, Vol.68, No.3, 2020, pp. 239–52. Doi: https://doi.org/10.31577/sd-2020-0015.

Kantor, Tadeusz. *A Journey Through Other Spaces: Essays and Manifestos, 1944–1990*, ed. and trans. M. Kobialka. University of California Press, 1993.

Lehmann, Hans Thies. *Postdramatic Theatre*. Routledge, 2006.

Lepage, Louise. "Posthuman Perspective and Postdramatic Theatre: the Theory and Practice of Hybrid Ontology in Katie Mitchell's The Waves," *Cultura, Lenguaje Y Representación / Culture, Language and Representation*. ISSN 1697–7750 · Vol VI, 2008, pp. 137–149.

Lepage, Louise. "Rethinking Sarah Kane's Characters: A Human(ist) Form and Politics," *Modern Drama*, Vol.57, No.2, 2014, pp. 252–272.

Locke, John.*An Essay Concerning Human Understanding*. Edited with an Introduction, Critical Apparatus and Glossary by Peter H. Nidditch.Oxford University Press, 1975.

Motal, Jan. "Behind the Curtain of Phylogeny: From Theatrical Anthropocentrism to Interspecies Appreciation," *The Slovak Theatre*, Vol. 67, No. 3, 2019, pp. 240–257. DOI 10.31577/sd-2019–0014.

O'Sullivan, Simon. "Cultural Studies as Rhizome—Rhizomes in Cultural Studies." In Herbrechter, S. (ed.) *Cultural Studies, Interdisciplinarity and Translation*. Rodopi, 2002, pp. 81–93.

Szondi, Peter. *Theory of Modern Drama*, trans. M. Hays. University of Minnesota, 1987.

IV
POST-PHILOLOGIES

18

Post-Theory and Post-Translation Studies

Evrim Doğan Adanur

Analyzing Post-theory in relation to studies in translation is conducive in the new millennium, since translation provides a wider arena in terms of the necessity for the inclusion of a larger world and diverse cultures beyond the Eurocentric. Moreover, the study of the cultural and ideological power relations in the process and output of translation, together with interdisciplinary approaches to it, provides applicable possibilities to theory in general. Even though a working theory of translation apart from the normative and prescriptive notions with wider theoretical applications has started to be discussed in the last century and the emergence of translation as a field of academic study encompassing the theoretical and applied fields was proposed in the 1970s, the practice of translation has been a debate since antiquity, which provided a base to later formulations.

The "how" of translation has been a popular subject since Cicero, Horace, and St. Jerome, who contested the corollaries of translation, juxtaposing the "word-for-word (verbum pro verbo)" with the "sense-for-sense (sensum pro sensu)" approaches. Debates on this binary continued through the centuries, where the main discussion was related to the translations of Ancient Greek and Latin texts and Bible translations.

During the rise of the national and vernacular languages in Europe, the early modern era produced novel approaches to translation. Étienne Dolet in *La manière de bientraduired'une langue enautre* ("How to Translate Well from One Language into Another" 1540) proposed essential translation principles including how translation must be handled in a scientific way and the importance of the usages of the target language together with the formal and lingual aspects of the original text (Bassnett 2013, 63-64). His principles opposing the contemporary translation practice in terms of his emphasis on the style of the target text and avoiding a literal translation for the sake of the vernacular became one of the reasons for his conviction for heresy and ensuing execution. Such a strategy also is used by George Chapman, who, in his English translation of the *Iliad*, followed domestication strategies, introducing a "Renaissance Homer" (Bassnett 2013, 22). In the seventeenth century, John Dryden wrote on the different types of translation arguing they be "metaphrase," "paraphrase," and "imitation," with a preference to paraphrase, especially concerning the translation of poetry (Dryden 17).

German translator Friedrich Schleiermacher, in the aftermath of Romantic discussions of the vital power of imagination and notions regarding "translatability" and "untranslatability," introduced the importance of the relationship between the source text and the target reader, and suggested that the translator either "leaves the writer alone as much as possible and moves the reader toward the writer, or he leaves the reader alone as much as possible and moves the writer toward the reader," preferring the former strategy (42). Schleiermacher's position elevates the source text and proposes that a separate sub-language be created in literary translation. Such views were followed by Dante Gabriel Rosetti, who defended the priority of the linguistic and formal aspects of the source text.

During the Victorian era, the necessity of a focus on the source text gained even more importance. The archaic language created in a target text through an effort to keep all the elements of the original text was preferred by critics and translators like Matthew Arnold, Thomas Carlyle, and Edward Fitzgerald. The primacy of the source language text was elevated, and translation was seen as a tool to upgrade the value of the source text language and culture.

With the turn of the twentieth century, the insistence on the juxtaposition of the *original* and the *translated* continued. Walter Benjamin, in "The Task of the Translator" (1923), wrote about the reciprocity between languages and argued that the translation is the "continued life" of the original text suggesting that "no translation, however good it may be, can have any significance as regards the original" (73, 72). The afterlife of the original, that is translation, for Benjamin provides an "ever-renewed latest and most abundant flowering" (73). Following Schleiermacher and Benjamin, in 1937, José Ortega y Gasset wrote "The Misery and the Splendor of Translation" in which he suggested that translation be not handled as a "magic manipulation" of one language of another, but rather as a different literary genre (109).

The 1950s and '60s saw a more linguistic-oriented approach to translation studies replacing the literary approach, especially through Eugene Nida and Andréi Federov. The theorists mainly dwelled on the notion of *equivalence* in translation. In the wake of structuralism, semiotic and linguistic approaches to translation arose with the aim of bringing a systematic approach to translation studies leading to theory, as a discipline, also named *traductologie*, separating itself from the practice of translation, especially through Eugene Nida's *componential analysis*, evaluating the components in the two languages for verbal equivalence. Roman Jacobson's semiotic approach and Jean-Paul Vinay and Jean Darbelnet's semantic approach dwelled on the kinds and lingual procedures of translation. Focusing on the core aspects of linguistics, Jakobson discussed the notion of translatability and equivalence between two languages, claiming that any concept can be rendered in any language, disregarding the culture or language specific concepts in praise for the universal aspects of language.

The notion of equivalence continued to be at the center of translation studies in the 1960s and 1970s. Werner Koller and Eugene Nida proposed a typology of equivalence. Eugene Nida, while working on Bible translations, underlined the importance of the cultural, together with the linguistic, proposing that paraphrasing would eliminate cultural differences whenever there is no shared referent. The cultural knowledge of the translator, Nida proposed, would help solve problems in translation through the translator's understanding of the ethnological and cultural contingent, by the semantic analysis of meaning across languages. Apart from the pragmatic equivalence, Nida worked on formal and dynamic equivalence in which the cultural elements, together with the linguistic, are to be studied to evaluate the context of a text. Analyzing the surface and deep structures, Nida proposed that the target text should create the same effect in the target culture as the source text did in the original culture (*Toward a Science of Translating*, 1964).

Likewise, Peter Newmark, in his *Approaches to Translation*, proposed a distinction between two types of translation: *semantic*, which is related to the linguistic equivalence, and *communicative*, which is related to the text's relative effect on the target culture. Juliane House, in *A Model for Translation Quality Assessment*, also tackled the cultural significance of the text through her discussions of "overt" and "covert" translations, still debating certain elements of linguistic equivalence.

George Steiner progressively suggested that all forms of communication were acts of translation and argued that a credible translation between languages would be a futile attempt, since all translation would be molded with the subjectivity of the translator. In *After Babel*, Steiner offered a hermeneutical approach instead of a linguistic one, proposing that the purpose of language is not simply communicating but also reconstructing meaning, as any form of communication is through understanding, which is maintained through translation across times and places (29).

The focus of studies in translation increasingly shifted from the significance of the source text to that of the target text, from the understanding of translation as a linguo-cultural phenomenon to a culturally driven, autonomous product that engenders new possibilities. In the 1970s, Katherina Reiss and Hans J. Vermeer introduced a more functionalist and pragmatic approach to translation. Naming their approach *Skopostheorie*, they dwelled on the importance of the text types that determine the type of translation. Positing that linguistic equivalence would not be adequate since translation was not "merely and not even primarily a linguistic process," they proposed looking "somewhere else" (qtd. in Nord, *Translating* 10). Skopos theory rejected the idea of translation as a form of transcoding and defined it as a form of "purposeful human activity:" what determines the translation phenomenon is the prospective function of the target text, produced in that target culture. Focusing on the situation of the target text and the cultural background of the target text user, the skopos, purpose, of the target text, as opposed to that of the source text, was examined. Christiane Nord proposed that the "function of the target text is not arrived at automatically from an analysis of the source text, but is pragmatically defined by the purpose of the intercultural communication," that is, translation (*Text Analysis* 9). The functionalist approach also brought about a study of the procedures of translation in a given culture. Proposing that it is neither the author nor the translator, but the *initiator*, who starts the translation process, the functionalist critics underlined the importance of the *situation* of the target text, which is always different from the source text. The ideological and economic aspects of the target text situation are therefore brought under scrutiny.

The notion of *deforming tendencies*, another important contribution to translation studies, was offered by Antoine Berman, who, in his "Translation and the Trials of the Foreign" (1984), argued that the *domestication* strategies as opposed to *foreignization* techniques in translation bring about the assimilation of the source text and language into the target text audience and culture. In his view, translation is "the trial of the foreign," which builds a bridge between the self-same and foreign, where there is a trial for the target culture with the foreign text, and a trial for the foreign text by being offered in a different context (284). In the notion of the *negative analytic* of translation, Berman proposed that translated texts tend to produce a "text that is more 'clear', more 'elegant', more 'fluent', more 'pure' than the original" through "ethnocentric, annexationist translations and hypertextual translations (pastiche, imitation, adaptation, free rewriting), where the play of deforming forces is freely exercised. Every translator is inescapably exposed to this play of forces, even if he (or she) is animated by another aim" (296, 286).

James S. Holmes pronounced the necessity of studies in translation as a distinct field of academic study in his seminal "The Name and Nature of Translation Studies" (1972). His call for a new academic discipline that requires a classification separate from the purely linguistic and the literary proved popular, shifting the focus of translation studies from the prescriptive, normative, and linguistic to cultural and descriptive paradigms, embracing both the theoretical and applied aspects of translation. Holmes offered a scientific division of translation studies into two main parts: *pure*, including the theoretical and descriptive studies, and *applied* studies that cover translation criticism, translator training and aids, in order to include all forms of studies in translation through the centuries (71).

Another change from the merely linguistic aspects of translation was offered by Itamar Even-Zohar and Gideon Toury. Even-Zohar proposed the *polysystem theory*, while Toury introduced *descriptive translation studies*, both offering a target-oriented approach. In polysystem theory, "different literatures and genres, including translated and non-translated works, compete for dominance" and translated literature is observed in "a system operating in the larger social, literary and historical systems of the target culture" (Munday 21, 189). No matter how he based his theories on the formalist approach, Even-Zohar describes polysystem theory as "a multiple system, a system of various systems which intersect with each other and partly overlap, using concurrently different options, yet functioning as one structured whole, whose members are interdependent." Therefore, polysystem theory studies how the target culture selects works for translation and how "translation norms, behaviour and policies are influenced by other co-systems" (qtd. in Munday 190). Toury pointed out the significance of the translations in the social and literary systems of the target culture as the "facts of target cultures: on occasion facts of a peculiar status, sometimes even constituting identifiable (sub)-systems of their own" (qtd in Munday 175). In order to situate the translation's larger role in the target culture, Toury calls for a three-phase methodology: look for the significance or acceptability of the target text in the target culture system, analyze source text and target text pairs through textual analysis, and try to find generalizations and patterns between the pairs in order to reach a systematic understanding (Munday 175). Descriptive translation studies, therefore, deals with the study of product, function, and process (Munday 17).

The polysystem theory was pursued by Theo Hermans, Susan Bassnett, and André Lefevere. Susan Bassnett's *Translation Studies*, first published in 1980, brought together diverse approaches to translation studies including the linguistic, philosophical, and literary, bringing a historical approach to the discipline. Theo Hermans edited *The Manipulation of Literature: Studies in Literary Translation* (1985), which introduced a "new paradigm" in translation studies. In the introduction to the volume, Hermans reacts against what he calls "naively romantic concepts of 'artistic genius', 'originality', 'creativity', and a severely restricted notion of what constitutes a 'national literature'" (7). If, Hermans resumes, this genius is directly related to a national language, the literature produced by it would "assume an aura of sacred untouchability," and translating the original text therefore be "condemned as a foolhardy and barely permissible undertaking, doomed from the start and to be judged, at best, in terms of relative fidelity, and at worst as outright sacrilege" (7-8). Hermans proposes that translations either create a "separate subsystem, with its own characteristics and models, or be more or less fully integrated into the indigenous system" or even that "they may form part of the system's prestigious centre or remain a peripheral phenomenon; they may be used as 'primary' polemical weapons to challenge the dominant poetics, or they may shore up and reinforce the prevailing conventions" and "all translation implies a degree of manipulation of the source text for a certain purpose" (10).

The contributors to Hermans's volume were later called "The Manipulation School." Studies in translation increasingly exhibited a "move from translation as text to translation as culture and politics" (Munday 198). *The cultural turn* announced by Mary Snell-Hornby in her article in *Translation/History/Culture* (1990), edited by Bassnet and Lefevere, became the umbrella for different viewpoints, including the practice of translation in the contemporary scene and "the power exercised in and on the publishing industry in pursuit of specific ideologies, feminist writing and translation, translation as 'appropriation', translation and colonization, and translation as rewriting, including film rewrites" as Munday explains (198). Their aim is to examine the text and translation activity in relation to "the larger issues of context, history and convention." or what we would now call identity politics (*Translation/History/Culture*, 11).

In the preface to *Translation/History/Culture: A Sourcebook*, André Lefevere and Susan Bassnett proclaim that translation studies would bring together diverse fields such as "linguistics, literary study, history, anthropology, psychology and economics," underlining the interdisciplinary prospects of the field (xi). A novelty of the Manipulation School is seeing translation as "a rewriting of an original text," which they see as manipulation in relation to dynamics of power in a given culture. Translation, through refractions, is a means to carry a work of literature from one system to another. (13). Such a manipulation of literature relates to some ideology and poetics and is determinant in the "evolution of a literature and a society," introducing "new concepts, new genres, new devices." Therefore, they argue, "the history of translation is the history also of literary innovation, of the shaping power of one culture upon another," with a simultaneous power to "repress innovation, distort and contain" (xi). "In an age of ever increasing manipulation of all kinds," Bassnett and Lefevere maintain, "the study of the manipulative processes of literature as exemplified by translation can help us toward a greater awareness of the world in which we live" (xi). Moreover, in *Translation, Rewriting, and the Manipulation of Literary Fame*, Lefevere proposes that—due to the determinants in the target culture, and as a result of the preferences resulting from the variables in the target culture—all translation is a form of rewriting. He posits three factors controlling the translation mechanism: ideology, patronage, and poetics. And he suggests that as the most "recognizable" type of rewriting, translation "is potentially the most influential because it is able to project the image of an author and/or those works beyond the boundaries of their culture of origin" (9). Another important aspect of his book is that it also analyzes translations from non-Anglophone cultures. Lefevere points out that during translations to English, the language of power, the translators prefer to "rewrite . . . in terms of a system their potential audience would be able to understand" (77). Therefore, domestication strategies are followed in translations *to* the English language.

The predilection of foreignization instead of domestication strategies in translation, where adequacy is expected in translation to Western languages and equivalence is sought for in translations from Western languages, is further scrutinized by Lawrence Venuti in *The Translator's Invisibility: A History of Translation* (1995). Venuti argued that domestication is a means to reduce the source text ethnocentrically to the target culture while foreignization is "ethnodeviant," celebrating the linguistic and cultural differences of the text (125). Venuti further criticizes the British and American publishers who "have reaped the financial benefits of successfully imposing English language cultural values on a vast foreign readership, while producing cultures in the United Kingdom and the United States that are aggressively monolingual, unreceptive to foreign literatures" (12).

Gayatri Spivak offered the notion of *translatese*, which is the standardization of "Third World" voices in English translations. In her "The Politics of Translation," she handles the ideological consequences of the current *politics of translation*, "currently gives prominence to English and the other 'hegemonic' languages of the excolonizers" (Munday 210). She also discusses the function of the translator from a psychoanalytical perspective in "Translation as Culture."

In the last decade of the twentieth century, translation studies was nourished by the consolidation of a variety of disciplines, including postcolonial and gender studies, leading to multi- and interdisciplinary approaches. The stronghold of cultural approaches to translation also led translation studies to intersect with "post" debates. For instance, Sherry Simon has suggested that "contemporary feminist translation has made gender the site of a consciously transformative project, one which reframes conditions of textual authority" which is a result of the *cultural turn* in translation studies (qtd in Munday 208).

Siri Nergaard and Stefano Arduinere evaluated this "turn" in translation studies and in 2011 proposed a new term, "post-translation studies," inclusive of the widened studies in translation. This term is adopted by Edwin Gentzler in his *Translation and Rewriting in the Age of Post-Translation Studies* (2017). Gentzler deals with the rewritings and adaptations of texts into other cultures in an attempt to erase the hierarchy of the source text over the target text. What Gentzler promotes is the fluidity of the difference between the original, translation, rewriting, and even adaptation. The focus of his view of post-translation studies is not a comparison between the source text and the target text, but an analysis of how the end product reshapes the understanding of the source text through the integration of the rewriting into the original text and culture. Gentzler values all the phases of the translation process—pre-translation, translation, and post-translation—arguing that "the cultural context of translation can tell us much more about the translation itself" (*Translation* 5). He posits translation as the core of almost all disciplines, whose importance is to increase, since "[c]ontemporary and increasingly interdisciplinary studies of translation suggest that the borders transgressed in translation tend to be more multiple and permeable than traditionally conceived" (*Translation* 5). In this manner, post-translation in the extreme would deal with the erasing of the borders and rethinking translation "as an always-ongoing process of *every* communication" (*Translation* 5). This way translation would be "viewed less as a temporal act carried out between languages and cultures and instead as a precondition underlying the languages and cultures upon which communication is based" (5). Gentzler continues his arguments, progressively asking:

> What if we consider the political, social, and economic structures as built upon translation? What if we view the landscape—the parks, buildings, roads, memorials, churches, schools, and government organizations—not as solely monocultural, but also as a product of post-translation effects? (*Translation* 5)

Seeing the text, and the culture, as a product of rewriting, Gentzler analyzes the quest of *A Midsummer Night's Dream* from Germany to northern Europe and Russia, returning in a different genre. Other works whose journeys he analyzes are *Faust*, *À la recherche du temps perdu*, and *Hamlet*—all analyzed in their "counter-culture, cannibalized, postcolonial, and feminist contemporary versions" (*Translation* 16).

Re-examining the historical roots of translation theories, Gentzler finds most to be somehow dependent on equivalence and suggests that even Even-Zohar and Toury could not escape the traditional roots of formalism (*Contemporary* 411). Gentzler finds poststructuralist paradigms, especially deconstruction, offering new possibilities. Derrida's insistence on translation as "the origin of philosophy," and how translation creates the original since all texts are rewritten and reconstructed by each reading, provides a new approach to the analysis of each translation of a text (qtd. in Gentzler, *Contemporary* 416). It is Derrida who broke with the traditionalism of Formalism through the suggestion that in each linguistic system, different languages operate (*Contemporary* 466). Translation, therefore, would bring, in Derrida's words, a "regulated transformation of one language by another, of one text by another" (qtd. in Gentzler, *Contemporary* 469).

Susan Bassnett, in her foreword to Erwin Gentzler's *Translation and Rewriting in the Age of Post-Translation Studies*, suggests that the prefix in the term post-translation studies means not an "end to translation studies," but a call for "expansion of its self-imposed boundaries, so that the field can reach out to other disciplines and become more open to ideas about translational issues coming from researchers who may not be primarily engaged in translation" (Foreword ix). Explaining Gentzler's motives, she suggests that his paradigm "demands a questioning of older definitions of translation, and an end to trying to distinguish between so-called originals, translations, and rewritings" (Foreword ix).

The "Ethical Turn" of post-theory overlaps with the "cultural turn" in translation studies, a turn that is based on the cultural, sociological, and economic aspects of translation. Recent studies related to translation that include gendered, postcolonial, psychoanalytical, and ecocritical approaches, together with attention to the ideological processes of translation, including the study of the translator, and analyses of the definitive function of translation in different cultures offer new directions and new arenas to theory in the new millennium. Regarding translation as production, post-translation studies deal with the impact of translation in different cultures. Since the idea of a world literature or comparative literature seems chimerical without translation, with the inauguration of transdisciplinary approaches to translation, post-translation studies can help reinvent theory by offering larger fields of study.

Edwin Gentzler quotes Paul Engle to define the significance of translation in the current state of the world:

> As this world shrinks together like an aging orange and all peoples in all cultures move closer together (however reluctantly and suspiciously) it may be that the crucial sentence for our remaining years on earth may be very simply:
>
> TRANSLATE OR DIE.
>
> The lives of every creature on the earth may one day depend on the instant and accurate translation of one word. (qtd in Gentzler, *Contemporary* 47)

REFERENCE LIST

Bassnett, Susan. *Translation Studies.* 1980. forth ed. Routledge, 2013.

Bassnett Susan and André Lefevere, eds. *Translation, History, and Culture.* Pinter Publishers, 1990.

Bassnett Susan and André Lefevere. Preface. 1992. *Translation/History/Culture: A Sourcebook* edited by André Lefevere, Routledge, 2003, pp. ix-xii.

Bassnett, Susan. Foreword. *Translation and Rewriting in the Age of Post-Translation Studies,* Edwin Gentzler, Routledge, 2017, pp. viii-xi.

Berman, Antoine. "Translation and the Trials of the Foreign." 1984. *The Translation Studies Reader,* edited by Lawrence Venuti, Routledge, 2004, pp. 284–297.

Dryden, John. "On Translation" in *Theories of Translation,* edited by Rainer Schulte and John Biguenet, The University of Chicago Press, 1992, pp. 17–31.

Gentzler, Edwin. *Contemporary Translation Theories.* 2nd ed. Multilingual Matters, 2001, iBooks.

———. *Translation and Rewriting in the Age of Post-Translation Studies.* Routledge, 2017.

Hermans, Theo. Introduction. "Translation Studies and a New Paradigm." 1985. *The Manipulation of Literature: Studies in Literary Translation,* edited by Theo Hermans, Routledge, 2014, pp. 7–15.

Holmes, James S. "The Name and Nature of Translation Studies." 1975. *Translated!: Papers on Literary Translation and Translation Studies,* edited by James S. Holmes, Rodopi, 1998, pp. 66–80.

House, Juliane. *A Model for Translation Quality Assessment.* Gunter NarrVerlagTübingen, 1977.

Munday, Jeremy. *Introducing Translation Studies,* 4th ed., Routledge, 2016.

Nida, Eugene A. *Toward a Science of Translating: With Special Reference to Principles and Procedures Involved in Bible Translating.* Brill, 1964.

Nord, Christiane. *Text Analysis in Translation: Theory, Methodology, and Didactic Application of a Model for Translation-Oriented Text Analysis.* Rodopi, 1991.

———. *Translating as a Purposeful Activity: Functionalist Approaches Explained.* St. Jerome P, 1997.

Ortega y Gasset, José. "The Misery and the Splendour of Translation," *Theories of Translation,* edited by Rainer Schulte and John Biguenet, The University of Chicago Press, 1992, pp. 93–112.

Schleiermacher, Friedrich. "On the Different Methods of Translating." *Theories of Translation,* edited by Rainer Schulte and John Biguenet, The University of Chicago Press, 1992, pp. 36–54.

Spivak, Gayatri. "The Politics of Translation." 1992. *The Translation Studies Reader,* edited by Lawrence Venuti, Routledge, pp. 397 – 412.

———. "Translation as Culture." In *Translation—Reflections, Refractions, Transformations,* edited by Paul St-Pierre and Prafulla C. Kar, John Benjamins, 2007, pp. 263–277.

Steiner, George. *After Babel: Aspects of Language and Translation.* 1975. Oxford UP, 1998.

Venuti, Lawrence. *The Translator's Invisibility: A History of Translation.* 1995. 2nd ed., Routledge, 2016.

Vermeer, Hans J. "Is Translation a Linguistic or a Cultural Process?" *Ilha do Desterro,* vol. 28, no. 2, 1992, pp. 37–49.

19

New Directions in Corpus Linguistics

Meltem Muşlu

Saussure's foundation of semiotics as a new discipline and his seminal courses on grammar, generally regarded as the starting point of structural linguistics, revolutionized the study of language in the twentieth century. The next major turn in linguistics emerged when Chomsky set the rules of "universal grammar" by distinguishing the linguistic faculty from other cognitive abilities and proposed that all languages have a common structural basis. In contrast to Chomskyan cognitivism, "Cognitive approaches," rising in the 1980s, embraced meaning-based and function-oriented perspectives in language as a mental mirror of the world and a means of making sense of the world. Cognitive approaches evolved, in time, to "psycholinguistic approaches," which focused on the process of language production and comprehension. Today, corpus linguistics (CL hereafter) as the study of language using large collections of machine-readable texts called corpora comes into the forefront. As Sinclair (*Corpora in Language Teaching* 1) points out, when the first electronic corpora were being formed in the early 1960s, a shift in the focus of linguistic theory from the study of empirical data to the study of the mental processes was taking place. Despite its popularity now, at first, CL was not considered a useful method by some linguists and applied linguists. For instance, most Chomskyan linguists rejected the idea of using real contextual data instead of using native speakers' judgments of grammaticality in certain sets of constructed sentences, as well as the idea of "context-free grammar, which seeks to explain how speakers know to distinguish grammatical from ungrammatical irrespective of possible contexts of use" (Middeke et al. 380). However, as Meyer states, linguists are now far more open to using corpora for both descriptive and theoretical language studies. McCarthy describes CL as "cutting edge change in terms of scientific techniques and methods" (125). Today, corpora have been widely used in many fields—such as literature, sociolinguistics, psycholinguistics, translation, and language teaching—directly or indirectly related with linguistics—which, in turn, opens new areas of research or offers new insights to traditional research. In the light of these, the purpose of this chapter is to link the relevance of corpus studies to (post)theory and studies in humanities and medical sciences. Rather than attempting to do a comprehensive overview, the chapter will focus on the application of corpora in three different fields to exemplify the broad framework corpus studies can be applied to: literature, (critical) discourse analysis, and medical sciences. Considering that most of the chapters in this book on post-theory covers literature, focusing on the application of corpora in literary studies would be relevant. CL can contribute to the descriptive inventory of literary stylistics and (critical) discourse analysis by facilitating more empirical descriptions of language use. Although it seems irrelevant, considering the interdisciplinary/transdisciplinary nature of science in the "modern" ages, the potential usage of CL in health to diagnose some illnesses is also briefly touched upon. The secondary aim of the chapter is to briefly discuss the challenges and limitations of corpus linguistics and suggest some solutions.

A shift from the idea of language located in the mind of the ideal speaker to the idea of language located in society's collective memory may be considered as the foundation upon which CL is established. In the last five decades, with the acceleration in the development of computer technology to process speed and storage capacity of electronic data, the structured compilation of written or transcribed speech texts, and the development of more powerful corpus tools used in annotation, analysis, and statistics, CL has undergone a remarkable revival. It has started to shed a different light upon the debates on whether CL is a method, or a theory, or as Tognini-Bonelli characterizes, "corpus-based or corpus-driven" (65) form of language study. Corpus-based linguistics refers to testing or exemplifying theories and descriptions formulated before corpus studies, and corpus-driven linguistics refers to any inductive, bottom-up research which uses raw corpus data. The new methodologies and methods enrich theories and scientific perspectives by working with corpus data, conducting experiments, or researching evidence collected by introspection, logical argumentation, corpus analysis, and experimental tests (Middeke et al.). As Tognini-Bonelli puts forward, "corpus linguistics has become a new research enterprise and a new philosophical approach to the linguistic enquiry" (1), leading to a qualitative change in our understanding of language by combining data gathering activities, computational methods, and theorizing. Following Sinclair (*Trust the Text*), scholars such as Hoey, Stubbs, Teubert, and Aaarts (among others) view corpus as a theory.[1] For instance, Teubert defines CL as "a theoretical approach to the study of language" (2). Similarly, Stubbs proposes that "a corpus is not just a tool, but a major concept in linguistic theory" (*Corpus Linguistics* 301) and "Quantitative information on language use not only reveals new facts, but also helps to solve problems which have been at the heart of the discipline for the last hundred years" ("On Text" 130). On the contrary, McEnery et al. and McEnery and Hardie view CL as a philosophical approach and they reject the idea that it has the status of a theory. Rather they believe that "*all* corpus linguistics can justly be described as corpus-based" (McEnery and

Hardie 6) rejecting the binary distinction between corpus-based and corpus-driven linguistics.[2] Below, the contribution of corpus studies to different fields is discussed referring to its challenges, limitations, and the role of (post)theory in analysis.

One of the distinctive features of modern linguistics is its interdisciplinary nature. Corpus linguistics has become one of the dominant approaches in linguistics research applying various methods to different fields. For instance, although "corpora entered the classroom from the backdoor" (Bernardini 15) and its pedagogical value and theoretical potential were neglected for a long time, as Anthony states, CL is increasingly used in language learning classrooms. Similarly, as Stubbs ("Conrad in Computer") points out, either linguists or literary critics have neglected stylistics for different reasons. However, corpus stylistics is also becoming very popular.

According to Green, "Corpus stylistics is the study of literary style via computational tools applied to machine-readable literary works. It combines the science of linguistics with literary studies and, . . . is one of the growing interdisciplinary fields between the traditional and digital humanities" (283). Corpus stylistics combines different approaches-corpus linguistics and literary stylistics and contributes to the understanding of language and literature, certain periods, and cultures. Corpora can provide invaluable data for literary and stylistic analysis by providing comparative information through quantitative data. Mahlberg uses the term "corpus theoretical approach" describing CL as "an approach to the description of English with its own theoretical framework" (*English Nouns* 2). McIntyre and Walker state that:

> What corpus linguistics offers to stylistics is a set of theories and analytical methods for exploring large quantities of language data. What stylistics offers to corpus linguistics is a set of theories, models and analytical frameworks that may be deployed in the interpretation of corpus data and corpus-derived results. (*Corpus Stylistics* 315)

According to Stubbs ("Conrad in Computer"), unique individual texts can be explained only by comparing them with what is normal and expected in general language use; "what happens millions of times is necessary in order to understand the 'unique.'" (5). Corpus stylistics is "an approach that can link in with the concerns in literary stylistics and criticism" (Malhberg and McIntyre 216). Thus, it is not a field that challenges traditional literary studies. In the past, intuition and intelligent handling were predominant. However, the use of digital methods in literary studies has made the analysis more systematic and technologically equipped (Ganascia). Corpus analysis validates subjective critical analysis since quantitative analysis guides qualitative analysis (McIntyre and Walker, "Corpora, Poetry, Drama" 522). That is, corpus techniques do not outperform manual analysis and they should not replace it. Vice versa, it complements the manual analysis by covering additional aspects of a text and adding further techniques to the stylisticians' toolkit. With the help of this, analyzing the style associated with individual authors and works can get easier and less complicated (Malhberg and McIntyre *Corpus Stylistics*). To make correct interpretations, however, a quantitative approach to data analysis on its own is not enough. Qualitative analysis with good knowledge of linguistics beyond what the computer can produce, such as keyword lists, collocations, and so on, is needed. Depending on the purpose, corpus methods and stylistics analysis can be integrated into different ways. One of the direct ways of integrating corpus methods and stylistics analysis is using pre-existing large corpora (reference corpus) to support or challenge an intuitive response to a text (McIntyre and Walker, *Corpus Stylistics* 26). Another way is "treating the target text (or, indeed, texts) as a corpus in its own right" (*ibid* 111) instead of comparing the target text(s) with a reference corpus. In this way, patterns that cannot be discovered through qualitative analysis alone can be discovered. For instance, by conducting a very detailed textual analysis, Mahlberg ("Dickens' Fiction") examines the techniques of characterisation, body language, and speech presentation in Charles Dickens' novels.

Although complex quantitative research designs are used in CL today, even the very basic tools of the field, such as frequency lists, word lists, and keywords, have provided insights into literature. For instance, in his study on Conrad's *Heart of Darkness*, Stubbs ("Conrad in Computer") uses word lists and collocations to have a solid grasp of Conrad's important themes and style markers. He stated that the most frequent words he found, such as *seem, like, looked, something,* and *sometimes,* reflect the vagueness and the sense of the inscrutable, which are Conrad's stylistic markers. Similarly, Scott and Tribble analyzed the distinctive words used in Shakespeare's play *Romeo and Juliet* through keywords analysis. Culpeper also analyzed *Romeo and Juliet,* but his study focused on the distinctive keywords used by each character in the play. He constructed a comparison corpus consisting of the utterances produced by the other characters in the play and found both expected and surprising findings.

Fischer-Starcke analyzed Jane Austen's *Northanger Abbey* by describing the distinctive keywords in the novel. In the analysis, two different comparison corpora were used: one consisting of Austen's six novels, and one consisting of other fictional texts written by Austen's contemporary authors. With this approach, the distinctive words used in a particular literary work can be identified. Many other corpus stylistics studies can be found in the literature; Jacobs, Koristashevskaya, Oliveria, Leech, Mahlberg and McIntyre, Mahlberg ("Clusters and Dickens"), Muşlu, O'Halloran ("Literary Evaluation"), and Viana and Zyngier to name a few.[3]

Some very inspiring corpus stylistics projects have also been running. One of them is The CLiC Dickens Project (Mahlberg et al. "CLiC") which started in 2013. The project shows how computer-assisted methods can be used to study literary texts. Both linguistic and literary analysis, for example, how readers perceive fictional characters, can be applied to texts. As part of the project, a web-based application was designed to specifically analyze literary texts. Mahlberg points out another contribution of corpus stylistics:

> Corpus stylistics can also contribute to the exploration and development of descriptive tools that aim to characterize meanings in texts. For the analysis of a work of literature the individual qualities of the text and relationships with other texts play a role. The

concept of local textual functions provides possibilities to explore textual features from various points of view. ("Bridging the Gap" 240)

Another project—Encyclopedia of Shakespeare's Language[4]—examines Shakespeare's language in detail. The project aims to reveal the usage of words and other linguistic units in Shakespeare and the language of his period. With this comparative method, the distinctive features of Shakespeare's language, how his contemporary audience would have perceived his language, or as Culpepper brings forward, his supposedly big contribution to English vocabulary can be revealed.

The development of postmodernism is often connotated as "turn to discourse" or the "linguistic turn" in science. It was when the notions of "discourse," "rhetoric" and "language" were used interchangeably. Accordingly, another area in which CL is highly integrated is (critical) discourse analysis. Trappes-Lomax defines discourse analysis as "the study of language viewed communicatively and/or of communication viewed linguistically . . . involving reference to concepts of language *in use*, language *above or beyond the sentence*, language as meaning *in interaction*, and language in *situational and cultural context*" (134). However, as he states, critical discourse analysis (CDA henceforth) is a political enterprise seeking not only to understand the social world but also to transform it by relying on theories, such as poststructuralist, feminist, postcolonial, and Foucault's philosophy of knowledge/power among others. Khosravi Nik states that "CDA is inherently both eclectic and interdisciplinary, and requires a set of linguistic analytical tools as well as a theory (or theories) which can help to contextualise and relate the findings to the society"(55). However, according to O'Halloran, CDA is

> a multi-disciplinary set of practical approaches which investigates how language use can contribute to the reproduction of social and economic inequality, how language use can persuade listeners and readers to (re)produce the values and agendas of the relatively powerful which may not be in the interests of the relatively powerless. (*Posthumanism* 6)

For instance, CDA can be used to study sexist or racist relations. According to him (*ibid*), CDA cannot be done without having political commitments. Similarly, Partington ("Political Language") explains the benefits of using corpus-assisted approaches in CDA stating that it deepens our understanding of (political) language from different scientific perspectives, from linguistic and political perspectives in his case. Wodak and Meyer see social inequality as a problem, therefore; CDA can be considered a problem-oriented form of discourse analysis. CDA relies on close analysis of a small number of texts; however, corpus-based approaches have been applied to examine discourses of large political texts (Fairclough, Partington *Political Argument*) and discourses of the disadvantaged, for instance, immigrants/refugees/asylum seekers (Baker et al., Baker and McEnery, Blinder and Allen, Gabrielatos and Baker, Soto-Almela and Alcaraz-Mármol, Taylor), and LGBT+ members.[5] Considering the scope of this book, instead of focusing on these studies, however, I would like to focus more on how corpus linguistics and CDA methods can provide an adaptable quantitative window on Discourse (with big D defined by Foucault). In doing so, O'Halloran's approach will be used as a sample.[6]

Referring to Rosi Braidotti's idea that our lives are becoming more *post*human since more intelligent technology has been transforming life, portable and wearable technologies are becoming an indispensable part of humans, and the boundary between human and nonhuman is becoming unsharp, O'Halloran states that his method presents a posthuman critical thinking and a posthuman CDA since to create alternative critical subjectivities (which he defines as discursive and ethical subjectivities), decentring of human subjectivity is required, which can be attained through interfacing with machines. Analyzing large collections of texts with CL tools, such as concordance lines, "can provide relatively convenient insight into 'big D' Discourse" (33).

O'Halloran states that "Corpus linguistics can be seen as part of the digital humanities" (68) or if it is needed to put it less controversially, digital humanists can use analytical techniques in CL since they are easy to apply. Saying this, he also touches upon the debate on whether CL is a method or a theory. He states that compared to technically sophisticated analytical frameworks in linguistics, CL consists of a set of techniques and principles to analyze electronic data with easy-to-learn terminology. Having said that, he does not consider CL only a method. Rather he claims that "it has produced important insights into language use" (5). When analyzing the data, the researcher has the option of not annotating the data, that is not using detailed metalinguistic text description (e.g., parts-of-speech tagging, transcribing, or coding). Scholars supporting the idea of corpus being a theory (corpus-as-a theory/corpus-driven), such as Sinclair, are against annotation believing that the linguist's interaction with the corpus data is the only correct source of making a generalization and explaining language. O'Halloran emphasizes that when he says CL (tools) is easy to learn and apply, he does not diminish the value of metalanguage. On the contrary, he states that depending on the researcher's goal, such detailed description should/can be done (as he did when explaining how d/Discourse can do ideological work). Whether the analyzis is corpus-based or corpus-driven depends on the purpose of the researcher. More and more scholars in the humanities are using software to make it easier to gather, analyse and understand the data. O'Halloran asserts that "Transformation is key. Digital humanities scholars use software to transform the habitual way of researching and teaching" (5), and "while the humanities are digitising, they are also undergoing mutation into *post* humanities" (70).

Focusing on the transformational and transdisciplinary nature of science today, finally, I would like to exemplify how CL, which is increasingly used in (digital) humanities and social sciences, can also be used in medical sciences. There are many kinds of corpora that may contain spoken or written language, contemporary or old texts, texts from one language or more languages depending on their use: Parallel (translation), synchronic or diachronic, general, reference, monolingual or multilingual, and learner corpora. Among these, learner corpora can be used in medical sciences. Learner corpora are electronic collections of texts produced by learners of a language and are used to study the mistakes and problems learners have when learning a foreign language. Besides learner corpora, researchers can compile their own corpora depending on their purpose. An interdisciplinary approach combining clinical linguistics, psychology, and CL, for example, can be used in to diagnose some illnesses such as dyslexia, social anxiety disorder, and dysorthographia, or evaluate the efficacy of a treatment. Psychology aims at diagnosing, treating, and preventing cognitive, emotional, and behavioral problems, whereas clinical linguistics analyze the language used by patients with any disorder, such as aphasia, Alzheimer's, schizophrenia, and autism. A diverse interdisciplinary approach and input—combining their own methods with CL methods—can help clinicians and researchers gain a more comprehensible insight into the relationship between the language produced by patients, their (clinical) diagnosis, and treatment. One of the studies conducted to detect a learning disorder was done by Diez-Bedmar. In her study, she explains and illustrates how a learning disorder, dysorthographia, can be detected when conducting computer-aided error analysis (annotating corpus for errors using a comprehensive error classification) and concludes that failure to recognize symptoms of this disorder may lead to making incorrect interpretations, for example, misleadingly attributing the errors a student makes to their language acquisition process rather than to their learning disorders. On the other hand, correct interpretations lead to taking timely precautions, such as seeking psychological help and undergoing appropriate treatment. In another study, Garcia-Lopez et al. studied patients with social anxiety disorder and tried to examine if a corpus-based linguistic analysis of the adolescents' descriptions of their social feared situations before and after the treatment is correlated with their treatment outcome. They found a close relationship between the sensitivity of treatment outcome and adolescents' use of language when describing their feeling when facing a social situation. They concluded that the linguistic analysis of patients' discourse might be useful when evaluating treatment efficacy and future studies may help to detect patients' risk of dropping treatment. Studies using CL methods to detect dyslexia or decrease reading difficulties were also conducted. For instance, in their study, Gala et al. present a new parallel corpus that can be used by people interested in text simplification, such as researchers, teachers, and speech therapists, to decrease difficulties in children learning to read. The results showed that the words targeted for simplification were well-chosen, substituted with considerably easier alternatives, and the manual simplifications reduced reading errors significantly.

CONCLUSION

The studies mentioned above present a small array of different fields and disciplines CL can congregate. The whole world is getting more digital; therefore, humanities and social sciences should move with the times, adapt, change, and innovate, which can (only) be possible with interdisciplinary and transdisciplinary work. There are more tools to test the validity of previous theories or to come up with new ones. As expressed above, corpus stylistics is not a field that competes with traditional literary studies; rather, it can provide invaluable data for literary and stylistic analysis by providing comparative information through quantitative analysis and complementing manual analysis with new techniques. Similarly, as Hunt emphasizes, compared to manual ideological analysis, CL offers a degree of objectivity and efficiency providing statistical support for interpretations, opening the possibility of analyzing much larger quantities of data with a set of tools especially helpful in lexical analysis without sacrificing social sensitivity and the micro-level nuances of discourse analysis. Before post-theory, deconstructivism was the dominant approach, which uses philosophical reflection and therefore nonempirical. However, CL is empirical, and thus, it has statistical relevance. When abstract notions such as literary work, culture, and theory are combined with CL methods, they (can) become statistically more relevant. However, rather than multidisciplinary work, interdisciplinary and/or transdisciplinary work can bring more insights to understanding of different fields. Through the engagement with literary criticism, CDA, and medical sciences, for example, corpus linguists can develop new more specific methods and resource; similarly, literary scholars, discourse analysts, or people in health sciences may profit from corpus methods. For instance, corpus stylisticians should work with literary scholars to better understand and interpret the data they gathered. With the advancement in the digital humanities, further "multimodal" levels are added to the analysis; new technologies that visualize data are used; new applications and software are created. Therefore, it will not be surprising that all research in humanities will be digitized in one way or another. Although these innovations will bring new challenges, they can be easily solved with interdisciplinary or transdisciplinary work. For instance, multimodal corpora (collections of video and speech recordings with transcriptions and gesture, hand, and body language annotations) brought new challenges to annotate and understand the data. Yet, it also brought new insights to the understanding of the public discourse. It is a challenge to analyze "digitalised language"—the language used in social media or multiplatform messaging apps like WhatsApp in which emotions are expressed with emojis or prosodic features are marked with uppercase letters. However, they are valuable sources that can be added to the "collective memory" of society. As Flowerdew states, "CL techniques helped us to understand how various language choices and patterns operate at a text-linguistic level" (178). More interdisciplinary/transdisciplinary work, and training researchers with multiple skills, such as from teaching literature and cultures to teaching coding, understanding huge and multimodal data to small and old data, analyzing texts from one genre to texts from various fields would be more straightforward and efficient. This inter/transdisciplinary work would not only help researchers understand the world better, but also help them find more funding for their research. Considering the competitiveness of finding sources in humanities and social sciences, this would also provide a good opportunity for funding.

NOTES

1. See Sinclair *Trust the Text* for a more detailed discussion on his core ideas as corpus-as a theory.
2. See McEnery and Hardie for a detailed critic of Sinclair and his followers on corpus as a theory vs. as a method, chapters six and eight specifically.
3. See also Römer, Chollier, and Biber for the use of corpora in literature.
4. See http://wp.lancs.ac.uk/shakespearelang/.
5. See Baker and Motschenbacher.
6. See O'Halloran (*Posthumanism*) for a more detailed description of his proposed method. The book presents how CDA, theory, and CL can be linked describing the evolution of DA from Kant to Derrida and the evolution of CDA from its roots into the posthuman age. O'Halloran explains why he rejects some of Derrida's philosophy and why his ideas are closer to Deleuze and Guattari with various demonstrations of his method.

REFERENCE LIST

Anthony, Laurence. "A Critical Look at Software Tools in Corpus Linguistics." *Linguistic Research*, vol. 30, no. 2, 2013, pp. 141–161.

Baker, Paul. "Language, Sexuality and Corpus Linguistics: Concerns and Future Directions."*Journal of Language and Sexuality*, vol. 4, no. 2, 2018, pp. 263–279.https://doi.org/10.1075/jls.17018.bak

Baker, Paul and Tony McEnery. "A Corpus-Based Approach to Discourses of Refugees and Asylum Seekers in UN and Newspaper Texts." *Journal of Language and Politics*,vol. 4, no. 2, 2005, pp. 197–226.

Baker, Paul, et al. "A Useful Methodological Synergy? Combining Critical Discourse Analysis and Corpus Linguistics to Examine Discourses of Refugees and Asylum Seekers in the UK Press." *Discourse & Society*, vol. 19, no. 3, spring 2008, pp. 273–306. https://doi.org/10.1177/0957926508088962.

Bernardini, Silvia. "Corpora in the Classroom: An Overview and Some Reflections on Future Developments." *How to Use Corpora in Language Teaching*, edited by Sinclair, John. John Benjamins Publishing, 2004.

Biber, Douglas. "Corpus Linguistics and the Study of Literature Back to the Future?" *Scientific Study of Literature*, vol. 1, no. 1, 2011, pp. 15–23. https://doi.org/10.1075/ssol.1.1.02bib.

Blinder, Scott, and William L. Allen. "Constructing Immigrants: Portrayals of Migrant Groups in British National Newspapers, 2010–2012." *International Migration Review*, vol. 50, no. 1, 2016, pp. 3–40. https://doi.org/10.1111/imre.12206.

Chollier, Christine. "Textual Semantics and Literature: Corpus, Texts, Translation." *Signata*[Online], vol. 5, 2014, pp. 77–99. https://doi.org/10.4000/signata.461.

Culpeper, Jonathan. "Keyness: Words, Parts-of-speech and Semantic Categories in the Character-talk of Shakespeare's Romeo and Juliet." *International Journal of Corpus Linguistics* vol. 14, no. 1, 2009, pp. 29–59. DOI:10.1075/ijcl.14.1.03cul.

Diez-Bedmar, Maria Belen. "Detecting Learning Disorders in Students' Written Production in the Foreign Language: Are Learner Corpora of Any Help?" *Porta Linguarum*, vol. 15, 2011, pp. 35–54. DOI: 10.1177/0963947005048873

Fairclough, Norman. *New Labour, New Language?* Routledge, 2000.
Fischer-Starcke, Bettina. "Keywords and Frequent Phrases of Jane Austen's Pride and Prejudice: A Corpus-Stylistic Analysis." *International Journal of Corpus Linguistics*, vol. 14, no. 4, 2009, pp. 492–523.
Flowerdew, Lynne. "Corpus-Based Discourse Analysis." *The Routledge Handbook of Discourse Analysis*, edited by J. Paul Gee and M. Handford. Routledge, 2012.
Gabrielatos, Costas and Paul Baker. "Fleeing, Sneaking, Flooding: A Corpus Analysis of Discursive Constructions of Refugees and Asylum Seekers in the UK Press, 1996–2005." *Journal of English Linguistics*, vol. 36, no. 1, 2008, pp. 5–38.DOI: 10.1177/0075424207311247
Gala, Nuria, et al. "Alector: A Parallel Corpus of Simplified French Texts with Alignments of Misreadings by Poor and Dyslexic Readers." *Proceedings of the 12th Conference on Language Resourcesand Evaluation*, edited by Calzolari, N., et al. European Language Resources Association, 2020.
Ganascia, Jean-Gabriel, "The Logic of the Big Data Turn in Digital Literary Studies." *Frontiers Digital Humanities*, vol. 2, no. 7, 2015. https://doi.org/10.3389/fdigh.2015.00007.
Garcia-Lopez, Luisjoaquin, et al. "Treatment Change in Adolescents with Social Anxiety Disorder: Insights from Corpus Linguistics." *Ansiedad y Estres*, vol. 17, no. 2–3, 2011, pp. 149–155.
Green, Clarence. "Introducing the Corpus of the Canon of Western Literature: A Corpus for Culturomics and Stylistics." *Language and Literature: International Journal of Stylistics*, vol, 26, no. 4, 2017, pp. 282–299.
Hunt, Sally. "Representations of Gender and Agency in the *Harry Potter* Series." *Corpora and Discourse Studies Integrating Discourse and Corpora*, edited by P. Baker and T. McEnery. Palgrave, 2015.
Jacobs, Arthur M. "Explorations in an English Poetry Corpus: A Neurocognitive Poetics Perspective."*Frontiers in Digital Humanities*, 2018.https://arxiv.org/abs/1801.02054v1.
Khosravinik, Majid. "Actor Descriptions, Action Attributions, and Argumentation: Towards a Systematization of CDA Analytical Categories in the Representation of Social Groups."*Critical Discourse Studies*, vol. 7, no. 1, 2010, pp. 55–72.
Koristashevskaya, Elina. "Semantic Density Mapping: a Discussion of Meaning in William Blake's Songs of Innocence and Experience." 2014, University of Glasgow, MRes thesis.
Leech, Geoffrey. "Virginia Woolf Meets Wmatrix." *Études de Stylistique Anglaise*, vol. 4, 2013, pp. 15-26. DOI: 10.4000/esa.1405.
Mahlberg, M.,et al. "CLiC Dickens: Novel Uses of Concordances for the Integration of Corpus Stylistics and Cognitive Poetics." *Corpora*, vol. 11, no. 3, 2016, pp. 433–463.
Mahlberg, Michaela and Dan McIntyre. "A Case for Corpus Stylistics: Ian Fleming's *Casino Royale*." *English Text Construction*, vol. 4, no. 2, 2011, pp. 204–227.
Mahlberg, Michaela, "Clusters, Key Clusters and Local Textual Functions in Dickens." *Corpora*, vol. 2, no. 1, 2007, pp. 1–31.
Mahlberg, Michaela. "Corpus Stylistics: Bridging the Gap between Linguistic and Literary Studies." *Text, Discourse and Corpora Theory and Analysis*, edited by M. Stubbs and W. Teubert. Continuum, 2007.
Mahlberg, Michaela. *Corpus Stylistics and Dickens's Fiction*. Routledge, 2013.
Mahlberg, Michaela. *English General Nouns: A Corpus Theoretical Approach*. John Benjamins, 2005.
McCarthy, Michael. *Issues in Applied Linguistics*. Cambridge University Press, 2001.

McEnery, Tony, and Andrew Hardie. *Corpus Linguistics: Method, Theory and Practice*. Cambridge University Press, 2012.

McEnery, Tony, et al. *Corpus-Based Language Studies: An Advanced Resource Book*. Routledge, 2006.

McIntyre, Dan and Brian Walker. "How Can Corpora Be Used to Explore the Language of Poetry and Drama?" *The Routledge Handbook of Corpus Linguistic*, edited by O'Keeffe A, and McCarthy, M. Routledge, 2010.

McIntyre, Dan and Brian Walker. *Corpus Stylistics Theory and Practice*. Edinburgh University Press, 2019.

Meyer, F. Charles. *English Corpus Linguistics: An Introduction*. Cambridge University Press, 2004.

Middeke, Martin, et al. *English and American Studies: Theory and Practice*. Springer, 2012.

Motschenbacher, Heiko. "Corpus Linguistics in Language and Sexuality Studies: Taking Stock and Looking Ahead."*Journal of Language and Sexuality*, vol. 7, no. 2, 2018, p. 145–174. https://doi.org/10.1075/jls.17019.mot.

Muşlu, Meltem. "A Corpus-Based Analysis of William Blake's *Songs of Innocence* and *Songs of Experience*." *English Studies in the 21st Century* Edited by Antakyalıoğlu, Z., Asiatidou, K., Gündüz, E. İ., Kavak, E., and Almacıoglu, G., Cambridge Scholars Publishing, 2020, pp. 244–261.

O'Halloran, Kieran. "Corpus-Assisted Literary Evaluation." *Corpora*, vol. 2, no. 1, 2007, pp. 33–63.

O'Halloran, Kieran. *Posthumanism and Deconstructing Arguments: Corpora and Digitally-driven Critical Analysis*. Routledge, 2017.

Oliveira, Jasmine S. "Robert Frost's Poems: Some Light from Corpus Analysis." *Revele*, vol. 7, 2014, pp. 125–140. DOI: 10.17851/2317-4242.7.0.125–139.

Partington, Alan. "Corpus Analysis of Political Language."*The Encyclopedia of Applied Linguistics*, edited by Carol A. Chapelle. Blackwell Publishing Ltd., 2013. DOI: 10.1002/9781405198431.wbeal0250

Partington, Alan. *The Linguistics of Political Argument: The Spin-Doctor and the Wolf-Pack at the White House*. Routledge, 2003.

Römer, Ute. "Where the Computer Meets Language, Literature, and Pedagogy: Corpus Analysis in English Studies." *How Globalization Affects the Teaching of English: Studying Culture Through Texts,* edited by Gerbig, A. and Anja M.W., E. Mellen Press, 2006.

Scott, Mike and Christoper Tribble. *Textual Patterns: Key Words and Corpus Analysis in Language Education*. John Benjamins, 2006.

Sinclair, John. "Introduction." *How to Use Corpora in Language Teaching*, edited by Sinclair, J. McH., John Benjamins Publishing, 2004.

Sinclair, John. *Trust the Text: Language, Corpus and Discourse*. Routledge, 2004a.

Soto-Almela, Jorge and GemaAlcaraz-Marmol. "Victims or Non-Humans: Exploring the Semantic Preferences of Refugees in Spanish News Articles." *Language & Communication*, vol. 69, 2019, pp. 11–25. doi.org/10.1016/j.langcom.2019.05.001.

Stubbs, Michael. "On Texts, Corpora, and Models of Language." *Text, Discourse and Corpora*, edited by M. Stubbs and W. Teubert. Continuum, 2007.

Stubbs, Michael. "Conrad in the Computers: Examples of Quantitative Stylistic Methods." *Language and Literature*, vol. 14, no. 1, 2005, pp. 5–24.

Stubbs, Michael. "Review of T. McEnery and A. Wilson (1996): *Corpus Linguistics*." *International Journal of Corpus Linguistics*, vol. 2, no. 2, 1997, pp. 296–302.

Taylor, Charlotte. "Investigating the Representation of Migrants in the UK and Italian Press: A Cross-Linguistics Corpus-Assisted Discourse Analysis." *International Journal of Corpus Linguistics,* vol. 19, no. 3, 2014, pp. 368–400. DOI: 10.1075/ijcl.19.3.03tay.

Teubert, W. "My Version of Corpus Linguistics." *International Journal of Corpus Linguistics,* vol. 10, no. 1, 2005, pp. 1–13.

Tognini-Bonelli, Elena. *Corpus Linguistics at Work.* John Benjamins Publishing, 2001.

Trappes-Lomax, Hugh. "Discourse Analysis." *The Handbook of Applied Linguistics,* edited by Davies, A. and Elder, C., Blackwell Publishing, 2004.

Viana, Fausto Fabiana and Zyngier Sonia. "Corpus Linguistics and Literature: A Contrastive Analysis of Dan Brown and Machado de Assis." *Textos e leituras: Estudosempiricos de lingua e literature (Texts and Readings: Empirical studies of language and literature),* edited by Zyngier S, Viana V., and Jandre J., Publit, 2007.

Wodak, Ruth and Michael Meyer. "Critical Discourse Studies: History, Agenda, Theory and Methodology." *Methods of Critical Discourse Studies,* edited by R. Wodak and M. Meyer. 3rd ed., SAGE Publications, 2016.

20

Translinguism in the Context of Language Teaching in the Twenty-First Century

New Approaches and New Practices

Gamze Almacıoğlu

Second language education started to be implemented by putting it on systematic foundations in the middle of the twentieth century. In this process, different but fundamentally abstractive and restrictive approaches and practices were predominant in subjects such as the role and use of the mother tongue, bilingualism, or multilingualism. Speech was a priority in the early days of second language teaching, but written language learning was left behind. Starting from the 1960s and '70s, oral-auditory exercises were used extensively in second language teaching. Written exercises were mimetic and repetitive. In the education of the students, structure, form, syntax, and grammar were given priority. In a system with a high concentration of such applications, the focus was not on using real language. This led to a lack of knowledge for students about how language and communication work in real applications. In the late 1970s and '80s, second language education focused on the importance of communication and language use for participation in certain discourse communities. Although the importance of communication and the use of language suitable for communication types was recognized and new approaches and applications were developed, highlighting language learning to enter a discourse community also opened the way for other problems. This attitude put pressure on students to give up their native language practice to become practitioner members of new discourse communities. According to Phillipson (173), the monolingual approach used in Anglo-American English teaching is not cognitively, linguistically, and educationally valid. Pennycook (*Global Englishes*) stated that the indirect or direct support of English through education policies, which he described as "the language of international capitalism" (43), caused the education, business, and social environment to take shape in favor of a monolingual elite.

This change in second language education paved the way for the perspectives and practices of postmodernist philosophy. Postmodernism, which showed its effects in second language education in the 1990s, is defined by Fahim and Pishghadam as subjective; irrational; unscientific; oriented toward local demands; constructivist; populist; consisting of a combination of parts; advocating to be better, not the best; nonlinear; not generalizable; oriented toward practices, not theories; concrete; and a structure that contains not a single form but many varieties (36). These features of postmodernism managed to influence many disciplines and directly affected education, especially second language education. Winch and Gingell explained the reflection of postmodernism in education as "increasing the impact of innovative approaches and strengthening the emphasis on learner centeredness, learner autonomy, problem-solving within the framework of group and project work, learning by gaining experience and critical thinking, and subject integration in a multicultural context" (175–78).

By the twenty-first century, approaches and practices based on native language or bilingualism began to replace second language education models based on monolingualism with the concept of translingualism. The reason was that translingualism had an impact on many human areas. This perspective was applied to pedagogy, daily social interaction, communication, linguistics, visual arts, music, transgender discourse and so on. The growing body of work gave the impression that such an approach could define any somewhat unconventional application. Translingualism is important to be seen as an explanatory of postmultilingualism practices observed in the twenty-first century and as a structure that forms the basis of these practices. Translingualism offers a new interdisciplinary (transdisciplinary) research perspective beyond artificial distinctions between linguistics, psychology, sociology, and so on. Therefore, it requires analytical methods that focus more on how language users organize their resources that create diversity and multiple meanings than treating languages as discrete and complete systems. For instance, although the concept of translanguaging originated in bilingual education, it has been taken up in second language studies and applied linguistics. Understanding how these fields define translanguaging and its pedagogical uses gives a broader view of language practices and potential ways instructors could use their language practices in the classroom. Translanguaging is defined as the use of different languages together in the most general sense. Translanguaging includes the thought processes behind language production, effective communication, language function, and its use. According to Cummins ("Rethinking" 223), although different languages' syntactic, morphological, or grammatical structures are different, some cognitive and linguistic characteristics underlie all languages. These properties are transferred from one language to another.

Garcia (143) emphasizes that translanguaging is not about language itself but communication. Translanguaging does not focus on the correct and competent use of language. Rather, this concept is related to students using all their language resources and linguistic skills together to help them research new knowledge and concepts, make connections between ideas, or understand others during communication. Translanguaging requires a critical look at the monolingual approaches Cummins ("Teaching for" 70) called the "two-solitudes" approach, in which languages are kept separate by precise lines in language education and the monolingual education policies that propose these approaches.

Canagarajah (*Translingual*) focused on the definition of performative competence rather than communicative competence. According to this new definition, it is "interaction-based and procedural, rather than a set of learnt (propositional) resources as in communicative competence"(174–75).It focuses on the concept of "alignment" which "connects semiotic resources, environmental factors and human subjects in relation to one's own communicative needs and interests in order to achieve meaning and focuses on how much more than what is the communication" (174–75). Cook also used the concept of multicompetence rather than communicative competence to examine the L2 user as a whole; he defines multicompetence as "the knowledge of multiple languages in the same mind or in the same community" (447). According to him, in the examination of linguistic proficiency, the language user should be considered a whole, not an incomplete speaker of L2 (447). Luk and Bialystok (607) also stated that languages are not separate and independent but that both languages' language vocabulary experiences interact.

With these new approaches and perspectives, terms like translation, transfer, code-switching, and so on, that have previously been defined in different ways and positioned in different places in second language education have been reinterpreted. Even the basic concepts such as competence that form the basis of them have been re-examined. In summary, these hybrid uses, which are not among the general principles of standard second language education and are often avoided, have come up again with the emphasis on the possible benefits of translanguaging in second language education and formed part of the translingual theory. Wei explains the added values of the concept by highlighting the "trans" prefix to "languaging" by referring to:

—the fluid practices that go beyond, i.e., transcend, socially constructed language systems and structures to engage diverse multiple meaning-making systems and subjectivities,
—the transformative capacity of the Translanguaging process not only for language systems but also for individuals' cognition and social structures; and,
—the transdisciplinary consequences of re-conceptualizing language, language learning, and language use, and working across the divides between linguistics, psychology, sociology, and education. (27)

Translingualism, by definition and nature, is a linguistic ideology that believes "language boundaries are fluctuating and in a constant revision" (Horneret al. 287). This approach is important in verifying the students' linguistic identity and not missing the learning opportunity provided by the linguistic diversity in the classroom (Jain 492). While the translingual approach focuses on "mutual intelligibility," it also puts context ahead of fluency. Unlike a monolingual approach, the translingual approach promotes code-meshing, code-switching, and language hybridity. Differences in a language or between languages cannot always be seen as boundaries but can also be considered new sources for generating meaning (Horneret al. 287). Hence, translingualism sets forth that languages are associated with individuals and, therefore, they are living organisms.

Translingualism underlines the alterity of language systems over concepts such as "standard written English" and "unaccented speech." Not all linguistic or textual substandard uses are errors that need to be corrected. "Not every instance of nonstandard usage by a student is an unwitting error; sometimes it is an active choice motivated by important cultural and ideological considerations" (Canagarajah, "The Place" 609). The past decade has seen a gradual increase in second language scholars theorizing translingualism toward a rhetoric of translingual writing. As a result, it is one of the most popular and current theoretical and pedagogical models for bringing up the issues like language difference, the standardization of language use and linguistic inequality. For instance, Kellman ("J. M." 164) was among the first researchers to use the term translingualism. According to him, translingual writers are authors who can express themselves in multiple verbal systems. It is important to rely on L1 in the early stages of writing and go beyond English-only policies where Standard English is the only variation (Fu 30).

According to Canagarajah ("Lingua Franca" 98), translingualism is indispensable for understanding verbal and semiotic sources in communication. Translingualism revisits verbal and semiotic resources that interact to produce new structures and meanings beyond the structuralist and functional meanings. Therefore, translingualism as an analytical concept also offers new ways to evaluate literary uses of language. Postcolonial literature gave birth to a new narrative paradigm: translingual literature—texts by authors using more than one language or a language other than the primary language. Language use is an instrumental strategy for representation and identity construction in the post-apartheid era. According to Fairclough (116) and Foucault (156), this is because language reflects power relations in social contexts. Hall (4) also sees language as an important tool in identity construction, and thus the concepts of self and belonging are "languaged." With the emergence of translingual literature, the definition of translingualism "as the purposive and artful reproduction within one language of features from another language" (Scoot 75) became more prominent. Some of the most important translingual authors of the twentieth century are Joseph Conrad, Samuel Beckett, and Vladimir Nabokov. Each represents a unique example of translingualism. It is natural for newcomers (mostly migrants) to assimilate into a new home, often by learning the language. For instance, Milan Kundera had already established himself as a leading Czech novelist when, in his forties, he resettled in France and began writing in French. "Because of linguistic dexterity, translingual writers are uniquely equipped for auto translation."(Kellman "Literary" 340). Notable examples of authors who translated themselves are Beckett, Brink, Dinesen, Dorfman, and Nabokov. Within the scope of this book, it could not be crossed without mentioning how translingualism emerged and developed in the field of literature in terms of literary works and authors. As can be understood from the term translanguaging, which is incorporated into the theory of translingualism, language interacts directly or indirectly (mostly directly) with all human phenomena. The changes and transformations created by different language use in literature have also affected other areas. Translingual literary studies have increasingly attracted academicians from various disciplines, including comparative literature, linguistics, language pedagogy, psychology, history, and so on. Since more detailed discussions and reviews about the field of literature will be discussed in the relevant chapters, we can continue to examine the main subject of this article, "the process and progress of translingualism in language teaching."

In this process, the effectiveness of practices that have been widely used in the past and which keep second language teaching separate has been questioned again. Various researchers have begun to question the validities of limiting languages and monolingual teaching approaches in language teaching processes. Anderson (in Creeseand Blackledge 112) called for more flexible approaches to language teaching methods that respond to contexts that do not easily fit existing patterns. Thus, in the recent period, the holistic approach that addresses language teaching in a broader and more flexible framework has come to the fore as an option for traditional language teaching approaches in the context of multilingualism.

The holistic approach to language teaching differs from the monolingual approach in many aspects. The holistic approach addresses the languages used by the individual as a whole, not separately, in the contexts in which multiple languages are taught and suggests that L1 and L2 contribute to each other in acquiring language skills in language teaching. The holistic approach reflects Cummins's ("Interdependence" 74) "interdependence principle." According to this principle, the development of languages is interconnected, and it is important to integrate new knowledge into existing cognitive structures in the teaching of languages because previous knowledge is the basis for interpreting new information ("Teaching through" 12). Experts who advocate this view believe that L1 should be encouraged in the expression of courses other than language lessons to make and expand students' conceptual knowledge in language teaching. Thus, more can be achieved by providing cross-language transfer in understanding the subject and developing weak language (Baker 5).

Cenoz and Gorter (1-15) argue that given all the language vocabulary of the speakers, they can activate their linguistic resources, which will be more effective than learning languages separately. According to Cummins ("Teaching for" 72), these two languages feed each other if the educational environment allows students access to both languages. According to the ECML network site, each learner creates their own language repertoire in different languages they know or use. Skills gained in one language can be used to learn another. There are complementariness and interaction between languages. In the holistic approach, languages are not treated separately, and their contribution to each other is considered the development in vocabulary.

Various phenomena, such as the transfer of some language skills from one language to another and the interaction between languages, require addressing related topics as a whole in teaching multiple languages. The basic framework of holistic approaches is the interlingual links that integrate different languages and the curriculum that offers course contents in different languages. All linguistic information of speakers is considered so that multiple language learners can enable their linguistic resources and become more effective language learners than when languages are learned separately. There are various language teaching models in most countries to raise the next generations of the twenty-first century to be rich in languages. According to Helot and Cavalli, using L1 and L2 together in language education is an innovative approach to integrated teaching science aimed at uncovering all possible convergences between the linguistic and cultural resources of students, their own languages, educational languages, and additional languages (two or more languages) in the curriculum (485). In fact, this definition considers the individual who learns more than one language, the languages s/he has developed during the learning process, and the relations between these languages, and considers the linguistic and cultural repertoire of the learner as a whole.

By discussing differences as riches, some educators of the past have been prevented from characterizing the purpose of education as ensuring that all students learn the same concepts and skills in the same way over the same period, and instead the prediction that the purpose of education is to ensure that all students reach the next level by pushing their personal boundaries and reveal their potential at the highest level has started to gain weight. One of the types of teaching that has adopted this point of view is called differentiated teaching. This approach accepts different individual characteristics such as students' precognition, interest, and learning styles; allows everyone to succeed by developing designs suitable for these characteristics; and aims to improve students' self-regulation, problem-solving, communication, and cognition skills in the learning process.

Hall (4) defines differentiated teaching as identifying all different characteristics and maximizing each student accordingly. Similarly, Gregory and Chapman (3) define differentiated teaching as a philosophy that refers to teachers planning according to their students' individual differences rather than a tool. It is necessary to consider the different readiness of the students in second language teaching, whether they have an interest in the target language, strategies for learning a second language, and plan and design the teaching according to these factors. Differentiated education considers the personality of the student without ignoring the whole group. Thus, the teacher accompanies the student step by step in language education. This method also treats the student as a whole. By offering a student-tailored education process with differentiated learning tools, students can acquire language skills appropriate for their level. Thus, the student acts independently and participates effectively in their learning process.

Children can choose from various clothes that match their changing bodies, styles, and preferences throughout life. Without any explanation, we understand that this relaxes them and allows them to express their evolving personality. For students with different readiness levels and interests in school, differentiating or adapting teaching is also more relaxing, engaging, and remarkable. Uniform teaching that suits everyone, although they are the same age chronologically, will inevitably come in abundance, just like one-size-fits-all clothing, or hit their feet like tight shoes, according to students with different needs. Differentiated teaching argues that it is possible to create classes where the facts of the diversity of students in a class can be addressed together with the realities of the curriculum.

The consequence of practices such as the holistic approach (which covers applications like bi/multilingual education and differentiated teaching) with translingualism has been possible when the twenty-first century began to look at everything (nature, politics, economy, psychology, differences, rights, technology, education, language, etc.) that human beings interact with from a generally different perspective. Scholars in the field of education have become aware of the need to modify or reconstruct the educational systems to develop the requisite knowledge, skills, and dispositions necessary to satisfy the need of twenty-first-century learners.

Partnership for Twenty-First Century Learning (P21)and OECD, considering the role of these skills in this age, have worked together for Education 2030 to translate transformational competencies and other key concepts into a set of specific constructs so that teachers and schools can better incorporate them into curricula. "Framework for Twenty-First Century Learning" (P21) illustrates that learning and innovation skills include critical thinking and problem solving, communication, collaboration, and creativity (4 Cs); life and career skills need flexibility and adaptation (another popular term "resilience" in psychology and education in the twenty-first century), initiative and self-direction, social and cross-cultural skills, productivity and accountability, leadership and responsibility; information, media, and technology skills cover the abilities to access and evaluate information, use and managing information, analyze media, create media products, and apply technology effectively. When twentieth- and twenty-first-century learning is compared, while there is content learning in the twentieth century, there is learning the tools and skills to remake the content to become the producer and creator in the twenty-first century. To narrow the subject to second language learning, ACTFL has presented the twenty-first-century learning framework in detail under the heading of "World Languages Twenty-First Century Skills Map." In this century's approach,

> Unlike the classroom of yesteryear that required students to know a great deal of information about the language but did not have an expectation of language use, today's classroom is about teaching languages so that students use them to communicate with native speakers of the language. This is what prepares them to use their language learning as a 21st century skill. (ACTFL)

In summary,

> In the twenty-first century, foreign language education is not only contributing to students' career and college readiness, but it also helps develop the individual as language learners take a new and more invigorating view of the world, a world that understands that they are better because of their knowledge about the people who share many of the

same hopes and dreams for their future, but it is with a different set of perspectives on the world. It's only through the language of the people that we can truly understand how they view the world. What makes this a language student is a twenty-first century skilled learner. (ACTF)

In short, political, social, economic, and technological changes affect the language teaching process. Thanks to the developments in social sciences, the definitions of learning, teaching, student, and teacher have been renewed. Today, learning refers to more than a change in behavior. The student is an active participant in the learning process, and the teacher is a consultant. Teaching is diversified with different methods, techniques, and materials. At this point, individual differences between students are effective. Although students are expected to show certain characteristics according to their age, student profiles are very diverse today. In this case, it is difficult for a single learning method or technique to succeed. Therefore, learning and teaching environments should be organized according to all these different characteristics. In this sense, an example from Canagarajah's (*Translingual* 498-99) study can illustrate that the different use of a preposition in English may not be an error but rather a product of the non-native language users' mother tongue and indeed essentially their lifestyle. His study shows that Indian students use the prepositions "in-on" interchangeably in their writings like "I'm in the bus" or "I'm on the bus," although teachers keep correcting them. When the students were asked why they continued this usage, they said that people are likely to be both "on" and inside the bus since India is crowded. In this case, using the right preposition may not be necessary; it can even be confusing.

Also, with the increasing use of technology, people have moved from page to screen, thus changing the way people use language. New literacies emerged as people produced, wrote, visualized, and manipulated language in new ways (Synder128). Social media has become an effective technology-based communication way in people's lives, especially in the professional field. Social networking sites are seen as productive sites that bring together participants from many identities. For example, Lam (460) examined the important role of communication, in which language and culture are integrated, in the transmission via computer. This language pattern is called "hybridization of language."

Another term, linguistic "(n)ethnography," is the result of a combination of two methods: "netnography" (Kozinets 85), (virtual ethnographic analytic frameworks) and "linguistic ethnography" (Dovchin 60), which considers the emergence of translingual applications as both offline and online. Employees from diverse cultural and linguistic backgrounds use technology to increase access to social networks that can connect many users of the world's languages. One of the frequently used writing products is online chat platforms. For example, WhatsApp is one of many other online media used for communication. Computer-mediated communication is "communication that takes place between human beings via the instrumentality of computers" (Herring 1), and it shows that people use online language differently according to different situations and purposes. Although English comes first among the international languages used on these platforms, language users of different cultures and mother tongues use some structures from their own language by placing them in English. In his study, You (in Brooke 75) examined how young Chinese employees use Chinese and English codes to create a "domestic diaspora community." The article population use nonofficial or nonstandard abbreviated and spoken English forms on this platform, in stark contrast to their professional self. Lam (460) refers to it as a "textual identity."

On the other hand, Canagarajah and Dovchin ("The Everyday" 135) chose Facebook as the main research site due to its widespread popularity to look at the online linguistic behaviours of young Mongolian-Kazakh Facebook users. They stated that "It plays a significant role in the daily linguistic repertoires of people around the world (de Bres 312), involving semiotic, heteroglossic, and linguistic creativity." And "language examples produced by Facebook users can be defined as 'translingual English' or 'codemeshing', where the online users twist, mix, and bend the standardised form of English" (136).

Today, it is obvious that social media is used more and more by young people to communicate with each other and in business environments. These environments provide spaces for young people where information and popular culture can be shared without borders and barriers (such as distance, different perspectives or as our subject: different languages). For this reason, social media offers a rich field of study that includes many eccentric uses of languages and allows these uses to be examined. Translingual phrases such as "Spiderpig"—blending of movie title "Spiderman" and "pig"; "nuekiller"—the fusion of "nuclear" and "killer"; "the rise of Xboars"—the tranformation of "The rise of Renegade X," a popular teen fantasy fiction; and "Boarzilla" (the English word "boar" with the Japanese word "Godzilla") referring, perhaps, to the "Godzilla-like boars from Japan" (Canagarajah and Dovchin, "The Everyday" 138) are creative examples of language uses in which English meshes with cultural resources of global youth culture. "English is understood not so much through fixed grammar, but rather its use shows how individuals can creatively mobilise and transcend different linguistic resources at their disposal and adopt different negotiation strategies to make meanings" (138).

Current linguistic trends in sociolinguistic research and applied linguistics have also influenced studies in language education and revealed the necessity of new approaches and practices in this field. Adherents of this perspective recognize the paradigm shift regarding the logical practice of "translingual English" in the classroom as having great potential to increase the effectiveness of English language learning and teaching processes (Canagarajah, *Translingual* 499). The introduction of "translingual English" in the classroom can link social, cultural, community, and linguistic areas of students' lives (Creese and Blackledge 112). It can help language educators understand their students' multiple desires, identities, and aspirations involved in "multiple ways of speaking, being, and learning" (Pennycook 157). This can allow us to see the world through the eyes of youth and create alternative learning opportunities (Dovchin 60). As Pennycook notes, "Languages will flow and change around us, new combinations of languages and cultures will be put together, texts will be sampled and mixed in ever new juxtapositions" (158). In other words, "Students are in the flow; pedagogy needs to go with the flow" (Pennycook158).

Curriculums that integrate different languages and establish interlingual connections in multilingual teaching may be more effective than programs that treat languages as separate departments (Helot and Cavalli 475). Kramsch considers the multilingual perspective developed from a holistic approach to be revolutionary for "questioning all the fundamentals of theoretical and applied linguistics and the traditional and national foundations of foreign language teaching" (109) Kramsch's statement is a pretty good one because the adoption of the multilingual perspective requires radical and structural changes in education policies and practices.

Language teaching policies should emphasize approaches developed according to the new requirements of the twenty-first century instead of education systems shaped according to the worldview of the nineteenth century (Helot and Laoire 14). It is necessary to move forward by comparing the past and the point reached in the twenty-first century and then by thinking about what direction the world will move in the future and how we should prepare the learners and develop applications in this direction. "We are currently preparing students for jobs that don't yet exist. . . using technologies that haven't been invented. . . in order to solve problems we don't even know are problems yet" (Riley in "Redlands Daily Facts"). As this quote shows, most of what we do is based on predictions. All predictions may turn out to be wrong in the future. "For students starting a four-year technical degree this means. . . half of what they learn in their first year of study will be outdated by their third year of study" (community.mis.temple.edu). So, what does it mean all? How should we integrate education policies and systems into this process, which some have called "The Age of Artificial Intelligence"? What needs to be done is to be aware of all these possibilities and try to be a part of the change.

This world, reshaped not only by artificial intelligence but also by many factors, is now a hybrid world. In addition to technology, it is also transformed psychologically and sociologically. The tool in which all characteristics of man are reflected and transferred is the language s/he uses. The translingual approach is a good alternative for differences within and across all languages. "It adds recognition that the formation and definition of language and language varieties are fluid. Further, this approach insists on viewing language differences and fluidities as resources to be preserved, developed, and utilized. Rather than responding to language differences only in terms of rights, it sees them as resources" (Horner et al. 304). Something different should be done to make a difference. Educating today's individuals in yesterday's way would be stealing from their tomorrows.

REFERENCE LIST

ACTFL Twenty-First Century Skills Map. Retrieved from https://www.actfl.org/sites/default/files/resources/21st%20Century%20Skills%20Map-World%20Languages.pdf, on December 20, 2020.

Baker, Colin. *Foundations of Bilingual Education and Bilingualism*(5th Ed.). Multilingual Matters, 2011.

Brooke, Ricker Schreiber. "I Am What I Am: Multilingual Identity and Digital Translanguaging." *Language Learning & Technology*, 2015, pp.69–87.

Canagarajah, A. Suresh. "The Place of World Englishes in Composition: Pluralization Continued." *College Composition and Communication*, vol. 57, no.4, 2006, pp. 586–619.www.jstor.org/stable/20456910.

———. "Lingua Franca English, Multilingual Communities, and Language Acquisition." *The Modern Language Journal*, vol. 91, no.1, 2007, pp. 934–938. https://doi.org/10.1111/j.0026-7902.2007.00678.

———. *Translingual Practice*. Routledge, 2013.

Canagarajah, A. Suresh and Sender, Dovchin. "The Everday Politics of Translingualism as a Resistant Practice." *International Journal of Multilingualism*, vol. 16, 2019. DOI: 10.1080/14790718.2019.1575833

Cenoz, Jasone, and Gorter, Durk. "Towards a Holistic Approach in the Study of Multilingual Education." *Multilingual Education: Navigating Between Language Learning and Translanguaging*, edited by J. Cenoz and D. Gorter, Cambridge University Press, 2015, pp. 1–15.

Cook, Vivian. "Multi-competence." *The Routledge Encyclopedia of Second Language Acquisition*, edited by P. Robinson, Routledge, 2013, pp. 447–451.

Council of Europe "Common European Framework of Reference for Languages: Learning, Teaching, Assessment." 2001, Retrieved fromhttps://rm.coe.int/1680459f97, onNovember 17, 2020.

———. "Plurilingual and Intercultural Education: Definition and Founding Principles."2018, Retrieved from https://www.coe.int/en/web/platform- plurilingual-intercultural-language education/the-founding-principles-of-plurilingual-and-intercultural-education, on November 17, 2020.

Creese, Angela, and Blackledge,Adrian."Translanguagingin the Bilingual Classroom: A Pedagogy for Learning and Teaching?" *The Modern Language Journal*, vol. 94, 2010, pp. 103–115.

Cummins, Jim. "Interdependence of First and Second Language Proficiency in Bilingual Children." *Language Processing in Bilingual Children*, edited by E. Bialystok, Cambridge University Press, 1991, pp. 70–89.

———. "Rethinking Monolingual Instructional Strategies in Multilingual Classrooms." *Canadian Journal of Applied Linguistics*, vol. 10, 2007, pp. 221–240.

———. "Teaching for Transfer: Challenging the Two Solitudes Assumption in Bilingual Education." *Encyclopedia of Language and Education,* edited by J. Cummins and N. H. Hornberger, vol. 5: Bilingual education (2nd Ed.). Springer, 2008, pp. 65–76.

Cummins, Jim, and Persad, Robin. "Teaching Through a Multilingual Lens: The Evolution of EAL Policy and Practice in Canada." *Education Matters*, vol. 2, 2014, pp. 3–40.

de Bres, Julia. Introduction: Language Policies on Social Network Sites. *Language Policy*, vol. 14, no. 4, 2015, pp. 309–314.

Dovchin, Sender. *Language, Media and Globalization in the Periphery: The Lingua Scapes of Popular Music in Mongolia*. Routledge, 2018.

European Centre for Modern Languages of the Council of Europe (2018). Plurilingual and Interculturaleducation. Retrieved from https://www.ecml.at/Home/tabid/59/language/en-GB/Default.aspx, on November 16, 2020.

Fahim, Mansoor, and Pishghadam, Reza. "Postmodernism and English Language Teaching." *Iranian Journal of Applied Language Studies*, vol. 1, no. 2, 2011, pp. 27–54. DOI: 10.22111/ijals.2011.51.

Fairclough, Norman. "Language and Ideology." *Trabalhosem Linguistica Aplicada*, vol. 17, no, 1, 1991, pp. 113–131.

Foucault, Michel. *Discipline and Punishment*. Vintage Books, 1995.

Fu, Danling. *Writing Between Languages: How English Language Learners Make the Transition to Fluency, Grades 4–12*. Heinemann, 2009.

García, Ofelia. "Education, Multilingualism and Translanguaging in the Twenty-First Century." *Social Justice Through Multilingual Education*, edited by T. Skutnabb–Kangas et al. Multilingual Matters, 2009, pp. 140–158.

Gregory, H. Gayle, and Chapman, Carolyn. *Differentiated Instructional Strategies. One size doesn't fit all.* Corwin, 2002.

Hall, T. "Differentiated Instruction. Effective Classroom Practices Report." National Center on Accessing the General Curriculum, CAST, U.S. Office of Special Education Programs, 2002, Retrieved from http://www.cast.org/ncac/classroompractice/cpractice02.docon, on November 15, 2020.

Helot, Christine, and Marisa, Cavalli. "Bilingual Education in Europe." *Encyclopedia of Bilingual and Multilingual Education*, edited by O. Garcia, A. Lin, and S. May, Springer International Publishing, 2017, pp. 472–487.

Helot, Christine, and Laoire, M. O. "Introduction: From Language Education Policy to a Pedagogy of the Possible." *Language Policy for The Multilingual Classroom: Pedagogy of The Possible*, edited by C. C. Helot, and M. O. Laoire, Multilingual Matters, 2011, pp. 11–25.

Herring, Susan. C. "Introduction." *Computer-Mediated Communication: Linguistic, Social and Cross-cultural Perspectives*, edited by S. C. Herring, John Benjamins, 1996, pp. 1–12.

Horner, Bruce, et al. "Opinion: Language Difference in Writing—Toward a Translingual Approach." *College English*, vol. 73, no. 3, 2011, pp. 303–321.

Jain, Rashi. "Global Englishes, Translinguistic Identities, and Translingual Practices in a Community College ESL Classroom: A Practitioner Research Reports." *TESOL Journal*, vol. 5, 2014, pp. 490–518. https://doi.org/10.1002/tesj.155.

Kellman, Steven. "J. M. Coetzee and Samuel Beckett: The Translingual Link." *Comparative Literature Studies*, vol. 33, no. 2, 1996, pp. 161–172. www.jstor.org/stable/40247052.

———. "Literary Translingualism: What and Why?". *Polylinguality and Transcultural Practices*, vol. 16, no. 3, 2019, pp. 337–346. WEB. DOI: 10.22363/2618-897X-2019-16-3-337-346

Kozinets, Robert. *Netnography: Redefined*. Sage, 2015.

Kramsch, Claire. "Authenticity and Legitimacy in Multilingual SLA." *Critical Multilingualism Studies*, vol.1, 2012, pp. 107–128.

Lam, Wan Shun Eva. "L2 Literacy and the Design of the Self: A Case Study of a Teenager Writing on the Internet." *TESOL Quarterly*, vol. 34, no. 3, 2000, pp. 457–82.

Luk, Gigi, and Bialystok, Ellen. "Bilingualism Is Not a Categorical Variable: Interaction Between Language Proficiency and Usage." *Journal of Cognitive Psychology*, vol. 25, no.5, 2013, pp. 605–621. DOI: 10.1080/20445911.2013.795574.

OECD. The Future of Education and Skills: Education 2030. 2018. Retrieved from https://www.oecd.org/education/2030/E2030%20Position%20Paper%20(05.04.2018). pdf,on December 20, 2020.

P21P21's Framework for Twenty-First Century Learning. 2007. Retrieved from http://www.p21.org/our- work/p21-framework, on December 12, 2020.

Pennycook, Alastair. "English in the World/The World in English." *Power and Inequality in Language Education,*edited by J. W. Tollefson,pp.34–58. Cambridge University Press, 1995.

———. *Global Englishes and Transcultural Flows*. Routledge, 2007.

Phillipson, Robert. *Linguistic Imperialism*. Oxford University Press, 1992.

Redlands Daily Facts, November 23, 2009. Retrieved from https://www.redlandsdailyfacts.com/2009/11/23/a-new-model-of-liberal-learning-for-the-21st-century/, on December 25, 2020.

Scoot, Patrick. "Gabriel Okaro'sthe Voice: The Non-Ijo Reader and the Pragmatics of Translingualism." *Research in African Literatures*, vol. 21 no. 3, pp. 75–88, https://www.jstor.org/stable/3819635.

Synder, Ilana. *Page to Screen: Taking Literacy into the Electronic Era*. Routledge, 1998.

Wei, Li. "Translanguaging as a Practical Theory of Language." *Applied Linguistics,* vol. 39, no: 1, 2018, pp. 9–30.http://doi.org/10.1093/applin/amx039.

Winch, Christopher, and Gingell, John. *Philosophy of Education: The Key Concepts*. Routledge, 1999. https://doi.org/10.4324/9780203026076.

21

Language Education within and after the Post-Method Era

Vildan İnci Kavak

INTRODUCTION

In the nineteenth and early twentieth century, knowledge was mostly considered absolute, stable, and out there to be discovered (Gilbert 67). Yet, the rest of the twentieth century was characterized by rampant tension and deep mistrust in science, politics, and economic systems as established concepts and norms left their places to fluid, complex, and uncertain notions and views, mostly constructed in social contexts (67). In other words, knowledge has been an unstable product of ever-changing and contested processes, requiring participants' time/energy and constant modifications. This paradigm shift in the centuries-old epistemological, ontological, and relational justifications of life gave rise to an umbrella term, postmodernism. Postmodernism was essentially a literary and cultural movement that originated in France in the post-war period. This artistic and cultural movement marked a continuation of and a reaction to modernism, which explored (the confines of) reasoning, rationality, experimentalism, idealism, subjectivity, and high culture. As Peter Childs states, "the hegemony of realism was challenged by modernism and then postmodernism as alternative ways of representing reality and the world" (3). Jean-Michel Rabaté argues that historians "use 'modernity' to refer to a direct route from Descartes to the Enlightenment in a movement of thought that rejected religious authority and ended up stressing the political freedom allied with scientific knowledge" (9). For thinkers such as Charles Baudelaire, Gustave Flaubert, Stéphane Mallarmé, and Friedrich Nietzsche, "'modern' involves not only an anti-authoritarian stance opposing classical conventions but also revulsion in front of bourgeois society on the rise" (Rabaté 10). While modernism was mostly a literary and art movement that emerged in the early twentieth century, modernity as a concept stood for the adoption of new technologies and scientific breakthroughs, a self-conscious search for knowledge and truth, and a renunciation of the archaic politics and societal systems. On the other hand, the age of postmodernity was "a time of constant change, multiplicity, fluidity and uncertainty" (Andreotti 7), in which knowledge, identity, and culture are socially and spatially constructed, unstable, and in constant crisis. Postmodernism approaches reality as a social construct because the reality of any phenomenon is created exclusively among its participants (Ahmadian and Rad 593). Therefore, the latter half of the twentieth century witnessed that truth was not containable and was prone to infinite revisions; therefore, it could be constructed, deconstructed, and replaced interminably (Trilling and Hood 5, Hargreaves 18, Lankshear and Knobel 167). Below is a summary of postmodernism characteristics as a cultural concept by Fahim and Pishghadam:

- Postmodernism is based on constructivism as there is no absolute truth; the truth is determined by the participants of the context through social interactions.
- It rejects absolutism but defends relativism as knowledge is not fixed and static, as science has shown in modernism. There are more probabilities than certainties, so we can only reach the better option for the context because there is no best.
- It is against theories because none is better than the other; thus, inquiries must be answered pragmatically.
- It does not accept expertise as a concept because knowledge is created between participants mutually in social dialogues. Thus, the idea that a knower/expert teaches the other/inexperienced is not true.
- It rejects major/global realities because it is highly culture- and context-sensitive. In short, knowledge is not universal, so it cannot be generalized. Each context is distinctive, and its knowledge should be evaluated in its own terms. Local needs and diversities should be considered and respected.
- It replaces objectivism with subjectivism. Scientific disciplines are not only affected by physical laws but by the rules of society (34-36).

The underlying relativism, pluralism, and indeterminacy of postmodernist theories and the so-called postmodern culture have unprecedentedly influenced various education disciplines such as language education. As a possible way out of the challenges arising in the arena of language education with the impact of postmodern policies, guidelines, and their classroom implementations, Kumaravadivelu proposed a contemporary model in which macro and microstructures guide and frame the ideas that came along with a fusion of diverse models in language education and other disciplines (Kumaravadivelu, *Understanding Language Teaching* 201). In this model, he maintains that researchers and practitioners develop an awareness of macrostructures (cultural, political, and historical) that shape and reshape the microstructures of pedagogic enterprises (Kumaravadivelu 201). Macrostrategies prompted by macrostructures are "general plans derived from currently available theoretical, empirical, and pedagogical knowledge related to L2 learning and teaching" (201). The model, in this respect, aimed to melt global values and ideologies in the pot of local and context-sensitive variables shaped under the umbrella term, "glocalisation" (Ahmadian and Rad 592, JesicaDwi Lusianov 360), which is used for global but localised processes to meet social, cultural, and economic needs. In this way, local plans can be utilized to achieve global standards, which can also be maintained as macrostructures (Patel and Lynch 223). This approach exemplifies the educational trend that critiques the recent developments in art and humanities and their impact on education. The new thinking has proposed that modern and post-modern educational models should communicate with each other constructively and interactively by incorporating scientific reasoning and universal methodologies with more individualised and diversified pedagogies. Consequently, a dialogical (and collaborative) turn has emerged in language teaching and raised the urgency of a swift transformation into more inclusive and responsive models. In the light of the above discussion, the rest of the chapter will survey the recent developments in teaching by enquiring what might and should come after postmodern educational models and discussing the expediency of a more collaborative approach to contemporary language teaching.

FOREIGN LANGUAGE TEACHING METHODOLOGY AND THE POST-METHOD TURN

An evident impact of postmodernity can be traced in recent educational models and practices, particularly within the concepts of "post-methodology" and the "glocalisation" of English language education. To begin with, methods or methodological approaches have never been utilized and implemented in their purest forms in language classrooms since they have never been derived from classroom practices. In most cases, they have been implemented in the classroom, but they were ignorant of classroom realities (Pennycook 606, Richards and Rodgers, "Approaches and Methods in Language Teaching" 244). To illustrate, Audio-lingualism or the Audiolingual Method was popularized in the 1950s to respond to the US service members' need to learn different languages in short periods in World War II. The method was founded principally on the behaviorist assumption that conditioning was the key to learning and the structural linguists' emphasis on grammar in language teaching. It was strongly criticized because the Audiolingual Method presented limited options to learners for natural interaction, verbal fluency, and authentic practices (Pennycook 603). Learners were considered as stimulus-response mechanisms whose learning was an immediate outcome of classroom drills. In a reaction to such a methodology, linguists stressed the functional and communicative potential of language. They advocated a more interactional approach to language teaching, paving the way for Communicative Language Teaching (CLT). The theorists of CLT favored communicative proficiency to the syntactical and structural composition of language. CLT targeted communicative competence and stressed the interdependence of four skills in communication (Stern 456); However, CLT's excessive attention to speaking and listening posed a threat to developing reading and writing skills (Horowitz 141). Additionally, the method was not suited to foreign contexts as most teachers and learners fail to develop native-like proficiency in the non-native settings where the foreign language is mostly taught as an academic and professional component. In the same way, most of the reputable methods such as "The Direct Method," "Grammar-Translation Method," "The Structural Approach," "Suggestopedia," "Total Physical Response," "The Silent Way," "Community Language Learning," "Task-Based language Learning" or "The Natural Approach" have appealed to proponents and opponents (Larsen-Freeman, "Recent Innovations" 51-69). Most of these methods have been "out-of-date" or even "dead" today (Allwright 168). Accordingly, the method is no longer a key and dependable construct in language teaching and what is needed is not really "an alternative method" but "an alternative to method" (Liu 175). This increasing awareness appears to be coupled with a resolve to name the current state of foreign or second language teaching as "the postmethod condition" (Kumaravadivelu, "The Postmethod Condition" 27).

Kumaravadelivelu has proposed certain strategies and parameters for the postmethod condition of teaching pedagogy. He claimed that the postmethod pedagogy covers ten macro strategies: maximization of learning opportunities, facilitation of negotiated interaction, minimization of perceptual mismatches, activation of intuitive heuristics, fostering language awareness, contextualization of linguistic input, integration of language skills, promotion of learner autonomy, raising cultural consciousness, and ensuring social relevance (32). All these strategies reject the best method's inquiry, highlighting the importance of how local needs can be addressed carefully and the current practices can be adapted to different contexts. Kumaravadelivelu also identified three parameters under the postmethod theory: "particularity," "practicality," and "possibility" ("Toward a Postmethod Pedagogy" 538). The first suggests that a teaching program "must be sensitive to a particular group of teachers teaching a particular group of learners pursuing a particular set of goals within a particular institutional context embedded in a particular socio-cultural milieu" (538). In other words, a teaching program should be context-sensitive. The second supports the conviction that theory and practice should collaborate and work for an identical goal. Therefore, knowledge needs to emerge from the practice, and the practice should feed in the knowledge. There should be action in thought and thought in action, highlighting the criticality of reflection and action, action research, and more responsive practices. The last parameter is "possibility," which means that learners are the source of experience, so they shape and are shaped by knowledge emerging in the process. Their experience feeds into the classroom practices just like how they are fed by a broader social, economic, and political setting they live in. Learners' and teacher's identities are formed and reformed in this cycle. On the whole, postmethod pedagogy draws on some of the dualistic qualities of postmodern educational systems, such as localism/particularism, egalitarianism/pluralism, and flexibility/adaptability.

Several scholars have claimed that the shifts in academia and its structures have affected disciplines and practitioners by transforming the way they see their profession and its constituents (Gilbert 70, Gee 22, Edwards and Usher 20, and Cope and Kalantzis 164–195). Kumaravadivelu defines this state of mind with the words: "We have moved from a state of 'awareness' toward a state of 'awakening'" ("TESOL Methods" 75). We are now more aware that methods-based education must be more responsive to local provisions, value teacher/learner views, and admit the criticality of macrostructures molding and transforming the micro-structures of teaching and learning. As most up-to-date teachers are introduced to the technology later than their students, they often struggle to identify students' needs. While these students can reach all information easier and quicker through digital aids than teachers, they utilize digitally-mediated modes and instruments as their new learning norm. This incongruity between teachers and learners causes the latter to lose interest in the lessons, eventually resulting in a prevalent disappointment and failure in foreign language teaching and linguistics, if not all educational disciplines.

A post-method practitioner thus should be conscious of what is going on in their class. They should be able to research to have a better insight into class variables such as learner's interests, worries, attitudes, and so on, which "encourages the teacher to engage in a carefully crafted process of diagnosis, treatment, and assessment" (Brown 13). The teacher should be alert to any such instances as "what works and what does not, with what group(s) of learners, and for what reason, and assessing what changes are necessary to make instruction meet its desired goals" (9). That's why "teachers should not hesitate to research by developing and using investigative abilities derived from the practices of exploratory research" (Allwright 127), teacher research cycle (Freeman and Freeman 19), classroom observation, and discourse analysis (Kumaravadivelu, "Critical Classroom Discourse Analysis" 457). According to Holec, in this new state of education, a learner should be independent, keen, and manage to learn individually (3). Autonomous learners demand autonomous teachers. Teachers are expected to have not only competence but confidence as well. They should also be willing to devise and employ their individual theory of practice. Given the sociopolitical conditions, these practices should respond to their own educational settings and conditions peculiarities. Since teachers' professional and personal knowledge is made from what they gain through official and individual routes of educational experience, this feeds into teacher autonomy and shapes it.

WHAT ARE NEW PATTERNS OF LANGUAGE EDUCATION IN THE POST-POSTMODERN ERA?

Leicester claims that modern and postmodern education methodologies are untenable and functionless when used individually (78). The absolute truth (Phillips-Bell

98) and the relativist doctrines are not flawless and coherent (Lawson 83). Thus, education programs based on either of them would also lack some key constituents. While modernist programs position some groups as more prestigious and popular and marginalize less privileged forms of knowledge and understanding (Hirst 120), postmodernist programs encourage plural perspectives in multicultural education. Still, only some groups can be paid attention to (Walkling 90). The boundaries are more blurred in modern educational contexts, and there is no need for labels and tags. Thus, new schemes emerged such as "adult education," "lifelong education," "reflective practitioner" (Schön 55), and "radical pedagogy" (Giroux 14), show different human experiences and intersubjectivity in education. Additionally, a recent concept named "glocalization" has been introduced to the field of language education as a reconciling concept to settle the clash between globalisation and localization by echoing the slogan "think globally, act locally." According to Weber, glocalization is "a mix of global frameworks and local practices, [. . .] which greatly increases the potential for independent learning by merging worldwide knowledge and local knowledge" (cited in Gurko132). Nevertheless, Moss notes that "glocalisation does not represent the intermediate or transitional idea or a period between the local and global level but rather as the use of global standards to describe the goals and consequently make local plans to achieve these standards" (cited in Ahmadian Rad 594). That is, microstrategies are localized, context-specific, and needs-oriented classroom practices, and they derive from macrostrategies to meet local and individual necessities. Gurko defended the concept by stating that glocalization can "greatly increase the potential for independent learning by merging worldwide knowledge and local knowledge" (132). This is fundamentally based on the universal values of equity and equal distribution of powers. From the perspective of glocalization, all systems and communities should be accepted and valued as key entities because the way individuals experience the world differs in a degree of flexibility and variability. Local concepts are also equally important as they can even change universal norms. The controversy on the use of mother tongue in language classrooms can provide an example for foreign language education. Mother tongue use has frequently been condemned or banned from classrooms for the sake of a higher degree of proficiency, which can be noted in the case of Communicative Language Teaching.

Postmodern educational policies have supported relativism and marginalized social groups in different contexts, but they ignored the emerging needs of modern societies. Considering the limitations of modernist and postmodernist pedagogies, not only one best option but a collection of possible valid options for each fast-changing context should be identified. Gadamer suggests the re-conceptualization of methods and strategies.

> As tools, methods are always good to have. But one must understand where these can be fruitfully used. Methodical sterility is a generally known phenomenon. Every once in a while, for instance, we find tried and true or merely fashionable methods applied in a field where they are simply unproductive. (*Gadamer in Conversation* 41)

Therefore, it would be better to benefit from methods if they are used judiciously. In a world after the demise of postmodern philosophies and politics, it could be hard to accept reliable methodologies or permanent answers. Still, some answers can work provisionally and more successfully. This can present an optimal balance between modernism's essentialist philosophical stance and postmodernism's "chaotic carnival" (Snir 299-311). In this context, learners' aims should be personalized. Johnson and Paulston describe learner roles in an individualized language-learning program. The learner should be:

- the planner of his/her own learning programme and take responsibility for what he/she does in the classroom.
- the monitor and evaluator of his or her own progress.
- the member of a group and learns by interacting with others.
- the tutor/student of other learners and teachers (39-46).

Many of the newer methodologies tend to posit a reconsideration of the learner's contribution to the learning process (Richards and Rodgers) on multiple components of the education system such as "the types of learning tasks, the degree of control learners need, the patterns of learner groupings, the degree to which learners influence the learning of others, the view of the learner as a processor, performer, initiator, problem-solver, etc." (244).

Above all the issues mentioned above of theoretical compromises and collaborative approaches to education, the unexpected entry of COVID-19 into our agendas has presented a completely new challenge. The pandemic has profoundly reformed various aspects of language teaching. Face-to-face education has been abandoned hastily, and virtual/technology-based teaching systems and platforms have been introduced to all levels of education around the world. Most educators are forced to utilize and learn new skills in distance education due to frequent updates on practices and expectations in a period of vigilance, chaos, and unpredictability. Accordingly, how teachers and students in online classes can be supported requires closer attention to lessen the unforeseeable damage to disadvantaged, underachieving social groups, national literacy programs, and international students caused by abrupt school closures. Thus, a new pedagogy incorporating emerging remote learning and teaching systems on local and global scales is supposed to address these uncertainties and ensure the involvement of these groups in the planning and making of policies and curricula in the coming years. As an urgent need, the teacher education should also be reconsidered and consolidated, so prospective teachers can be equipped to "make their own informed decisions in relation to the contributions they can make in their contexts in dialogue with colleagues, learners, parents and the wider society" (Andreotti 12).

The pandemic can also present some unexpected benefits in foreign language teaching. The recent research evinced that "[a] possibility for English language teaching during and after the pandemic is that of translingual practices and pedagogy" (Yi and Jang 2). In contrast to monolingual or structuralist practices, "translingual practices are more hybrid, dynamic, and spontaneous language and literacy practices that involve traversing multiple languages and orchestrating diverse semiotic resources and modes" (2). As an offshoot of translanguaging theory, translingualism sees learners' linguistic repertoire as a whole and individually unique. It rejects monolingual language teaching methods by offering a more autonomous, individualized, and creative teaching environment. Translanguaging allows students to protect their identity and feel more positive about learning a language as they are accepted (Cummins 9). The learner's main language and culture have particular importance in a new language. This establishes a mentally positive approach to learners who can thus feel more liberated from the artificiality of monolingual environments in the foreign language learning context. Considering that online education mostly ignores the individualised needs and mental factors, more flexible and inclusive teaching models such as a translingual language teaching method can have the potential to compensate for the humanistic inadequacies of language teaching through distance learning tools.

Nevertheless, it is still unclear how language educators will adapt to the emergency remote language teaching models after the pandemic. Distance teaching may function disparately in various contexts. "Online teaching is characterised by different modalities (e.g., fully online; blended) and modes of communication (e.g., synchronous, asynchronous), remote teaching may actually rely on or avoid technology for instructional purposes" (Moser et al.6). At this point in history, in-service training, online workshops, free teaching and learning tools, technology-incorporated teaching tools, and distance assessment methods dominate education. Yet, a more systematic and methodological approach to post-pandemic education will be central to the successful realization of educational objectives more than ever in history.

CONCLUSION

This chapter offers a compass rather than a straightforward guide for current problems surrounding the field of education on the whole and foreign language education in particular. Adapting new frameworks (i.e., cognitive adaptation, epistemological pluralism, localisation of objectives, etc.) to the existing programs and systems is an intimidating and often unattainable task. In the post-method age, a corporation of modern or postmodern pedagogies has been promoted. All education stakeholders have been encouraged to maintain an ongoing dialogue on various elements of education (schemes, learner/teacher needs, resources, tools, modes, etc.) more prolifically and comprehensively. There will be multiple answers, risks, solutions through the de- and re-construction of concepts since circumstances alter and new disputes arise day by day. For that reason, we, as educators, should change our perspectives on the potential of change and uncertainties in education just as Kahaney stated, "if change can be viewed as a component in an ongoing process called 'learning' instead of as a product or a 'thing,' then it would be easier to have a different relationship to change itself" (193). Brown stated that "the profession has at last reached the level of maturity where we recognize the complexity of language learners in multiple worldwide contexts demands an eclectic blend of tasks, each tailored for a particular group of learners studying for particular purposes" (*Principles of Language Learning and Teaching* 172). Therefore, the ultimate aim should not be to reach merely a unique and temporally working solution for all because even the most popular language education methods and strategies have been short-lived and without much impact in the rapid pace of the modern world.

Even though teachers often look for a silver bullet in the form of simple updates or quick fixes, it would not be possible to provide them with all-in-one keys in the post-postmethod teaching world. When the methodology is juxtaposed with post-methodology in language teaching, the former is typically static and spatiotemporally constrained, allowing limited room for individuation, revision, and advance in time. Rancière elaborates on how teachers should take the concept of method:

> A method means a path: not the path that a thinker follows but the path that he/she constructs, that you have to construct to know where you are, to figure out the characteristics of the territory you are going through, the places it allows you to go, the way it obliges you to move, the markers that can help you, the obstacles that get in the way. Examining a method thus means examining how idealities are materially produced. (114)

To recap, methods are beneficial if they can adjust to new circumstances and embrace the local variables. In a post-postmodern world, it would be hard to develop dependable, long-term methodologies or permanent answers, and the key will be on adaptability, mobility, and particularity. As Kahaney puts it, "instead of experiencing resistance to change as an obstacle, we as teachers could come to expect resistance to change as part of the learning process and thus plan for various kinds of and degrees of resistance" (193). In this state of interruptions and unpredictability due to pandemics, socio-economical, and cultural crises, the postmodern models and practices of language teaching, including post-methodology and glocalization, can offer some limited success in English language education. However, as various postmodern schemes lack absolute foundations and borders, they would be frameless, more eclectic, and heterogeneous. Instead, approaches and methods respecting the significance of the human subject, the value of global objectives, and the diversity of local needs can offer a possible solution to challenges in language education. The examples of translingual language teaching practices value learners' individual differences and mental involvement in the learning process. A functional synthesis of conflicting teaching philosophies and attitudes is on-demand more than ever in history.

REFERENCE LIST

Ahmadian, Mehrshad, and Saeedeh Erfan Rad. "Postmethod Era and Glocalized Language. Curriculum Development: A Fresh Burden on Language Teachers." *Journal of Language Teaching & Research* vol. 5, no. 3, 2014, pp.592–598.

Akbari, Ramin. "Reflections on Reflection: A Critical Appraisal of Reflective Practices in L2 Teacher Education." *System* vol. 35, no. 2, 2007, pp. 192–207.

Allwright, Dick. "The Characterisation of Teaching and Learning Environments: Problems and Perspectives." *Foreign Language Research in Cross-cultural Perspective. John Benjamins Publishing Company: Amsterdam*, 1991, pp. 161–173.

———. "Integrating 'Research' and 'Pedagogy': Appropriate Criteria and Practical Possibilities." *Teachers Develop Teachers Research*, 1993, pp. 125–135.

Andreotti, Vanessa. "Global Education in the '21st Century': Two Different Perspectives on the 'Post-' of Postmodernism." *International Journal of Development Education and Global Learning* vol. 2, no. 2 2009, pp. 5–22.

Brown, H. Douglas. *Principles of Language Learning and Teaching*. vol. 4. New York: Longman, 2000.

———. "English Language Teaching in the 'Post-Method' Era: Toward Better." In *Methodology in Language Teaching: An Anthology of Current Practice* vol. 9, 2002, pp. 9–18.

Childs, Peter. *Modernism*. Routledge, 2016.

Cope, Bill, and Mary Kalantzis. "Multiliteracies: New Literacies, New Learning." *Pedagogies: An International Journal*, vol. 4, no. 3, 2009, pp. 164–195.

Cummins, Jim. "Language and Identity in Multilingual Schools: Constructing Evidence-based Instructional Policies." *Managing Diversity in Education*. Multilingual Matters, 2013, pp. 3–26.

Edwards, Richard, and Usher, R. *Postmodernism and Education*. London: Routledge, 1994.

Fahim, Mansoor, and Reza Pishghadam. "Postmodernism and English language teaching." *Iranian Journal of Applied Language Studies*, vol. 1, no. 2, 2011, pp. 27–54.

Freeman, Donald, and Donald J. Freeman. *Doing Teacher Research: From Inquiry to Understanding*. Heinle & Heinle Pub, 1998.

Gadamer, Hans-Georg. (2001) *Gadamer in Conversation: Reflections and Commentary* (Ed. and Trans. R.E. Palmer) New Haven and London: Yale University Press.

Gee, James Paul. "What Video Games Have to Teach Us About Learning and Literacy." *Computers in Entertainment (CIE)* vol.1, no. 1, 2003, pp. 20–25.

Gilbert, Jane. "Equality and Difference: Schooling and Social Democracy in the Twenty-First Century." *Critical Literacy: Theories and Practices*, vol. 4, no. 1, 2010, pp. 66–77.

Giroux, Henry. "The Hope of Radical Education." *What Schools Can Do: Critical Pedagogy and Practice*, 1992, pp. 13–26.

Gurko, Krista L. "What Does LORI Say? Comparing the Availability and Characteristics of Learning Objects on One 'Worldwide' and Two African Open Educational Resource Websites." *Proceedings of the First International Symposium on Open Educational Resources: Issues for Localisation and Globalisation.* 2011.

Hargreaves, Andy. *Teaching in the Knowledge Society: Education in the Age of Insecurity*. Teachers College Press, 2003.

Hirst, Paul H. "Liberal Education and the Nature of Knowledge." *Philosophical Analysis and Education*, vol. 2, 1965, pp. 113–140.

Holec, Henri. *Autonomy and Self-Directed Learning: Present Fields of Application: Autonomieetapprentissageautodirige: Terrains d'applicationactuels: Project No. 12: Learning and Teaching Modern Languages for Communication*. Council of Europe, 1988.

Horowitz, Daniel. "Process, Not Product: Less Than Meets the Eye." *TESOL Quarterly*, vol.20, no. 1, 1986, pp. 141–144.

Johnson, Francis Charles, and Christina Bratt Paulston. *Individualising the Language Classroom: Learning and Teaching in a Communicative Context*. Jacaranda Press, 1976.

Kahaney, Phyllis. "Afterword: Knowledge, Learning and Change." *Theoretical and Critical Perspectives on Teacher Change*, 1993, pp. 191–200.

Kumaravadivelu, Bala. "A Postmethod Perspective on English Language Teaching." *World Englishes*, vol. 22, no. 4, 2003, pp. 539–550.

———. "The Postmethod Condition: (E)merging Strategies for Second/Foreign Language Teaching." *TESOL Quarterly*, vol.28, no. 1, 1994, pp. 27–48.

———. "TESOL Methods: Changing Tracks, Challenging Trends." *TESOL Quarterly*, vol. 40, no. 1, 2006, pp. 59–81.

———. "Toward a Postmethod Pedagogy." *TESOL Quarterly*, vol. 35, no. 4, 2001, pp. 537–560.

———. *Understanding Language Teaching: From Method to Postmethod*, Lawrence Erlbaum Associates, Inc., Publishers, Mahwah, New Jersey, 2006.

Kumaravadivelu, Bernard. "Critical Classroom Discourse Analysis." *TESOL Quarterly*, vol.33, no. 3, 1999, pp. 453–484.

Lankshear, Colin, and Michele Knobel. *New Literacies: Changing Knowledge and Classroom Learning*. Open University Press, 2003.

Larsen-Freeman, Diane. "Recent Innovations in Language Teaching Methodology." *The ANNALS of the American Academy of Political and Social Science*, vol. 490, no. 1, Mar. 1987, pp. 51–69.

Lawson, Kenneth H. "The Semantics of 'Truth': A Counter-Argument to Some Postmodern Theories." *International Journal of Lifelong Education*, vol. 19, no. 1, 2000, pp. 82–92.

Leicester, Mal. "Post-Postmodernism and Continuing Education." *International Journal of Lifelong Education*, vol. 19, no. 1, 2000, pp. 73–81.

Liu, Dilin. "Comments on B. Kumaravadivelu's The Postmethod Condition:(E)merging Strategies for Second/Foreign Language Teaching: Alternative to or Addition to Method?." *TESOL Quarterly*, vol. 29, no. 1, 1995, pp. 174–177.

Lusianov, JesicaDwi. "Post-Method Era and Glocalization in Language Teaching and Learning."*Forth International Conference on Language, Literature, Culture, and Education (ICOLLITE 2020)*.Atlantis Press, 2020.

Moser, Kelly M., Tianlan Wei, and Devon Brenner. "Remote Teaching during COVID-19: Implications from a National Survey of Language Educators."*System* 97, 2021, pp. 1–51.

Patel, Fay, and Lynch, Hayley. "Glocalization as an Alternative to Internationalisation in Higher Education: Embedding Positive Glocal Learning Perspectives." *International Journal of Teaching and Learning in Higher Education,* vol. 25, no. 2, 2013, pp. 223–230.

Pennycook, Alastair. "The Concept of Method, Interested Knowledge, and the Politics of Language Teaching." *TESOL Quarterly*, vol. 23, no. 4, 1989, pp. 589–618.

Phillips-Bell, M. "Multicultural Education: A Critique of Walkling and Zec." *Journal of Philosophy of Education*, vol. 15, no. 1, 1981, pp.97–105.

Rabaté, Jean-Michel. "Philosophy."*A Companion to Modernist Literature and Culture*, edited by David Bradshaw and Kevin J. H. Dettmar, John Wiley & Sons, 2008, pp. 9–18.

Rancière, Jacques. "A Few Remarks on the Method of Jacques Rancière." *Parallax*, vol. 15, no. 3, 2009, pp. 114–123.

Richards, Jack C., and Theodore S. Rodgers. *Approaches and Methods in Language Teaching*. Cambridge University Press, 2014.

Schön, Donald A. *Educating the Reflective Practitioner: Toward a New Design for Teaching and Learning in The Professions.* Jossey-Bass, 1987.

Snir, Itay. "Making Sense in Education: Deleuzeon Thinking against Common Sense." *Educational Philosophy and Theory*, vol. 50, no. 3, 2018, pp. 299–311.

Stern, Hans Heinrich. *Fundamental Concepts of Language Teaching.* Oxford: Oxford University Press, 1983.

Trilling, Bernie, and Paul Hood. "Learning, Technology, and Education Reform in the Knowledge Age or We're Wired, Webbed, and Windowed, Now What?." *Educational Technology*, 1999, pp. 5–18.

Walkling, Philip H. "The Idea of a Multicultural Curriculum." *Journal of the Philosophy of Education*, vol. 14, no. 1, 1980, pp. 87–95.

Yi, Youngjoo, and Jinsil Jang. "Envisioning Possibilities amid the COVID-19 Pandemic: Implications from English Language Teaching in South Korea." *TESOL Journal*, vol.11, no. 3, 2020, pp.1–5.

Appendix

Tables of Differences

EDITOR'S NOTE

The tables below were materialized during the editorial process when my readings of "post-theory," "post-postmodernism," and "posthumanism" intensified and accumulated. The idea was generated from Ihab Hassan's inspiring table that listed the differences between "modernism" and "postmodernism" where he drew "on ideas in many fields—rhetoric, linguistics, literary theory, philosophy, anthropology, psychoanalysis, political science, even theology—and [. . .] many authors—European and American—aligned with diverse movements, groups and views" (Ihab Hassan, *The Dismemberment of Orpheus: Toward a Postmodern Literature*. The University of Wisconsin Press, 1982, p. 268). Although Hassan was appreciated for his definitions, discussions, and comparisons of postmodernism, and very much celebrated for his books back in the 1990s, the acclaim for his table of differences had been much less. It is because in the social sciences, the most dangerous, risky, and unscholarly inclinations are generalization, reductionism, and oversimplification. Still, in humanities, we all fancy tables that would miraculously disperse the mists and demonstrate the nuances. It is no surprise that I could not resist the temptation. Like Hassan, therefore, I should note that these rubrics can be contested or remain insecure and equivocal. The target concepts, "post-theory," "post-postmodernism," and "posthumanism," are still subject to current debates and in the process of formation. So, the proposed comparisons may collapse, or differences may shift in time, and, in that, I am placing myself at the mercy of the readers. Some terms were intended to be playful and humorous to remind the suggestive nature of the material. However, if, despite the perils, the tables should be of any use to anyone, then I will consider the risk worth taking.

Zekiye Antakyalıoğlu

Table A.1. Theory/Post-Theory

Theory	Post-Theory
Productive	Re-productive
Radical	Reactionary
Philosophical	Political
Schizophrenic	Hysteric
Cold War	War against/as terrorism
Astute	Audacious
Genesis	Legacy
Revolutionary	Rebellious
Eminent	Subsidiary
Diagnostic	Curative
Late capitalism	Wild capitalism
Perverse	Cordial
Introvert	Extrovert
Anti-humanist	Posthumanist
Différance	Dissidence
Trace	Destination
Meticulous	Disarranged
Amoral	Moral
Critical	Auto-critical
Textuality	Actuality
Cultural	Natural/Environmental
Stars	Satellites
Orpheus	Cassandra
Critique of philosophy	Critique of theory
Linguistics	Ethics
Nietzschean	Spinozist
Interdisciplinary	Multidisciplinary
Sceptical	Responsible
Disinterested	Committed
Deconstructive	Constructive
Apathy	Empathy
Desire	Demand
Objet petit a	Object
Absence	Presence
École	Hub
Seminar	Workshop
Individual	Network

Table A.2. Modernism/Postmodernism/Post-Postmodernism

Modernism	Postmodernism	Post-Postmodernism
Form	Perform	Re-form
Representation	Presentation	Demonstration
Hierarchy	Equality	Solidarity
Figurative	Self-reflexive	Literal
Sign	Signifier	Signified
Distance	Participation	Collaboration
Creation	Recreation	Production
European	Global	Planetary
Epistemology	Ontology	Hauntology
Thesis	Hypothesis	Synthesis
Presence	Absence	Remnant
Anti-Realist	Anti-Modernist	Realist-Modernist
Work	Text	Counter-text
Transcendence	Immanence	Telos
Present	Past	Future
New	Neo	Next
Symphony	Polyphony	Cacophony
Syndrome	Complication	Diagnose
Endure	Enjoy	#Resist
Despondency	Frivolity	Responsibility
Authenticity	Inauthenticity	Facticity
Angst	*Jouissance*	Urge
Utopia	Heterotopia	Dystopia
Human	Anti-human	Posthuman
Left-wing	Liberal	Green
Elitist	Populist	Socialist
National	International	Transnational
Meta-récit	Petit-récit	Digi-récit
Colonialism	Post-colonialism	Neocolonialism
Irony	Parody	Sincerity
Construction	Deconstruction	Reconstruction
Universal	Multiversal	Transversal
Self	Self/Other	Other
Relativity	Contingency	Reality
Geist	Zeitgeist	Poltergeist
Disssident	Complicit	Covenant
Individual	Dividual	Dual
Scene	Mise-en-scene	Anthropo-scene
Sight	Sight-seeing	Hindsight
Subject	*Objet petit a*	Object
Need	Desire	Demand
Garden	Theme-park	Wild-life
Form	Content of the form	Content
Ideologist	Conformist	Activist

Table A.3. Humanism/Posthumanism

Humanism	Posthumanism
Universalist	Transversalist
Essentialist	Pragmatist
Binary	Symbiosis
Being	Becoming
Singularity	Multiplicity
Cosmos	Chaosmos
Racial	Antiracial
Man	Actant
Heterosexual	Nonbinary gender
Settler	Nomad
Hierarchical	Egalitarian
Majority	Minority
Individual	Assemblage
Euro-centric	World-centric
Rational	Relational
Deal	Entangle
Cognitive	Intuitive
I	We
Them	Us
Potestas	*Potentia*
Law	Justice
Dualist/Cartesian	Monist/Spinozist
Progress	Transformation
Arrogant	Modest
Confront	Embrace
Anthropocentric	Post-Anthropocentric
Oedipal	Anti-Oedipal
Species	Trans-species
Space	Interspace
Materialist	Matter-realist
Manifesto	Proclamation
Bios	Bios-Zoe
World	Planet
Lack	Plenitude
Obedience	Rebellion
Territorialize	Deterritorialize
Resort	Environment
Hegemony	Network
Colonize	Sympathize
Action	Interaction
Attunement	Transposition
Totality	Diversity
Egotism	Altruism
Preserve	Change
Keep	Share

Humanism	Posthumanism
Border	Threshold
Profit	Nonprofit
Molar	Molecular
Positioned	Embedded
Dominate	Negotiate
Transcendence	Immanence
Fatalist	Vitalist
Capitalist	Anticapitalist
World as Stage	World as Home
Religious	Nonreligious
Consumerism	Sustainability
Doomsday	Anthropocene
Genesis	Eternal recurrence
Chronos	Aion
Bourgeoisie	A people to come
Liberal democracy	Bios-zoe-egalitarianism
Human	Life
Identity	Liquid identity
Anthropos	Nonunitary subject

Index

accountability, 90–94
actant, 74, 139, 264
affect, 35–37, 47, 103, 155–62, 179, 182; affective, 35–38, 103, 142, 153–62
Agamben, Giorgio, 80, 85–96, 153
agential, 66, 67, 72, 100; agential realism, 103–8
aion, 94–95, 265
Alaimo, Stacy, 78–79, 101, 105–8
animal, 66, 72–73, 89–95, 99–105, 114–19, 203; animality, 85, 89–92
Anthropocene, 104, 107,109, 113–22,
anthropocentric, 65–66, 72, 79, 80, 82, 86–87, 94, 119, 125, 147, 205, 208
anthropos, 78–82, 265
antihumanism, 76, 82, 103, 202,
Arnold, Matthew, 9–19, 214
assemblage, 67, 93, 103, 264

Barad, Karen, 67–70, 79–80, 86, 103, 106–8
bare life, 80, 85–96
Bauman, Zygmunt, 25–26, 86
biopolitics, 85–87, 91, 95
bios, 80–82, 85–96
Bloom, Harold, 133, 145
Boehmer, Elleke, 51, 53–60

Braidotti, Rosi, 2–3, 78–83, 85–96, 99–109, 206, 228

capitalism, 33–40, 65, 86, 115–17, 154–62, 166, 169, 178, 182, 202, 235
Capitalocene, 113–21
Caruth, Cathy, 47–49,
chronos, 94–95
Chthulucene, 113–21
Cixous, Helen, 43, 195
CL. *See* Corpus Linguistics
CLT. *See* Communicative Language Teaching
code, 128–32, 237
Communicative Language Teaching (CLT), 251–53
conatus, 37, 93
contemporary fiction, 54, 153–62, 165
contingency, 125–35
corpora, 223–30
corpus, 126, 133, 223–30; corpus linguistics, 223–30; corpus stylistics, 224–29
correlationism, 125–26
critique, 12–18, 43–50, 55–57, 76–82, 85–89, 141–46, 159–60, 169–72, 177–80, 262

cyborg, 67, 77–78, 88, 99, 102–6, 202, 204

deconstruction, 23, 47, 50, 80, 101, 109, 127, 141, 145, 156, 170, 181, 200, 202, 206–8, 220
Deleuze, Gilles, 33–41, 43, 47, 67, 78, 86–96, 100, 108, 141, 201–2
Derrida, Jacques, 24, 44, 81, 86, 100, 141, 143, 202, 220
Dickens, Charles, 126–33, 142, 226

ecocentric, 113–14
ecocriticism, 18, 23, 58, 81, 82, 105, 113
ecology, 36, 116, 191; ecological, 13, 18, 66, 74, 78, 82, 86, 88, 99, 154, 157
economy, 34, 39, 115, 149, 154, 177, 241
Eliot, T.S., 10, 15, 18, 148, 187
empathy, 21–31, 38, 48, 88, 157, 180–83
environment, 68, 70, 77, 79, 99, 106, 114–21, 188, 191, 193, 202, 235, 239, 264
epistemology, 71–74, 76–80, 105–8, 263
ethical, 92–96, 154–61, 169–72, 180, 228; ethical turn, 21–30, 220; ethics, 22–31, 40, 78, 85–96, 107, 154, 157, 165, 169–70
ethos, 2, 24, 26, 85–86

fascism, 33–41
Felski, Rita, 50, 140, 146–49
feminism, 36, 47, 58, 80, 99–9. See also post-feminism
fossil, 104, 114–16, 125–34
Foucault, Michel, 35, 75, 86, 100, 140–41, 202, 206, 227, 238
Freud, Sigmund, 43–48, 69–73, 189, 202

gender, 22, 47, 58–61, 76, 80, 100–8, 154, 188–93, 206, 219
glocalisation, 251–54
Guattari, Felix, 33–34, 38, 43, 78, 86, 90, 102–3, 105, 201

Haraway, Donna, 67, 69, 86, 100, 103–106, 117–20, 202, 204
Hartman, Geoffrey, 47, 49, 139, 146,
Hassan, Ihab, 76, 165, 203, 206, 261
homo sacer, 80, 85–96

humanism, 9–19, 65– 66, 71–73, 81–82, 85, 87, 90, 101, 103, 188, 201–8. See *also* posthumanism
hybrid, 67, 75–76, 105, 191, 202–208, 237, 244, 256; hybridisation, 57–61, 83,190, 242; hybridity, 55, 59, 167, 191, 208, 237

immanence, 86, 262, 263
intra-action, 67–68, 107–108
irony, 43, 50, 146, 155–156, 170, 172, 177, 179

Jameson, Fredric, 44, 165–166, 169, 173, 202
jouissance, 51, 72, 263

kairos, 94–95

Lacan, Jacques, 43–50, 66–74, 140
Leavis, F. R., 10–17
Levinas, Emanuel, 21–28, 141
liberal humanism, 9–19, 82, 188
liminality, 153–54, 182
Lyotard, Jean-François, 141, 173

Marx, Karl, 43, 47, 89, 143, 145, 189–90
materiality, 23, 67–72, 78–82, 104, 106–07, 161
Meillassoux, Quentin, 126–34
metaaffective, 160–62
metamodernism, 156, 167, 177–84
metaxis, 180–84
microfascism, 33–41
modernism, 167–68, 178, 187, 195, 207, 249, 263
modernity, 65–68, 82, 168–69, 249,
Moi, Toril, 130, 140, 144, 146
moral, 22–31, 38, 87, 90, 145–46, 156, 172, 178, 180; morality, 22–31, 43, 88, 90

Nancy, Jean-Luc, 141–142, 147, 149
neoliberal, 34, 154, 157–62, 166, 177
new materialism, 105, 107, 119; new materialist, 76–81, 103, 107

The New Sincerity, 35, 155–56, 171, 177–78
Newbolt Report, 10–19
nomadic, 83, 85–96, 100, 102, 109, 195
non-human, 75–82, 100–2, 130, 145, 147, 155
Nussbaum, Martha, 27, 30, 37

ontology, 75, 79–80, 85–87, 95, 103–7, 125, 131, 133, 162, 173, 177, 182, 189, 207, 263
OOF (Object Oriented Feminism), 107
OOO (Object Oriented Ontology), 107, 125–26, 132

performativity, 68–69, 79, 139
Plantationocene, 117–20
poetry, 15, 129, 142, 148, 187–95, 201, 214, 225
politics, 2, 22, 30, 35–40, 47, 54, 86–96, 101–7, 118, 126, 153–63, 165, 167, 177, 183, 191–92, 207, 217–18, 241, 249, 255
post-anthropocentric, 65, 79, 87, 264
postcolonial, 47, 49, 51, 53–61, 190, 219–20, 227, 238; postcolonialism, 50–61, 80, 101
postdramatic, 199–208
post-feminism, 50, 177
posthuman, 23, 66, 75–82, 85–96, 99–109, 119, 199–208, 228; posthumanism, 65–74, 75–82, 85–96, 100–9, 201–7, 227
post-method, 249–57
postmodernism, 14, 50, 54, 101, 103, 110, 155–58, 165–74, 177–84, 202, 227, 235–36
post-postmodernism, 155, 157, 161, 165–74, 177–84, 261–63
poststructuralism, 22–23, 54, 67, 85, 101, 103, 140, 157
post-theory, 14, 54–55, 77, 79, 83, 85, 113, 141, 148–49, 189, 195, 213, 220, 224, 230, 261–62
post-translation, 213–20

potentia, 85–96, 264
potentiality, 85–96
potestas, 87–88, 264
psychoanalysis, 31, 43–50, 66–74

Rabaté, Jean-Michel, 2, 46–47, 50, 249
relationality, 67–68, 72, 86–87, 92–93, 146, 169
rhizomatic, 75, 78, 109, 194, 201, 203–8
rhizome, 85–96, 105, 201, 203, 207
Richards, I.A., 10–19, 142

Sedgwick, Eve Kosofsky, 12, 18, 35
sincerity, 154–61, 171–72, 177–83, 263
speculative realism, 125–26
Spinoza, Baruch, 37, 40, 100; Spinozist, 86–87, 90, 103, 262, 264
structuralism, 67, 139–40, 214
stylistics, 224–29. *See also* Corpus stylistics
subjectivity, 10, 19, 37, 43, 65–74, 79, 81, 87–93, 100–3, 107, 127, 140–42, 148, 159, 162, 215, 228, 249
sustainability, 65, 88, 90, 93–94, 114, 265
sympathy, 27, 33–41, 154

threshold, 89–96, 265
transhumanism, 77–78, 201
translanguaging, 236–38
translingualism, 235–45
transpositions, 85–96, 100, 10n1
trauma, 47–50, 60, 160

van den Akker, Robin, 35, 156, 178–82
Vermeulen, Timotheus, 35, 156–61, 178–82
vitality, 92–93, 102–3, 105, 109n1, 265

Wallace, David Foster, 155, 158, 170–73, 180

Zizek, Slavoj, 45, 51, 72
zoe, 80–82, 85–96, 102, 109n1, 264–65. *See also* bios
zoe-centered, 80, 87, 92

About the Contributors

Evrim Doğan Adanur's current research examines a range of different approaches to Shakespeare and early modern drama. Her recent focus is the relationship between temporality and genre in Shakespeare. She is a graduate of Hacettepe University (BA), American University, Washington, DC (MA), and Ankara University (PhD). Teaching English studies for over twenty years, she formerly chaired the Department of Translation and Interpretation at Beykent University and is currently working as the founding chair of the Department of English Language and Literature at Fenerbahçe University in Istanbul.

Başak Ağın, PhD, is Associate Professor of English Literature at TED University, Ankara, Turkey. Her monograph, *Posthümanizm: Kavram, Kuram, Bilim-Kurgu* (2020, Siyasal) [Posthumanism: Concept, Theory, Science-Fiction], explores and exemplifies posthumanism through literary and filmic analyses. She edited M. Sibel Dinçel's Turkish translation of Simon Estok's *The Ecophobia Hypothesis* (2018, Routledge) and co-edited the volume *Posthuman Pathogenesis: Contagion in Literature, Arts, and Media* (2022, Routledge) with Şafak Horzum. Her research articles have appeared in scholarly journals such as *Neohelicon, Translation Review, CLCWeb*, and *Ecozon@*.

Selen Aktari-Sevgi is an Assistant Professor at the Department of American Culture and Literature, the director of the MA program in American Culture and Literature and of the Centre for Irish Studies in Başkent University, Ankara, Turkey. She holds a PhD in English literature from Middle East Technical University in Ankara, Turkey. Her main research interests are postmodern and contemporary British, Irish, and American fiction, gender studies, memory and trauma studies, and theories of affect. She has delivered papers on the works of contemporary writers such as Angela Carter,

Jeannette Winterson, Emma Donoghue, Anne Enright, Sara Baume, Julian Barnes and Ian McEwan. Her recent publications are a book chapter titled "Liminality and Affective Mobility in Anne Enright's *The Green Road*" in *Women on the Move: Body, Memory and Femininity in Present-Day Transnational Diasporic Writing* (Routledge, 2019) and an article titled "Unweaving the Shroud of Mourning: Don DeLillo's *The Body Artist*" (Çankaya *University Journal of Humanities and Social Sciences*, 2021).

Aylin Alkaç received her PhD in English literature from the Department of Western Languages and Literatures at Boğaziçi University, where she teaches. Her research focuses on contemporary fiction and literary theory with specific emphasis on Lacanian psychoanalytical theory.

Gamze Almacıoğlu received her PhD in English language teaching from Çukurova University, Adana. She is currently a lecturer at Gaziantep University, Turkey. Her main research interests are second language learning and teaching, first language acquisition, and pragmatics.

Zekiye Antakyalıoğlu is a professor and chair of English literature at Gaziantep University, Turkey. Her work primarily focuses on the theory of the novel, contemporary fiction, postmodernism, and modernism. She is the writer of two Turkish books: *Roman Kuramına Giriş* (2013) [An Introduction to the Theory of the Novel] and *Bir Düşün Sonu: Milan Kundera Üzerine Bir İnceleme* (2017) [The End of a Dream: An Analysis of Milan Kundera's Works].

Nurten Birlik teaches English literature, in the Department of FLE, Middle East Technical University. She has a book titled *Coleridge's Conversation Poems and Poems of High Imagination*. She has also co-authored a book titled *Lacan in Literature and Film*. She has published numerous articles on British Romantic poetry, Lacanian theory, modernism, and posthumanism.

Ivan Callus is Professor of English at the University of Malta. He has published extensively in the fields of contemporary fiction, poststructuralist literary theory, comparative literature, and posthumanism. He co-edits the journal *CounterText: A Journal for the Study of the Post-Literary*, published by Edinburgh University Press.

Mehmet Ali Çelikel completed his MA in English literature at Hertfordshire University in 1997, and his PhD in English studies at Liverpool University in 2001. His research interests include postcolonial literature, the fiction of Salman Rushdie, J.M. Coetzee, Arundhati Roy, and Hanif Kureishi. He is the writer of two Turkish books: *Sömürgecilik Sonrası İngiliz Romanında Kültür ve Kimlik* [Culture and Identity in the Postcolonial British Fiction, 2011], and *Çağdaş İngiliz Yazınında Küreselleşme, Göç ve Kültür* [Globalisation, Migration and Culture in the Contemporary British Literature, 2017]. He is currently a professor and chair in the Department of English at Marmara University, Turkey.

Rahime Çokay Nebioğlu holds her PhD in English literature from Middle East Technical University, Turkey. She is the author of *Deleuze and the Schizoanalysis of Dystopia*. She is a former Fulbright scholar in the Literature Program at Duke University. She continues her research as a visiting postdoctoral scholar at Duke University. Her research interests include utopian studies, Deleuze studies, modernisms, twenty and twenty-first centuries, the contemporary novel, history of the novel, comparative literature, critical theories, literature and philosophy, and political theory.

Cian Duffy is professor and chair of English Literature at Lund University, Sweden. He has published widely on various aspects of the intellectual life and cultural history of Europe during the eighteenth century and Romantic period, with special focus on the works of the Shelley circle, on landscape and travel writing, on the sublime, and on Nordic Romanticism. His work has also examined aspects of the prehistory of literary theory in the Romantic period. He is currently editing *The Cambridge Companion to the Romantic Sublime*. His latest monograph, *British Romanticism and Denmark*, came out from Edinburgh University Press in 2022.

Ela İpek Gündüz, PhD, is an Assistant Professor of English Literature at Gaziantep University, Turkey. Her main interests and researches are neo-Victorian literature, the contemporary British novel, adaptations, and gender studies. She authored several articles on Neo-Victorian literature, gender studies, and the contemporary British novel. Her recent works include "The Piano: a Neo-Victorian Specula(risa)tion." *Filming the Past, Screening the Present* (2021), and "Ever After: A Neo-Victorian Retrospection." *English Studies in the 21st century* (2020).

Mesut Günenç received his PhD in postdramatic theater and published articles in different journals, especially on contemporary British drama. He has published book chapters titled "Passions of William Shakespeare's Lesser-Known Characters: Tim Crouch I, Shakespeare" and "Victimized Woman: Sarah Kane's Phaedra's Love," "Kim Daha Çok İngiliz: Jez Butterworth'ün *Jerusalem* Adlı Oyunu" [Who is More English? Jez Butterworth's *Jerusalem*] and a book titled *David Hare'in Oyunlarında Post-Truth Söylem* [Post-Truth Discourse in the Plays of David Hare] in 2019.

Vildan İnci Kavak works as a lecturer at Gaziantep University, Turkey. She received her BA, MA, and PhD degrees in English language teaching. She is also a holder of Cambridge DELTA. Her research interests are translanguaging, conversation analysis, teacher professional development, first and second language acquisition, and teaching English to young learners.

Enes Kavak is currently working as an assistant professor at Gaziantep University and is a founding member of Theatre and Drama Network (TDN) in Turkey. He holds a PhD in English literature from the University of Leeds in the United Kingdom. His doctoral research titled "Spectacle, Performance and New Femininities in the Plays of Suffrage Playwrights between 1907 and 1914" focuses on Edwardian women's political theater. He is the co-editor of edited volumes titled *English Studies in the 21st Century* and *New Readings in British Drama: From the Post-War Period to the Contemporary Era*. His recent research focuses mostly on suffrage literature, dramatic theories, contemporary drama, and theater.

Meltem Muşlu is currently working as an Assistant Professor at the University of Gaziantep, English Language and Literature Department. She previously worked at different universities in the United States and Turkey. Her research interests include corpus stylistics, (critical) discourse analysis, and second language acquisition.

Bran Nicol is Professor of English Literature and Head of the School of Literature and Languages. His books include *The Private Eye* (Reaktion, 2013); *Postmodern Fiction: An Introduction* (Cambridge University Press, 2009); and *Stalking* (Reaktion, 2006), which was translated into Italian, Japanese, and Korean, *Iris Murdoch: The Retrospective Fiction* (Palgrave, second edition, 2004) and *D.M. Thomas* (Writers and their Work, 2002). He also edited the collection, *Postmodernism and the Contemporary Novel* (Edinburgh University Press, 2002), and co-edited *Crime Culture* (Bloomsbury, 2010). His main interests are modern and contemporary British, European and American fiction, literary theory, and "crime culture." He has presented his research in these areas at universities around the world.

Aytül Özüm received her PhD from Hacettepe University, Ankara (Turkey), where she currently works as a professor in the Department of English Language and Literature. Her research interests are gender studies, empathy studies, the modern and postmodern English novel, literary theory, and cultural studies. Her publications include: *Angela Carter ve Büyülü Gerçekçilik* [Angela Carter and Magical Realism, 2009], a co-edited volume *İngiliz Edebiyatında Toplumsal Cinsiyet* [Gender in English Literature, 2018], a co-edited volume *Edebiyat ve Kültürde Yalnızlığın 16 Hâli* [16 States of Loneliness in Literature and Culture, 2021] and articles and book chapters both in English and Turkish on George Eliot, Angela Carter, A.S. Byatt, Nâzım Hikmet, Bilge Karasu, Onat Kutlar, Orhan Pamuk, and Peter Ackroyd. She co-organized two multidisciplinary conferences called "Yalnızlık 2018" [Loneliness 2018] and "Korku 2019" [Fear 2019] held in Ankara.

Emrah Peksoy holds a PhD in English literature and works as an assistant professor at Kahramanmaras Istiklal University, Turkey. He teaches critical reading, literary forms, and theory. His research interests include critical theory, distant reading, speculative realist aesthetics, literatures in English, and world literature. His research appeared in various recognized journals.

Seda Şen is assistant professor at Başkent University, Department of American Culture and Literature. She completed her PhD in 2018, her dissertation title being "Constructing Modernist Poetics: Transnational Representations of London in the Poetry of Ezra Pound and T. S. Eliot." Her research interests include modernist poetry, Anglo American poetry, interdisciplinary urban studies, graphic narratives, contemporary poetry and performance, creative reimaginations of memory, and literary cartography.

Cenk Tan works as a lecturer doctor at the Department of Foreign Languages at Pamukkale University, Denizli, Turkey. His areas of interest include speculative fiction, science fiction, ecocriticism, contemporary novel, film studies, and continental philosophy. Having published preliminary articles in these areas, Cenk specializes in environmental humanities and is enthusiastic to conduct research on indigenous studies.

www.ingramcontent.com/pod-product-compliance
Lightning Source LLC
Chambersburg PA
CBHW020112010526
44115CB00008B/797